A SEMANTIC AND STRUCTURAL ANALYSIS OF JAMES

SIL International

SEMANTIC AND STRUCTURAL ANALYSIS SERIES

JOHN BANKER, GENERAL EDITOR

A SEMANTIC AND STRUCTURAL ANALYSIS OF JAMES

George and Helen Hart

The Greek text used in this SSA is from the fourth revised edition
of the United Bible Societies' *Greek New Testament*.

© 2001 by SIL International

Library of Congress Catalog No. 2001088914
ISBN: 1-55671-118-2
Printed in the United States of America

All Rights Reserved
No part of this publication may be reproduced, stored in a retrieval system, or transmitted in any form or by any means—electronic, mechanical, photocopy, recording, or otherwise—without the express permission of SIL International, with the exception of brief excerpts in journal articles or reviews.

Copies of this and other publications of SIL International may be obtained from

International Academic Bookstore
7500 West Camp Wisdom Road
Dallas, TX 75236, USA

Voice: 972-708-7404
Fax: 972-708-7363
E-mail: academic_books@sil.org
Internet: http://www.sil.org

CONTENTS

Acknowledgments vii

Abbreviations viii

GENERAL INTRODUCTION 1
The Theory on Which a Semantic and Structural Analysis Is Based 1
Format and Conventions 1
The Use of a Semantic and Structural Analysis 2
The Nature of Propositionalization 2

INTRODUCTION TO THE SEMANTIC STRUCTURE OF THE EPISTLE OF JAMES 5
The Importance of Recognizing the Communication Situation 5
Authorship of James 5
The Recipients 6
Occasion and Purpose of the Letter 6
Genre 6
Overview: Thematic Units and Their Theme Statements 9

THE SEMANTIC UNITS OF THE EPISTLE OF JAMES 13
The Epistle 1:1–5:20 13
Epistle Constituent 1:1 (Opening of the Epistle) 14
Epistle Constituent 1:2–5:18 (Body of the Epistle) 16
    Part Constituent 1:2–18 18
        Division Constituent 1:2–12 19
        Division Constituent 1:13–18 35
    Part Constituent 1:19–5:11 44
        Division Constituent 1:19–20 46
        Division Constituent 1:21–27 49
        Division Constituent 2:1–13 59
        Division Constituent 2:14–26 73
        Division Constituent 3:1–18 87
        Division Constituent 4:1–17 109
        Division Constituent 5:1–11 133
    Part Constituent 5:12–18 149
        Division Constituent 5:12 151
        Division Constituent 5:13–18 154
Epistle constituent 5:19–20 (Closing of the Epistle) 162

Bibliography 167

Charts:
Paragraph-Pattern Types 3
Chart of Communication Relations 4
The Constituent Organization of James 8

ACKNOWLEDGMENTS

Many have contributed to *A Semantic and Structural Analysis of James*. Several noteworthy earlier drafts were prepared in the 1970s under the able supervision of John Beekman, who, along with John Callow, developed the theory behind the present series. The drafts made by J. O. Ekstrom, Ralph Hill, and Catherine Rountree were consulted from time to time during the preparation of this volume. Also consulted was the analyzed translation of James produced by Neva Miller and Catherine Rountree in 1989 for use in translation workshops around the world.

We are profoundly grateful to our general editor, John Banker, who not only did a careful edit of this work, but was also a willing and tireless consultant throughout its production. Without his expertise and insights we could never have completed the work. We also profited from our colleagues Ellis Deibler, John Tuggy, and Robert Sterner, who were always willing to evaluate and offer suggestions on specific problems. James E. Mignard reviewed the SSA from a Greek perspective and made helpful observations on the general content. Copy editor Betty Eastman reviewed an early draft of the first chapter and gave significant advice on the general formatting of SSAs. After the work was completed, she edited the entire manuscript for consistency and accuracy. Her careful attention to all details was invaluable. The Computer Department at Waxhaw also deserves special thanks for their instruction in the use of computers and the patient assistance by specialists when help was needed. Dick Blight in the Translation Department at Dallas has done an excellent job in preparing the camera-ready copy.

Most of all, we thank the Lord for the wisdom and strength he gave day by day as well as for the spiritual blessings received through the insights gained in our study. We trust that others will profit from using this SSA not only personally but also in communicating these crucial truths to others.

ABBREVIATIONS IN THE DISPLAYS

[DOU]	doublet		[MTY]	metonymy
(exc)	exclusive		¶ PTRN	paragraph pattern
[HEN]	hendiadys		[PRS]	personification
[HYP]	hyperbole		[RHQ]	rhetorical question
[IRO]	irony		(sg)	singular
[LIT]	litotes		[SIM]	simile
[MET]	metaphor		[SYN]	synecdoche

ABBREVIATIONS IN THE TEXT

BAGD*	Bauer, Arndt, Gingrich, Danker
BDF	Blass, Debrunner, and Funk
CBW	C. B. Williams
CEV	Contemporary English Version
GNT	Greek New Testament (Aland et al.)
JB	Jerusalem Bible
JBP	J. B. Phillips
KJV	King James Version
NAB	New American Bible
NASB	New American Standard Bible
NBV	New Berkeley Version
NCV	New Century Version
NEB	New English Bible
NIV	New International Version
NJB	New Jerusalem Bible
NLT	New Living Translation
NRSV	New Revised Standard Version
REB	Revised English Bible
RSV	Revised Standard Version
SSA	Semantic and Structural Analysis
TEV	Today's English Version (Good News for Modern Man)
TNT	Translator's New Testament
UBS	United Bible Society
WEY	Weymouth

*BAGD will be cited by the following formula: page number, period, entry citation (e.g., BAGD, 405.12bβ).

GENERAL INTRODUCTION

The Theory on Which a Semantic and Structural Analysis is Based

This analytical commentary on the Epistle of James is based on the theory of semantic structure set forth in *The Semantic Structure of Written Communication* by Beekman, Callow, and Kopesec (1981). *Man and Message* by K. Callow (1998) presents a broader basis for this theory.

This Semantic and Structural Analysis (SSA), like the other studies in the series, has been prepared with the needs of the Bible translator in view, though it should be useful to all serious students of God's Word. It aims to arrive at the meaning the original writer intended to communicate to the original recipients, but it differs from most other commentaries in that it is based on a particular theory of the structure of meaning. Consequently, a consistent and comprehensive approach to the analysis of the meaning is applied to the total document, whether that meaning is conveyed by the smallest segments of the written communication (words and their component parts) or whether it is conveyed by the largest segments (paragraphs and combinations of paragraphs).

In an SSA the Greek text is analyzed in terms of its semantic units, from the highest level to the lowest. Each of these units is presented first as a display. Following the display, the unit's structure is discussed: its intent, paragraph pattern or macrostructure, boundaries, coherence, prominence, and theme. For a unit on the lowest level (i.e., a single paragraph or propositional cluster), exegetical notes are also given.

This SSA does not include a detailed section on the theory and presentation of semantic and structural analyses as some of the earlier SSAs do (Colossians, 2 Thessalonians). Readers may refer to the Colossians or 2 Thessalonians SSA for this information. The James SSA, however, does include a chart of communication relations and a chart of paragraph patterns, providing easy access to these important tools. (A separate manual explaining the theory, presentation and use of SSAs is being prepared for future publication.)

Format and Conventions

Each semantic unit of James will be displayed as a chart, with the discourse structure and relational structure shown at the left and the referential contents at the right. Readers should note the following conventions:

1. Italics in the propositions of the display designate implicit material that has been supplied. In some cases, however, it has been difficult to decide what is implicit material and what is actually a component of the meaning of the Greek word or words being translated.
2. Parentheses are used to enclose alternate renderings, for example, 'my God (*or*, God whom I *worship*)'. But if both alternates are a single word, they are separated simply by a virgule: 'teach/counsel'. Parentheses are also used to enclose specifications for pronouns, as in 'you(sg)' or 'we(exc)'.
3. Square brackets indicate the clarification of an antecedent, for example, in proposition 3:15a: 'Those who have such attitudes [14a]'. Square brackets also enclose abbreviations for figures of speech that occur in the Greek, for example, '[MET]' for metaphor.
4. In an orienter-content relation where the content consists of more than one proposition, the content label is not used in most cases; rather, the reader is alerted in the left side of the display to the orienter-content relation by the use of a vertical dotted line. The content consists of everything on the vertical line to which the dotted line connects, that is, each proposition of the multipropositional unit immediately below the orienter. See 3:4a–e in the 3:1-12 display for an example.
5. Bolding in the propositions of the display indicates words that are forefronted in Greek and therefore emphatic, as, for example, '**you**' in proposition 2:6a. At the beginning of a note, where the words are already bold, an emphasized word is indicated by underlining.
6. A dagger (†) following certain words or phrases in the propositions of the display indicates that suggestions for translation or alternate renderings are given in the notes.

In this SSA a distinction is made between communication relations on the lower propositional levels and paragraph-pattern relationships on the highest level within the paragraph. The paragraph-pattern type in any paragraph will be based on the author's intent for that paragraph. For example, when the author comes to a point in the discourse where he wants to directly affect the audience's behavior, he will use a hortatory paragraph pattern. Because of this change from SSAs published before 1990, the reader will find that a supportive subparagraph unit in a hortatory paragraph that would have been labeled grounds in earlier SSAs is now labeled *basis*, and the corresponding supported unit is labeled APPEAL rather than HEAD or EXHORTATION, as before. Similar changes have been made in other types of paragraph patterns. (For more on paragraph patterns see Tuggy 1992 and also our chart of paragraph pattern types on page 3.)

Another change in this SSA is that the label NUCLEUS is used instead of HEAD for nuclear units. Also, whenever a nuclear unit has a different relation to two or more nonnuclear units on the same vertical line, the nuclear unit is given a double label (e.g., see 3:2d in the 3:1–12 display), rather than a single label, as was done by the earlier SSA authors.

The Use of a Semantic and Structural Analysis

To a translator who must not only determine the meaning of a passage but also resolve a myriad of translation problems, it may seem like drudgery to wade through the detailed reasoning backing up the exegetical decisions in an SSA. On the other hand, the detailed reasoning is necessary to determine the best analysis. Any interpretation should be backed up with solid reasoning, and there is no way this can be done without detailed analysis, including reference to the Greek text. To determine whether or not the reasoning is solid, the translator has the option of studying the analysis following each display. The notes, especially, are helpful. They explain such things as the reason for supplying implicit information.

But instead of reading every part of the SSA some translators first read the propositions in a display along with other commentaries, versions, and helps; where there is obvious agreement, they may move ahead with confidence. (Greenlee's 1993 *Exegetical Summary of James* lists commentaries that support the various interpretations.) But where there is a difference between the display's renderings and those of other commentaries, the notes on that particular verse or portion of a verse should be consulted to see what led to the decision represented in the display. Translators should then be better able to make their own judgment as to the best interpretation.

To further facilitate discretionary reading of the notes, certain words or phrases are marked in the display with a dagger (†); suggestions for their translation or alternate rendering are given in the corresponding note. The renderings in the display work together with the notes to provide the information translators need. Since the propositions are limited in the information they can provide, the notes contribute to a fuller understanding of them.

To obtain the greatest benefit from an SSA, the discussions of "Intent and Paragraph Pattern" should also be consulted: they orient the reader to the biblical author's development of his argument or thesis. Any part of a book or discourse is best understood in its complete context, and it is the "Intent and Paragraph Pattern" discussion of a given semantic unit that helps the SSA user to see the unit in its broader context.

The Nature of Propositionalization

It must be understood that the SSA display text is not, strictly speaking, a translation. Rather, it expresses the analysis of the meaning of the Greek text in English surface-structure form with various restrictions. For instance, abstract nouns are avoided as much as possible by changing them into verbs and adding obligatory case roles. Finite forms of the verb are normally used rather than participles. Words are used only in their primary senses. For live metaphors, the full meaning of the figure intended by the original author is given. As a result, the sentences do not always sound natural, as in a good translation they should. The inclusion of implicit material often makes them sound overloaded with information and too interpretive. But the primary purpose of the display text, remember, is to be a source of information, not a model to be translated word for word into a real language.

The propositions more closely approximate the patterns of non-Indo-European languages than those of English or Greek. Thus, if the receptor language naturally uses abstract nouns in more or less the same way English or Greek does, it would be expected that the use of abstract nouns in a translation would be more natural and effective than the form of the display text. But if the receptor language does not normally use abstract nouns, the display text form may indeed be helpful since its patterns and obligatory elements are those of verb constructions, not abstract nouns. But even in these languages the display text form ought not be followed word for word; instead, the translator must seek to follow the patterns of the receptor language.

Likewise, the implicit material provided in the display text is not intended to be translated in its entirety. Only that which is necessary in the receptor language should be used in translating.

Readers of this SSA need to be alert to the fact that, in the propositions, all third person singular masculine pronouns whose referent is an unnamed human being refer to both sexes. (A few such pronouns refer to named persons: Abraham, in 2:21; Job, in 5:11; and Elijah, in 5:17.) In James' letter there are an unusual number of these "gender-inclusive" pronouns, especially of the indefinite pronoun τις 'anyone'; James uses them to present principles of conduct and individual responsibility. But rendering them to show the inclusiveness would distort James' message. Changing to the third person plural, for instance, would require plural verbs and the focus on individual behavior would be entirely lost; and changing to second person plural would erase the distinction in the Greek text between third person singular masculine forms and the many second person plurals that also occur. Thus for this SSA it was deemed best to reflect the Greek usage. Translators can then choose an appropriate rendering in their particular target language, remembering that in some languages the inclusive concept *is* best expressed by another pronoun—the second person plural pronoun, perhaps, or the first person plural inclusive.

		SOLUTIONALITY	CAUSALITY	VOLITIONALITY
IDEAS	EXPOSITORY −sequence	+problem (exp)+SOLUTION ±evidence^n ±(complication+SOLUTION) [(objection+REFUTATION)/ query+RESPONSE)]	+cause^n+EFFECT; +major+minor+INFERENCE; +evidence^n+INFERENCE; +PRINCIPLE+application^n	+justification^n+CLAIM
IDEAS	NARRATIVE +sequence	+problem+RESOLUTION ±resolving incident^n ±(complication+RESOLUTION)	+occasion+OUTCOME	+step^n+GOAL
EMOTIONS	EXPRESSIVE −sequence	+problem (emo)+SOLUTION ±seeking/belief ±(complication+SOLUTION)	+situation^n+REACTION ±belief	+belief^n+CONTROL
EMOTIONS	DESCRIPTIVE +sequence	+problem (dsc)+SOLUTION ±experience^n ±(complication+SOLUTION)	+situation^n+REACTION	+description^n+DECLARATION
BEHAVIOR	HORTATORY −sequence	+problem (hrt)+APPEAL ±basis^n ±(complication+SOLUTION)	+basis^n+APPEAL; +APPEAL+application^n; +basis^n+COMMISSIVE	+motivation+ENABLEMENT^n; +motivation^n+APPEAL
BEHAVIOR	PROCEDURAL +sequence	+problem (prc)+SOLUTION ±step^n ±(complication+SOLUTION)	+APPEAL+outcome	+STEP^n+accomplishment

Paragraph-Pattern Types in Various Discourse Genres (With a few exceptions one formula serves for each paragraph-pattern type; alternate formulas are separated by a semicolon.)

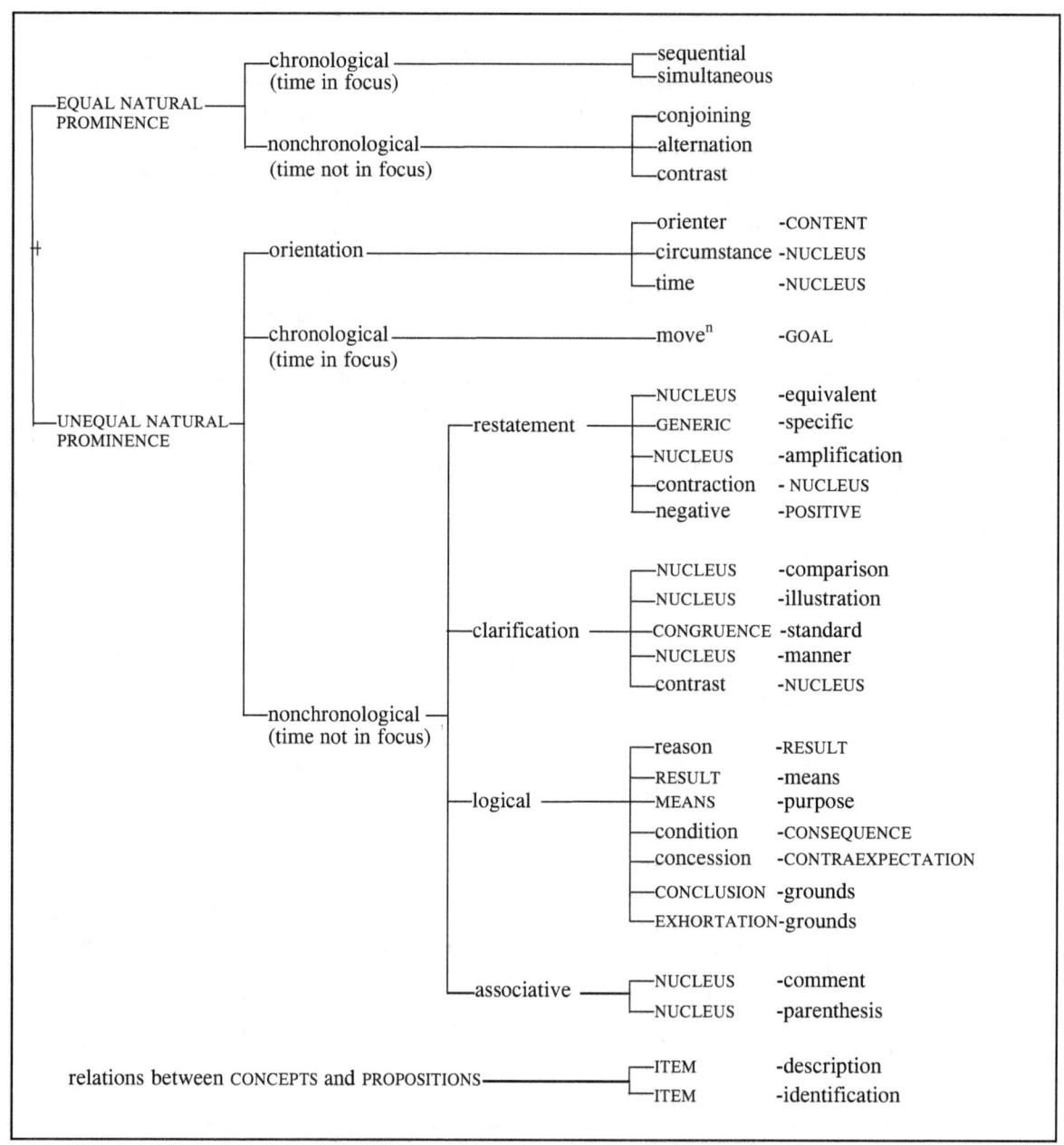

Chart of Communication Relations

Notes:
1. The relations are given in the chart in the usual order in which they are found in New Testament Greek.
2. The naturally prominent member of a paired relation is shown in full capitals. When the writer uses marked-prominence devices to increase the prominence of the normally less prominent member, both members will be shown in full capitals in the display.
3. NUCLEUS-amplification and contraction-NUCLEUS are the same communication relation, but with a difference in the position of the nucleus.
4. In the displays ITEM is shown as a gloss enclosed in single quote marks.

INTRODUCTION TO THE SEMANTIC STRUCTURE OF THE EPISTLE OF JAMES

The Importance of Recognizing the Communication Situation

A written document reflects the situation in which it was written: the general historical situation and the particular situation of the writer and recipient(s). It also reflects the personality and beliefs of the writer and the knowledge and assumptions that he or she brings to the document concerning the circumstances of the letter's recipients. It is therefore of value to the translator to be familiar with the communication situation, since it provides the background against which various exegetical decisions are made. The author of the Epistle of James speaks with great authority and refers to many specific situations that the recipients are facing.

Authorship of James

At least four men called James are mentioned in the New Testament, but only two are worthy of consideration as the possible author of this epistle. One of these is the son of Zebedee, one of the Twelve; and the other is Jesus' half brother, who became the leader of the Jerusalem church. But since the Apostle James was killed in A.D. 44, which would hardly have allowed time for the conditions referred to in the epistle to have developed, this leaves only James the Lord's brother as the likely author of the letter.

Although the church fathers attribute the Epistle of James to James the Lord's brother, the question of authorship has long been debated. Modern critical scholars who reject the traditional view have proposed various alternatives and date the epistle after the death of the Lord's brother. Yet there is much evidence, both externally and internally, to support the traditional view. Some commentators (e.g. Tasker, Oesterley) date the epistle A.D. 60–62, but the majority (e.g., Moo, Mayor, Kistemaker, Hiebert, Blue) favor an earlier date: A.D. 45–48. (For a comprehensive treatment of the subject, see Hiebert, pp. 13–28, or Moo, pp. 19–30.)

The main arguments against the traditional view of authorship are: (1) the excellent Greek; (2) scant reference to the person, life, and teaching of Jesus Christ; (3) no overt claim to apostolic authority or relationship to Christ; (4) Hellenistic features; (5) the perceived disagreement between James and Paul in the teaching on faith and works; and (6) the recipients' condition, which seems to point to a time after the destruction of Jerusalem. These arguments have led some (e.g., Ropes, Dibelius, Laws) to propose various alternatives, most of which depend on a later date, either the end of the first century or during the first half of the second. One view proposes that some unknown teacher published the letter under the pseudonym of James. An alternative view, proposed by Spitta, contends that the epistle was originally a Jewish document that was given a Christian veneer by the insertion of reference to Jesus Christ. This theory fails to recognize the Christian assumptions that lie behind much of the epistle (Tasker, p. 34).

The principal arguments for the traditional view are as follows:

1. External evidence, namely the testimony of the church fathers, supports this conclusion. Though not very early, it is consistent in maintaining that James the Lord's brother wrote this epistle.
2. The fact that the author felt no need to identify himself and yet speaks with such authority suggests that he was a well-known figure.
3. The author's Jewish background, as evidenced in the epistle by the use of the word 'law' and the appeal to the Old Testament for support in his arguments, is consistent with the traditional view.
4. There are striking similarities between this epistle and James' Acts 15:13–21 speech.
5. Conditions among the recipients are consistent with the traditional view, reflecting conditions following the stoning of Stephen rather than after the destruction of Jerusalem in A.D. 70 (Dockery).
6. The simplicity of the church organization favors an early date.

In answer to the first objection to the traditional view, although the Greek of James is undeniably more polished than most New Testament Greek, it is entirely conceivable, according to Kistemaker (pp. 8–9), that a Palestinian Jew could have written idiomatic Greek. Moo (p. 24) points out that its quality should not be exaggerated. As for the objection from those who claim scant Christian content, they simply fail to recognize the great number of the teachings of Jesus that *are* alluded to (Sloan). Davids (1982: 47–48) lists thirty-six references to specific verses in the Synoptics. Furthermore, the author's purpose did not require him to discuss basic Christian doctrines, since the problems of the recipients were not doctrinal errors but rather the failure to apply their beliefs to their daily lives. The Hellenistic features are not evidence against the traditional authorship, since Paul used the same Hellenistic literary devices, including diatribe. The claim of conflict between James' and Paul's teaching overlooks their use of key terms with different meanings and the fact that they were addressing different problems. (See the notes on 2:14d and 2:21c for a fuller discussion.)

The Recipients

In the first verse of the first chapter the recipients of the letter are identified as ταῖς δώδεκα φυλαῖς ταῖς ἐν τῇ διασπορᾷ 'the twelve tribes in the dispersion'. There are three different interpretations of this phrase: (1) A few commentators (e.g., Adamson) think James was addressing all Jews living outside of Palestine. (2) Other commentators (e.g., Laws, Ropes, Ward) interpret the phrase figuratively to be a reference to all Christians as the new Israel. (3) The majority (e.g., Martin, Moo, Davids 1982) say that James was writing to Jewish Christians living outside of Palestine. The first view is improbable because the whole letter assumes that the recipients were believers in Jesus Christ. The second view deserves consideration, since there appears to be a parallel with 1 Pet. 1:1, in which the noun διασπορά 'dispersion' clearly includes Gentile believers. However, Adamson (p. 49) contends that the force of the article, omitted in 1 Pet. 1:1, shows that the term in James "is still non-technical and is used concretely of the dispersed Jews." Furthermore, the Jewishness of the epistle makes a figurative interpretation improbable. The third view is preferable because the author assumes his readers' knowledge of the Old Testament and its authority. Furthermore, he uses a monotheistic confession to summarize 'doctrine' in 2:19 (Moo, p. 30). He also uses the word 'synagogue' in 2:2.

From internal evidence we know that the recipients were believers and that many of them were poor. They were suffering from religious, social, and economic persecution.

Occasion and Purpose of the Letter

James is not addressing a single group of Christians but various congregations scattered far and wide throughout the Roman world. The occasion for this letter seems to fit the situation of Acts 11:19–21 in which many Jewish Christians were scattered as a result of the persecution connected with the stoning of Stephen. The verb used in Acts 11:19 is a cognate of διασπορά 'dispersion'. Since James was the head of the Jerusalem church, it is "entirely natural that he would address a pastoral letter to these believers from his 'home' church who were scattered abroad because of persecution" (Moo, p. 33).

The purpose of this epistle is stated in 1:4, "that you may be mature and complete, not lacking anything." James' concern is practical, to help the believers live up to their faith with unreserved obedience to Christ their Lord. To accomplish this purpose he had to correct errors and misunderstandings that resulted in conduct unworthy of true Christian faith. He exhorts them to bravely endure trials, obey God's commands, demonstrate faith by their compassionate actions and speech, repent of their sins, and respond to life's problems with prayer (see the theme for the epistle on p. 9).

Genre

Because of its opening greeting, the book has traditionally been referred to as an epistle, but it lacks personal references as well as the customary conclusion. This has led to considerable conjecture concerning its genre. Some conclude that it is a religious and moral tract or a homily sent in the form of a letter for general edification. But the constant use of first and second person pronouns suggests a letter, and the lack of personal references may well be due to its being a circular letter (see p. 13, "Structure of the Epistle" under the display of the whole epistle).

The contents of the book identify it with the genre of hortatory literature. The Epistle of James has a greater frequency of imperatives than any other book in the New Testament. In the present analysis of twenty-four paragraphs in the book, eighteen are considered hortatory, and all but one of the eight sections are hortatory.

A number of commentators (e.g., Ropes, pp. 12–14) point out that the literary style of the epistle has many similarities to the Hellenistic diatribe, a colloquial genre used to instruct general audiences. It featured rhetorical questions, conditional sentences, alliteration and assonance, analogies, and short sayings. However, some characteristic features of Hellenistic diatribes, such as bitter sarcasm and name-calling, are absent from James' letter. Although there are obvious similarities in style, the fundamental ideas are far more closely connected with Jewish thinking. In fact, the synagogue sermons also made use of some of these devices. The epistle as a whole is far too Jewish and biblical to be considered a Hellenistic diatribe (Adamson). Rather, it is a pastoral letter demonstrating deep insight into the recipients' spiritual condition and exhorting them to remedial action.

THE CONSTITUENT ORGANIZATION OF JAMES

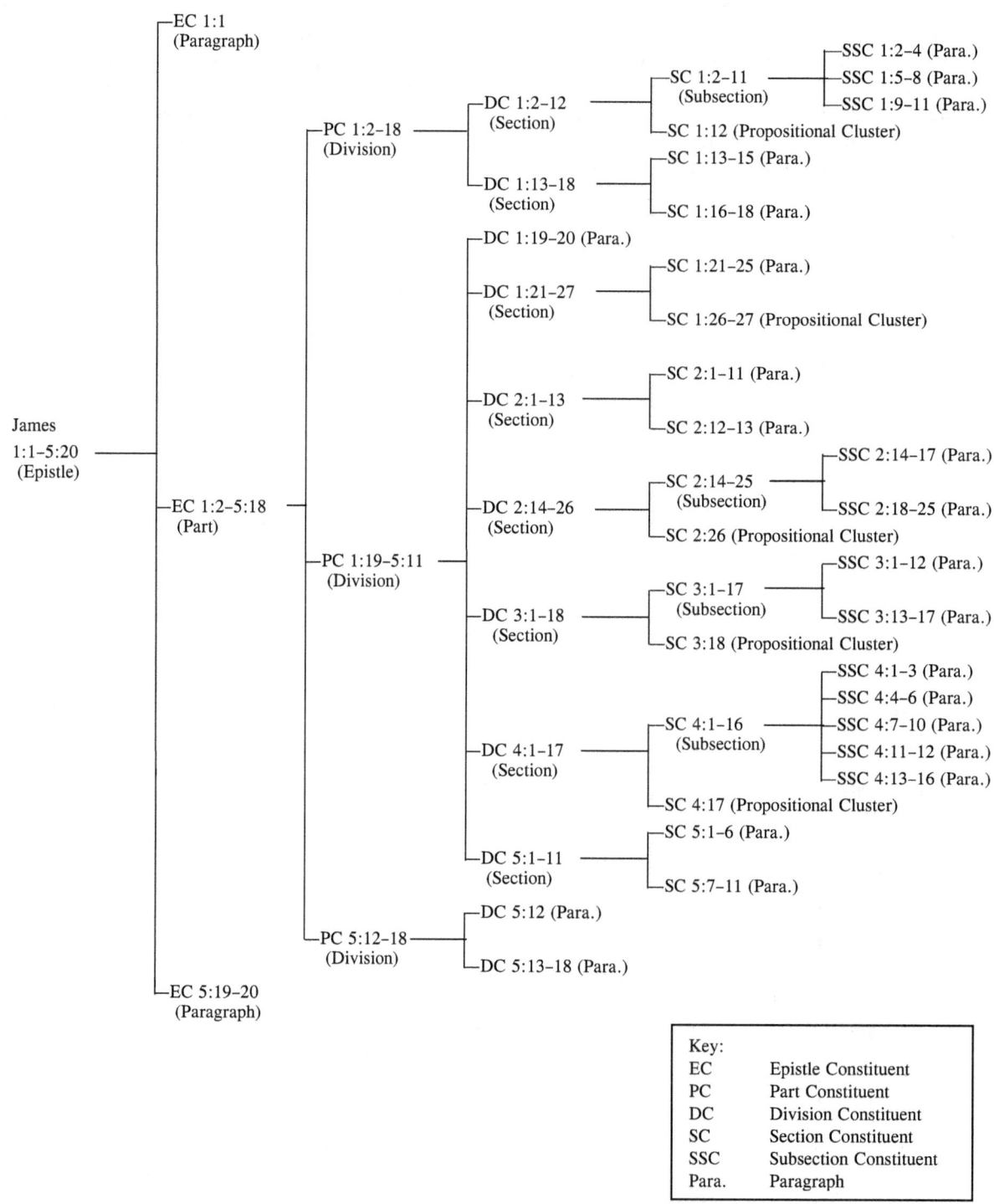

INTRODUCTION

OVERVIEW: THEMATIC UNITS AND THEIR THEME STATEMENTS

JAMES 1:1–5:20 (Epistle)
Theme: I, James, am writing to God's scattered people. When you experience difficulties, only rejoice and keep on bravely enduring them. Do what God commands in his message rather than just listening to it. Stop honoring some people more than others. Only by doing good can a person prove that he truly trusts in God. You should strive to speak rightly to others and do good, acting peaceably toward others, to demonstrate that you are truly wise. You are fighting among yourselves because of your evil desires. Be sad because you have sinned, and humble yourselves before God. Wait patiently for the Lord to return and judge all people fairly, even the rich who oppress you. Ask God to help you and pray for each other.

EPISTLE CONSTITUENT 1:1 (Paragraph: Opening of the Epistle)
Theme: I, James, am writing this letter to Jewish people who trust in the Lord Jesus Christ (or, to all God's people) who are scattered throughout the world. Greetings!

EPISTLE CONSTITUENT 1:2–5:18 (Part: Body of the Epistle)
Theme: When you experience difficulties, only rejoice and keep on bravely enduring them. Do what God commands in his message rather than just listening to it. Stop honoring some people more than others. Only by doing good can a person prove that he truly trusts in God. You should strive to speak rightly to others and do good, acting peaceably toward others, to demonstrate that you are truly wise. You are fighting among yourselves because of your evil desires. Be sad because you have sinned, and humble yourselves before God. Wait patiently for the Lord to return and judge all people fairly, even the rich who oppress you. Ask God to help you and pray for each other.

    PART CONSTITUENT 1:2–18 (Hortatory Division: General Appeals of 1:2–5:11)
    Theme: When you experience difficulties, only rejoice and keep on bravely enduring them. If a person wants to do evil, he should not think that God is tempting him to do so, since it is his own evil desire that causes him to do evil.

        DIVISION CONSTITUENT 1:2–12 (Hortatory Section: Nucleus$_1$ of 1:2–18)
        Theme: When you experience difficulties, only rejoice and keep on bravely enduring them. If you want to act wisely when trials come, ask God to help you, and firmly trust him. He will reward the person who bravely endures difficulties.

            SECTION CONSTITUENT 1:2–11 (Hortatory Subsection: Appeal of 1:2–12)
            Theme: When you experience difficulties, only rejoice and keep on bravely enduring them. If you want to act wisely when trials come, ask God to help you, and firmly trust him. Believers who are poor and those who are rich should both value most what God has done for them.

                SUBSECTION CONSTITUENT 1:2–4 (Hortatory Paragraph: Generic Appeal of 1:2–11)
                Theme: When you experience difficulties that test whether or not you will continue to trust God, only rejoice and keep on bravely enduring them in order that you may be all that God intends you to be.

                SUBSECTION CONSTITUENT 1:5–8 (Hortatory Paragraph: Specific Appeal$_1$ of 1:2–11)
                Theme: If you want to act wisely when trials come, ask God to help you, and firmly trust him.

                SUBSECTION CONSTITUENT 1:9–11 (Hortatory Paragraph: Specific Appeal$_2$ of 1:2–11)
                Theme: Believers who are poor and those who are rich should both value most what God has done for them rather than focusing on their material resources that will disappear.

            SECTION CONSTITUENT 1:12 (Expository Propositional Cluster: Basis of 1:2–11)
            Theme: God blesses those who bravely endure difficulties; he will reward them by causing them to live eternally.

        DIVISION CONSTITUENT 1:13–18 (Hortatory Section: Nucleus$_2$ of 1:2–18)
        Theme: When difficulties happen, if a person wants to do evil, he should not think that God is tempting him to do so, since it is his own evil desire that causes him to do evil and God does only good for us.

SECTION CONSTITUENT 1:13-15 (Hortatory Paragraph: Appeal of 1:13-18)
Theme: When difficulties happen, if a person wants to do evil, he should not think that God is tempting him to do so, since it is his own evil desire that causes him to do evil.
SECTION CONSTITUENT 1:16-18 (Hortatory Paragraph: Basis of 1:13-15)
Theme: Stop thinking falsely that God tempts you to do evil, since God does only good for us.

PART CONSTITUENT 1:19-5:11 (Hortatory Division: Specific Appeals of 1:2-5:11)
Theme: Do what God commands in his message rather than just listening to it. Stop honoring some people more than others. Only by doing good can a person prove that he truly trusts in God. You should strive to speak rightly to others and do good, acting peaceably toward others, to demonstrate that you are truly wise. You are fighting among yourselves because of your evil desires. Be sad because you have sinned, and humble yourselves before God. Wait patiently for the Lord to return and judge all people fairly, even the rich who oppress you.

DIVISION CONSTITUENT 1:19-20 (Hortatory Paragraph: Introduction to 1:21-5:11)
Theme: Every one of you should eagerly pay attention to God's message and should not speak hastily nor get angry hastily.

DIVISION CONSTITUENT 1:21-27 (Hortatory Section: Appeal$_1$ of 1:19-5:11)
Theme: Do what God commands in his message rather than just listening to it. Those who show compassion on the weak and do not act immorally truly worship God.

SECTION CONSTITUENT 1:21-25 (Hortatory Paragraph: Appeal of 1:21-27)
Theme: Therefore stop doing all kinds of evil, and do what God commands in his message rather than just listening to it. God will approve of those who do what he wants them to do.
SECTION CONSTITUENT 1:26-27 (Expository Propositional Cluster: Axiomatic Basis of 1:21-25)
Theme: Those who show compassion on the weak and do not think or act immorally truly worship God and receive his approval.

DIVISION CONSTITUENT 2:1-13 (Hortatory Section: Appeal$_2$ of 1:19-5:11)
Theme: Stop honoring some people more than others, since you are disobeying God's law that we should love one another. God will not act mercifully to those who do not act mercifully toward others.

SECTION CONSTITUENT 2:1-11 (Hortatory Paragraph: Appeal of 2:1-13)
Theme: Stop honoring some people more than others, since you are not treating people the way God treats them and you are disobeying God's law that we should love one another.
SECTION CONSTITUENT 2:12-13 (Hortatory Paragraph: Motivational Basis of 2:1-11)
Theme: Continually act mercifully toward others, since God will not act mercifully to those who do not act mercifully toward others.

DIVISION CONSTITUENT 2:14-26 (Expository Section: Basis of 1:21-2:13 and 3:1-5:11)
Theme: Only by doing good to others can a person prove that he truly trusts in God, since it is useless for one to say that he trusts in God if he does not do what God commands.

SECTION CONSTITUENT 2:14-25 (Expository Subsection: Claim of 2:14-26)
Theme: Anyone who says he trusts in Jesus Christ but does not act compassionately to others is not truly trusting in him. Only by obeying God and doing good to others can a person prove that he trusts in him.

SUBSECTION CONSTITUENT 2:14-17 (Expository Paragraph: Nucleus$_1$ of 2:14-25)
Theme: Anyone who says he trusts in Jesus Christ but does not act compassionately toward others is not truly trusting in him.
SUBSECTION CONSTITUENT 2:18-25 (Expository Paragraph: Nucleus$_2$ of 2:14-25)
Theme: But someone may claim that one person is saved because he trusts in God and another person is saved because he does good to others. In answer to that, the inadequacy of faith without good deeds is demonstrated by the example of demons. From the examples of Abraham and Rahab we can see that only by obeying God and doing good to others can a person prove that he truly trusts in him.

SECTION CONSTITUENT 2:26 (Expository Propositional Cluster: Axiomatic Justification of 2:14-25)
Theme: It is useless for one to say that he trusts in God if he does not do what God commands.
DIVISION CONSTITUENT 3:1-18 (Hortatory Section: Appeal₃ of 1:19-5:11)
Theme: You should all strive to speak rightly, since what you say has a powerful effect on others. So don't boast that you are wise if you are jealous of others and self-seeking. Those who act peaceably toward others will cause the whole community to act righteously.
　SECTION CONSTITUENT 3:1-17 (Hortatory Subsection: Appeal of 3:1-18)
　Theme: Not many of you should become ones who habitually teach, since God will judge teachers with greater scrutiny than others. You should all strive to speak rightly, since what you say has a powerful effect on others, often destructive. So don't boast that you are wise if you are jealous of others and self-seeking.
　　SUBSECTION CONSTITUENT 3:1-12 (Hortatory Paragraph: Nucleus₁ of 3:1-17)
　　Theme: Not many of you should become ones who habitually teach, since God will judge teachers with greater scrutiny than he will judge others. You should all strive to speak rightly, since what you say has a powerful effect on others, often destructive and hypocritical.
　　SUBSECTION CONSTITUENT 3:13-17 (Hortatory Paragraph: Nucleus₂ of 3:1-17)
　　Theme: Don't boast that you are wise if you are jealous of others and self-seeking. Rather, do good to demonstrate that you are truly wise, acting peaceably and compassionately toward others.
　SECTION CONSTITUENT 3:18 (Expository Propositional Cluster: Axiomatic Basis of 3:1-17)
　Theme: Those who act peaceably toward others will cause the whole community to act righteously.
DIVISION CONSTITUENT 4:1-17 (Hortatory Section: Appeal₄ of 1:19-5:11)
Theme: You are fighting among yourselves because of your evil desires. Be sad because you have sinned, and humble yourselves before God. If anyone knows the right thing that he ought to do yet doesn't do it, he is sinning.
　SECTION CONSTITUENT 4:1-16 (Hortatory Subsection: Appeal of 4:1-17)
　Theme: You are fighting among yourselves because of your evil desires and you have become God's enemies. He opposes the proud but helps those who act humbly. Therefore be sad because you have sinned, and humble yourselves before God. Stop speaking evil against each other and don't boast about what you will do in the future.
　　SUBSECTION CONSTITUENT 4:1-3 (Expository Paragraph: Basis₁ of 4:7-10)
　　Theme: You are fighting among yourselves because of your evil desires and you are never getting what you want because you pray with wrong motives.
　　SUBSECTION CONSTITUENT 4:4-6 (Expository Paragraph: Basis₂ of 4:7-10)
　　Theme: You are unfaithful to God and are acting as evil people do, so you have become God's enemies, but God wants to help you. He opposes the proud but helps those who act humbly.
　　SUBSECTION CONSTITUENT 4:7-10 (Hortatory Paragraph: Generic Appeal of 4:1-16)
　　Theme: Therefore submit yourselves to God and resist the devil. Stop doing and thinking wrongly, and be sad because you have sinned. Indeed, humble yourselves before God and he will exalt you spiritually.
　　SUBSECTION CONSTITUENT 4:11-12 (Hortatory Paragraph: Specific Appeal₁ of 4:7-10)
　　Theme: Stop speaking evil against one another and thus condemning each other. Only God has the right to condemn others.
　　SUBSECTION CONSTITUENT 4:13-16 (Hortatory Paragraph: Specific Appeal₂ of 4:7-10)
　　Theme: You should not boast about what you will do in the future, since life is transitory; rather, you should plan to do whatever God wants you to do, since boasting about what you want to do, rather than considering the will of God, is sinful.
　SECTION CONSTITUENT 4:17 (Expository Propositional Cluster: Axiomatic Basis of 4:1-16)
　Theme: Certainly if anyone knows the right thing that he ought to do yet doesn't do it, he is sinning.

DIVISION CONSTITUENT 5:1-11 (Hortatory Section: Appeal$_5$ of 1:19-5:11)
Theme: The rich people who oppress you should weep because God will punish them. Therefore wait patiently for the Lord to return and judge all people fairly. Do not complain against each other lest he judge you when he returns. God blesses those who patiently endure suffering.

SECTION CONSTITUENT 5:1-6 (Expository Paragraph: Basis of 5:7-11)
Theme: The rich people who oppress you should weep because they will suffer much. God will punish them because they have unjustly caused others to suffer.

SECTION CONSTITUENT 5:7-11 (Hortatory Paragraph: Appeal of 5:1-11)
Theme: Therefore wait patiently for the Lord Jesus Christ to return and judge all people fairly. Do not complain against each other lest he judge you when he returns. From the examples of the prophets and Job we know that God blesses and rewards those who patiently endure suffering.

PART CONSTITUENT 5:12-18 (Hortatory Division: Concluding Appeals of 1:2-5:18)
Theme: Always tell the truth. Whatever your circumstances are, pray and God will help you. So confess your sins to each other and pray for each other.

DIVISION CONSTITUENT 5:12 (Hortatory Paragraph: Appeal$_1$ of 5:12-18)
Theme: Don't say, "If I am lying, may God punish me." Instead, always tell the truth lest God condemn you.

DIVISION CONSTITUENT 5:13-18 (Hortatory Paragraph: Appeal$_2$ of 5:12-18)
Theme: Whatever your circumstances are, pray with faith and God will certainly help you, both physically and spiritually. So confess your sins to each other and pray for each other, since God answers prayer.

EPISTLE CONSTITUENT 5:19-20 (Hortatory Paragraph: Closing of Epistle)
Theme: If anyone turns from God's true message, you believers should counsel him to once again obey God so that God will forgive his many sins.

THE SEMANTIC UNITS OF THE EPISTLE OF JAMES

JAMES (Epistle)

THEME: I, James am writing to God's scattered people. When you experience difficulties, only rejoice and keep on bravely enduring them. Do what God commands in his message rather than just listening to it. Stop honoring some people more than others. Only by doing good can a person prove that he truly trusts in God. You should strive to speak rightly to others and do good, acting peaceably toward others, to demonstrate that you are truly wise. You are fighting among yourselves because of your evil desires. Be sad because you have sinned, and humble yourselves before God. Wait patiently for the Lord to return and judge all people fairly, even the rich who oppress you. Ask God to help you and pray for each other.

MACROSTRUCTURE	CONTENTS
opening	1:1 I, James, am writing this letter to Jewish people who trust in the Lord Jesus Christ (or, to all God's people) who are scattered throughout the world. Greetings!
BODY	1:2–5:18 When you experience difficulties, only rejoice and keep on bravely enduring them. Do what God commands in his message rather than just listening to it. Stop honoring some people more than others. Only by doing good can a person prove that he truly trusts in God. You should strive to speak rightly to others and do good, acting peaceably toward others, to demonstrate that you are truly wise. You are fighting among yourselves because of your evil desires. Be sad because you have sinned, and humble yourselves before God. Wait patiently for the Lord to return and judge all people fairly, even the rich who oppress you. Ask God to help you and pray for each other.
closing	5:19–20 If anyone turns from God's true message, you believers should counsel him to once again obey God so that God will forgive his many sins.

STRUCTURE OF THE EPISTLE

Much has been written about whether or not the Epistle of James is actually a letter. The book begins with a typical epistolary introduction, uses the personal pronouns 'you' and 'we', and frequently calls the recipients 'my brothers', but it lacks the personal references and closing remarks that commonly occur in New Testament epistles. Ropes (p. 1) concludes that it is a religious and moral tract having the form, but only the form, of a letter. Moo (p. 38) considers it a brief sermon or extraction drawn from a series of sermons sent to the dispersed church in the form of a letter, whereas Kistemaker (p. 3) classifies it as a general epistle because of the lack of personal remarks. Obviously this is an unusual type of letter, but it is, nevertheless, a letter.

Adamson (p. 202) throws light on the *closing*, which commentators invariably point out as a problem. He says, "All our NT Epistles end with a direct message to the hearers, of greeting, blessing, warning (as 1 John) or, as the Epistle of James, of encouragement and reward." Since most of the epistles were written by Paul, one tends to consider his style as the norm. However, although James does not have a formulaic closing, it does have an appropriate closing (see "Intent and Paragraph Pattern" below the 5:19–20 display). Thus it is clear that the Epistle of James has the three characteristic parts of a letter: an *opening* (1:1) that is a brief address and greeting, a BODY (1:2–5:18) that contains the basic message James wants to communicate, and a *closing* (5:19–20) that is an appeal to action, characteristic of James' style throughout.

PROMINENCE AND THEME

The BODY of the epistle is clearly its most prominent part. While it has more natural prominence, since it carries the main message of the discourse, the *opening* is also important because it identifies the writer and the recipients. Therefore the theme of the epistle is based on the *opening* and the BODY's most prominent information. The recipients are identified in the theme as "God's scattered people" for brevity's sake (see the note on 1:1b–c).

EPISTLE CONSTITUENT 1:1 (Paragraph: Opening of the Epistle)

> *THEME: I, James, am writing this letter to Jewish people who trust in the Lord Jesus Christ (or, to all God's people) who are scattered throughout the world. Greetings!*

RELATIONAL STRUCTURE	CONTENTS
AUTHOR	1:1a *I, James, serve God and the Lord Jesus Christ.*
ADDRESSEES — 'Jewish believers'	1:1b *I am writing this letter* to Jewish people *who trust in the Lord Jesus Christ (or*, to all God's people)
— identification	1:1c who are scattered throughout the world.
GREETING	1:1d *I greet you all.*

INTENT AND STRUCTURE

Verse 1 of James' letter is in the pattern typical of the opening of a Greek letter of the time. In the Greek text, 1:1 is a single sentence in which the subject with its modifying stative phrase identifies the author, the indirect object identifies the recipients, and what appears to be some type of direct object in the form of an infinitive is the greeting. There is no other verb in the Greek, but the main purpose of James in addressing the specified recipients is to indicate that it is to them that he is writing the message of the letter, rather than that he is only greeting them at this point. The components 1a, 1b–c, and 1d are coordinate. Based on their semantic content they are labeled AUTHOR, ADDRESSEES, and GREETING.

The author's purpose in writing an opening was to identify himself and his recipients and to establish rapport with them so that they would not only read but also heed the contents. By the description 'servant of God and the Lord Jesus Christ' he not only established rapport but also conveyed the authority needed.

NOTES

1:1a *I, James, serve God and the Lord Jesus Christ.* The letter from James opens with a simple, direct greeting without the blessing that commonly occurs in most other epistles. The author introduces himself simply as James, or Jacob, a name common among Palestinian Jews during the first century. The fact that James identifies himself only by name and as δοῦλος 'servant, slave' implies that he was already well known to his readers. The designation δοῦλος indicates a relationship of submission to the absolute authority of God. It is a term of humility; yet there is a certain authority that comes from the One he represents (Moo). James' service is described as both to God and to the Lord Jesus Christ. The only other occurrence of Jesus' full name is in 2:1. The word 'servant' stands at the end of the phrase, making prominent the identity of his heavenly Masters (Levinsohn, p. 94). Although he says nothing about his human relationships or ecclesiastical position, most commentators identify him as Jesus' half-brother who became the leader of the congregation in Jerusalem (see p. 5, "Introduction").

1:1b–c *I am writing this letter* There is no finite verb in the Greek that would relate the writer to the recipients, so this implicit information is supplied in the display.

to Jewish people *who trust in the Lord Jesus Christ (or*, to all God's people) who are scattered throughout the world. The phrase ταῖς δώδεκα φυλαῖς ταῖς ἐν τῇ διασπορᾷ 'to the twelve tribes in the dispersion' was commonly used to identify the Jewish people who had been scattered during the Captivity. Here the term specifies the recipients of the epistle. Many commentators (e.g., Mayor, Hiebert, Martin) insist that this refers to Jewish believers only. Others (e.g., Ropes, Laws, Tasker) believe that the phrase is used figuratively to indicate all Christians, both Jewish and Gentiles. Alford makes a very relevant comment:

> . . . nor can there be any reasonable doubt that this Epistle was addressed to Jewish Christians in the first place. Not however to them, as distinguished from Gentile Christians: for the two classes appear to have been not as yet distinct.

This is assuming the early date of writing (see p. 5). The TEV has "all God's people". In the light of Alford's observation, this rendering does not necessarily reflect a figurative interpretation. For this reason both alternatives are given in the display, as well as in the theme.

1:1d *I greet you all.* The formulaic χαίρειν 'greetings' here was common in thousands of ancient papyri, although it is not found in the address of any other apostolic epistle. It does occur in Acts 15:23 in the letter drawn up under James' direction to the Gentile churches.

BOUNDARIES AND COHERENCE

The initial boundary of the 1:1 unit coincides with the beginning of the discourse. Verse 1 is an unusually terse greeting, but it does identify the writer and the recipients of the letter. The first finite verb of the epistle, an imperative ἡγήσασθε 'consider it (joy)' in v. 2, marks the beginning of the next unit, the BODY of the epistle. In 1:2 is also the first of many occurrences of the vocative ἀδελφοί μου 'my brothers'. It is evident that a major change of topic is often accompanied by a vocative, as some commentators recognize (e.g., Davids 1989:37 and Loh and Hatton, p. 11).

PROMINENCE AND THEME

There does not seem to be evidence that any of the three coordinate components of the 1:1 paragraph is more prominent than the others. Therefore the 1:1 theme statement has been drawn from each one.

EPISTLE CONSTITUENT 1:2–5:18 (Part: Body of the Epistle)

THEME: When you experience difficulties, only rejoice and keep on bravely enduring them. Do what God commands in his message rather than just listening to it. Stop honoring some people more than others. Only by doing good can a person prove that he truly trusts in God. You should strive to speak rightly to others and do good, acting peaceably toward others, to demonstrate that you are truly wise. You are fighting among yourselves because of your evil desires. Be sad because you have sinned, and humble yourselves before God. Wait patiently for the Lord to return and judge all people fairly, even the rich who oppress you. Ask God to help you and pray for each other.

MACROSTRUCTURE	CONTENTS
GENERAL APPEALS	1:2–18 When you experience difficulties, only rejoice and keep on bravely enduring them. If a person wants to do evil, he should not think that God is tempting him to do so, since it is his own evil desire that causes him to do evil.
SPECIFIC APPEALS (contains peak units)	1:19–5:11 Do what God commands in his message rather than just listening to it. Stop honoring some people more than others. Only by doing good can a person prove that he truly trusts in God. You should strive to speak rightly to others and do good, acting peaceably toward others, to demonstrate that you are truly wise. You are fighting among yourselves because of your evil desires. Be sad because you have sinned, and humble yourselves before God. Wait patiently for the Lord to return and judge all people fairly, even the rich who oppress you.
CONCLUDING APPEALS	5:12–18 Always tell the truth. Whatever your circumstances are, pray and God will help you. So confess your sins to each other and pray for each other.

INTENT AND MACROSTRUCTURE

Throughout the 1:2–5:18 *BODY* of his epistle James' intent is to affect the actions and attitudes of the readers. Following the second exhortation in the epistle, ἡ δὲ ὑπομονὴ ἔργον τέλειον ἐχέτω 'let endurance have its perfect work' (1:4), there is a purpose clause that provides the author's general intent and purpose: ἵνα ἦτε τέλειοι καὶ ὁλόκληροι, ἐν μηδενὶ λειπόμενοι 'in order that you may be perfect and entire, lacking in nothing'. Spiritual maturity would radically affect their behavior and attitudes.

The overall structure (macrostructure) of the epistle's *BODY* consists of three units, the first being *GENERAL APPEALS* (1:2–18), which focus on the trials of life, a matter of great concern to the recipients in their situation. The second is *SPECIFIC APPEALS* (1:19–5:11), which primarily deal with particular problems in the lives of the church members that hinder spiritual growth. The third unit is *CONCLUDING APPEALS* (5:12–18), concerned with oaths, prayer, and healing, as well as brief references to several other motifs of the epistle. These *CONCLUDING APPEALS* are different from the *SPECIFIC APPEALS* in that they are not primarily prohibitionary but rather have an encouraging theme.

As to genre, there is no question as to the hortatory nature of the epistle. It has a greater frequency of imperatives than any other New Testament book. James' purpose is clearly not so much to inform as to command, exhort, and encourage (Moo, p. 36).

There are two peaks in the epistle, both of which occur in the *SPECIFIC APPEALS* unit. The first is 2:14–26, which is the expository peak of the 1:19–5:11 division; the second is 4:1–17, the hortatory peak of the entire epistle. (The characteristics of these peaks will be discussed later under the respective units.)

BOUNDARIES AND COHERENCE

The initial boundary of 1:2–5:18 is discussed under 1:1. Its final boundary is considered to be at the end of 5:18 for the following reasons:

1. The 5:19–20 unit is the last sentence in the book, and we would expect some type of closure.
2. James' primary goal in the epistle has been spiritual maturity, not only for the individual but also for the entire community. In 5:19–20, the final two verses, he urges the readers to reclaim the wanderer, which implies putting into practice all the exhortations of the whole letter.
3. A change of topic from an illustration of effective prayer in the Old Testament to the spiritual restoration of erring brothers is accompanied by the final occurrence of the vocative, ἀδελφοί μου 'my brothers'.

In view of these things, we see that these two verses serve as an excellent conclusion, advising the readers to do for each other what the author has tried to do for them (Johnson).

It is significant that there is remarkable agreement between commentators and linguistic analysts as to the identification of the epistle's paragraphs. However, when scholars try to outline James or determine its major divisions, there is much divergence of opinion. For example, Ropes (pp. 4-5) posits three high-level divisions after the initial verse of greeting: 1:2-2:26, "On Certain Religious Realities"; 3:1-18, "On the Teacher's Calling"; and 4:1-5:20, "Worldliness and the Christian Conduct of Life Contrasted." Hiebert, on the other hand, proposes four major units all built around the single theme of faith (pp. 42-46): 1:2-18, "The Testings of Personal Faith"; 1:19-3:18, "The Test Marks of a Living Faith"; 4:1-5:12, "The Reactions of Living Faith to Worldliness"; and 5:13-20, "The Reliance of Living Faith on God." Others, such as Burdick and Stulac, have as many as eight major units.

The reason for these differences is that James, unlike Paul (e.g., in Romans and Ephesians), does not follow a clearly defined outline. Paul's ideas are presented linearly, while James' tend to be cyclical. In chapter one James lays down a series of themes that he subsequently develops. Same or similar themes are widely scattered in the discourse. But this does not mean that James' letter was put together in a haphazard manner. To the contrary, it is integrated in a pattern that reflects the realities of life.

This sort of cyclical presentation may be harder to analyze than a linear presentation, at least for the Western mind, and to try to outline it in the traditional way gives a distorted view of the Epistle of James. To subsume too much under one general heading, as Ropes does in his first division, obscures the full message of James.

Our analysis highlights the way James uses his themes to point out the spiritual problems of the readers and to encourage and motivate them toward spiritual maturity. With great fervor James points to heartfelt repentance as the solution to their problems and urges the believers to pray for each other. He then concludes with a plea for restoring any in the community who have wandered from the truth.

Coherence in the 1:2-5:18 BODY is achieved by the author's consistently adhering to the effect on his audience that he intends (see "Intent and Macrostructure"). Semantic coherence is seen in the many motifs that "continually crop up, like musical motifs in a symphony or opera" (Moo, p. 39). Some of the key ones are: faith (1:3, 6; 2:1, 5, 14-26; 5:15); trials (1:2, 12; 5:13); endurance (1:3-4, 12; 5:11); wisdom (1:5; 3:13-17); perfection (1:4, 17, 25; 2:22; 3:2); prayer (1:5-6; 4:2-3; 5:13-18); the Word (1:18, 21-23; 2:8, 23; 4:5); speech (1:19, 26; 2:12; 3:5-10; 4:11; 5:12, 16); the rich (1:10-11; 2:6-7; 5:1-6); the law (1:25; 2:8-12; 4:11); righteousness (1:20; 2:21, 23-25; 3:18; 5:6, 16); salvation (1:21; 2:14; 4:12; 5:15); humility (1:9-10; 4:6, 10); sin (1:15, 21; 2:9; 3:8; 4:1-4, 8, 17; 5:15-16); judgment (2:4, 12-13; 3:1; 4:11-12; 5:9, 12); and repentance (4:7-10; 5:16, 19-20, as well as exhortations throughout the book that call for a change of negative behavior).

Terry used a similar list of recurring words and topics to determine eighteen sections that he listed clockwise around a circle. As he noted repetition of the concepts in other parts of the epistle, he drew lines between the linked sections. Thus he determined a pattern of discourse structure. By means of these intersectional links he ultimately connected all the sections in a spider-web fashion, and he concluded that this is what holds the book together (see table 6 on p. 118 of his article). Fry also identified recurring themes, plotting their occurrence throughout the book and perceiving structure in the epistle based on them. He concluded with a quasi-chiastic outline organized around the main theme of "The Testing of Faith."

PROMINENCE AND THEME

All three components in the 1:2-5:18 BODY of James' epistle are conjoined, hence naturally prominent. Therefore the theme statement is derived from all three.

PART CONSTITUENT 1:2–18 (Hortatory Division: General Appeals of 1:2–5:11)

THEME: When you experience difficulties, only rejoice and keep on bravely enduring them. If a person wants to do evil, he should not think that God is tempting him to do so, since it is his own evil desire that causes him to do evil.

MACROSTRUCTURE	CONTENTS
POSITIVE APPEAL	1:2–12 When you experience difficulties, only rejoice and keep on bravely enduring them. If you want to act wisely when trials come, ask God to help you, and firmly trust him. He will reward the person who bravely endures difficulties.
NEGATIVE APPEAL	1:13–18 When difficulties happen, if a person wants to do evil, he should not think that God is tempting him to do so, since it is his own evil desire that causes him to do evil and God does only good for us.

INTENT AND MACROSTRUCTURE

Following a brief greeting James plunges directly into one of the basic themes of his epistle. He is concerned principally with the way his readers who are trusting in Jesus Christ react to the difficult circumstances that they face in life and how their attitude and reactions will affect their spiritual lives. Thus the 1:2–18 division is hortatory, and it is composed of two hortatory sections. In the first (1:2–12) James exhorts the believers to react positively to the problems they face, because that will bring about spiritual maturity in their lives now and reward for them in the life to come. In the second (1:13–18) he warns of the consequences of reacting negatively because that would bring spiritual death. Furthermore, God's purpose in allowing difficult circumstances is not to cause them to sin but to make them into the kind of people he wants them to be.

BOUNDARIES AND COHERENCE

The initial boundary of 1:2–18 was discussed under 1:1. The phrase ἀδελφοί μου 'my brothers', which occurs frequently throughout James at the beginning of a new unit, is first used in 1:2. The beginning of the next unit is at 1:19, marked by a slightly varied repetition of the vocative, ἀδελφοί μου ἀγαπητοί 'my beloved brothers', followed by a series of exhortations about a new topic, the application of the 'message' to their individual lives.

The unit's lexical coherence is shown by the use of the noun πειρασμός 'trial/temptation', the cognate verb, and the negated cognate adjective ἀπείραστος 'untempted'. These forms occur in 1:2, 12, 13 (four times), and 14, where they function as the basic topic of both the positive section and negative section of this unit, and they do not occur elsewhere in James. A related concept is found in the adjective τέλειος 'complete, perfect', which occurs in 1:4 and 1:17 and describes God's goal for the testing and the anticipated effect of his help in the lives of believers. The semantic domain of giving and receiving also provides coherence to the unit: 'giving' and 'will be given' in 1:5; 'will receive' in 1:7 and 'receive' in 1:12; 'gift' in 1:17 (twice). The contrast between spiritual life in 1:12 and spiritual death in 1:15 also shows the coherence of the two components of the 1:2–18 unit.

PROMINENCE AND THEME

The two constituents of 1:2–18 are equally prominent due to their parallel structure, the first (1:2–12) being positive and the second (1:13–18) negative. Thus the themes of both are combined, with only slight modification, to form the theme of 1:2–18.

DIVISION CONSTITUENT 1:2–12 (Hortatory Section: Nucleus₁ of 1:2–18)

THEME: When you experience difficulties, only rejoice and keep on bravely enduring them. If you want to act wisely when trials come, ask God to help you, and firmly trust him. He will reward the person who bravely endures difficulties.

MACROSTRUCTURE	CONTENTS
APPEAL	1:2–11 When you experience difficulties, only rejoice and keep on bravely enduring them. If you want to act wisely when trials come, ask God to help you, and firmly trust him. Believers who are poor and those who are rich should both value most what God has done for them.
motivational basis	1:12 God blesses those who bravely endure difficulties; he will reward them by causing them to live eternally.

INTENT AND MACROSTRUCTURE

With the 1:2–12 hortatory section James now begins the letter's BODY. Here he establishes a pattern that he uses frequently through much of the book—a hortatory unit followed by a generic comment about the topic of the unit. Commentators have suggested that these generic comments were traditional sayings familiar to the readers and thus supportive to James' theme. These final statements of each section, such as the one in 1:12, function semantically as the *motivational* or *axiomatic basis* of the preceding APPEAL. This pattern is one of the criteria that we used to determine all but one of the sections from 1:2 through 5:11.

The internal structure of 1:2–12 is an APPEAL (1:2–11) and a *motivational basis* (1:12). The promise of a future reward for patiently enduring present difficulties would be a strong motivation to obey the exhortations given in 1:2–11.

BOUNDARIES AND COHERENCE

The initial boundary of the 1:2–12 unit has been discussed under 1:1. The final boundary is following 1:12, which is the *motivational basis* of the APPEAL in 1:2–11. In 1:13 a new topic begins about negative reactions to testing and the results of reacting in that way. There is also a change of genre at 1:13 from expository back to hortatory.

There is a difference of opinion regarding whether v. 12 should be connected with what follows or with what precedes, either on the paragraph or macrostructural level. Some commentators and versions consider v. 12 as a part of vv. 12–15 (e.g., Ward, Tasker; TEV, RSV, REB) or of vv. 12–18 (e.g., Davids 1982, Laws). Others consider it as a part of 1:2–12 at the macrostructural level (e.g., Blue, Hiebert, Burdick), and this is preferable for the following reasons:

1. Verse 12 functions as the motivational basis for 1:2–11, a pattern observed throughout the epistle.
2. Although the lexical linkage between 1:12 and 1:13 is obvious, semantically 1:12 has closer ties with what precedes it. The topic of trials introduced in 1:2 continues through 1:12. Only in 1:13 is temptation addressed, a different topic.
3. The argument begun in 1:3 about the way testing produces endurance is drawn to a close in 1:12 (Johnson).

Lexical coherence is shown by the use of the noun πειρασμός 'trial/temptation' (in the sense of difficult external circumstances) in vv. 2 and 12 and also by the following words in the same semantic domain: δοκίμιον 'testing/genuineness' in 1:3 and the cognate adjective in 1:12; and ὑπομονή 'endurance' in 1:3 and the cognate verb in 1:12. The focus of the 1:2–12 unit is on enduring trials, which involves reaching the goal (1:4) and receiving the reward (1:12).

PROMINENCE AND THEME

The 1:2–12 unit is predominantly positive. The four imperatives in the APPEAL (1:2–11) have to do with how one should rightly react to the difficulties in life. The importance of a proper attitude toward trials is reinforced by the *motivational basis* (1:12), which promises God's approval and reward for those who heed these exhortations. In most hortatory units both the APPEAL and *basis* are prominent enough that both should be included in the theme statement, as here.

SECTION CONSTITUENT 1:2–11 (Hortatory Subsection: Appeal of 1:2–12)

THEME: When you experience difficulties, only rejoice and keep on bravely enduring them. If you want to act wisely when trials come, ask God to help you, and firmly trust him. Believers who are poor and those who are rich should both value most what God has done for them.

MACROSTRUCTURE	CONTENTS
GENERIC APPEAL	1:2–4 When you experience difficulties that test whether or not you will continue to trust God, only rejoice and keep on bravely enduring them in order that you may be all that God intends you to be.
specific appeal₁	1:5–8 If you want to act wisely when trials come, ask God to help you, and firmly trust him.
specific appeal₂	1:9–11 Believers who are poor and those who are rich should both value most what God has done for them rather than focusing on their material resources that will disappear.

INTENT AND MACROSTRUCTURE

In the 1:2–11 subsection the author states the correct positive reaction that believers should have in facing difficult circumstances. The internal structure of the unit is GENERIC-specific: there is a GENERIC APPEAL (1:2–4) and two *specific appeals* (1:5–8 and 1:9–11). The GENERIC APPEAL urges believers to react positively to circumstances of life so that they may reach the goal of spiritual maturity, which is the theme of the entire epistle. The two following paragraphs are specific applications to situations faced by these believers in their lives. In the first, 1:5–8, godly wisdom that is acquired through prayer is discussed. Godly wisdom and prayer are topics that are further elaborated in chapters 3 and 5. In the second paragraph, 1:9–11, the problem of riches and poverty is discussed and then further elaborated in chapters 2 and 5. The common thread that runs through all three of the components of 1:2–11 is that the believers should have a proper attitude and spiritual values regardless of their circumstances.

BOUNDARIES AND COHERENCE

The initial boundary of the 1:2–11 unit has been discussed under 1:1. The beginning of the next unit at 1:12 is marked by a change of topic: from the poor and the rich to the promise of a reward to those who react properly to difficult circumstances. There is also a change of genre from hortatory to expository and a change of tense from aorist and future to present. In addition, at a higher macrostructural level, 1:12 functions as the *motivational basis* of the 1:2–11 unit (see "Intent and Macrostructure" of 1:2–12).

The lexical and semantic coherence between 1:2–4 and 1:5–8 is brought about by the tail-head linkage in vv. 4 and 5 with the verb λείπω 'lack'. In addition, the topic of faith, which is presented in v. 3 (in the subsection's first paragraph, 1:2–4) recurs in v. 6 (in its second paragraph, 1:5–8); and the opposite of faith is expressed both by the verb διακρίνω 'doubt, waver' and the metaphor of a wave, also in v. 6. The subsection's final paragraph (1:9–11) deals with another trial faced by the readers, poverty; and the correct attitude toward material circumstances is presented. (This is developed later in 5:1–11.)

PROMINENCE AND THEME

The theme statement of the 1:2–11 unit is drawn from each of its component paragraphs. Most prominent is the GENERIC APPEAL (1:2–4), since it is more comprehensive, but also included are the two *specific appeals* (1:5–8 and 1:9–11), which are applications of the principles stated in the first paragraph.

SUBSECTION CONSTITUENT 1:2–4
(Hortatory Paragraph: Generic Appeal of 1:2–11)

THEME: When you experience difficulties that test whether or not you will continue to trust God, only rejoice and keep on bravely enduring them in order that you may be all that God intends you to be.

¶ PTRN RELATIONAL STRUCTURE	CONTENTS
APPEAL₁ — CONTRAEXPECTATION	1:2a My fellow believers, only rejoice,
└─ concession	1:2b *even when you* experience various kinds of difficulties,*
┌─ orienter	1:3a *since you need to realize more and more*
│ ┌─ circum- ─ MEANS	1:3b that whenever *God allows* you to experience difficulties
│ │ stance └─ purpose	1:3c *in order to* test whether or not you will continue to trust *him,*
│ │ ┌─ condition	1:3d *if you continue to trust him,*
basis ── CONTENT ── NUCLEUS ── CONSEQUENCE	1:3e you will be able to bravely endure difficulties.
APPEAL₂ (MEANS)	1:4a And keep on enduring difficulties bravely *by trusting him more and more firmly* [PRS]
basis ── POSITIVE (purpose)	1:4b in order that you may become all God intends you to be [DOU] (*or, spiritually* mature and complete),
└─ negative	1:4c not lacking any good quality. [LIT]
	*Unless otherwise marked, 'you' in the display text is always a plural reference in this SSA.

INTENT AND PARAGRAPH PATTERN

James' intent in the 1:2–4 paragraph is to affect the readers' actions and attitudes. To accomplish this James uses two positive exhortations (2a–b and 4a), the second built upon and complementary to the first. The paragraph is therefore hortatory, its principal constituents being two APPEALS and their *bases*. This is by far the most common paragraph pattern throughout the book.

The *basis* for the first APPEAL (3a–e) gives the premise for reacting joyfully to trials. The *basis* for the second (4b–c), instead of consisting of a grounds construction beginning with a conjunction such as γάρ 'since' or ὅτι 'since', consists of a purpose construction introduced by the conjunction ἵνα 'in order that'. This purpose construction is a motivational purpose acting as the *basis* for the APPEAL. This *basis* states the theme and goal of the entire book. James expects his audience to react positively to all circumstances in their lives, even the difficult ones, so that they will become mature—all that God intends them to be.

NOTES

1:2a My fellow believers, The vocative ἀδελφοί μου 'my brothers' is used by James, in slightly varied forms, fifteen times in this short book. Usually it occurs at the beginning of a new unit and occasionally within a unit to mark something he wants to emphasize. In 2:1 he clarifies the sense in which he uses this term: "My brothers, as believers in our glorious Lord Jesus Christ" (NIV). In the displays ἀδελφοί μου 'my brothers' is rendered as 'my fellow believers'.

only rejoice, The imperative verb ἡγήσασθε 'consider, regard' is in the aorist tense, not present, as might have been expected. The aorist indicates either that they are to adopt this attitude toward trials once and for all as a result of a deliberate conscious decision (Hiebert, Moo), or that each case is to be considered as an occasion for joy (Ropes, Adamson). Either view is possible. Many versions use "consider" or "count" here.

In the Greek the noun phrase πᾶσαν χαράν 'all joy' is fronted, indicating emphasis. It has been taken by some commentators (e.g., Mayor,

Moo) to mean an attitude of joy in the highest degree; others (e.g., Hiebert, Huther, Laws) take it to mean only joy, unmixed with other reactions. The second alternative seems preferable, since this is the first *APPEAL*, which is positive, and is best understood as contrasting with the prohibited reaction in the negative *APPEAL* in 1:13 (see the comments on the macrostructure of 1:2–18). James is saying that one should respond with only joy in contrast to those who respond by blaming God for their difficulties. JBP makes this higher-level contrast explicit: "don't resist them as intruders, but welcome them as friends!" In some languages a more natural translation might be 'only rejoice', as in the display. James is calling for the sort of positive attitude toward trials that views them as opportunities for growth in the Christian life and so accepts them as occasions for rejoicing (Hiebert).

1:2b *even* when you experience various kinds of difficulties, The noun πειρασμός 'trial/temptation' has two basic meanings. It can be (1) external afflictions that may test a person's character or (2) an attempt to cause someone to sin. The majority of commentators think that in the context of this paragraph James is focusing on external afflictions rather than temptations, although some (e.g., Oesterley, Adamson) think that both are involved. The first view seems preferable for the following reasons:

1. The verb περιπίπτω 'fall into' in its other two New Testament occurrences (Luke 10:30, Acts 27:41) refers clearly to external circumstances.
2. In the following verse (1:3) the same concept is referred to as 'the testing/genuineness of your faith' and this would imply a testing rather than a temptation.
3. The use of the indefinite temporal construction introduced by ὅταν 'whenever', the qualification of ποικίλος 'various', and the aorist subjunctive mode of the verb would all suggest that James refers to the common difficulties of life as well as to the adversities that Christians encounter as the result of their faith (Moo).

The adjective ποικίλος 'various' is emphatic because it is separated from its noun and occurs clause-finally. It stresses the diversity of the testings.

The communication relation between 2a and 2b could be considered NUCLEUS-circumstance. However, some commentators (e.g., Manton) mention that joy is not the natural reaction to difficulties, implying a CONTRAEXPECTATION-concession relation. That is why it may be helpful to make this relation explicit by the use of a mild concessive connector such as '*even* when'.

1:3a *since* you need to realize more and more Many versions and commentators translate the participle γινώσκοντες 'knowing' as though James' readers already understood what he was about to say (TEV and NIV have "because you know"). While this verse does indicate the grounds or basis of the previous exhortation, the present participle may well indicate that his readers, although not ignorant of the truth being set forth, needed to continue to realize it in their personal experience. The verb γινώσκω 'know' suggests a knowledge grounded in personal experience. That is, as they react joyfully when they face trials, they will come to more fully realize that the testing of their faith develops endurance (Hiebert).

1:3b–c that whenever *God allows* you to experience difficulties *in order to* test whether or not you will continue to trust *him*, Commentators disagree on the meaning of the noun δοκίμιον 'testing/genuineness' here. Some (e.g., Laws, Ropes) think that the process of testing is what is in focus and that it is the testing of their faith that produces endurance. Others (e.g., Mayor, Martin) think that the focus is upon the means of testing the genuineness of their faith. Still others (e.g., Adamson, Blue) say that the focus is upon the result of testing; that is, the part of their faith proved to be genuine is what produces endurance. The semantics of this abstract noun is very complex and its meaning is further complicated by the fact that it is personified, being the agent of the main verb κατεργάζεται 'causes, produces'. The rendering in the display is an attempt to unscramble the semantic mismatch and to make clear that these three foci are not mutually exclusive but each is a part of the stated or implied information in the author's argument.

One meaning component of the word 'testing/genuineness' is the *means* of testing, which is correlated with the noun πειρασμός 'trial/temptation' in 1:2b. The implied agent of the testing is God, who allows trials to test their faith and reveal its true nature. That it is a *process* is partially indicated by the use of the present tense in both the participle 'knowing' and the main verb 'causes, produces'. These difficulties are certainly the means of the testing, but the process of testing itself is also necessary to produce the desired effect. Furthermore, the *result* of testing is reflected in 3d-e, since only genuine faith develops endurance. In 1 Pet. 1:7, the only other place where δοκίμιον is used, the result of testing is more clearly in focus. Here, although all three senses may be thought of as present, it is the process of testing that is more in focus.

The thing that is being tested is faith. In this context the noun πίστις 'faith' refers not to the objective content of the gospel but subjective confidence in God and his message. James is saying that the purpose for which God allows difficulties to come into their lives is to increase their faith or steadfastness.

1:3d *if you continue to trust him,* This proposition is supplied to express an implicit part of the author's argument. It is a condition that must be met or the intended outcome of the testing will not be accomplished.

1:3e you will be able to bravely endure difficulties. The object of the verb κατεργάζεται 'causes, produces' is the noun ὑπομονή 'endurance', which Louw and Nida define as "capacity to continue to bear up under difficult circumstances" (25.174). Although this is a noun form, it refers to an event concept and is expressed as a verb phrase in the display.

1:4a And keep on enduring difficulties bravely It is characteristic of James' style that he repeats a word or idea and then expands the concept. Here ὑπομονή 'endurance' is repeated along with the conjunction δέ. Commentators and versions are about equally divided in their interpretation of whether or not contrast is indicated by this occurrence of δέ. Levinsohn (p. 65) says, "The assertions of v. 4 build on those of v. 3, but are distinct." In v. 3 endurance is the quality resulting from the testing, whereas in v. 4 it is a further step in the process. The coordinate conjunction 'and' is used in the rendering here because a contrast relation might make the reader think that James is changing his instructions rather than just adding an additional step in the process. If, in a given language, it is too difficult to connect the two *APPEALS* by a form like 'and', it would be best to omit the conjunction, as in NIV, TEV, and some other versions.

In v. 3 'endurance' occurs without an article, whereas here it is used with an article to signal that it was previously mentioned. It is also personified, functioning as the subject of the imperative verb ἐχέτω 'let have'. James seems to be emphasizing that this perseverance is not just a passive attitude but is, in contrast, an active quality that should bring results in their lives. The noun phrase ἔργον τέλειον 'perfect/full work' focuses on the process of allowing or enabling endurance to produce fully what God intends for our lives. It may refer to the development of perfect endurance (Huther, Johnson), but more probably the reference is to the development of the perfect character described in the following clause (Tasker, Laws). James reminds his readers that they should keep on trusting God so that endurance achieves its ultimate goal.

by trusting him more and more firmly Since endurance itself is aspectual, a process that continues over time, it implies an action and the action is trusting. Ropes says, "The constancy here referred to is constancy in faith, from which completed character may be expected to spring."

1:4b in order that you may become all God intends you to be (*or, spiritually* mature and complete), A positive purpose clause here states the final outcome they should realize. It is introduced by ἵνα 'in order that' and is the *basis* for the second APPEAL in the paragraph. Again James, in characteristic style, repeats a word and then proceeds to expand the concept. The word τέλειος 'complete, perfect', which occurs in the two parts of the verse and links them, expresses what God expects from this process of testing and endurance. Some commentators argue that the goal of 'perfection' is unattainable in this life and is therefore an eschatological goal to be attained only in the coming age. However, the present tense 'may be' implies not merely a future goal but a present progressive attainment. This is in accord with the entire book. James is most concerned with the daily actions of those who make a profession of faith. Hiebert says, "Maturity of character is not the result of the number of trials encountered but the way in which those trials are met, allowing them to achieve their divinely intended impact on us." The theme of maturity keeps recurring and could be considered a motif that helps to tie the whole book together.

The second adjective ὁλόκληροι 'complete' carries the idea of 'whole, intact'. Here, used in an ethical sense, it would mean all of those virtues that should characterize the mature believer. Moore (p. 59) calls 'perfect' and 'complete' a near-synonymous doublet. Based on this, the first of the alternative renderings in the display is one generic phrase.

1:4c not lacking any good quality. As an intensifier James adds an equivalent negative here, ἐν μηδενὶ λειπόμενοι 'not lacking anything'. This is litotes, in which an affirmative idea is expressed by the negation of its antonym. However, the negative is retained in the display because a positive restatement would be tautological. Moreover, James often states the same idea in positive and negative form for emphasis. The translator should use the vernacular form that will bring out this emphasis.

BOUNDARIES AND COHERENCE

The opening boundary of the 1:2–4 unit has been discussed under 1:1. The beginning of the next unit in 1:5 is marked by a change of topic: from the proper attitude toward trials to prayer for wisdom. There is a tail-head linkage between v. 4 and v. 5; the final word of v. 4, λειπόμενοι 'lacking', is carried over as λείπεται 'lacks' in the first phrase of the 5–8 paragraph, which is in a specific-GENERIC relation to this paragraph.

The lexical coherence of 1:2–4 is shown by πειρασμός 'trial' in v. 2 and several words in vv. 3 and 4 in the same semantic domain: δοκίμιον 'testing/genuineness' (v. 3), ὑπομονή 'endurance' (v. 3 and v. 4), and τέλειος 'perfect, complete' (v. 4, twice). The trials are the occasion; endurance is the expected reaction; perfection is the desired result or outcome of the situation. These words do not occur again until 1:12, which is the *motivational basis* of the 1:2–11 subsection.

PROMINENCE AND THEME

The two APPEALS of 1:2–4 have natural prominence and thus are included in the theme. The 3c purpose clause in the *basis* of the first APPEAL is also included, since faith is basic to the argument of the whole paragraph. Also included is the purpose clause in the *basis* of the second APPEAL, holding up spiritual maturity as the goal for Christian living.

SUBSECTION CONSTITUENT 1:5-8
(Hortatory Paragraph: Specific Appeal₁ of 1:2-11)

THEME: If you want to act wisely when trials come, ask God to help you, and firmly trust him.

¶ PTRN	RELATIONAL STRUCTURE	CONTENTS
APPEAL₁ — *motivational basis₁* — *motivational basis₂*	condition — CONSEQUENCE — NUCLEUS₁ — NUCLEUS₂	1:5a If anyone of you does not know *what he should do to endure trials well*,†
		1:5b he* should ask God *what he should do*,
		1:5c *since* God wholeheartedly helps† all people *who ask*
		1:5d and *since* he does not reproach [LIT] anyone *for asking*;
		1:5e and *if anyone asks*, God will help him know *what he should do*.
APPEAL₂ — *basis*	circumstance — NUCLEUS — POSITIVE / NEGATIVE — NUCLEUS — NUCLEUS / comparison — amplification — CONCLUSION — ORIENTER / CONTENT — grounds₁ — grounds₂	1:6a But *when anyone asks God*,
		1:6b he should firmly trust *God*.
		1:6c He should not doubt *that God wants to help him always*,
		1:6d since anyone who keeps doubting God is *unstable*
		1:6e like a wave of the sea that goes back and forth when the wind blows. [DOU] [SIM]
		1:7a Indeed that person *who doubts* should not think
		1:7b that the Lord will do anything *that is requested by him*,
		1:8a *since he is* a person who cannot decide *if he will commit himself to God*
		1:8b *and is* unstable in all he does.

*In all displays 'he' means 'he or she' except when its referent is a particular man (see p. 3).

INTENT AND PARAGRAPH PATTERN

James' intent in 1:5-8 is to continue to affect the reactions of the readers to their trials. The unit consists of two APPEALS (5a-b and 6a-c), the first supported by two *motivational bases* (5c-d and 5e) and the second by its *basis* (6d-8b); hence the unit is a hortatory paragraph. The APPEALS are two specific ways by which the readers are to put into action the advice of the previous paragraph. The first APPEAL, that they should pray, is elaborated later, in 5:13-18; and the topic of faith that is so crucial in the second APPEAL is again in focus in 2:14-26.

NOTES

1:5 Some commentators (e.g., Oesterley) see no connection between this paragraph and the preceding one. Moo says, "[W]e should probably not tie verses 5-8 too closely to verses 2-4." But that some thought sequence is implied is clear from the use of the conjunction δέ 'and/but'. It functions here to indicate a switch of topics to wisdom, as indicated by the conditional clause εἰ δέ τις ὑμῶν λείπεται σοφίας 'if anyone of you lacks wisdom'. TEV and NCV have "but," JBP "and," but most versions (e.g., NIV, REB, RSV, JB) omit the conjunction. It is likewise omitted in the display.

Another signal of a transition is the repetition of the verb λείπω 'lack'. Repetition of a key word or thought in a tail-head linkage is a device that James uses frequently between closely related units. The common overall theme here is how the believer should handle trials.

1:5a If anyone of you does not know The noun σοφία 'wisdom' represents a cognitive event and is therefore rendered as a clause. James' idea of wisdom here comes from the Old Testament, especially the beginning chapters of Proverbs. It is not general knowledge of things but rather understanding what God wants people to do. Hiebert says, "It is the moral discernment that enables the believer to meet life and its trials with decisions and actions consistent with God's will." This conditional clause does not imply that James did not know whether there were those who had the need or not; rather, it assumes the reality of the need. The use of the indefinite pronoun τις 'anyone' indicates that acknowledging that lack is an individual matter. The topic of wisdom is further developed in 3:13-17.

what he should do to endure trials well, In the Greek the content of the wisdom is implicit and must be supplied from the context. A concise summary of the immediate context (1:2-4), like the one supplied here, may be required for the full proposition to be understood. Some commentators (e.g., Hiebert, Tasker) say that this wisdom would also include other situations in life in which one needs to know the will of God and how to apply it: 'if anyone of you does not know what God wants him to do'. Such a broader content would also be acceptable. Without understanding the biblical view of wisdom intended here, this verse is subject to misinterpretation, as though God had promised to give the believer unlimited knowledge.

1:5b he should ask God *what he should do,* The present tense of the verb αἰτείτω 'ask' indicates that the action is to be continuous or repeated. The object of 'ask', though unstated, is clear from the context. The proposition reflects the author's emphasis on conduct in this epistle.

1:5c *since* **God wholeheartedly helps all people who ask** The word διδόντος 'giving' is a participle functioning as an attributive to θεοῦ 'God'. This puts the focus upon the character of God himself and not on the giving. James is saying that one of the bases for the exhortation in 5b is this characteristic of God. This relation is expressed in the display by the conjunction 'since'. The present tense indicates that it is God's nature to be continually giving. The word 'giving' here is to be understood in its causative sense. In many languages 'giving' would not collocate with 'wisdom', and a word such as 'teach' or 'help to know' may be necessary. In the display, simply 'help' is used, for brevity's sake, without the full form of the causative, since the full form occurs in 5e. The adjective πᾶσιν 'to all' sets the scope of God's giving, but the context implies a limitation: it is available to all *who ask*. The adverb ἁπλῶς 'unreservedly/generously' used in this context stands in contrast with 'two-souled' in 1:8a (Moo) and is rendered 'wholeheartedly'.

1:5d and *since* **he does not reproach anyone** *for asking***;** James here reinforces the positive 5c statement by means of litotes, the negation of a negative concept, in this case 'reproaching'. It might be translated as 'since God is very eager to help you', but this would be tautological. Note that although the reason for the 'reproaching' (ὀνειδίζοντος) is not expressed in the Greek, in many languages it will have to be expressed. Commentators suggest 'for asking', 'for lacking wisdom', or 'for bothering him'.

1:5e and *if anyone asks,* **God will help him know** *what he should do.* The implicit conditional clause is supplied here to remind the translator that this is a part of James' argument. If it is omitted in translating, the translator needs to do a comprehension check to be sure that the readers remember that this is a condition of God's helping anyone.

The Greek is καί δοθήσεται αὐτῷ 'and it will be given to him'. When such a clause follows an imperative, it often expresses the result of carrying out the action of the imperative (cf. Phil. 4:9) and may function semantically as a motivational basis for the command, as here. The implicit object of the verb is supplied here from the context: 'what he should do'.

1:6a-b But *when anyone* **asks** *God,* **he should firmly trust** *God.* In this context there is a semantic contrast, shown in English versions by "but" as the translation of δέ. In 5e the promise is that if they ask for wisdom, God will help them, *but*, in contrast, James says, a lack of faith may hinder this promise from being fulfilled.

The verb αἰτείτω 'let him ask' is repeated here from v. 5, indicating that this is another exhortation to the readers. However, there is mismatch between the grammar and the semantics. The new information is contained in the noun πίστις 'faith', which is an event and best expressed as a verb. This becomes the second APPEAL of this paragraph, while the lexical content of the imperative 'let him ask' may function semantically as the circumstance for the new concept of trust that James focuses on for the remainder of the paragraph. This second APPEAL of the paragraph is stated first positively (in 6b) and then negatively (in 6c). The exact content of this trust needs to be extracted from the context. Commentaries are almost equally divided between two views of what the object of this faith is: (1) It is the confidence that he will receive his request (e.g., Oesterley, Huther). (2) It is steadfast faith in God (e.g., Hiebert, Ropes, Davids 1994). Although the first alternative appears obvious in the immediate context, when one looks at the broader context (especially 1:2–4 and 1:12) and sees that the basic theme of the whole unit (1:2–12) is the testing and approval of faith in God, then the second alternate becomes preferable. The issue is not just God's answering a particular prayer of a person but rather that person's faith, which is an attitude of committal to and dependence on God. He must believe not only that God is able to grant requests but also that he answers in harmony with his own character and purpose.

1:6c He should not doubt *that God wants to help him always*, The verb διακρινόμενος 'doubt' in 6c is further evidence of the mismatch in 1:6a-b. This verb is a negative restatement of 'trust'. The participial form carries imperative force just like its positive contrast 'trust' in 1:6b. Literally, it means 'divide'. The picture is of a divided mind, a mind torn between competing desires or emotions within (Hiebert). This negative statement is James' way of clarifying what faith is by stating how a person acts who does not have faith. Again, commentaries are equally divided about what should not be doubted (see the two options in the note on 1:6b). The second option—steadfast faith in God—is again preferred because of the context, that is, that one should not doubt God's good will toward man (Laws, Davids 1989). This is the same concept that is expressed in 1:17. The present tense of the participle implies that the indecision has become habitual. The rest of the paragraph (vv.6–8) develops this contrast between faith and doubt.

1:6d since anyone who keeps doubting God is unstable Here the conjunction γάρ 'for' introduces a series of propositions, from 1:6d to 1:8b. It indicates that these propositions function as the *basis* for the 1:6b-c APPEAL. Propositions 6d-e are an illustration of doubt. They describe the attitude and actions of the doubting person by comparing them to waves (see the note on 6e).

1:6e like a wave of the sea that goes back and forth when the wind blows. The two verbs ἀνεμιζομένῳ 'being driven by the wind' and ῥιπιζομένῳ 'being tossed about' used here to describe the action of a wave are considered by many to be synonyms. Moore (p. 60) calls them a doublet. All the commentators agree that the point of similarity here is instability or unfixed direction. Since faith is a stable committal to God, its antithesis, doubt, is the *lack* of a stable commitment to him.

1:7a Indeed that person *who doubts* should not think Some commentators (e.g., Hiebert, Ward) think that the conjunction γάρ 'for' is here introducing a second reason why a person should ask in faith and not doubt. Other commentators (e.g., Martin, Laws, Ropes), however, consider it to be introducing an explanation or a confirmation of a previous statement, which is another use of γάρ (Dana and Mantey, p. 242). Moreover, only KJV, RSV, and NRSV have a conjunction that expresses reason here. Therefore it seems preferable to consider this proposition an explanation of the previous statement. It continues the comparison of the doubting man to a wave and does not seem to be a distinctly new idea. Thus 7a-8b function as an amplification of 6d-e.

Although the verb in the verb phrase μή . . . οἰέσθω 'let not suppose' is imperative, the proposition functions as the ORIENTER of the CONTENT in 7b, so that instead of presenting an additional appeal, it intensifies the CONTENT that it introduces. The ORIENTER is considered of equal prominence with the CONTENT, since it is not simply an introducer of the CONTENT but contains both an imperative and the negating particle that qualifies the CONTENT as something not to be accepted as true.

The verb 'suppose' implies a subjective or unwarranted judgment (Hiebert). Here it is in the present tense and is used with the particle μή 'not'. Brooks and Winbery say, "The present imperative with μή is used to stop an action already in progress. . . . The word 'stop' may be used in the translation to bring [this] out . . ." (p. 127). However, as Greenlee (p. 41) points out, whether it is something already in progress or something not yet being done can be determined only from the context. The former would give 'stop doing this', the latter 'don't be doing this'. BAGD (516.III.3) describes the latter as "expressing a command that is generally valid," that is, a general truth. In deciding whether or not to use the word 'stop', the translator should consider James' intent. Was it to focus on a particular situation that needed strong reprimand or was it to state a general principle? Here it seems to be a general principle.

The noun phrase ἄνθρωπος ἐκεῖνος 'that person' serves to identify the subject of 'suppose' as the person who was mentioned as doubting. It has a suggestion of disapproval, as in Mark 14:21 and Matt. 12:45 (Ropes).

1:7b that the Lord will do anything *that is requested by him,* Most commentators think that ὁ κύριος 'the Lord' here refers to God the Father, since the prayer for wisdom in 1:5 is addressed to God. Lenski, however, holds that since the title 'Lord' is given to Jesus Christ in 1:1, the reference is to him. Either is possible but the former is more probable. As to the pronoun τι 'anything', its meaning may be limited to the thing requested; God does give general benefits to all people. This implicit information is supplied in the display.

1:8a *since he is* a person who cannot decide *if he will commit himself to God* The adjective δίψυχος 'two-souled' is a graphic word that some think was coined by James. It is not found in Greek literature before the date of his writing. However, the idea of being of two minds is a common Old Testament concept and is also in the teaching of Jesus (Matt. 22:37). The word adds to the characteristics of the doubting person that he is vacillating, lacking total allegiance to God. Some languages have an idiom to express this concept. The implicit content of the cognitive event is rendered in the display in terms of commitment. Davids (1989) says, "The promises of the gospel all assume a commitment of the individual to, and trust in, God. . . ."

Some versions (e.g., RSV, NRSV, TEV, NCV) translate vv. 7 and 8 together, making v. 8 the expanded subject of 'will receive': 'the doubter should not think that a double-minded man, unstable in all his ways, will receive anything'. But Tasker says that this is not the most natural rendering in view of the Greek word order. The phrase ἀνήρ δίψυχος 'double-minded man' can also be regarded as appositive to ὁ ἄνθρωπος ἐκεῖνος 'that person' in v. 7; as such, it sets forth a graphic description of his character (Tasker). Hiebert suggests that a dash at the end of v. 7 followed by the appositive words would be more forceful, but it is more natural in most languages to supply a copulative verb, as in the display.

Some (e.g., Laws, Martin; NIV, REB, WEY) consider this phrase simply a further and pejorative description of the doubter, but there is also a logical relationship between 7a-b and 8a-b. Huther refers to the "reason why the doubter is not heard"; based on his view, the communication relation between 7a-b and 8a-b is CONCLUSION-grounds, hence 'since'. Moo says, "'That man', 'that doubter' must not expect that God will respond to his requests, for he is insincere and inconsistent in his allegiance to God."

The change here from ἄνθρωπος 'person/man' to ἀνήρ, the primary meaning of which is 'man' (i.e., male), but which may also be translated 'person', is thought by most (e.g., Ropes, Hiebert) to be merely for stylistic variety with no difference in meaning. Mayor suggests that when these two words are used for 'person', ἄνθρωπος is a general term and ἀνήρ is more commonly used with some descriptive word, as in 1:12, 1:23, and 2:2. This may well be true (BAGD, p. 66.4), but such a distinction would probably not affect a translation.

1:8b *and is* unstable in all he does. The adjective ἀκατάστατος 'unstable' conveys the thought of being unsettled or lacking foundation. It is qualified by the phrase 'in all his ways', which is a Hebraism depicting his personal conduct. It encompasses all the varied aspects of a person's life. Davids (1989) says, "There is a basic instability within that will eventually become evident in behavior."

BOUNDARIES AND COHERENCE

The opening boundary of the 1:5-8 unit has been discussed under 1:2-4. The beginning of the next unit at 1:9 is marked by a change of topic: from faith and doubting to rich versus poor and height versus humiliation.

Semantic coherence is evidenced by the contrast between πίστις 'faith' in 1:6 and διακρίνω 'doubt' in 1:6 (twice) and words in the same semantic domain, ἀκατάστατος 'unstable' in 1:8, δίψυχος 'two-souled' in 1:8, as well as the illustration about waves in 1:6.

PROMINENCE AND THEME

The two *APPEALS* in 1:5-8 are more naturally prominent than the *bases*, so the theme is taken from the *APPEALS*.

SUBSECTION CONSTITUENT 1:9–11
(Hortatory Paragraph: Specific Appeal₂ of 1:2–11)

THEME: Believers who are poor and those who are rich should both value most what God has done for them rather than focusing on their material resources that will disappear.

¶ PTRN — RELATIONAL STRUCTURE	CONTENTS
APPEAL₁	1:9 The believer who is poor/humble should take pride† in *the fact that God* considers him very valuable (*or*, has exalted him *spiritually*), [MTY]
APPEAL₂	1:10a and the believer who is rich should take pride in *the fact that* he humbles himself† *in order to trust in Jesus Christ* (*or*, but the rich person *can only* take pride *in the fact that God* will humble him *in the judgment* [IRO]),
basis — NUCLEUS — NUCLEUS	1:10b since he *and his riches* [MTY] will pass away
└ comparison	1:10c just as a wild flower *withers*. [SIM]
┌ circumstance	1:11a When the sun rises,
├ comparison — NUCLEUS	1:11b the scorching heat/wind dries the plant and the flower falls
└ amplification	1:11c and it is no longer beautiful.
└ amplification — NUCLEUS	1:11d In the same way the rich person will die [MET] while he is busy working, *leaving behind his riches*.

INTENT AND PARAGRAPH PATTERN

James' primary intent in the 1:9–11 paragraph is to affect the attitude of the readers toward riches. This is a motif that is further developed in 2:1–13, where there is a detailed discussion of the believers' favoring the rich while neglecting the poor, and again in 5:1–11, which includes a warning to the rich and encouragement for the poor.

The 1:9–11 paragraph is composed of two APPEALS (1:9 and 1:10a), followed by the *basis* of the second APPEAL (1:10b–11d); thus it is a hortatory paragraph. In it James reminds both the poor and the rich about what they should value most in their lives. He does so here in the midst of a unit on how they should react toward their trials. The implication seems to be that the believers value wealth so highly that a lack of it is a trial—they need to be reminded of what they should really value and they need to be warned of the danger of loving wealth, which is not lasting.

NOTES

1:9 Some commentators (e.g., Oesterley) think that there is no connection between this paragraph and the preceding one. However, the use of δέ 'and/but', as in 1:5, implies that there is a sequence of ideas of some kind, although the precise connection is not indicated. A few commentators (Alford, Lange) consider this as antithesis; however, the majority (e.g., Adamson, Huther) regard it as simple transition. NASB translates it "but"; in all other versions the relation is left implicit, as in our rendering here. Because James does not finish the topic of the positive reaction to difficult circumstances until v. 12, it is clear that in vv. 9–11 he is building on and developing what he has already said. This helps support the decision to consider this paragraph the second specific example of the 1:2–4 GENERIC APPEAL (see "Intent and Macrostructure" of 1:2–11).

The believer who is poor/humble Commentators are divided in their opinion about which sense of the adjective ταπεινός 'poor/lowly' is in focus here. Since it is contrasted in 1:10 with the rich, the sense of 'poor' is certainly in view. However, in this verse it is also used in connection with the noun ὕψος 'high position' and the verb καυχάομαι 'take pride in'; thus the sense of a low social status is intended as well. In reality, the two concepts are integrally related, since in most cultures a high social status is given to the wealthy while a low social status is given to the poor. Note that James does not mean a particular lowly brother but lowly brothers in general. In translation, one should consider whether it is more natural to use singular or plural here.

should take pride in *the fact that God considers him very valuable (or,* has exalted him *spiritually),* The Greek word ὕψος 'high position' is a noun, but in this context it involves an event and/or attributive concept. The agent of this action is God, since the use of the noun phrase ὁ ἀδελφός 'the brother' here implies a spiritual application. This term occurs frequently in the epistle and is always used in a Christian rather than biological sense (see the notes on 1:2 and 2:1). Although a few commentators (e.g., Oesterley) interpret this exaltation as a change in fortune that has resulted in the poor becoming rich, the vast majority (e.g., Mayor, Davids 1982, Tasker) consider it a reference to the poor man's present spiritual status as a Christian. So James is saying that it is God who makes this value judgment to raise the believer to a position of high spiritual value and the believer is to recognize this. Hiebert vividly summarizes: "He may be financially poor, looked down upon by the world, and considered a nobody, but in the eyes of God he has a position of lofty dignity."

The verb καυχάομαι 'boast, take pride in' can be used negatively with the meaning of arrogant boasting, but it is frequently positive, as here. The present imperative indicates that the believer should adopt this as a characteristic response. It parallels the command of 1:2, 'only rejoice' when trials come. Here the believer is asked to react positively with pride to a specific trial, that is, economic or social deficiency. He must realize that God's approval is far more important than wealth, which will very quickly pass away. In some languages it might be more appropriately translated 'be glad about' or 'rejoice'.

1:10a and the believer who is rich The particle δέ 'and/but' along with the fronted noun phrase ὁ πλούσιος 'the rich one' indicates a switch of topics, from 'the poor brother' to 'the rich one'. Note that the word 'brother' is not repeated following the phrase 'the rich'. There are two main views regarding this: (1) that both the poor and rich are Christians and that James is giving each appropriate spiritual advice; (2) that the rich one is not a Christian and is identified with the non-Christian rich addressed in 5:1–6. While the second view is held by some (e.g., Huther, Martin, Davids 1982), the first view is preferred for the following reasons:

1. This is the meaning that is most natural to the structure of the Greek sentence, since the parallel structure of the argument implies that both 'the poor' and 'the rich' relate to the same noun, 'brother', and both would be subjects of the verb 'take pride in'.
2. The second view would seem to assume that there were no rich people in the church, whereas 1 Tim. 6:17–19 and other passages indicate that there were rich believers.
3. The second view would make this statement to unbelievers intensely ironical; and although James does use irony, he seems to be completely sincere here.

Most commentators (e.g., Moo, Ropes, Hiebert) hold the first view. The first view is reflected also in a number of versions (NIV, TEV, NEB, JB). But although it is the view preferred here, there is enough support for the second view to present it as a valid alternative in the display. It must be noted, however, that the implications of the alternative view affect the rendering of the rest of the proposition, and therefore it will be discussed separately at the end of this note following the citation of the alternative rendering.

should take pride in *the fact that* he humbles himself *in order to trust in Jesus Christ* The prepositional phrase ἐν τῇ ταπεινώσει αὐτοῦ 'in the humiliation of him' is an event concept and must be propositionalized as a clause, requiring that the agent and the nature of the humiliation be specified. Some (e.g., Ropes, Oesterley) suggest that the experience of humiliation is economic or social: the rich one may lose some of his riches and be ostracized by his former rich friends. While this may have been true in the experience of many, it seems best to see the focus of the statement as figurative, not material. If the exaltation of the poor brother has a spiritual basis, the experience of the rich brother's being humbled should also be understood spiritually. This is a statement of true Christian values. As the poor brother should overlook his poverty to focus on his value in God's eyes, so the rich brother should overlook his earthly riches to accept the true humility that is a necessary part of his faith in Christ. James repeats this thought explicitly and in more detail in 4:10, "Humble yourself before the Lord and he will lift you up," and by implication in 4:13–16, where the attitudes of boasting and bragging are condemned.

If this concept of humiliation is expressed as a verb, it may be necessary to express the agent of the verb. Most versions that use a verb form translate it as a passive and do not express the agent. In the display it is translated as a reflexive, making the individual himself the agent. Since this is a part of the APPEAL, it would be much more in agreement with the paragraph's hortatory genre to have the person himself as the agent. In 4:10, which is a semantic equivalent, this same root is translated as a reflexive in most versions, 'humble yourself'. If in the receptor language it is difficult to translate the concept of self-abasement, it could be translated as 'The rich believer should take pride in the fact that God has caused him to be lowly in order to follow him'.

(**or, but the rich person** *can only* **take pride in the fact that God will humble him** *in the judgment*), Although this alternate rendering is not the preferred one, it is based on a valid view. Stulac (pp. 190-201) gives a scholarly presentation of this view that the rich one was not a believer, and it is true that πλούσιος 'the rich (person)' could be functioning as a noun here. The main arguments for this view are:

1. James omits the term 'brother' when he introduces the rich man, whom he compares to a plant that withers and dies.
2. In other parts of his epistle James leaves the impression that the rich do not belong to the Christian fellowship (see 2:6-9 and 5:1-6).
3. James is addressing believers who were poor and oppressed by the rich. It is conceivable that the prospect of the future judgment of the rich would be an added comfort to the recipients of this letter.

If this view is taken, the propositionalization of the irony would have to be expressed nonfiguratively, as in the display. The prospect of his destruction in the end would be substantiated by 10b. But the translator who chooses to see this as irony should do a thorough comprehension check to be sure the receptor audience understands the rendering.

1:10b since he *and his riches* **will pass away** The subordinate conjunction ὅτι 'because, since' introduces the *basis* for the second APPEAL of this paragraph. James here states the *basis* for putting one's trust in Christ and not in riches. Some commentators (e.g., Laws, Kistemaker) and most versions interpret the verb παρελεύσεται 'will pass away' as 'will die' with the reference being to the rich man's death. Others (e.g., Ropes, Bratcher; JB) see this as a metonymy; that is, πλούσιος ... παρελεύσεται 'the rich one will pass away' means 'his riches will pass away'. Still others (Tasker, Adamson) think that the two views are not mutually exclusive and that it is referring to both the man and his wealth. The final view is preferable, since the whole paragraph treats the proper Christian perspective on wealth.

1:10c just as a wild flower *withers.* In the noun phrase ἄνθος χόρτου 'flower of grass', the noun χόρτος includes any small plant growing in the wild, but the focus is more on the flower of the plant. The point of similarity in this simile is transitoriness: both the bloom and the man with his wealth will disappear. The plant may last a short time, but the bloom is of even shorter duration.

1:11a When the sun rises, In this context, rather than introducing a reason for 10c, the function of the conjunction γάρ is to introduce an elaboration of the figure of the fading flower in 10b-c. In so doing, it also shows that v. 11 functions as an amplification of the 10b-c NUCLEUS.

11b the scorching heat/wind dries the plant and the flower falls The noun καύσων 'burning heat' may refer to the heat of the sun or the scorching hot wind, which is how the Septuagint renders Jon. 4:8 (Mayor, Moo). Either of these would be acceptable. However, the focus of the passage is the effect on the plant—its very temporary life. In translating, a culturally relevant term that will keep this focus should be considered. All four verbs, ἀνέτειλεν 'rose', ἐξήρανεν 'dried', ἐξέπεσεν 'fell off', and ἀπώλετο 'perished', are in the aorist, which though it is the tense generally used to present the action as an historical event, is "gnomic," indicating that the events are characteristic of what always happens (Hiebert). English would use the general present for this; some languages would use the habitual aspect.

The picture here (also used in 1 Peter 1:24) is probably drawn from Isa. 40:6-8. The terminology—'flower of the grass', 'dries up', 'falls'—is the same as well as the point of similarity, namely transitoriness, but the application is different. James applies it specifically as a value statement about the place of wealth in the Christian's life.

1:11c and it is no longer beautiful. The word εὐπρέπεια 'beauty' augments the point of similarity, transitoriness. Some think it could imply the attractiveness of wealth, but the primary focus is still on temporariness. Though it is an abstract noun in the Greek, it is rendered as an adjective in the display. The verb ἀπώλετο 'perished' is likewise expressed as a modifer, 'no longer': 'no longer beautiful'.

1:11d In the same way the rich person will die while he is busy working, *leaving behind his riches.* The verb μαρανθήσεται 'will fade away' is used metaphorically here—the comparison is to a flower. In reference to a person, it means death. To see it only as death, however, would miss the main focus of the paragraph (see the note on 1:10b). After all, the poor man dies as well as the rich. What is implicit in the argument is brought out well by Hort, who says that James means "not death absolutely but death as separating riches from their possessor and showing them to have no essential connection with him" (quoted by Adamson, p. 66). The rich need to be reminded not of the certainty of death but of the transitoriness of wealth (Ropes).

While some commentators (Moo, Tasker) think the expression ἐν ταῖς πορείαις αὐτοῦ 'in his (business) pursuits' refers to business trips made by the rich man, most (e.g., Ropes, Davids 1982, Laws) regard it as a generic term for business activity. It emphasizes that his business was his highest priority.

BOUNDARIES AND COHERENCE

The initial boundary of the 1:9-11 unit has been discussed under 1:5-8. The final boundary at 1:12 has been discussed under the macrostructure of 1:2-11.

Verses 9-10 are grammatically coherent in that one verb, καυχάσθω 'let boast' (v. 9), is an exhortation addressed to both the humble brother in v. 9 and the rich one in v. 10. The semantically contrastive nouns ὕψει 'high position' (v. 9) and ταπεινώσει 'humiliation' (v. 10) also lend coherence, as does the illustration in vv. 10-11 comparing the transitoriness of flowers with the rich man and his riches that will fade.

PROMINENCE AND THEME

The most prominent components of the 1:9-11 paragraph are the two *APPEALS,* in which one verb, καυχάσθω 'let boast', is addressed to both the poor and the rich. The theme statement includes a summary of these two *APPEALS* plus the 10b NUCLEUS of the second *APPEAL*'s *basis*, which is also naturally prominent.

SECTION CONSTITUENT 1:12
(Expository Propositional Cluster: Basis of 1:2–11)

THEME: God blesses those who bravely endure difficulties; he will reward them by causing them to live eternally.

RELATIONAL STRUCTURE	CONTENTS
GENERIC ——— 'people'	1:12a God blesses† the people
└── identification — NUCLEUS	1:12b who bravely endure difficulties;
└── amplification	1:12c by doing so, they have proved *that they truly trust him.*
SPECIFIC ——— NUCLEUS	1:12d He will cause them to live *eternally,* which will be their reward.
└── amplification	1:12e He has promised this *reward* to those who love him.

INTENT AND STRUCTURE

At the macrostructure level the 1:12 unit functions as the *motivational basis* of the 1:2-11 *APPEAL* (see "Intent and Macrostructure" for 1:2-12). Here James encourages his readers by promising a reward if they heed his exhortations. The basic structure of this unit is expository.

While the primary reason for deciding the relation between v. 12's two higher-level components is semantic, the function of ὅτι must also be considered, since ὅτι connects the two in the

Greek. Their nuclear subcomponents are 'blessed is the person who endures trials' and 'he will receive the crown of life'. Technically, these statements are not in a cause-effect relation but in a restatement relation, either generic-specific or nucleus-amplification. It is possible therefore that ὅτι here has a function akin to its use when it introduces content after an orienter. This would be expressed in English as 'that'. In such a context as the one here, the sense is somewhat comparable to 'in that' in English: 'Blessed are those who bravely endure difficulties in that they will receive the crown of life'. It is true that this type of construction can be more naturally expressed in English with 'because', as some versions have it: 'Blessed are those who bravely endure difficulties because they will receive the crown of life'. However, in semantic theory 'because' is an expression of reason or grounds, and this is not in view here. Perhaps the best way to express the relation is to omit any conjunction, as in CEV: "God will bless you, if you don't give up when your faith is being tested. He will reward you with a glorious life." Note the parallelism between "God will bless you" and "He will reward you," instead of one being the basis for the other.

NOTES

1:12a God blesses The word μακάριος 'blessed, happy' has its roots in the Old Testament, especially the Psalms and Proverbs. The term would be familiar to James also from the beatitudes of Jesus. It is the antonym of 'woes' in Luke 6:24–26. BAGD (p. 486) defines this word as "*blessed, fortunate, happy,* usu. in the sense *privileged recipient of divine favor.*" Although a number of versions (e.g., REB, TEV, NAB, JB) translate this word as 'happy', an equal number (e.g., NIV, RSV, WEY, CEV) use 'blessed'. In James 1:12 the latter seems preferable, since the focus is upon what God will do for people and not upon their reaction to it. Johnson says,

> Although the translation "happy" is certainly possible . . . , "blessed" is preferable not only because it can be distinguished from "happiness" . . . , but also because of its consistent use within the biblical tradition to describe the result of right relatedness of humans to God. . . .

While the Jews always avoided using the name of God, God was the unnamed agent of the blessing; hence the implicit agent is supplied here.

If 'happy', which has popular support, is preferred, a possible rendering would be 'Happy are the people who bravely endure difficulties; by doing so, they have proved *that they trust God. They are happy* because God will cause them to live eternally'. The communication relation between 12a–c and 12d–e would then be RESULT-reason rather than GENERIC-SPECIFIC.

the people The noun ἀνήρ 'man' here occurs without an article but with a descriptive clause following it; thus the meaning is 'man, mankind, people in general'. (See the final paragraph of the note on 1:8a for more on ἀνήρ.) In some languages the plural might be more appropriate, as some versions have it: "God blesses the people who patiently endure difficulties" (NLT). In the display the plural is used to make the third person references in the verse clearer.

1:12b who bravely endure difficulties; This proposition echoes 1:2–4. It is clear that πειρασμός 'trial/temptation' refers to outward difficulties here as it did there, rather than to temptation to sin, which would have to be resisted, not endured (Ropes). The verb ὑπομένει 'endures' is in the present tense, indicating that the faithful Christian characteristically remains steadfast and refuses to give up despite the trials of life. Such endurance is a sign of genuine faith.

1:12c by doing so, they have proved *that they truly trust him.* The conjunction ὅτι 'that, because' is the first word in the 1:12c–e subordinate clause. (For its function see "Intent and Structure" under the display of 1:12.) This conjunction is not rendered in the display, since the clause it introduces is in a restatement relation to 12a–b. The participial phrase δόκιμος γενόμενος 'having become approved' occurs before the main verb of the clause and makes an additional observation about those who persevere. Ropes says, "This is another way of saying ὑπομένει, not a further condition of receiving the crown." A participial phrase of the type used here may indicate time. Some versions render it so, for example, NIV's "when he has stood the test." There is, of course, an eschatological aspect to the reward in 12d, but it can be enjoyed in part during this present life (Tasker). James' primary focus here is upon the present attitude of those who will receive the reward.

BAGD (203.1) defines the adjective δόκιμος as "approved (by test), tried and true, genuine." It comes from the same root as δοκίμιον 'testing, genuineness' in 1:3, where it is used with 'of their faith', indicating that it is their faith that is being tested and approved. This implicit information from 1:3 has been supplied to clarify what it is that is being approved.

In the Greek the words 'having become approved' represent the perspective of the one who has endured the trials. This perspective is preserved by the rendering 'they have proved *that they truly trust him*'. (NCV is similar: "After they have proved their faith, God will reward them with life forever.") This proposition amplifies 12b. Bratcher suggests that this phrase might be combined with the preceding clause as one statement, such as 'the person who successfully endures all hardships and does not lose his faith'.

1:12d He will cause them to live *eternally*, which will be their reward. The verb phrase λήμψεται τὸν στέφανον τῆς ζωῆς 'he will receive the crown of life' is from the perspective of the one who has endured the trials, like 'having become approved' in 12c. But the reciprocal of 'he will receive' augmented by explicit reference to the implied agent of the giving, God, is used in the display since 'receive' does not have this sense in many languages or, if it could be used, is often unnatural.

The noun στέφανος 'crown' is used by Paul as a metaphor for the believer's reward. Such a crown was a head-wreath given to the winner in Greek athletic contests. Orthodox Jews abhorred such games, however, so it is unlikely that James had this sort of crown in mind for Jewish readers. In the Septuagint the word 'crown' was used to symbolize a special honor. It was usually given by a king to a friend as a mark of honor (Hiebert). Therefore, although Paul uses it as a live metaphor (e.g., 1 Cor. 9:25), in the Book of James it is a dead metaphor, meaning simply a reward, despite the fact that the NIV, RSV, and JB have 'crown'. Note that TEV, REB, NCV, and TNT do have 'reward'.

Commentators agree that in the phrase 'crown of life', 'life' is appositive to 'crown': 'a reward that consists of life'. In this context 'life' suggests much more than physical life, since it is something to be received in the future and it is based upon loving God. Hiebert says, "It is not merely escape from eternal condemnation, but the believer's eternal enjoyment of life as the approved of God in His presence."

1:12e He has promised this *reward* The specific agent of the verb ἐπηγγείλατο 'he promised' is not explicit in the Greek, although late textual variants filled out what may have seemed to be a lacuna by adding either κύριος or θεός. 'God' is the subject, however, based not on any textual variant, but on the fact that throughout Scripture he is always the agent, implied or otherwise, of blessing. There doesn't seem to be a specific verse in the Old Testament or in the Gospels to which James is referring here, so from that standpoint the agent could be either 'God' or 'Jesus'. Most commentators prefer 'God' as the agent. Thus, it appears, 'God' is the divine agent in this whole section, since he is named in 1:5, and the referent of τοῦ κυρίου 'Lord' in 1:7 is most likely also to him, since both θεός and κύριος refer to the one agent who is granting requests in 1:5-8.

The content of the promise is made clear in the Greek by the relative pronoun ὅν 'which', which refers back to 12c. In the display the specific referent of 'this', namely 'reward', is supplied from 12d.

to those who love him. This is the first mention of love in the Epistle of James. One might have expected a statement regarding faith here such as is stated in 1:3c, so James seems to be equating real Christian faith with loving God. Note that this is a common phrase in the Septuagint and later Jewish and Christian writings.

BOUNDARIES AND COHERENCE

The initial boundary of the 1:12 unit has been discussed under 1:2-11, and the beginning of the next unit at 1:13 under 1:2-12. This unit coheres in that it is one Greek sentence and a generic summary statement functioning as the *motivational basis* for 1:2-11.

PROMINENCE AND THEME

The theme of the 1:12 unit is drawn from both its GENERIC and SPECIFIC components. In a restatement relation such as this it is often difficult to see one as more prominent than the other.

DIVISION CONSTITUENT 1:13–18 (Hortatory Section: Nucleus₂ of 1:2–18)

THEME: When difficulties happen, if a person wants to do evil, he should not think that God is tempting him to do so, since it is his own evil desire that causes him to do evil and God does only good for us.

MACROSTRUCTURE	CONTENTS
APPEAL	1:13–15 When difficulties happen, if a person wants to do evil, he should not think that God is tempting him to do so, since it is his own evil desire that causes him to do evil.
motivational basis	1:16–18 Stop thinking falsely that God tempts you to do evil, since God does only good for us.

INTENT AND MACROSTRUCTURE

The 1:13–18 section is hortatory, being composed of an APPEAL with its *motivational basis*. James' purpose in this unit is to warn his readers that if they react negatively to the difficult circumstances they face, the result will be disastrous for their spiritual life. In the 1:13–15 APPEAL he admonishes them not to blame God for temptations to sin because the real source of evil is their own evil desire. In the 1:16–18 *basis* he reminds them that God is totally good and that his purpose in our lives is to do only good and not evil. This latter unit functions not only as a *motivational basis* for the 1:13–15 APPEAL, it also contains an APPEAL within it, which has to do with how the hearers should handle the main APPEAL. That is, it is not another main APPEAL.

BOUNDARIES AND COHERENCE

The opening boundary of 1:13–18 was discussed under 1:2–12. The beginning of the next unit at 1:19 is marked by a change of topic: from the source of temptation to remarks about speech and anger. The vocative ἀδελφοί μου ἀγαπητοί 'my dear brothers' is further evidence for a boundary at 1:19.

Semantic coherence comes from the discussion of the goodness and perfection of God in vv. 13, 17, and 18 in contrast with the temptation to do evil in 13–15. The verbs συλλαμβάνω 'conceive' in 1:15 and ἀποκυέω 'give birth' in 1:15 and 1:18, which are used metaphorically, provide lexical and semantic coherence. Sin is spoken of as producing spiritual death in 1:15, whereas God produces spiritual life to believers through the new birth in 1:18.

PROMINENCE AND THEME

In the 1:13–18 section the 1:13–15 APPEAL is naturally prominent. The theme of 1:13–18 is therefore the theme of this APPEAL, along with the final clause of the 1:16–18 *motivational basis*. The unusual APPEAL in 1:16 may well have been intended by James to give prominence to the statement that follows it, namely, that God does only good for us. Therefore it would be impossible to think that he would tempt us to do evil.

SECTION CONSTITUENT 1:13–15 (Hortatory Paragraph: Appeal of 1:13–18)

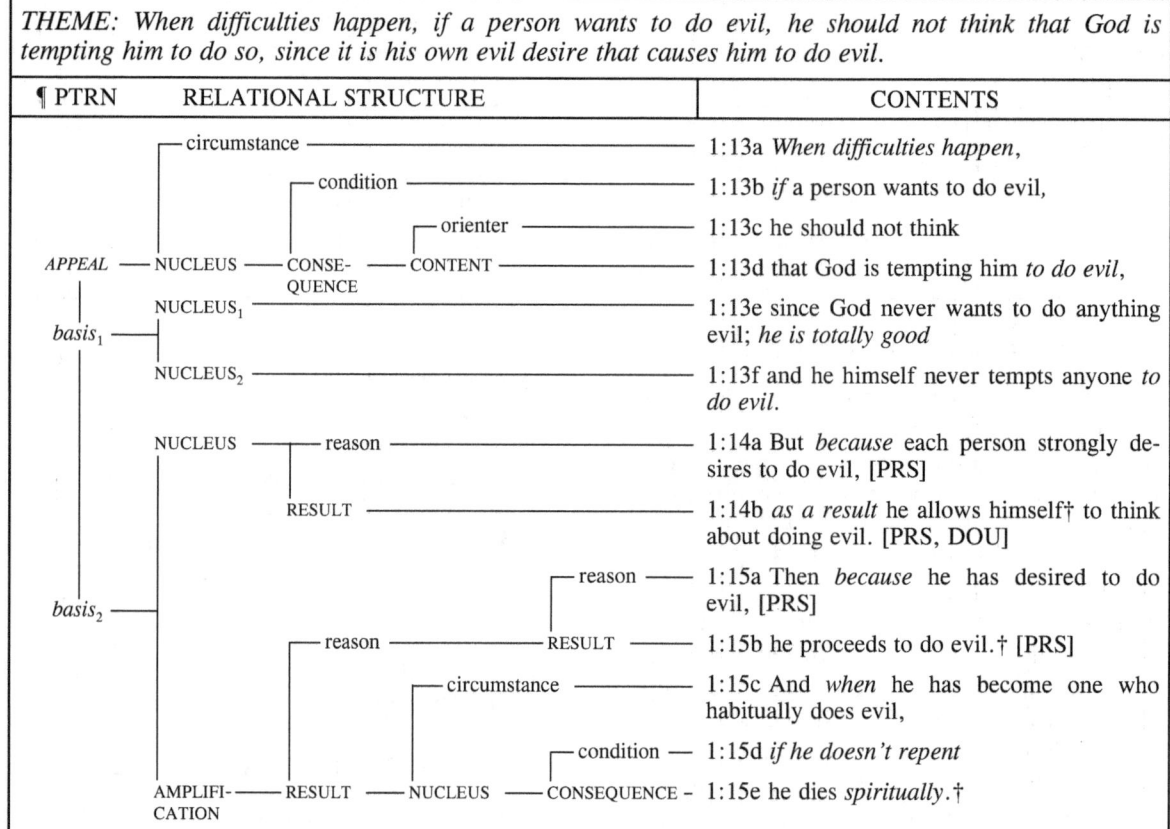

THEME: When difficulties happen, if a person wants to do evil, he should not think that God is tempting him to do so, since it is his own evil desire that causes him to do evil.

INTENT AND PARAGRAPH PATTERN

In 1:13–15 James proceeds to discuss the fact that the difficult circumstances of life can become the occasion for temptation. His intent here is to warn the readers not to seek an excuse for sin by accusing God of being responsible.

The 1:13–15 unit is a hortatory paragraph, consisting of an APPEAL (13a–d) and two *bases* (13e–f and 14a–15e). The contention in the first *basis* is that we should not blame God for temptation because God by his very nature cannot tempt. In the second *basis* the real source of temptation is named, our own evil desire, which ultimately leads to spiritual death.

NOTES

1:13a–b When difficulties happen, if a person wants to do evil, In 1:2 and 12 James uses the noun πειρασμός 'trial/temptation' in expressing the fact that God allows difficult experiences to come into our lives with the goal of our becoming spiritually mature. Here in 1:13 he uses the related verb form πειράζω 'try/tempt' and combines it with the thought of sin, which makes it clear that he is talking about an inner enticement to evil. Ropes says, "In the case supposed the person tempted either has yielded, or is on the point of yielding; he is called ὁ πειραζόμενος [the one being tempted], instead of ὁ ἁμαρτών [the one sinning], by a kind of euphemism." In the display the concept of 'difficulties' is retained because it is the circumstance for the temptation. The conditional conjunction 'if' is supplied because the experience of being tried carries with it the possibility of failure (Laws).

The passive participle πειραζόμενος 'being tempted' is translated as a passive in almost all English versions. If rendered as active, as many languages require, it is necessary to supply the agent. From vv. 14–15 it is clear that the person himself is responsible, so in the display this is expressed as a person's desire to do evil.

1:13c–d he should not think that God is tempting him *to do evil,* The verb in the phrase μηδεὶς ... λεγέτω 'let no one say' is a present imperative. Preceded by μηδείς, it may imply that James' readers had asserted that God was tempting them (cf. the note on 1:7a, next to last paragraph). The tendency to blame God for temptation and hence excuse succumbing to it is a theme with ample parallels in both Greek and Jewish literature (Laws). It would be possible to say 'stop saying/thinking that God is tempting you' here, but since it follows a participle (πειραζόμενος 'being tempted' in 13b) that semantically is a conditional ('if a person wants to do evil'), it seems preferable to render this as a general principle, as in the display.

1:13e since God never wants to do anything evil; *he is totally good* The conjunction γάρ 'for' introduces a twofold argument for rejecting the claim that God is the source of temptation. The first point is based upon his character: he is ἀπείραστος 'untemptable'. This negative adjective is derived from the passive form of the verb πειράζω 'tempt', which is used three times in this verse. The noun κακός 'evil' is used without an article and denotes things that have the moral quality of being harmful and damaging, the opposite of the morally good. Commentators differ in their interpretation of the adjective 'untemptable'. According to the majority (e.g., Moo, Hiebert), it means that God is not tempted by evil. It denotes the complete lack of desire for evil and is in contrast with πειραζόμενος 'being tempted' in 13b. This negative statement implies that God is totally good, and this is supplied in the display since the negative statement alone does not adequately portray the holy character of God. Laws says that "temptation is an impulse to sin, and since God is not susceptible to any such desire for evil he cannot be seen as desiring that it be brought about in man."

Two other possible interpretations of the phrase 'untemptable of/with evil' should be considered. A few commentators (e.g., Martin, Alford) argue that it is simply the equivalent of the classical ἀπείρατος derived from the verb πειράω 'try, experience', meaning that God is inexperienced in evil. But this is not acceptable since the meaning in this passage must be determined from the general force of the verb πειράζω 'tempt' (Mayor). The other view is held by Davids (1982): the phrase means that God should not be tested by evil people. He bases his view partially on such Old Testament passages as Deut. 6:16. But Moo says that Davids' view "has difficulty explaining *estin* ('is') and must give an unusual force to the genitive *kakōn*." This statement probably refers to the fact that κακός 'evil' as a substantive is normally used to describe evil things while πονηρός in substantive form is used to describe evil people. The traditional view is preferable in that it correlates with the central topic of the paragraph, temptation, and also because of the deliberate play on words, using a cognate of πειράζω 'try/tempt'.

1:13f and he himself never tempts anyone *to do evil*. The use of δέ 'and/but' here indicates that this is a continuation of the foregoing. This proposition is the second point of the argument rejecting the claim that God is the source of temptation: such a claim is contrary to the actions of God. (See the note on 1:13e for the first point.) The intensive pronoun αὐτός 'he/himself' gives marked prominence to God's being the one who is not the source of temptation. Although the pronoun 'himself' is omitted by some versions (e.g., NIV, JB), many include it (e.g., TEV, RSV, REB, NCV). While God does test people, as seen in the Old Testament (e.g., Abraham), it is never with evil intent (Tasker).

1:14a But *because* each person strongly desires to do evil, In 14a–15e James states the true source of temptation. This is the second *basis* for the 13a–d APPEAL. It begins with ἕκαστος δὲ . . . ὑπὸ τῆς ἰδίας ἐπιθυμίας 'But each person . . . by his own desire'. The majority of commentators and versions indicate the contrast here by translating δέ as 'but', 'rather', or 'instead'. Along with δέ there is frontingindicating that the argument develops through a switch of agents: from ὁ θεός 'God' to ἕκαστος 'each person'.

The word 'because' is supplied to express the reason-RESULT communication relation between 14a and 14b. The singular ἕκαστος 'each person' and ἰδίας 'his own' in the Greek show that being tempted is an individual matter.

The noun ἐπιθυμία 'desire, lust' is in itself a neutral term meaning strong desire, but in this context it is associated with sin and so is obviously negative. The word order in the Greek permits the phrase 'by his own evil desire' to be seen as closely connected either to the main verb, πειράζεται 'is tempted', or to the participles that follow it. Although a few associate it only with the main verb, the majority associate it either with the two participles that follow (Huther, Tasker) or with all three verbs (Ropes, Lenski). The latter seems best. While it belongs primarily with the main verb (for otherwise the contrast between God and 'evil desire' is weakened), it is secondarily the agent of the participles also (Ropes).

The preposition ὑπό 'by' implies direct agency and serves to personify 'evil desire' as the active agent of the tempting. However, a man's desires cannot function independently of the man himself. If, by his own volition, he dwells on those desires, he is being lured by those thoughts to a course of action, in this case, yielding to temptation. To avoid both the passive and personification, in the display 'each person' is made the subject of an active verb: 'each person strongly desires to do evil'. Several commentators (e.g., Moo, Tasker, Davids 1982, Hiebert) point out that it is significant that James does not blame the devil or other outside influence but focuses directly upon the individual's personal responsibility. This supports the decision in propositionalizing vv. 14 and 15 to make the individual himself the agent of all of the actions.

1:14b *as a result* he allows himself to think about doing evil. The finite verb πειράζεται 'is tempted' and the participles ἐξελκόμενος 'being drawn out' and δελεαζόμενος 'being enticed' are synonymous. The participles present temptation in vivid figurative language. The imagery here comes from fishing and perhaps also hunting, or it may refer to a harlot's activities as in Prov. 7:6–23. Commentaries vary greatly in the details of interpreting this imagery. One view is that there is a sequence of actions: first the drawing out of a person from his repose and second the alluring as with bait (Lenski, Oesterley) or as with a harlot (Mayor). Another view is that the two phrases are two aspects of the same process (Ropes, Hiebert). Most versions translate this with two phrases: "dragged away and enticed" (NIV), "attracted and seduced" (JB), "lured and enticed" (RSV), "drawn away and trapped" (TEV). However, Moore (p. 60) considers these two participles a synonymous doublet (conjoined by 'and'), and his interpretation is preferable. At the same time, in many languages it is impossible to personify 'evil desire' and have it act upon the person himself. In the display it is therefore rendered nonfiguratively. If the translator desires, the comparison could be stated as follows: 'Just as an animal is lured by bait, so a person is lured by his evil thoughts to do evil'. If the figure is retained in translation, care must be taken lest a complicated figure obscure the higher-level, more important contrast between the first *basis* (it is not God who causes sin) and the second *basis* (it is one's own evil desire that is the cause of sin).

It should also be noted that all verbs in this verse are in the present tense showing that the author is here focusing on the process of evil desire working in the hearts of people.

Since the communication relation between 14a and 14b is reason-RESULT, the phrase 'as a result' is supplied in the display.

1:15a Then *because* The adverb εἶτα typically indicates progression of some type, but the exact form of that progression will depend upon the context. If it is rendered here as 'then', the aorist participle συλλαβοῦσα needs to be rendered as 'because he has desired to do evil', as in the display. An option would be to omit 'then' and translate 15a–b as 'Because he desires to do evil, he proceeds to do evil'.

The thrust here is that evil desire results in sin, sin becomes habitual, and then the inevitable result is spiritual death. This progression is of a reason-result type. While versions tend to use temporal markers such as 'when' or 'after' for this progression, reason-result markers are better, except for 15c where 'when' suggests the progression from initial sin to continual sin.

he has desired to do evil, The phrase ἡ ἐπιθυμία συλλαβοῦσα 'evil desire having conceived' is the first part of a metaphor, the image of which has to do with the process of human reproduction. (It continues in 15b.) The point of similarity is the inevitability of the progression of the actions. Spelled out in full, the comparison would be 'as a woman conceives and gives birth to a child, so evil desire results in sin'. However, it may be impossible in many languages to make 'evil desire' the subject of the verb. Therefore, it seems best, as in 14a, to make the person himself the subject—it is the person who desires evil and yields to temptation. It is so rendered in the display, that is, nonfiguratively. This also helps to clarify the higher-level contrast between 13c–d and 14a–b: it is not God who is enticing you to do evil, but the person himself, desiring to do evil, who is the cause of sin.

1:15b he proceeds to do evil. The verb phrase τίκτει ἁμαρτίαν 'bears sin' completes this part of the human reproduction metaphor started in 15a. There are two views as to the tie between 'conceives' and 'gives birth': The first is that 'conceives' and 'gives birth' are the one process of producing sin (Adamson, Ropes). The second is that they are two distinct steps, in which allowing the desire to remain in the heart is conceiving and the actual act of sin is the birth

(Mitton, Hiebert). Although the second view seems preferable, it is difficult to express distinct stages nonfiguratively. The distinction between temptation in 14b and conception in 15a may overlap. A translator who would like to make conception distinct from birth might say 'Then because he has desired to do evil, he decides to do evil and then does so'. What is important is to clearly state the inevitable progression from evil desire to the act of sin. Ropes may be right when he says, "The two ideas have no independent significance in the figure." He refers to such passages as Gen. 21:2, "Sarah conceived and bore Abraham a son. . . ."

1:15c And *when* he has become one who habitually does evil, The extended human reproduction metaphor continues here, with the noun ἁμαρτία 'sin', which was the object in 15b, fronted and functioning as the subject. This is tail-head linkage, used immediately prior to the climax in 15e to highlight that event. The root of the verb ἀποτελέω 'become complete/full-grown' is τελέω 'complete'. It is the same root used in 1:4, where it expresses the fact that God intends good results from the proper reaction to trials. In contrast, this wrong reaction of doing evil results in death. Mayor says, "Sin when full-grown, when it has become a fixed habit determining the character of the man, brings forth death." The aorist participle ἀποτελεσθεῖσα 'having been fully formed' before the main verb indicates time prior to the main verb, so the temporal 'when' is used here even though there is a reason-RESULT relation between 15c and 15d-e.

1:15d *if he doesn't repent* Some commentators say that at this point in the paragraph there is an implication of a strong call to repentance. Thus there is the possibility of interrupting the decline into spiritual death by repenting. Adamson, in discussing the three stages of the progression from evil desire to death, refers to "the next step in sin's deadly fruition. *If* he yields to it. . . ." Hiebert says, "Unless its life and growth are terminated by repentance, sin will have its sure development until it becomes 'full grown'." This implicit idea is therefore supplied in the display.

Starting at 14a, there is a long complicated argument of five propositions leading to an inevitable result, spiritual death (14a–15e). All of this argument is the second *basis* for the APPEAL in 13a-d. If such a complicated discourse structure is not common in the target language, it may be helpful to supply the implicit information about repentance earlier, perhaps following 15a, for example: 'then because he has decided to do evil, if he does not repent, he proceeds to do evil.'

1:15e he dies *spiritually*. The verb ἀποκυέω 'give birth to' is a continuation of the human reproduction metaphor, a second birth in which sin is the mother of death. This personification is not retained in the display. The noun θάνατον 'death' is the object of the verb. It is translated 'death' in all versions, but commentators say the meaning is 'spiritual death' or 'eternal death'. The metaphor is rendered nonfiguratively here. It would be possible, at the conclusion of v. 15, to add a brief statement such as 'Just as when a woman conceives and when the child is fully formed, she bears it, so it is that if a person decides to do evil, he will do so and the inevitable result will be spiritual death.'

BOUNDARIES AND COHERENCE

The initial boundary of 1:13–15 was discussed under 1:2–12. The beginning of the next unit at 1:16 is marked by the occurrence of the vocative ἀδελφοί μου ἀγαπητοί 'my beloved brothers'. There is also a shift of focus in the subject matter: from the responsibility of man in 1:13–15 to God's positive character traits in 1:16–18, which makes the assumption that God is the author of sin completely false.

Lexical coherence consists in the use of πειράζω 'try/tempt' in v. 13 (three times) and v. 14. Note that it is used not in the positive or neutral sense of testing, but in the sense of an enticement to sin, hence the rendering 'tempt'. The related adjective ἀπείραστος 'untempted' is used in v. 13. This is the only occurrence of the word in the New Testament. Lexical items in the semantic domain of sin also add coherence: κακός 'evil' in v. 13, ἐπιθυμία 'lust' in vv. 14 and 15, and ἁμαρτία 'sin' in v. 15. Referential coherence is shown by the use of μηδείς 'no one' and οὐδείς 'no one' in v. 13 and ἕκαστος 'each one' in v. 14. They emphasize personal responsibility.

PROMINENCE AND THEME

The 1:13–15 theme statement is drawn from the naturally prominent features of the unit, the *APPEAL* with its orienter and the second *basis*, since it is the second *basis* that gives the real source of temptation to sin, namely one's own evil nature.

SECTION CONSTITUENT 1:16–18 (Hortatory Paragraph: Basis of 1:13–15)

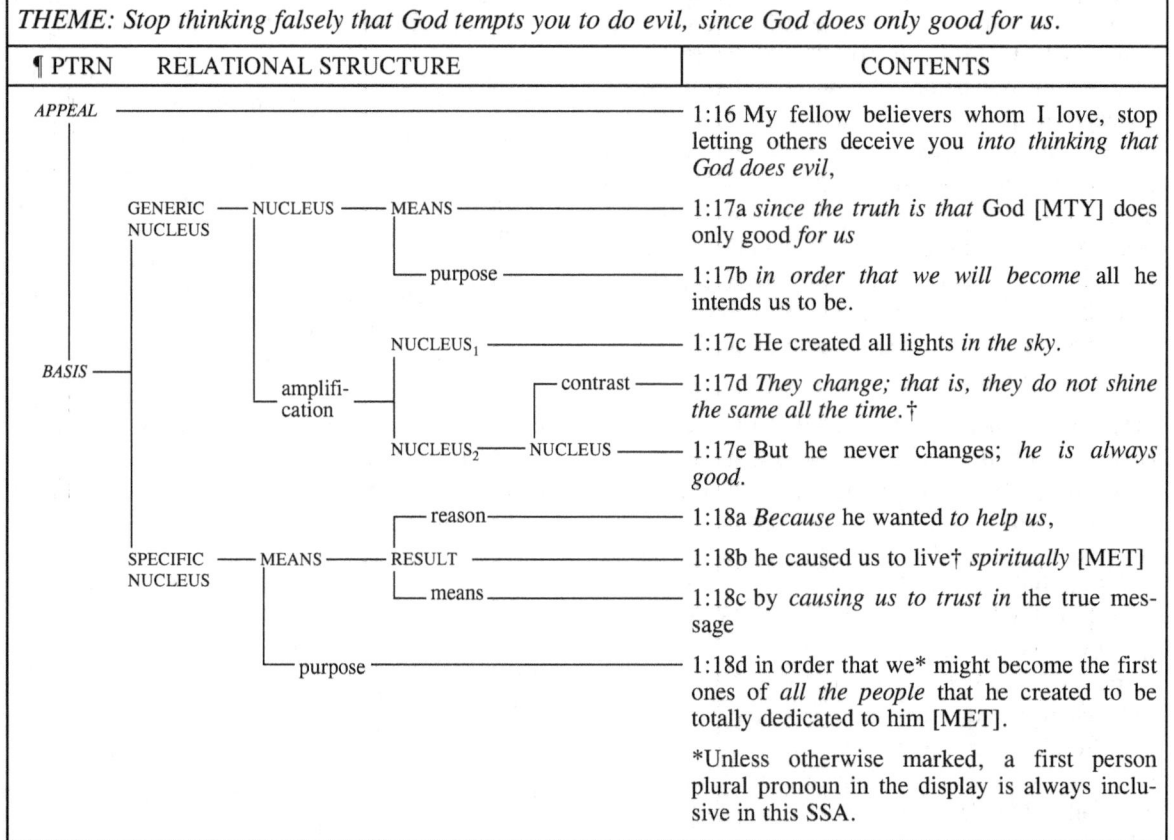

INTENT AND PARAGRAPH PATTERN

James' purpose in the 1:16–18 paragraph is to reinforce his warning against blaming God for temptation and sin by stressing God's total goodness and his beneficent activities in human affairs. The paragraph is structurally hortatory, since it contains an APPEAL in v. 16, but the most significant feature semantically is the BASIS (vv. 17–18) for the APPEAL. (See "Intent and Macrostructure" of 1:13–18 for the function of the APPEAL in this unit.) God is not only wholly good, but of his own will he caused us to live spiritually so that we would become partakers of his nature as a kind of firstfruits dedicated to God. All this precludes any divine purpose for evil in our lives.

NOTES

1:16 My fellow believers whom I love, The vocative here is the first of three vocatives in which the adjective ἀγαπητοί 'beloved' is added. It indicates James' extremely close relationship to the readers. Most versions translate this as 'my dear brothers'. In other languages an appropriate term of endearment should be used.

stop letting others deceive you *into thinking that God does evil*, The negative imperative μὴ πλανᾶσθε 'do not err' is a generic APPEAL: the deception referred to is not explicitly expressed. Some commentators (e.g., Oesterley) say that this verse refers back to vv. 13–15, warning against being deceived into thinking that God is the author of temptation. Others (e.g., Laws) say that it is cataphoric, meaning that they are not to be deceived into casting doubt on the good character of God. However, the majority (e.g., Hiebert, Moo, Stulac) say that this verse is transitional and may be connected with either or both, since the topic of the source of temptation is dealt with in both 13–15 and 16–18. In the display v. 16 is primarily connected with what follows, v. 17, in which the focus is on God's goodness. The very nature of God makes it inconceivable that he would tempt to evil (see "Prominence and Theme" for 1:13–18). As Huther says:

> A *new* line of thought, unconnected with the preceding, does not indeed begin with this verse; μὴ πλανᾶσθε must not therefore be considered, with Hornejus, Gebser, and others, only as the

concluding formula to what goes before.... The same formula is found in 1 Cor. vi. 9, xv. 33; Gal. vi. 7 (similarly 1 John iii. 7); in all those places it precedes a thought certain to the Christian conscience, by which a preceding expression is confirmed in opposition to a false opinion: this is also the case here.

The present imperative preceded by the negative particle μή indicates that some of the readers were prone to think unfairly about God (Hiebert). This is reflected in the display with 'Stop letting others deceive you'. It may also be stated as a general principle: 'Don't let others deceive you.' The context leaves both possibilities open.

1:17a *since the truth is* With v. 17 the BASIS of the 1:16 APPEAL begins. There is no conjunction in Greek showing this relation; but because 1:17 may be seen as the grounds for obeying the exhortation in 1:16, the words *'since the truth is'* are supplied to show the relation.

that **God does only good** *for us* The 1:16-18 paragraph picks up the theme from 1:5 of God's character as a giving God and develops it as a refutation of the wrong idea that God tempts men (1:13). 'God' is the appropriate agent in this proposition, since it is so indicated later in v. 17 ('the Father of lights'). This is confirmed by the adverb ἄνωθεν 'from above', which means divine origin; it is, in fact, a metonymy for God. The abstract noun 'gift' is not a thing concept, but an event, and is expressed in the display as what God does for people.

James uses two different nouns for 'gift' in this verse. Some commentators (e.g., Ropes, Moo) say that there is no significant difference in meaning between them and that the variation is for rhetorical effect only. The main purpose of such repetition is to place emphasis on the incomparable goodness of whatever comes from God (Johnson). Moore (p. 60) considers these two nouns a near-synonymous doublet, so it is perfectly acceptable to render them as a single concept. However, two concepts may well be seen here, for although they have the same verb root, they have different suffixes. The first, δόσις with the suffix of action, focuses on the act of giving. The second, δώρημα with the suffix denoting result, refers to the thing given (Hiebert, Mayor). There are two adjectives used with these nouns, which lends support to the view that there are two concepts here. The first adjective, ἀγαθός 'good', describes the giving as to its moral quality. Coutts (p. 108, quoted by Adamson, p. 68) says, "James has no philosophical answer to the problem of evil. He cannot explain why people are pushed almost beyond endurance but he offers a practical answer: faith in a God of pure goodness."

1:17b *in order that we will become* **all he intends us to be.** The second adjective, τέλειος 'perfect, complete' (see the note on 1:4), describes the gift as to its effect on the souls of men. This is James' answer to the wrong idea in 1:13 that God is the author of sin: God is the source of everything good, and his purpose for testing is to bring about spiritual maturity. The meaning of the adjective 'perfect' is expressed in the display as a purpose clause because it states the intent of God in allowing testing in our lives.

1:17c He created all lights *in the sky.* The noun phrase τοῦ πατρὸς τῶν φώτων 'the Father of lights' is a Jewish circumlocution to avoid the use of God's name. James used this title to remind his readers of God's creative power. In Job 38:28 the word 'father' is used in this same sense. Most versions retain the word 'father', but some do not (TEV, NCV, NLT). TEV, for example, has "from God, the Creator of the heavenly lights."

This phrase introduces the topic of 'lights', which is then used as a comparison to the nature of God. In the context the reference is obviously to the sun, moon, and stars. That they are lights in the sky is supplied in the rendering here.

1:17d *They change; that is, they do not shine the same all the time.* This proposition is an implication of the 17e statement that God does not change. There is an implied contrast: God never changes but the lights do. The noun παραλλαγή 'change' in 17e may refer to the regular movements of the heavenly bodies (Moo, Oesterley) or to variations in the intensity of light given (Hiebert, Alford, Ropes). Either interpretation is valid, but the latter seems preferable and is therefore given in the display as the manner of change referred to. The phrase τροπῆς ἀποσκίασμα 'shadow of turning' may refer to eclipses of the sun or moon (Alford, Davids 1982) or to clouds blocking light from above (Kistemaker, Davids 1982) or to nighttime alternating with daytime (Alford, Kistemaker). Commentators vary greatly as to the exact details of the change that the lights undergo, but these details are not significant for translation. If translators wish to express 'shadow of turning', they might add 'and the shadows that they cause also change'. The most important concern is that the details given not detract from the verse's focus on God's unchangeability.

1:17e But he never changes; *he is always good*. The implicit information supplied in the second half of this proposition is a positive restatement of God's immutability. More directly it would be 'he is always the same'. However, in the context the specific type of sameness is more forceful. This entire paragraph vindicates God's character in the face of those who doubted his goodness and reliability (Martin).

1:18a *Because* he wanted *to help us*, The Greek is an aorist participle, βουληθείς 'having willed'. The generic statement of 17a, 'God does only good for us', answers specifically the wrong idea of 13e that God tempts us to do evil. The full argument is that man 'by his own evil desire' chooses to sin (14a–b), which leads to spiritual death, but God 'by his own will' wants to cause us to live spiritually (18a–b). The communication relation expressed by the participle is best seen as causal, indicating the reason God gave us new life (Alford, Mayor). In the display this relation is expressed by 'because'.

The implicit 'to help us' is supplied because in some languages the verb 'want' requires an object, and a generic positive statement such as this may be grammatically necessary. The propositions following this one state more clearly what it is that God wanted to do.

1:18b he caused us to live *spiritually* The figurative use of the word for giving birth has been interpreted in various ways. The two main views are that it means (1) the creation of the world and/or mankind (Laws) or (2) the new birth, that is, entrance into spiritual life (Hiebert, Tasker, Mayor). The first seems unlikely since this figure is never used in the Old Testament to refer to the creation. Moreover, this meaning would be a divergence from the main topic of overcoming trials and temptations. The second fits the context much better, since it is the same word used in 1:15, where it is stated that if we react wrongly to testings, such sin brings forth death. Here God wills to bring forth spiritual life. This giving of birth is accomplished by means of 'the true message' (18c), which parallels 1:21, where it is said that this same message 'is able to save your souls'. The aorist tense here looks back to the time of conversion, the beginning of this new life (Hiebert).

This giving of birth metaphor is rendered non-figuratively in the display. If translators want to retain the figure, they might express it as follows: 'As a woman gives birth to a child, so God has caused us to live spiritually'. But care must be taken lest such an addition impede the flow of the argument in 1:16–18.

1:18c by *causing us to trust in* the true message The phrase λόγῳ ἀληθείας 'by a word of truth' is James' way of referring to the gospel, as most commentators agree; however, they differ in their interpretation of the genitive. Some (e.g., Huther, Kistemaker) say that 'truth' is an attribute of 'word': 'the true message'. Others (e.g., Hiebert, Mayor) say that it is an objective genitive: 'a message that proclaims the truth'. But from a semantic point of view these are essentially the same; both refer to the gospel message. Since 'God' is the actor and this is the means by which God accomplishes his purposes in our lives, it seems best to express our involvement in the process as 'trust in the true message'.

1:18d in order that we might become the first ones The word ἀπαρχή 'firstfruits' is an Old Testament term, also used by pagans. It refers to offering God the first part of a harvest and the firstborn of animals, dedicating them to him. It is used here figuratively as indicated by the indefinite adjective τινα 'a certain' (Adamson, Mitton, Ropes) and refers to Christians. James includes himself in this group by using the pronoun ἡμᾶς 'us' twice.

of *all the people* that he created The Greek is τῶν αὐτοῦ κτισμάτων 'of his creation'. There are two views as to what or who is referred to here. The first is that since the noun κτίσμα 'what has been created' is commonly used of the material creation, James has in mind the idea expressed by Paul in Rom. 8:19–22, that the creation will yet share in the benefits of our salvation (Hiebert, Davids 1982). The second view is that the meaning is restricted to people; that is, the reference is to the vast number of people who shall yet be brought to salvation through Christ (Oesterley, Huther).

If the first view were correct, it would mean that James suddenly diverges here from the previous topic to an altogether different one: from personal exhortations not to blame God for failures, recognizing instead that their failures are the fault of their own evil desires, to the topic of how all of creation will some day be redeemed through the truth of God. While this topic would fit well in the context of Romans 8, it does not fit well in the Epistle of James, characterized as it is by practical, down-to-earth instructions for meeting the problems of daily life. Thus the second view would seem much better here, and is the one on which the rendering in the display is based.

to be totally dedicated to him. Many commentators say that included in the concept of 'firstfruits' is that they were dedicated to God (Adamson, Bratcher); they were first not only in time but also first in honor. This can be expressed as being a special possession of God (Davids 1982; CEV, NLT).

BOUNDARIES AND COHERENCE

The initial boundary of the 1:16–18 unit was discussed under 1:13–15 and the closing boundary under 1:13–18. Hiebert and Blue are among the few commentators who, along with NLT and NRSV, make a paragraph break after 1:16 rather than after 1:15 as in the display. (Hiebert sees v. 16 as transitional but feels that it is linked primarily with what has gone before.) The majority opinion—that the break is before v. 16—is supported by v. 16's vocative and negative imperative. The editors of the fourth revised edition of the Greek New Testament concur. (Additional arguments are in the note on v. 16.)

The coherence of 1:16–18 is shown by the description of God's nature as well as by contrasting concepts. The reference in 1:17 to the continual changes in the heavenly lights is in sharp contrast to the changeless nature of God. A further contrast is between πλανάω 'deceive' in 1:16 and ἀλήθεια 'truth' in 1:18, the truth that characterizes God's message. The paragraph ends with the supreme proof of God's goodness, his provision of the new birth, not as a response to necessity but by his own choice.

PROMINENCE AND THEME

The 1:16–18 theme includes a representation of the *APPEAL* in 1:16 and *BASIS* in 1:17–18, since both are integral to a hortatory paragraph pattern and since the *BASIS* is also marked as prominent by its function at the macrostructure level (see "Intent and Paragraph Pattern" for 1:16–18).

PART CONSTITUENT 1:19–5:11
(Hortatory Division: Specific Appeals of 1:2–5:11)

THEME: Do what God commands in his message rather than just listening to it. Stop honoring some people more than others. Only by doing good can a person prove that he truly trusts in God. You should strive to speak rightly to others and do good, acting peaceably toward others, to demonstrate that you are truly wise. You are fighting among yourselves because of your evil desires. Be sad because you have sinned, and humble yourselves before God. Wait patiently for the Lord to return and judge all people fairly, even the rich who oppress you.

MACROSTRUCTURE	CONTENTS
introduction	1:19–20 Everyone of you should eagerly pay attention to God's message and should not speak hastily nor get angry hastily.
APPEAL₁	1:21–27 Do what God commands in his message rather than just listening to it. Those who show compassion on the weak and do not act immorally truly worship God.
APPEAL₂	2:1–13 Stop honoring some people more than others, since you are disobeying God's law that we should love one another. God will not act mercifully to those who do not act mercifully toward others.
BASIS (expository peak of 1:19–5:11)	2:14–26 Only by doing good to others can a person prove that he truly trusts in God, since it is useless for one to say that he trusts in God if he does not do what God commands.
APPEAL₃	3:1–18 You should all strive to speak rightly, since what you say has a powerful effect on others. So stop boasting that you are wise when you are jealous of others and self-seeking. Those who act peaceably towards others will cause them to act righteously.
APPEAL₄ (hortatory peak of the epistle)	4:1–17 You are fighting among yourselves because of your evil desires. Be sad because you have sinned, and humble yourselves before God. If anyone knows the right thing that he ought to do yet doesn't do it, he is sinning.
APPEAL₅	5:1–11 The rich people who oppress you should weep because God will punish them. Therefore wait patiently for the Lord to return and judge all people fairly. Do not complain against each other lest he judge you when he returns. God blesses those who patiently endure suffering.

INTENT AND MACROSTRUCTURE

The intent of the 1:19–5:11 SPECIFIC APPEALS of the 1:2–5:18 BODY has already been treated under 1:2–5:18. James' desire to affect the recipients' behavior is carried out by a series of APPEALS the purpose of which is that they reach spiritual maturity (1:4). Alford (p. 106 in his prolegomena) says,

> The main theme of the Epistle may be described as being the ἀνὴρ τέλειος, in the perfection of the Christian life . . . ; and his state and duties are described and enforced, not in the abstract, but in a multitude of living connexions and circumstances of actual life. . . .

The overall structure (i.e., macrostructure) of 1:19–5:11 is an *introduction* (1:19–20) and two APPEALS (1:21–27 and 2:1–13) followed by an expository unit that functions as a BASIS (2:14–26) for both of these APPEALS as well as for the three additional APPEALS that follow (3:1–18, 4:1–17, and 5:1–11). This BASIS emphasizes that the commands of the epistle, a hortatory epistle, should be carried out.

The *introduction* gives a preview of the SPECIFIC APPEALS, all of which deal with aspects of conduct that are inconsistent with the faith that the readers profess. The BASIS shows how godly conduct is an integral part of faith.

Partly because of its function at this higher level as the BASIS for all the SPECIFIC APPEALS, 2:14–26 is considered the expository peak of the 1:19–5:11 division (see "Intent and Macrostructure" under 2:14–26). The fourth APPEAL is the hortatory peak of the entire epistle (see "Intent and Macrostructure" under 4:1–17, also "Intent and Paragraph Pattern" under 4:7–10).

BOUNDARIES AND COHERENCE

The opening boundary of the 1:19–5:11 unit has been discussed under 1:2–18. The next unit is seen as beginning at 5:12 for four reasons:

1. The vocative ἀδελφοί μου 'my brothers' is used together with δέ.
2. As a number of commentators contend (e.g., Martin, Moo, Kistemaker), the introductory prepositional phrase πρὸ πάντων 'above all things' in 5:12 is intended to signal the final section of the letter. (Paul used the adverb λοιπόν 'finally' in 2 Cor. 13:11 similarly.)
3. There are no other obvious surface-structure markers of a paragraph or higher-level break until 5:19. Nevertheless, 5:13–18 seems to be quite different from the preceding material in the epistle in that it presents the positive way of working together as a community.
4. Although 5:12 and 5:13–18 are very different from each other, they can be considered a "miscellaneous topics" unit, as we take them to be. Such a unit is common toward the end of epistles, and this fact supports the unity of 5:12–18. (For further discussion of 5:12 and the unity of 5:12–18 see "Boundaries and Coherence" under the 5:12–18 unit and also the note on 5:12a.)

Some (e.g., Hiebert, Martin, Hill) consider 1:19–3:18 a high-level coherent unit with a major break at 4:1. Hill (p. 9) declares, "A new topic is clearly introduced with the rhetorical questions at 4:1. We are now dealing with behavior that is manifested in deplorable interpersonal relationships." But Davids (1982:26) rightly points out, "There is more of a communal focus in 4:1ff. in comparison to 3:1–18, but as Ward has shown, the whole of the epistle exudes a concern for communal interests, not an individualistic ethic."

Ekstrom (p. 5) proposes 1:19–4:17 as a high-level unit based on a chiastic structure as follows:

```
1:19-3:18 BE QUICK TO LISTEN (A), BE SLOW TO SPEAK (B), BE SLOW TO GET ANGRY (C)
    1:21-27 Receive God's Word, specifically 'obey it.'              Specific of A
    2:1-13 Don't show partiality.                                    Specific of 1:21-27
    2:14-26 If you profess to believe in God
            but don't act accordingly, God won't save you.           Grounds of 1:21-27
    3:1-12 Don't all of you desire to be teachers.                   Specific of B
    3:13-18 Live meekly if you claim to be wise.                     Specific of C

4:1-17 BE SLOW TO GET ANGRY (C'), BE SLOW TO SPEAK (B'), BE QUICK TO LISTEN (A')
    4:1-10 Submit yourself to God.                                   Means of C
    4:11-12 Don't criticize others.                                  Specific of B
    4:13-16 Don't boast about the future.                            Specific of B
    4:17 Do the good you know you should.                            Specific of A
```

There are many chiastic structures in the New Testament on all levels of discourse. Rountree acknowledges this in her analysis of the discourse structure of James; however, she points out, "the significance of such a structure is still in question. In James, it seems to me that such an analysis of the book obscures the real focus of the message."

Although the chiastic structure shown above is indeed remarkable, the themes are too vague to really reflect James' message. The inseparability of vital faith and deeds in 2:14–26 is not given proper emphasis. Furthermore, 3:1–12 addresses far more than the desire to be teachers; rather, it declares the powerful, often devastating effect of speech with far-reaching consequences. Perhaps even more significantly, the importance of repentance and restoration to fellowship with God in 4:7–10 does not have the focus it should have. In summary, while one way of looking at the Epistle of James is as a chiastic structure, it does not accurately represent either the author's focus or purpose in writing.

Coherence in the 1:19–5:11 unit has already been discussed under the 1:2–5:18 display. Further coherence is shown by the concept of community, a motif running throughout the entire division. Davids (1989:13) says, "James' primary concern is with the health of the community. . . . the author addresses the behavior of individuals because that behavior has an impact upon the life of the community." For James the elect community comprises believers who are mostly poor (2:5) and are facing a variety of difficult circumstances. Their showing of favoritism to the wealthy despite oppression by these very same rich people is breaking down the solidarity of the community (2:1–13) and revealing a defective faith (2:14–26). The community under pressure tends to split into bickering factions, a problem addressed in chapters 3 and 4. In chapter 5, James encourages the church to patiently await the return of Christ, who will judge all men fairly, including the rich. (For a fuller discussion see Davids 1989:12–21.)

PROMINENCE AND THEME

The *APPEALS* of 1:19–5:11 are naturally prominent, and the *BASIS* has marked prominence. Thus the theme is drawn from all of them. Since the *introduction* (1:19–20) is hortatory, it also has natural prominence, but because it does not clearly relate to all the *APPEALS*, it is better for each of the *APPEALS* to be represented individually in the theme rather than having the *introduction* represent them, or part of them.

DIVISION CONSTITUENT 1:19–20
(Hortatory Paragraph: Introduction to 1:21–5:11)

THEME: Every one of you should eagerly pay attention to God's message and should not speak hastily nor get angry hastily.

¶ PTRN	RELATIONAL STRUCTURE	CONTENTS
APPEAL₁	┌─ contrast ── ── NUCLEUS ──	1:19a My fellow believers whom I love, you know *this* [1:18], 1:19b but everyone of you should eagerly pay attention to *God's true message*
APPEAL₂		1:19c and should not hastily speak *your own thoughts*,
APPEAL₃	── EXHORTATION ─── │ ┌─ circumstance ─ └─ grounds ── NUCLEUS ──	1:19d nor hastily get angry, 1:20a since when anyone *of you* gets angry, 1:20b you are not doing what God wants you to do.

INTENT AND PARAGRAPH PATTERN

In his *GENERAL APPEALS* (1:2–18) James states the purpose of the epistle, spiritual maturity. This is brought out particularly in the final verse of 1:2–18, where he also states the means God uses to accomplish spiritual maturity, the 'word of truth'. Now in 1:19–20, using three comprehensive *APPEALS*, he introduces the *SPECIFIC APPEALS* unit of the epistle. This *introduction* gives a brief preview of the rest of the entire 1:19–5:11 division. It may also have a second function, to introduce the 1:21–27 unit, having to do with hearing and obeying the Word of God (see the notes on 19b and 21a for further details). The paragraph's three *APPEALS* (19b, 19c, and 19d–20b) mark it as hortatory. Only the third *APPEAL* has a grounds, which may be viewed as functioning as its *basis*.

In order to understand how the 1:19–20 unit functions as a preview, it is necessary to consider the general content of the *APPEALS* themselves. Many commentaries say that the content of 'hear' in the first *APPEAL* is expressed in the noun phrase λόγῳ ἀληθείας 'word of truth' from 1:18. It fits the context well to have James saying that they must eagerly hear the true message so that by means of it they can become the first of his redeemed creation (1:18) and become spiritually complete (1:4). However, for the two negative *APPEALS* about speech and anger there is a wide divergence of interpretation. Commentators make many references to parallel passages in Psalms, Proverbs, Ecclesiastes, and noncanonical Jewish literature, but almost nothing is said about the relationship of these topics to the rest of the letter itself. At the same time it should be noted that these three topics, the application of the Word, the control of speech, and the attitude of anger toward God and toward people, are three basic motifs of the entire letter, ones that are developed in the following chapters. (The specific details will be discussed later under the respective units.)

NOTES

1:19a My fellow believers whom I love, Here, at the beginning of the *SPECIFIC APPEALS* of the *BODY*, the fullest form of the vocative, ἀδελφοί μου ἀγαπητοί 'my beloved brothers', occurs for the second time (see the note on 1:16).

you know *this* [1:18], In the Textus Receptus v. 19 begins with ὥστε 'therefore', but the GNT has ἴστε 'know' with a B rating, which means that the UBS committee consider it almost certain. Most modern critical editions accept ἴστε 'know'. This verb form may be either indicative or imperative. Some commentators (e.g., Laws, Ropes, Davids 1982) interpret it as imperative with its primary reference being to the following imperatives, indicating that the reader should take special note of these admonitions. Interpreted this way, the function of the imperative would be as a *prominence orienter* to the following three *APPEALS*. This is best translated as "Remember this" (TEV) or "Take note of this" (NIV). Such an orienter might be expected at the beginning of the *SPECIFIC APPEALS* of an epistle. A number of versions take this view (RSV, TEV, NIV, JB, CBW, Goodspeed), and this is acceptable. However, other commentators (e.g., Alford, Mayor, Hiebert, Barclay) see the form as indicative, looking back at what was just said in v. 18. This view (followed by NASB, REB, TNT, and WEY) is supported by the occurrence of δέ after ἔστω 'let be', indicating that a further matter is to be presented (Hiebert). The only other two occurrences of ἴστε in the New Testament are in Eph. 5:5 and Heb. 12:17, and most commentators consider them to be indicative. While either interpretation is acceptable, the indicative is given in the display as more in keeping with the context.

1:19b but every one of you should eagerly pay attention to The function of δέ following the verb ἔστω 'let be' in v. 19 is to make it clear that a further matter is to be presented. However, δέ should probably not be understood as primarily introducing the new general topic. (This is normally the function of the vocative in James, but see 5:12). In this verse δέ is best understood as indicating the contrast between only knowing the Word and putting that knowledge into practice: 'be (ἔστω δέ) eager to hear', that is, be eager to pay attention to and obey. They must not stop with knowing about the source of their regeneration; they must allow the Word to continue to be evident in their lives (Hiebert).

The third person imperative in the present tense indicates that each believer is obligated to be continually doing the following instructions. The adjectives ταχύς 'quick' (here) and βραδύς 'slow' (19c-d) are more than time words. They describe the attitude governing the actions. For example, 'be quick to listen' means to be eager to receive and assimilate the message heard.

God's true message Some commentators (e.g., Moo, Davids 1982) take the 19b exhortation to be generic: be willing to hear the opinion of others. They cite various Old Testament and rabbinical parallels. However, more (e.g., Adamson, Ropes, Hiebert, Cranfield 1965a) connect it specifically to 'word of truth' in 1:18 and 'implanted message' in 1:21. In view of the immediate context and the fact that James continues in the following unit (1:21-27) with the same topic of the true message of God, the latter view is preferable. Although none of the versions make this explicit, our rendering follows the majority of commentators by supplying it as implied information. In chapter 2 James returns to this topic of heeding the message, especially in 2:14-26.

1:19c and should not hastily speak *your own thoughts*, This proposition is clearly contrastive with 19b. Not only are the adjectives ταχύς 'quick' and βραδύς 'slow' antonyms, but in 19b the action of hearing is encouraged and in 19c an aspect of speaking is discouraged. Again, some take this exhortation to be a generic one. For example, Laws says it refers to "strictures on unconsidered or passionate speech. . . ." However, in the context, the speaking as well as the listening may have to do with the message (Bratcher): one should not speak hastily without first considering what God has to say about the matter. The rendering in the display attempts to cover both of these possibilities by making the content of speech 'your own thoughts'. Slowness in relation to the tongue implies being able to control one's speaking so as to meet God's approval. There is a return to this topic in 1:26; and in chapter 3 James, in great detail, goes into the specifics of this broad statement.

1:19d nor hastily get angry, The noun ὀργή 'anger' implies more than a passing surge of temper. Rather, it denotes a persistent attitude of hatred or revenge (as in Matt. 5:22). If an outburst of passion had been intended, the word θυμός would have been more appropriate. A few commentators (e.g., Hiebert) think that James is concerned about anger in response to the hasty speech referred to in 1:19c. However, it is better to take this third imperative as a generic exhortation in view of the fact that James uses the whole of chapter 4 to discuss his readers' animosity toward one another and reprimand them for such an attitude with very strong language. It is quite in keeping with James' style to allude briefly to a topic to which he later returns in more detail.

1:20a since when anyone *of you* gets angry, Verse 20, introduced by the conjunction γάρ 'for', states the grounds for the preceding exhortation to not get angry. James personifies the noun ὀργή 'anger', making it the subject of the verb ἐργάζεται 'works/produces'. Since 'anger' represents an event or a state, it is rendered in the display as a verb in a circumstantial clause. Semantically the 20a-b unit is a generic statement regarding God's attitude toward human anger. The negative οὐκ with the present indicative verb is an expression of an abiding negative fact. The noun ἀνήρ 'man' is frequently used to distinguish man (i.e., a male) from woman, but here it is used without the article and thus is qualitative, meaning 'human wrath'. Propositions 20a-b are the grounds for the prohibition against anger, which is the only exhortation of the three that has a grounds. This is probably because it is the last of the three (Laws).

1:20b you are not doing what God wants you to do. Since the noun δικαιοσύνη 'righteousness' can mean 'justice' (NEB), some have suggested that this is a warning against thinking that man's anger can be excused because it is a tool of God's own just judgment. However, most commentators interpret the genitive in the phrase 'righteousness of God' as an objective genitive, hence righteous activity that meets God's approval. According to this view, 'working righteousness' is the opposite of 'working sin' in 2:9 and is a very common motif in this epistle.

BOUNDARIES AND COHERENCE

The initial boundary of the 1:19-20 unit was discussed under 1:2-18. The beginning of the next unit at 1:21 is indicated by a change from the generic imperatives of the *introduction* to the more specific exhortation focused on 'the implanted word'. Lexical coherence in 1:19-20 is shown by εἰς and εἰς τό 'for, with reference to', which occurs three times in v. 19, and the two nouns in vv. 19 and 20, ἄνθρωπος and ἀνήρ, both of which mean 'man/person'.

It should be noted that the majority of commentators take the initial διό 'therefore' in v. 21 as introducing the conclusion to v. 20. This would put v. 21 in the same paragraph as v. 20. Most versions follow this view and have 1:19-21 as a paragraph, as in the display below.

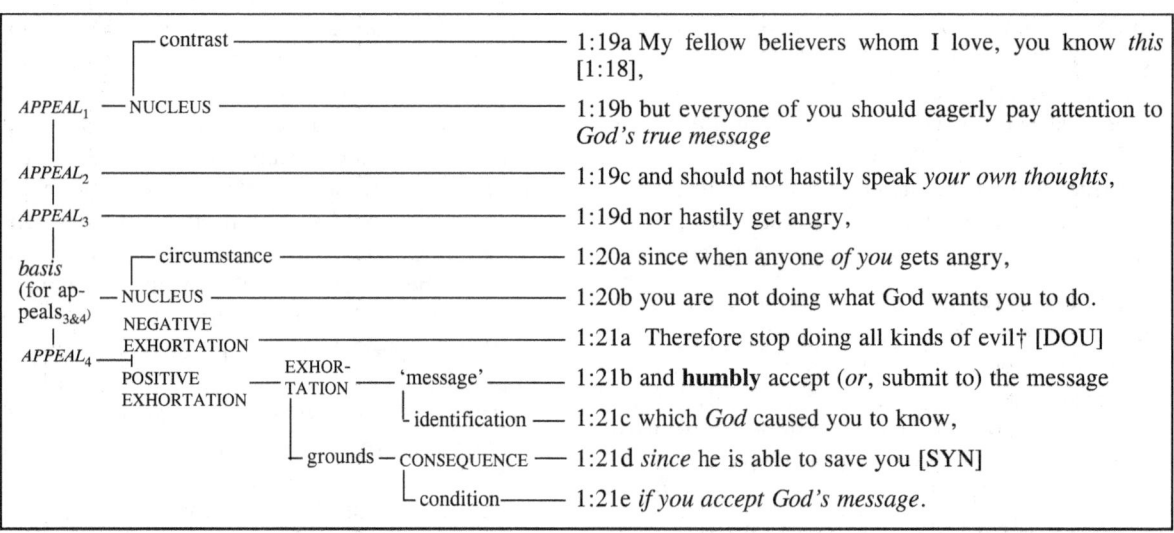

We reject such a paragraph division primarily because it does not seem logical that anger alone should be made the basis for stopping all kinds of evil and receiving the Word of God (see the note on 21a for more on this boundary and the implications of 'therefore'). But such an interpretation would not make any difference in translation; and, because of popular support, such a paragraph division would be acceptable in a translation.

PROMINENCE AND THEME

The three APPEALS in the 1:19–20 unit are naturally prominent. The theme is therefore taken from all of them.

DIVISION CONSTITUENT 1:21–27 (Hortatory Section: Appeal₁ of 1:19–5:11)

THEME: *Do what God commands in his message rather than just listening to it. Those who show compassion on the weak and do not act immorally truly worship God.*	
MACROSTRUCTURE	CONTENTS
APPEAL	1:21–25 Therefore stop doing all kinds of evil, and do what God commands in his message rather than just listening to it. God will approve of those who do what he wants them to do.
axiomatic basis	1:26–27 Those who show compassion on the weak and do not think or act immorally truly worship God and receive his approval.

INTENT AND MACROSTRUCTURE

The 1:21–27 section is the first APPEAL unit of the SPECIFIC APPEALS of the epistle. James' intent here is to affect the actions and attitudes of the readers so that the true message of God will make the change in their lives that he desires. Thus the section is hortatory. It is composed of an APPEAL (1:21–25) and an *axiomatic basis* (1:26–27). The APPEAL has to do with the reception of the Word and obedience to it. The *axiomatic basis* supplies motivation for paying attention to the 1:21–25 exhortations: it presents God's positive evaluation of those who obey his Word.

BOUNDARIES AND COHERENCE

The initial boundary of the 1:21–27 unit has been discussed under 1:19–20. The beginning of the next unit at 2:1 is indicated by the change of topic from obedience to God's Word to a warning against partiality and by the vocative expression ἀδελφοί μου 'my brothers', which James uses primarily at the beginning of new units.

The semantic coherence of the unit consists in a discussion of the topic of receiving the message of God and doing what it says so that the readers' lives will be changed. In addition, there is much correlation between the 1:21–25 hortatory paragraph and the 1:26–27 expository paragraph, which functions as an *axiomatic basis* for it. The negative exhortation in v. 21 is that they put away all evil, and v. 26 gives an example of evil, namely, not controlling their speech. In v. 22 those who only listen to the Word erroneously think that God will save them, and in v. 26 those who do not control their speech erroneously think that they worship God rightly. Also, the positive exhortation in v. 21 that they must submit to the message of God and so carry out its instructions correlates with v. 27, which gives two examples of what people must do if their worship of God is to be pleasing to him, namely, take care of the needy and maintain personal purity.

PROMINENCE AND THEME

The theme of 1:21–27 is taken from the APPEAL (1:21–25) and also from the *axiomatic basis* (1:26–27), since the APPEAL and *basis* are integral parts of hortatory units.

SECTION CONSTITUENT 1:21–25 (Hortatory Paragraph: Appeal of 1:21–27)

THEME: Therefore stop doing all kinds of evil, and do what God commands in his message rather than just listening to it. God will approve of those who do what he wants them to do.

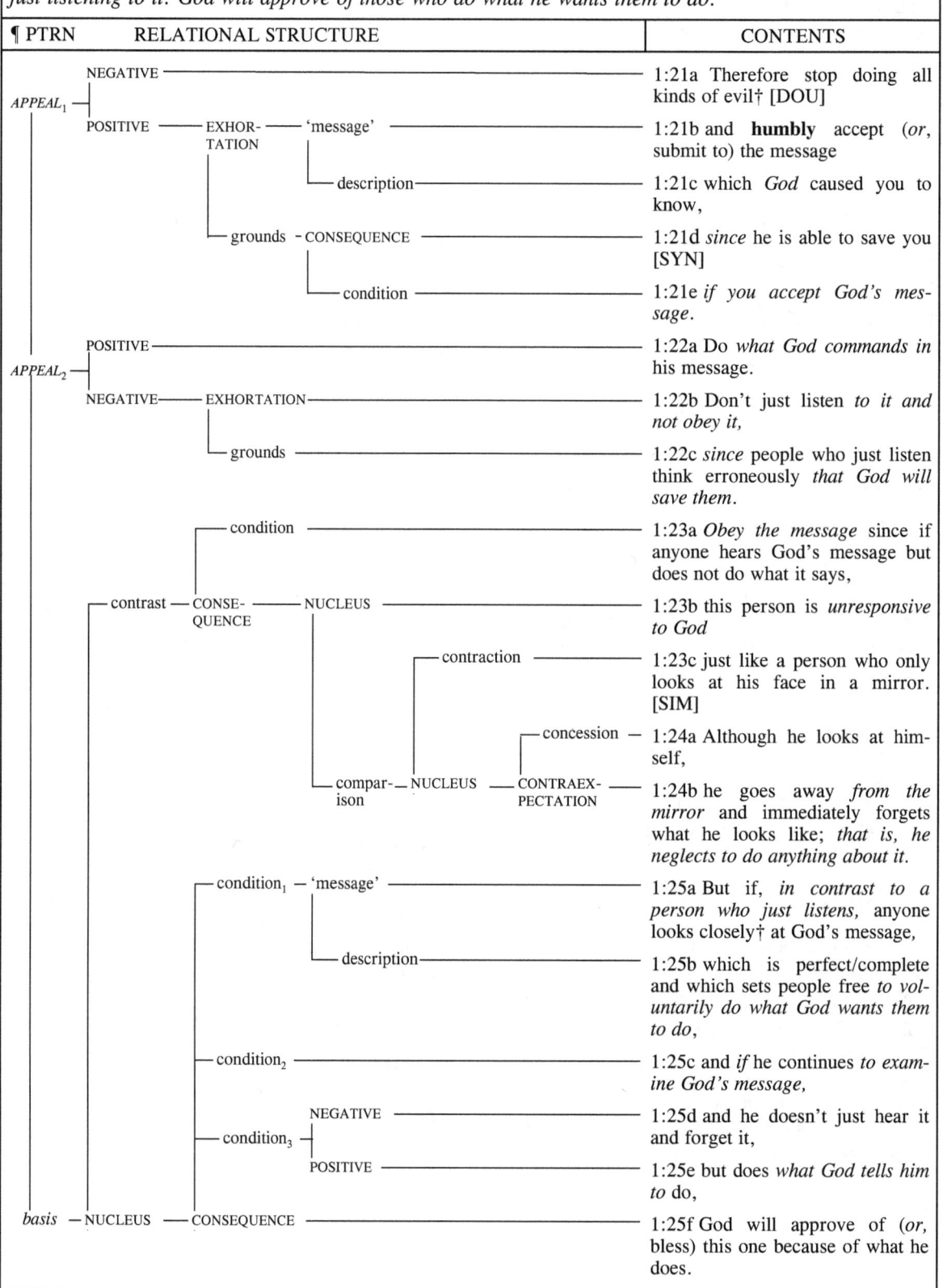

INTENT AND PARAGRAPH PATTERN

James' intent in the 1:21-25 paragraph is to affect the actions and attitudes of the readers so that they will respond to God's message by obeying it. Having finished the *introduction* (1:19-20), he now begins the first argumentative section of the 1:19-5:11 division. The paragraph consists of two coordinate APPEALS that are very similar in semantic content (see "Prominence and Theme" regarding the chiastic structure). Hence it is hortatory. The first APPEAL, in 1:21, serves to focus the readers' attention back on the concept of the word of truth first mentioned in 1:18. This concept, which remains in focus in 1:19-20, continues on here. The second APPEAL, in 1:22, is complementary, explaining how the message must be used in order to be effective in their lives. These APPEALS are followed by a *basis* (1:23a-25f) in which an illustration is used to make its point.

NOTES

1:21a Therefore Many commentators (e.g., Hiebert, Alford, Ropes) think that the conjunction διό 'therefore' is strictly inferential here. That is, it looks back to v. 20 and indicates that since anger does not accomplish what God wants us to do, the readers should stop doing evil and instead receive the implanted word with a humble spirit, which is the opposite of anger, treated in the final exhortation of vv. 19-20. While to connect v. 21 with 19-20 is grammatically possible, it would separate v. 21 from vv. 22-25. It is better to see v. 21 as part of 21-25 since the main verb of v. 21 ('receive') and the entire 21-25 paragraph are focused on the Word of God and the desired response to it.

A second view is that διό 'therefore' resumes and completes the thought of v. 18: God caused us to live spiritually by means of the true message; therefore we should get rid of all kinds of evil actions and obey the message (Moo). It is grammatically unusual for διό to refer back to a referent so far removed (two verses before)—the normal pattern is that it refers to the first possible previous referent.

A third view is possible: that διό is most directly connected with 1:19-20 as a whole. These verses not only give a preview of the rest of the entire division (1:21-5:11) but also function as the transition element to introduce the topic of the next unit, namely 21-27. This view is the preferred one for the following reasons:

1. The conjunction διό in v. 20 need not be seen as referring back to v. 18 only, since ἔστω δὲ πᾶς ἄνθρωπος ταχὺς εἰς τὸ ἀκοῦσαι 'let every man be swift to hear' is probably the most thematic element in v. 19, being the one chosen to start the unit. Most commentators say that the object of 'to hear' is the Word of God.
2. A conclusion or exhortation introduced by διό does not generally follow upon a unit that is in support of some other unit. Since γάρ in v. 20 shows that v. 20 supports v. 19, διό does not necessarily look back to v. 20 alone, as suggested in the first view. Rather, it moves the main argument along.
3. All commentators agree that the noun phrase τὸν ἔμφυτον λόγον 'the implanted word' in v. 21 refers to the same thing as the 'word of truth' in v. 18. The figure of giving birth in v. 18 is carried forward here in v. 21 by the 'planted' figure, which is rendered nonfiguratively in proposition 21c.

stop doing all kinds of evil The aorist plural participle ἀποθέμενοι 'putting away' is grammatically dependent upon the following imperative and partakes of its imperatival force (Hiebert, Mayor; also most versions). This is a negative exhortation that is followed by a positive exhortation in 21b, the two making up the first APPEAL of this paragraph. It involves the figure of stripping off garments. In Acts 7:58 this same participle is used in a literal sense, but generally in the New Testament it is used metaphorically in ethical exhortations, urging the readers to get rid of undesirable qualities or deeds. Since it is not a live metaphor, its meaning is given nonfiguratively in the display.

The word πᾶσαν 'all' means either 'every kind of' or 'every instance of'. The rendering in most versions implies 'every kind of'.

Moore (p. 60) treats ῥυπαρία 'filthiness' and κακία 'wickedness' as a near-synonymous doublet, although it should be noted that the grammatical coordination is between ῥυπαρίαν and περισσείαν 'abundance'. The word ῥυπαρία is used of dirty clothes or dirt on the body, but when used in a figurative sense, it refers to moral evil. If translators should want to preserve some of the figure, they could add 'that defile you'.

1:21b and humbly Humility stands in contrast to the anger warned against in v. 20. The prepositional phrase ἐν πραΰτητι 'in meekness' is fronted, thus emphasizing the need for a proper inner attitude toward the Word. This prominence should be shown in translating. In some languages it may be best to render it with a negative expression such as 'As you receive . . . , don't do it in a proud way' (Loh and Hatton).

accept (or, submit to) the message The main verb of 1:21, δέξασθε 'receive', has as its object the noun phrase τὸν ἔμφυτον λόγον 'the implanted word', the topic of the unit. The verb 'receive' does not signify a passive acquiescence to the message but rather a definite response to it. Though a few commentators (e.g., Oesterley) equate this receiving with initial acceptance of the gospel, most say it includes more than conversion. The aorist imperative form here indicates a decisive act resulting in the Word's becoming "an active working force in their lives" (Hiebert). In some versions it is rendered "submit"; some commentators use "obey."

1:21c which God caused you to know, With the adjective ἔμφυτος 'implanted', the figure now changes from clothing to planting a seed. Hort argued that this word must mean 'inborn', the original capacity for man to apprehend God's revelation, but other commentators (e.g., Mayor) point out that the reference is clearly to the Word of God, as in 4 Esdras 9:31, "For I sow my law in you and it shall bring forth fruit in you. . . ." In addition, James would have been familiar with the parable of the sower and the soils; and some of the vocabulary used in it, such as 'word', 'receive', and 'do', are used here as well and with the same basic theme. The figurative 'implanted' is rendered nonfiguratively in the display: 'which God caused you to know'. Moo says, "The command to *receive the implanted word*, then, is not a command to be converted . . . , but to accept its precepts as binding and to seek to live by them."

1:21d *since* he is able to save you This is an appositional clause: τὸν δυνάμενον σῶσαι τὰς ψυχὰς ὑμῶν 'that which is being able to save your souls'. It could be considered a description of the 'message of God' (Laws, Kistemaker); however, it also implies the reason for receiving the message (Adamson), as it provides the motivation for the exhortations ('accept' and 'do' God's message). Seeing it as grounds is more in keeping with the theme of this paragraph; thus the relation is labeled grounds in the display. The subject of δυνάμενον 'being able' is supplied, since in many languages a message cannot be the subject of a verb.

The noun phrase τὰς ψυχὰς ὑμῶν 'your souls' is commonly accepted as a Hebraism meaning the whole person. The phrase 'to save' refers in this context to the saving function of God's Word in delivering believers from the consequences of sin. Although the eschatological aspect of salvation is not excluded here, James' focus seems to be more on the daily application of the message of God to our lives so that we will become more mature spiritually (Ward).

1:21e *if you accept God's message.* This proposition is an implication of the verb δύναμαι 'be able', which is used together with the verb σῶσαι 'to save' in the final phrase of v. 21. The implication is that there is a condition to the act of saving; that is, in this context salvation is promised only to those who have obeyed the preceding exhortation to accept the message of God.

1:22a Do *what God commands in* his message. The Greek is γίνεσθε δὲ ποιηταὶ λόγου 'become doers of (the) word', in which ποιηταί 'doers' represents both people and an event. The event is rendered as a verb, 'do', and the content of the doing is the message of God. Since 'God's command' is an essential component of λόγος 'message', 'what God commands' is supplied.

Some commentators say that the conjunction δέ is adversative here, and some versions (e.g., JB, NRSV) translate it that way. However, the verb δέξασθε 'receive' in v. 21 and the event concept 'become doers' in v. 22 are both positive exhortations. They do not contrast; rather, v. 22 is a further development of what James means by receiving the message. The full meaning of the aorist imperative 'receive' in v. 21 is clarified by the verb phrase in v. 22 that begins with the present imperative γίνεσθε 'be, become': one should accept the precepts as binding and seek to live by them (Moo). The use of ποιηταί 'doers', a noun form for an event concept, emphasizes that "doing the message" should characterize their lives. Hiebert says, "A fair rendering would be 'Continue to be doers of the Word.'"

1:22b Don't just listen *to it and not obey it,* This proposition is the negative restatement of the exhortation in 22a. The real contrast in the v. 22 *APPEAL* is between ποιηταὶ λόγου 'doers of the word' and μόνον ἀκροαταί 'only hearers'. In some languages the usual word for 'hear' includes the idea of obeying. The implicit information 'and not obey it' is supplied to make the contrast clear.

1:22c *since* people who just listen think erroneously *that God will save them*. The participial phrase παραλογιζόμενοι ἑαυτούς 'deceiving yourselves' is reflexive and is so translated in all versions. However, it may be difficult or impossible in the target language to express the second person reflexive with the verb 'deceive'. If so, it may be necessary to rephrase in terms of false reasoning. The implied content of the erroneous thinking is taken from v. 21 ('which is able to save your souls').

The communication relation between 22b and 22c is EXHORTATION-grounds. This is expressed in the proposition by 'since'.

An alternative interpretation of the participle is that it has imperatival force, since it is dependent on the preceding imperative γίνεσθε 'become, be'. Semantically, this participial phrase is more closely related to 'be . . . not hearers only' than to 'be doers of the word'. With this in mind, it could be rendered as in the TEV, "Do not deceive yourselves by just listening to his word; instead, put it into practice."

1:23a *Obey the message* since The *basis* of the two APPEALS in vv. 21-22 is in vv. 23-25. This *basis* begins with an extended simile as an illustration of the result of the negative response warned against in v. 22. The conjunction ὅτι 'because, since' introduces it. James uses this illustration to enforce his point, which is 'obey the message'; these words are supplied here to refocus on the foregoing exhortations.

if anyone hears God's message but does not do what it says, Here the conjunction εἴ 'if' introduces a condition that assumes the existence of people who hear the message but do not let it affect their conduct. It would be valid to express this idea as 'anyone who'. Some versions (KJV, NRSV, CEV, NLT, WEY, CBW) use 'if'; others do not (NIV, TEV, JB, REB, JBP, NCV). NIV has "Anyone who listens to the Word but does not do what it says. . . ." In the display 'if' is used, not only because of the Greek but also to provide a structural parallel to v. 25, in which the conditional is definitely preferable.

1:23b this person is *unresponsive to God* This proposition is the NUCLEUS of a comparison relation. The verb ἔοικεν 'is like' expresses the comparison, which some (e.g., Laws) call a parable. It is more properly labeled an extended simile. In the display the implicit point of similarity, unresponsiveness, is supplied.

1:23c just like a person who only looks at his face in a mirror. There are three basic actions in the comparison: looking at himself, going away, and forgetting what he saw. The first action is expressed by κατανοοῦντι 'looking at, observing', a present active participle that implies a characteristic activity of the individual. The direct object of this action is the noun phrase τὸ πρόσωπον τῆς γενέσεως αὐτοῦ 'the face of his existence, birth'. It has been translated "his natural face" (KJV, RSV, NASB) or "the face nature gave him" (REB). These renderings are attempts to convey a component of γένεσις 'birth', but they are awkward. In actuality, γένεσις may only point out the sphere of mere material perception (Alford). NIV has "his face," as in the display. TEV's "himself" would also be acceptable.

1:24a-b Although he looks at himself, he goes away *from the mirror* and immediately forgets what he looks like; The conjunction γάρ 'for' usually expresses reason or grounds. In some versions it is translated "for" (KJV, NRSV, NASB), but most versions either omit it (TEV, REB, NCV) or have "and" (NIV, CEV). Since γάρ often marks simply an explanation, this is probably the case here. There are three verbs in this verse, and they present the three basic actions in the illustration. The first, κατενόησεν 'he looked at', repeats the action first mentioned in 23c. This verb and the two following ones, ἀπελήλυθεν 'he has gone away' and ἐπελάθετο 'he forgot', are connected by the coordinate conjunction καί 'and', which leaves the relation ambiguous. However, the implication is that the look revealed something needing attention but no response was given to it. Also, in the application of this comparison in v. 25 it is clear that a response was expected and would have been commended. So in the display the relation between 24a and 24b is labeled as a concession-CONTRAEXPECTATION.

The first verb, 'looked at', and the third one, 'forgot', are in the aorist tense. These are gnomic or timeless (Adamson), so they are translated as present tense. The middle verb, 'has gone away', is in the perfect tense, meaning that his departure without taking action has become a continuing state. This is best translated into English with the present tense. In some languages action verbs such as 'come' and 'go' obligatorily must express the destination or direction of movement. This implicit information is supplied in the display from the context.

The illustration effectively describes the attitude of the one who only hears. "First, he is illustrating the urgency of obedience.... Second, and more pointedly, James is illustrating the uselessness of passively receiving the Word." (MacArthur).

that is, he neglects to do anything about it. This implicit information is the most important point of the verse, being the result of the look in the mirror (Huther). One sense of the verb ἐπιλανθάνομαι 'forget' is 'neglect to do', which is more than just a lapse of memory. It is deliberately not responding to what has been seen.

1:25a But if, *in contrast to a person who just listens,* **anyone looks closely at God's message,** The conjunction δέ 'but' along with the fronted nominal clause ὁ ... παρακύψας ... ποιητής ... 'the one who looked ... (and became) a doer' indicates a switch of focus from the negative reaction to the message to the positive response to it. Since James started out with a condition-CONSEQUENCE presentation in 23a–24b, the communication relation within v. 25 is also condition-CONSEQUENCE, with three conditions preceding the 25f CONSEQUENCE. Even though 25a is not marked with εἰ 'if', semantically the condition-CONSEQUENCE presentation continues in the second part of the argument (i.e., 25a–f).

The verb παρακύπτω 'look closely' literally means 'bend over to look'. Some have suggested that James sets up a contrast in the manner of looking between this verb and κατανοέω 'look at, observe' in v. 24: the hearer glances hastily, while the doer considers more carefully. However, since κατανοέω is used in the sense of careful consideration in Luke 12:27, it is not likely that James intends any significant contrast by shifting verbs (Moo). Rather, the contrast is found between 'forgets' in 24b and 'continues' in 25c. In a number of languages it would be more natural to say 'read intently' or 'study carefully' rather than 'look closely' (Loh and Hatton).

James has not dropped his discussion of the 'message of God'. In 1:18 he calls it the 'word of truth', in 1:21 'the implanted word', in 1:22 the 'word', and here in 1:25 νόμος 'law', described in 25b as 'perfect/complete'. The 'law' to a Jew like James would normally mean the Mosaic law, which is also often called 'perfect/complete'. But here, as the context shows, it is the same as 'the word' in v. 22. In using the word 'law' to refer to the Christian message of the gospel, James is saying that Christians accept this body of truth taught by Jesus as the authoritative standard by which life is to be regulated (Davids 1982). This is in keeping with James' stress on the importance of doing the message of God.

1:25b which is perfect/complete and which sets people free *to voluntarily do what God want them to do,* This is the third occurrence in the letter of the adjective τέλειος 'perfect, complete'. The first, in 1:4, refers to the goal of spiritual maturity; the second, in 1:17, describes the good gifts God gives as to their effect on the souls of men. Here it is part of the description of God's message. The central idea is of wholeness, which demands integrity (Laws).

The noun ἐλευθερία 'freedom' is in the genitive case here. It is an objective genitive, meaning that this law gives freedom to those who accept it. A liberating power is at work within believers making it possible for them to be obedient. This obedience is not through compulsion (Tasker), so 'voluntarily' is supplied in the display to make this clear. (The same idea is found in Jer. 31:33.) Because there is a God-given motivation in those who love God (1:12), they are free to do what he has commanded because they have the desire to do so.

1:25c and *if* **he continues** *to examine God's message,* The participle παραμείνας 'continuing' is conjoined with the participle παρακύψας 'having looked into' in 25a. Since there is only one article governing the two participles, they have the same subject. They express complementary conditions for receiving the approval of God. This 'continuing' is in contrast with 'forgets' in v. 24. Note that 'continuing' is auxiliary in function and requires a main verb and object to be supplied from the context.

1:25d–e and he doesn't just hear it and forget it, but does *what God tells him to* **do,** A third aorist participle, γενόμενος 'becoming', completes the picture of the person described in v. 25. Two noun phrases are used with the participle to indicate what he has become. The first one is negative, οὐκ ἀκροατὴς ἐπιλησμονῆς 'not a hearer of forgetfulness'. (The genitive in this expression is a genitive of quality: he is not a forgetful hearer.) The second is positive, ποιητὴς ἔργου 'a doer of deeds'. These negative and positive phrases are functioning together as the third condition in the condition-CONSEQUENCE relation in this verse.

1:25f God will approve of (*or,* bless) this one because of what he does. The relative pronoun οὗτος 'this one' contrasts the person now described with the person who only hears in 23b. The adjective μακάριος 'blessed' does not mean 'prosperous' here; rather, it means the opposite of blameworthy (Ropes), hence 'approve' in the display. The prepositional phrase ἐν τῇ ποιήσει αὐτοῦ 'in his doing' probably refers to the man's conduct as a whole. It "views his whole life as a consistent doing. God wants more than isolated acts of obedience; the believer's entire life must be devoted to the incessant doing of His will" (Hiebert).

BOUNDARIES AND COHERENCE

The initial boundary of 1:21–25 is discussed under 1:19–20 as well as in the note for 21a. The beginning of the next unit at 1:26 is indicated by a change of topic: from doing what the message of God says to the new topic of true religion.

Coherence derives from the unit's topic, 'the word': λόγος occurs in vv. 21, 22, and 23, and its semantic equivalent, νόμον τέλειον 'perfect law', occurs in v. 25. Also there is a series of positive action verbs that have 'word' as their object: 'receive' in v. 21; 'do' with its cognate noun 'doer' in vv. 22, 23, and 25; and 'look closely at' and 'remaining' in v. 25. Also there are negative concepts used in contrast to 'doing': 'hear only' in vv. 22 and 23; 'a forgetful hearer' in v. 25.

There is a chiastic structure here that further ties the two *APPEALS* together as coordinate:

A (neg) Stop doing all kinds of evil. (21a)
   B (pos) Humbly accept the message of God. (21b)
   B' (pos) Become ones who do what God commands. (22a)
A' (neg) Don't only listen. (22b)

Many commentaries and most versions (e.g., Tasker, Davids 1982, Blue; NIV, TEV, REB, NCV) have divided the unit between v. 21 and v. 22, since they interpret the clause introduced by διό 'therefore' (v. 21) as relating only to v. 20 with the meaning that since a person's anger does not bring about righteousness, they should stop doing all kinds of evil. However, in the display we follow the interpretation that the clause introduced by 'therefore' (v. 21) is more intimately related to the following verses by virtue of the topic 'the word'. (See "Boundaries and Coherence" under 1:19–20 and the note on 1:21a for the complete discussion.) A boundary after v. 21 would disrupt the unity of the hortatory paragraph 1:21–25 and for that reason is not preferred.

PROMINENCE AND THEME

The two coordinate *APPEALS* in vv. 21 and 22 are naturally prominent. They are very similar to each other in semantic content, both being presented positively and negatively. The theme is taken from these coordinate *APPEALS* and their *basis*, which is also thematic since a *basis* is an integral part of the hortatory paragraph pattern.

SECTION CONSTITUENT 1:26–27
(Expository Propositional Cluster: Axiomatic Basis of 1:21–25)

THEME: Those who show compassion on the weak and do not think or act immorally truly worship God and receive his approval.

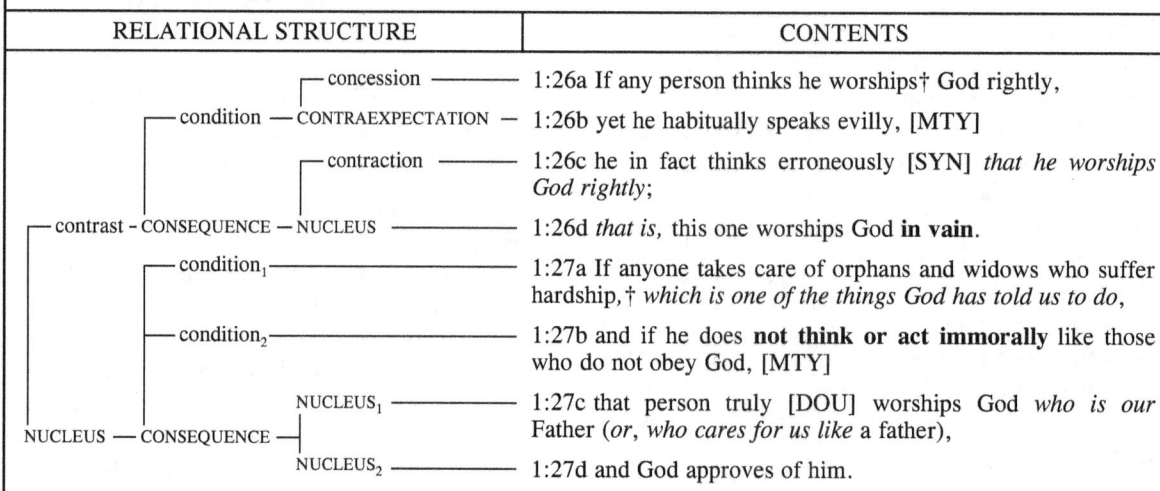

RELATIONAL STRUCTURE	CONTENTS
concession	1:26a If any person thinks he worships† God rightly,
condition — CONTRAEXPECTATION	1:26b yet he habitually speaks evilly, [MTY]
contraction	1:26c he in fact thinks erroneously [SYN] *that he worships God rightly*;
contrast - CONSEQUENCE — NUCLEUS	1:26d *that is*, this one worships God **in vain**.
condition₁	1:27a If anyone takes care of orphans and widows who suffer hardship,† *which is one of the things God has told us to do*,
condition₂	1:27b and if he does **not think or act immorally** like those who do not obey God, [MTY]
NUCLEUS — CONSEQUENCE — NUCLEUS₁	1:27c that person truly [DOU] worships God *who is our Father (or, who cares for us like* a father),
NUCLEUS₂	1:27d and God approves of him.

INTENT AND STRUCTURE

At the macrostructure level the 1:26–27 unit functions as the *axiomatic basis* of the preceding APPEAL (1:21–25). James assumes that the readers, who are fellow believers, want to worship God rightly and want to be approved by God. It is on the basis of this that he has been exhorting them to receive the message of God and obey it so that God may approve of them.

The internal structure is contrastive. Verse 26 is negative; it expresses what worship that is unacceptable to God is. In contrast, v. 27 expresses the kind of actions that characterize true worship and receive God's approval. Since the positive statement in 27a–d is more prominent, it is considered the NUCLEUS.

NOTES

1:26 This verse is an expositional argument. The point James wants to make is that if you are not controlling your tongue your religion is worthless. It is a syllogism. The major premise is: Anyone who does not control his tongue, that person's religion is vain. The minor premise is: You are not controlling your speaking. The conclusion is: Therefore your religion is vain.

1:26a If any person thinks he worships God rightly, The adjective θρησκός 'religious' occurs only here in the New Testament, but it was used widely in Greek religion and denoted the worship of gods. Its cognate noun form θρησκεία 'religion' occurs in vv. 26 and 27, and Paul used it in Acts 26:5 of his ceremonial worship as a Pharisee. The verb δοκέω 'think' refers to an individual's subjective opinion about himself. What is in view here is that the individual considers his actions to be what God wants, yet he has not met God's requirements in an important area of his life, specifically in the control of his speech (see the note on 26b). If, in the receptor language, the term for worship is closely connected to the posture a person takes in worship, such as bowing down, then it would be preferable to use a more generic phrase here such as 'follows God rightly' or 'truly obeys God'.

1:26b yet he habitually speaks evilly, The noun γλῶσσα 'tongue' is a metonymy for speech (see Louw and Nida, 33.74).

The participle χαλιναγωγῶν 'bridling' is a metaphor: the man's speech is compared to a wild horse. The point of similarity is control. In some versions (e.g., KJV, NIV, RSV, CBW, REB) it is translated as a live metaphor, but in even more (e.g., NEB, TEV, JB, CEV, NCV, WEY, JBP) as a dead metaphor, usually using the word "control." James does not state here what specific aspects of speech needed to be controlled, but the mention of it in this context would imply that God considers it important. Later he spends all of chapter 3 discussing this topic. Commentators speculate about what he is referring to, mentioning such things as anger and criticism (Davids 1982); lying, cursing, and filthy language (Kistemaker); slanderous words and boasting (Tasker). These negative statements about speech are taken from elsewhere in the epistle. In the display a generic term is used to characterize all of them: 'speaks evilly'. The present tense indicates that the condition is a continuing one.

We view the relation between 26a and 26b as concession-CONTRAEXPECTATION, but in many versions it is translated as a simple contrast: "but" (REB, CEV, and NCV). However, James seems to be saying that the two statements are inconsistent, not simply contrastive. Kistemaker, NIV, and NASB, translate the relation with "yet," in other words as a relation of concession (see BAGD, p. 392.I1g). A person who is worshiping God rightly would not be expected to speak in an evil manner, hence the concession-CONTRAEXPECTATION label.

1:26c he in fact thinks erroneously *that he worships God rightly;* In the participial phrase ἀπατῶν καρδίαν αὐτοῦ 'deceiving his heart', the word 'heart' refers to the person, especially his thoughts. A number of versions reflect this; for example, the NIV has "he deceives himself." It is best stated in terms of faulty reasoning (cf. 1:22c). The conjunction ἀλλά 'but', which introduces the phrase, connects it with the participial phrase in 26b, μὴ χαλιναγωγῶν γλῶσσαν αὐτοῦ 'not bridling his tongue'. Grammatically, these two participial phrases appear parallel as a part of the protasis. In form, they are nicely balanced constructions. However, semantically, 'deceiving his heart' in 26c is more parallel in thought to the clause in 26d: τούτου μάταιος ἡ θρησκεία 'the religion of this one (is) vain'. So we see the concept of self-deception as a part of the consequence of the evil speaking. This suggests that some other factor is forcing 26c into a participial form paralleling the 26b participial phrase. The tie between the two seems to be in the use of 'his tongue' and 'his heart', showing that James is focusing on the contrast between outward conduct and inward attitude.

Mayor supports this, likewise noting the difference between the semantic relations and grammatical form here: "We should rather have expected this to come in the apodosis: 'if any one thinks himself religious and yet does not bridle his tongue, he deceives himself, and his religion is vain.'" This strongly implies that it should be considered a part of the apodosis. Apparently agreeing with this, most versions (TEV, NIV, JBP, REB, NLT, CEV, NCV, NJB) also translate this as a part of the apodosis. Such an analysis makes 26c the beginning of the CONSEQUENCE relation, as shown in the display. Semantically, this fits the context better.

1:26d *that is,* **this one worships God in vain.** The genitive pronoun τούτου 'of this one' grammatically marks this clause as the apodosis. The clause, in fact, expresses the NUCLEUS of the CONSEQUENCE, as shown in the display. In the Greek the pronoun τούτου is forefronted as a point of departure, and the adjective μάταιος 'worthless/vain' is forefronted for emphasis. In English this emphasis might be expressed by a cleft construction: 'it is in vain that this one worships God'. Each language will have its own way to show such prominence.

1:27 In v. 27 James is not summarizing all that true religion involves. Rather, he presents the positive evidence of real religion in two respects, social concern and personal purity. The information in this verse is not given in the normal condition-CONSEQUENCE form in the Greek text. Nevertheless, there is an underlying condition-CONSEQUENCE relation, even though the elements that form the consequence are presented first. Notice that in the display the usual English word order of stating the condition first is followed.

1:27a If anyone takes care of orphans and widows who suffer hardship, *which is one of the things God has told us to do,* Most commentators, also BAGD (p. 298.2), say that the verb ἐπισκέπτομαι 'visit' implies visiting for the purpose of caring for the needs of these people. The present tense implies a continuing attitude rather than isolated acts. The prepositional phrase ἐν τῇ θλίψει αὐτῶν 'in their affliction' refers to the condition of the orphans and widows and shows the necessity of caring for them. These were the two groups most in need of aid because of their poverty and lack of legal status.

In most versions this is translated literally without indicating the relationship with the topic of the larger unit (1:21–27), namely, the necessity of obeying God's Word. This implicit relationship is supplied here: 'which is one of the things God has told us to do'. Care for orphans and widows is commanded many times in the Old Testament as a way of imitating God's care for them. James assumes the readers' familiarity with these Old Testament references, and this may be what prompted him to use these two classes of people as representatives of those most in need of help. An alternate way to express this specific reference to orphans and widows in a generic sense would be: 'If anyone takes care of *people* who are suffering much *such as* orphans and widows'. This proposition is the first condition of receiving God's approval.

1:27b and if he does <u>not</u> think <u>or</u> act <u>immorally</u> like those who do not obey God, Whereas the first condition for receiving the approval of God refers to one's conduct, the second refers to one's character. The adjective ἄσπιλος 'morally spotless' that occurs here is also used in 1 Pet. 1:19 to describe Christ. It is forefronted, emphasizing the necessity of personal purity as the most important thought in the final phrase of v. 27 (Lange); the forefronting of the pronoun ἑαυτόν 'himself' emphasizes the responsibility for personal cooperation with God's keeping power (Hiebert). Martin points out that ἄσπιλον 'morally spotless' matches ἀμίαντος 'undefiled' in the first part of the verse, which further explains the fronting of ἄσπιλον.

The noun κόσμος 'world' refers to mankind alienated from God and in rebellion against God's will (Hiebert), hence 'those who do not obey God' in the display.

1:27c-d that person truly worships God *who is our* Father (*or, who cares for us like a* father), and God approves of him. The Greek text underlying these two propositions comes at the beginning of v. 27, but because semantically these propositions are the consequence of the two conditions, the usual English order for that kind of construction is used.

True worship is here characterized by two adjectives, which form a positive-negative doublet (Moore, p. 60). The positive one, καθαρός 'pure', is used in a moral and religious sense (BAGD, p. 388.3b). The negative one, ἀμίαντος 'undefiled', denotes something not stained by moral evil. The phrase παρὰ τῷ θεῷ 'before God' means acceptable to God (Ropes) and in the display is expressed as an active verb: 'God approves of him'.

James refers to God here as πατήρ 'father'. In some languages such kinship terms are obligatorily possessed. Even some English versions translate it as 'our Father' here (NIV, REB, JB). In those languages for which the use of 'father' for God is problematical it might be better translated as 'who cares for us like a father', since the focus is on caring for the needy. Ropes says, "This designation of God is possibly used here because it is the care for God's fatherless ones (*cf.* Ps. 68:5) which is enjoined."

On the surface propositions 27c and d appear to be a definition of 'religion', but Moo cites Calvin: "he does not define generally what religion is, but reminds us that religion without these things he mentions is nothing. . . ."

BOUNDARIES AND COHERENCE

The initial boundary of 1:26-27 has been discussed under unit 1:21-25. The beginning of the next unit at 2:1 is marked by another change of topic, from true religion to a warning against partiality, and by the use of the vocative, ἀδελφοί μου 'my brothers', which is used in this letter primarily at the beginning of new units. There is also a change to hortatory genre.

Semantic coherence is shown in the single topic that is discussed. James assumes that as believers they all want to worship God rightly so that they will have God's approval. So he states one negative condition that will hinder this goal and two positive conditions that will accomplish the goal. All of this is a *motivational basis* for the preceding exhortations in 1:21-25.

PROMINENCE AND THEME

The most prominent constituent of the 1:26-27 unit is the NUCLEUS; therefore the theme is drawn from it. It consists of a condition-CONSEQUENCE construction. In such a structure both the condition and the CONSEQUENCE are included in the theme; otherwise the statement would be incomplete and not make sense.

DIVISION CONSTITUENT 2:1-13 (Hortatory Section: Appeal₂ of 1:19–5:11)

THEME: Stop honoring some people more than others, since you are disobeying God's law that we should love one another. God will not act mercifully to those who do not act mercifully toward others.

MACROSTRUCTURE	CONTENTS
APPEAL	2:1-11 Stop honoring some people more than others, since you are not treating people the way God treats them and you are disobeying God's law that we should love one another.
motivational basis	2:12-13 Continually act mercifully toward others, since God will not act mercifully to those who do not act mercifully toward others.

INTENT AND MACROSTRUCTURE

In the 2:1-13 section James changes from the generic topic of the need to obey God's message to a specific problem that existed among his readers at this time, namely, showing favoritism to the rich. His intent is to change their behavior so that they demonstrate to all people the same love that God has shown toward them. He points out that their showing favoritism is inconsistent with the mercy that God has granted them.

The 2:1-13 section, which is composed of an *APPEAL* with a *motivational basis*, is hortatory in genre. In the 2:1-11 paragraph James admonishes his readers to stop practicing favoritism to the rich, since they are breaking God's law of love. In the 2:12-13 paragraph he points out the implications for such conduct in the light of the coming judgment, so it provides motivation for their obeying the 2:1 *APPEAL* to stop honoring one person more than another. Within 2:12-13 there is also an *APPEAL*, which is a positive restatement of the main *APPEAL*. The function of this exhortation is to highlight the statement that follows it.

BOUNDARIES AND COHERENCE

The initial boundary of 2:1-13 was discussed under 1:21-27. The beginning of the next unit at 2:14 is marked by a change from the topic of partiality to a description of an ineffective faith without deeds. The use of the vocative, ἀδελφοί μου 'my brothers' and a change of genre from hortatory to expository also show that it is a new unit.

Some commentators (e.g., Davids 1982, Blue, Johnson) consider the entire second chapter a higher-level unit that develops a single argument. Johnson (p. 219) says, "From beginning to end, it concerns faith and its deeds." There are admittedly parallels between 2:1-13 and 2:14-26, such as the initial reference to faith in both (2:1 and 2:14), the similar hypothetical cases (2:2-3 and 2:15-16) ending in a rhetorical question (2:4 and 2:16), and the demonstration of the inconsistency of their reasoning (2:5-7 and 2:18-19). However, joining these two sections as a macrostructural unit is not preferable for the following reasons:

1. Similarities of style are to be expected in an epistle characterized by the diatribe method of argumentation.
2. Even the titles of those who propose such a macrostructural unit reveal that the subject matter of 2:1-13 and 2:14-26 is too diverse to adequately reflect a unified whole. Davids (1982) labels 2:1-26 "The Excellence of Poverty and Generosity" and Blue has "Serve with Compassion."
3. The vocative and the initial rhetorical question in 2:14-26 indicate a new paragraph.
4. The second section (2:14-26) is distinctive in its genre. It is the only section in the epistle that is expository; the others are all hortatory.
5. The 2:14-26 unit functions within the entire 1:19–5:11 division as the *BASIS* for all the *SPECIFIC APPEALS*, not only for 2:1-13.

Coherence in the 2:1-13 section is shown by references to νόμος 'law' in vv. 8, 9, 10, 11, and 12. Although it is clear by the modifiers that different laws are in focus, yet there is a common thread of law throughout the whole unit. In v. 8 it is the 'royal law' of love; in v. 12 it is 'the law of freedom', distinguished from the Mosaic law. The Mosaic law is referred to in vv. 9, 10, and 11, where the noun νόμος occurs without modifiers except for the article in vv. 9 and 10. Words in the semantic domain of judgment—κριτής 'judge' in v. 4, κρίνω '(to) judge' in v. 12, and κρίσις 'judgment' in v. 13 (twice)—also add coherence as do the two verbs of speech, λέγω 'say' in v. 3 (twice) and λαλέω 'speak' in v. 12.

PROMINENCE AND THEME

Since the *APPEAL* in 2:1-11 is naturally prominent, the theme of 2:1-13 is drawn from its most important components. Also included in the 2:1-13 theme is the second half of the 2:12-13 *motivational basis*; the prospect of God's judgment upon those who do not show mercy would be a strong impetus to refrain from honoring some while dishonoring others. Since the motivational material is found mostly in 2:13 (the *BASIS* in the 2:12-13 unit), only this second half of the *motivational basis* in 2:1-13 is included in the theme for 2:1-13. (The purpose of the exhortation in v. 12 is, as is implied by the οὕτως . . . ὡς construction, to serve mainly as a mechanism for conveying the motivational material.)

SECTION CONSTITUENT 2:1-11 (Hortatory Paragraph: Appeal of 2:1-13)

THEME: Stop honoring some people more than others, since you are not treating people the way God treats them and you are disobeying God's law that we should love one another.

¶ PTRN	RELATIONAL STRUCTURE	CONTENTS
APPEAL	grounds	2:1a My fellow believers, *since* you trust our Lord Jesus Christ, the one who is glorious,†
	EXHORTATION	2:1b stop honoring some people more than others.
basis₁	condition₁ — NUCLEUS₁ - 'person'	2:2a *To illustrate*, if (*or*, Suppose) a person enters your meeting
	description	2:2b who wears gold rings and fine clothes,
	NUCLEUS₂ - 'person'	2:2c and *if* a poor person also enters
	description	2:2d who wears shabby clothes,
	condition₂ — orienter	2:3a and *if* you show special attention to the one dressed in fine clothes by saying,
	NUCLEUS₁ - CONTENT	2:3b "Sit here in this good seat,"
	orienter	2:3c and *if* you say to the poor one,
	NUCLEUS₂ - CONTENT	2:3d "Stand there or sit on the floor," [MTY]
	NUCLEUS — CONSEQUENCE	2:4a you have obviously [RHQ] caused divisions in the church (*or*, you are obviously inconsistent);
	AMPLIFICATION	2:4b *that is*, you are thinking/judging evilly. [RHQ]
	prominence orienter	2:5a Listen *to me*, my fellow believers, whom I love,
	contrast — MEANS	2:5b God chose poor people whom *unbelievers consider to* have nothing of value [RHQ]
	purpose₁ — RESULT	2:5c *in order that he might bless them* abundantly
	REASON	2:5d *because* they trust *in him*

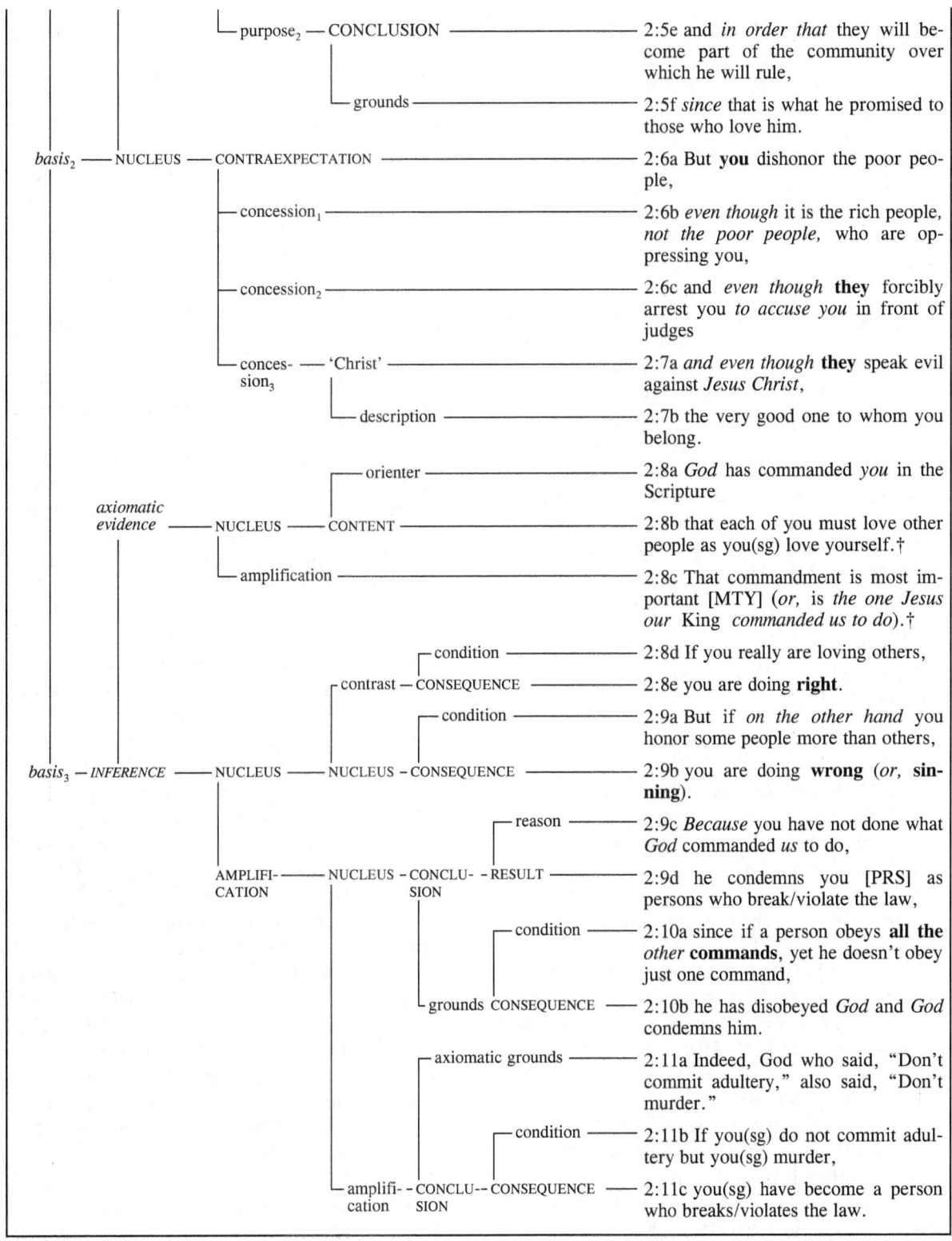

INTENT AND PARAGRAPH PATTERN

James' intent in the 2:1-11 unit is to affect the behavior of the believers so that they demonstrate to all people the same love that God has shown toward them. He points out that their showing favoritism to the wealthy is inconsistent with the mercy they have received from God.

This is a hortatory paragraph consisting of an *APPEAL* with three *bases*. The first *basis* (vv. 2-4), rather than giving a reason why the readers should obey the v. 1 *APPEAL*, shows how they may not be carrying it out, which would make them aware of the need to heed the *APPEAL*. In the second *basis* (vv. 5-7) God's treatment of the poor is contrasted with the readers' treatment of them, and reasons are given why it is inconsistent for them to favor the rich. The third *basis* (vv. 8-11) is even stronger: they should not show favoritism because to do so is disobedience to God and therefore sin. There is an embedded expository paragraph pattern in the third *basis* made up of an *INFERENCE* (2:8d-11c) and its *axiomatic evidence* (2:8a-c). In other words, the categorical command of God to love is clear (8a-c), and the *INFERENCE* of this is that obedience is acceptable (8d-e) whereas disobedience brings condemnation (9a-11c).

NOTES

2:1a My fellow believers, The vocative ἀδελφοί μου 'my brothers' again marks the beginning of a new unit and reveals James' personal relationship with the readers. It also expresses clearly that the basis of his strong exhortations and encouragements to them is their common relationship with Jesus Christ.

***since* you trust** The verb phrase ἔχετε τὴν πίστιν 'have the faith' has been variously translated. Some versions have the unnatural, literal "hold your faith" (NASB); but most have either "you believe" (REB) or "as believers" (NIV, TEV). Although 'have' is the imperative of the sentence, throughout the whole 2:1-11 paragraph James is concerned about their attitude toward others, referred to in the prepositional phrase ἐν προσωπολημψίαις 'with partiality/favoritism' (see the note on 2:1b). James forefronts it to signal that this is the topic of the unit. It occurs in the first position in the paragraph after the vocative. For this reason, the rendering in the display follows the many translations in which the concept of faith is subordinated, with the phrase regarding partiality being the main verb. Typical examples are: "as believers, don't show favoritism" (NIV) and "if you have faith . . . , you won't treat some people better than others" (CEV). Commentators are in general agreement that James is expressing the inconsistency of claiming faith in Jesus Christ while showing favoritism in their judgment of people based on external circumstances such as wealth. This attitude was condemned in the Old Testament (in Lev. 19:15 and many other passages). Such an attitude is also inconsistent with faith in Jesus Christ. Proposition 2:1a is the grounds for James' EXHORTATION in 1b, and this is expressed in the display by 'since' as the introducer of the clause.

our Lord Jesus Christ, the one who is glorious, This is one of only two times that the full name 'the Lord Jesus Christ' is mentioned in the epistle. Grammatically the noun phrase is composed of genitives: τοῦ κυρίου ἡμῶν Ἰησοῦ Χριστοῦ τῆς δόξης 'of our Lord Jesus Christ of the glory'. The relationship of 'of glory' to 'our Lord Jesus Christ' is ambiguous. Some commentators (e.g., Alford, Moo) think that 'glory' describes the word 'Lord' only: our Lord Jesus Christ, the Lord who is glorious. Others (e.g., Ropes, Martin, Huther) see 'glory' as describing the entire phrase: our glorious Lord Jesus Christ. A third view takes the word 'glory' to be in apposition to the preceding phrase so as to give another title to Jesus: our Lord Jesus Christ, who is the glory (e.g., Moffatt, Tasker, Mayor, Laws). According to this interpretation, Jesus is here compared to the Shekinah of the Old Testament; thus James is speaking of Christ as the glory in the midst of his people. The first view is not the best one because the whole name, 'the Lord Jesus Christ', is a well-accepted unit; moreover, 'the Lord' is followed by the genitive modifier 'of us', and it seems unlikely another genitive, 'of glory', would also modify 'Lord' (Huther). The second view is the one chosen for the display, for two reasons: One, the word order is best explained by this view; and two, it fits the context well that James should be emphasizing the inconsistency between faith in this glorious Person and their petty discrimination between the rich and poor (Ropes). However, the third view also fits the context and has good commentary backing, although no version consulted seems to express it. While 'glory' here may indeed be a veiled reference to the Old Testament Shekinah, the explanation of it, if this view is chosen, is so complicated that it would probably have to be put in a footnote or glossary instead of the text.

According to Buth (p. 6), 'glory' is equivalent to 'the Presence of God', and he suggests possible renderings, such as "in whom God has appeared," "in whom we see God," or "who makes God visible."

2:1b stop honoring some people more than others. While προσωπολημψίαις 'partiality/favoritism' is a noun, it refers to a kind of action or conduct of people and is therefore propositionalized as a verb. The phrase μή ἐν προσωπολημψίαις 'not with partiality' is forefronted in v. 1, which shows that it is the core topic of the entire paragraph. The verb ἔχετε 'have' that follows this phrase is a present imperative and is used with the negative μή 'not'; such a construction indicates that one should stop doing an action already in progress (Brooks and Winbery). As believers, they must stop showing partiality. Although this is the preferred rendering, stating this as a general principle would be acceptable: 'do not honor some people more than others.'

Westcott and Hort in their Greek text end this verse with a question mark. Goodspeed renders it, "Do you try to combine faith in our glorious Lord Jesus Christ with acts of partiality?" NRSV is similar. However, an imperative rendering, which is found in all ancient translations, is more forceful and more in keeping with James' hortatory style. The presence of γάρ 'for' in v. 2 and the implications of the negative μή (for a negative answer, if it were a question) also support interpreting the verb as an imperative.

2:2a *To illustrate,* On the paragraph level, γάρ 'for' here introduces vv. 2–4, which function as the *basis* for the APPEAL in 1b. Some commentators (e.g., Hiebert, Lange) see this as a causal usage, while others (e.g., Alford, Martin) see it as introducing an explanation. The latter function seems to be more in focus here because it introduces an illustration. Only the more literal versions (KJV, RSV, NASB) translate this conjunction; in the majority of versions (e.g., NIV, TEV, REB, CEV) "suppose" or a similar expression is used to introduce the illustration. In the display *'to illustrate'* is supplied to alert translators that they should use the appropriate means in a given language for signaling an illustration.

if (*or,* Suppose) The use of ἐάν 'if' suggests a hypothetical situation to some (e.g., Davids 1982, Moo, Hiebert), not an actual happening. But even Moo and Hiebert acknowledge the possibility that this really happened. In fact, there are good reasons for understanding vv. 2–3 as referring to something that happened regularly: (1) Beginning with v. 4 the indicative mood is used, indicating that James is talking about a real situation. (2) The situation described next, in vv. 6–7, clearly presents actual events happening to people in the church: the poor being oppressed by rich people. (3) James throughout the letter is dealing with real problems, not philosophical possibilities. The use of ἐάν may be James' way of conveying to his readers the hope that such ill-mannered practice will not take place any more (Martin, p. 63). While the grammar signals a hypothetical situation, the fact that James begins with a strong negative imperative and spends thirteen verses on this topic indicates that this was something that probably did happen at times. Although the conjunction 'if' occurs only once, the subjunctive mood in the verbs of vv. 2–3 shows that semantically 'if' is intended as an introduction to a series of conditions that explain in detail the contrast between attitudes and actions displayed in the assembly. The word 'Suppose' is given as an alternative to '*To illustrate,* if', since in English it commonly introduces an illustration.

The word order of the Greek text for 2:2a–4b is significant to the development of James' argument here. However, in translating this long, complex sentence into another language it may be best to restructure the material into smaller units. If the target language does not allow switching back and forth from rich to poor in the conditions, it may be necessary to present the rich man and how he is treated first and then the poor man and how he is treated. The natural grammatical order of the target language should be followed.

a person enters your meeting The noun συναγωγή 'synagogue, assembly' could refer to a place of Jewish worship; however, since this letter is clearly addressed to those who are 'brothers' because of their relationship in Christ, most scholars agree that 'synagogue' was the term used by the early Jewish believers for their assembly. The term denotes either the place of assembly or the company assembled. Some commentators say it is not necessary to decide whether a building or the congregation assembled is meant, but the display has 'meeting' because in the context the focus is on the reaction of the assembled ones toward the arrival of the two men.

Some commentators (e.g., Martin, Davids 1982) hold that this meeting was a judicial assembly of the church to deal with a dispute among its members. There are Jewish parallels of such a need for impartiality in which the litigants dressed themselves in fine clothes to impress the assembly. Furthermore, the forensic terms in v. 4 and v. 6 seem to support a law-court setting. However, most commentators (e.g., Kistemaker, Laws, Hiebert) conclude that it refers to a regular worship assembly. The text suggests that the two men were visitors, and it is unlikely that outsiders would have been present at a Christian judicial assembly (Moo). Laws says it is doubtful if the situation described allowed for "so precise a definition" as a judicial assembly. Either view is possible, but the second is preferable, since, as Kistemaker remarks, "The point of the example is to show that in a gathering of believers snobbery prevailed." However, the decision need not affect the translation.

2:2b–d who wears gold rings and fine clothes, and *if* a poor person also enters who wears shabby clothes, The adjective χρυσοδακτύλιος 'gold-fingered' does not suggest just one ring but rather a number of rings, a sign of social status. The next adjective, λαμπρός 'shining', refers either to glittering color or ornaments, and in this case to the elegant clothes worn by the wealthy. In the description of the poor man, the adjective ῥυπαρός 'filthy' is better rendered 'shabby', since the focus is on the social status of the man as a beggar and therefore destitute, not upon a neglect of hygiene. It is fronted in its phrase because it contrasts with 'fine' in the immediate context (Levinsohn, p. 95). It is clear that the entire 2:1–11 unit is focused on the contrast of believers' reactions toward the rich and toward the poor. At this point, instead of using the word 'rich' James chooses to refer to the rich by two graphic characteristics: as 'gold fingered' (i.e., wearing many gold rings), and as wearing fine clothing. Then the poor are referred to and described as dressed in shabby clothing. This may be done to stress the fact that these believers were judging based upon outward appearance rather than upon inward qualities (Hiebert).

2:3a–d and *if* you show special attention to the one dressed in fine clothes by saying, "Sit here in this good seat," and *if* you say to the poor one, "Stand there or sit on the floor," The verb ἐπιβλέπω 'pay attention to' is in the subjunctive mood, indicating that this is a continuation of the conditional sentence begun in 2:2a. In English a repetition of the conjunction 'if' is required. It is significant that there is no verb in 3c–d (about the treatment of the poor man) to parallel and contrast with the verb 'pay attention to' in 3a regarding the preferential treatment of the rich man. Only the verb εἴπητε 'you say' is repeated. The response to each of the visitors is highlighted, first by the repetition of the verb 'you say' and second by the repetition of the free pronoun σύ 'you' in the direct speech. The different treatment of the two people is indicated by a series of contrastive terms: 'sit' versus 'stand', 'here' versus 'there', and 'well' versus 'under my footstool'.

The adverb καλῶς, which follows Σὺ κάθου ὧδε 'you sit here', can mean either 'well' or 'please' (an expression of courtesy). Some commentators and versions (e.g., Ropes; TNT) prefer the latter, as it was often used this way in the papyri. However, most commentators and versions view it as a reference to the good seat that was offered. This is preferable, as it gives a better contrast between the attitudes shown toward the rich and poor (Adamson).

There are several variant readings of the remark to the poor man. The Textus Receptus has στῆθι ἐκεῖ ἢ κάθου ὧδε 'stand there or sit here' before 'under my footstool'. Modern textual critics agree that this longer reading was introduced to provide a neater parallelism. There is disagreement as to whether ἐκεῖ 'there' should follow 'stand' or 'sit'. The original was probably 'Stand there or sit under my footstool', which would be on the floor (Laws). The GNT has this reading with a B rating, indicating that the UBS committee considers it almost certain. Hence it is used in the display.

2:4a you have obviously caused divisions in the church This clause functions as the apodosis of the two preceding verses; that is, it is the CONSEQUENCE of the complex conditions. Since the verb διεκρίθητε 'you discriminate' is used with the negative οὐ, most commentators think it is a rhetorical question expecting an affirmative answer; hence it is expressed as a statement in the display. The exact meaning of this verb depends upon its relationship with the phrase ἐν ἑαυτοῖς 'among/in yourselves'. The reference may be to their outward conduct if the preposition is translated 'among' (Kistemaker, Davids 1982). The meaning would be that their actions toward the rich and poor are discriminatory, and this is something clearly condemned by God in the Old Testament. The majority of translators take 'among yourselves' as referring to discriminatory practices in the Christian community (Loh and Hatton). TEV renders it "you are guilty of creating distinctions among yourselves." Such conduct made unjustified divisions in their assemblies (Hiebert).

(**or, you are obviously inconsistent**); An alternative meaning of the phrase ἐν ἑαυτοῖς is 'in yourselves', denoting an inner attitude (Ropes, Martin, Cranfield 1965a). What this attitude is has already been suggested in 1:6, where James uses the verb διακρίνω to mean the divided, conflicting thoughts of a person who lacks faith. A reference to such inner conflict fits the present context well, hence is given in the display as an alternative rendering. Moo says James may be "tracing the sinful behaviour pictured in verses 2-3 back to its sinful motives." Either rendering has good commentary backing, but the first is preferable because in the immediate context the focus is actions and relationships in the group. (Later, in 2:5-11, James turns to focus on the inner attitudes that were the motivation for the wrong actions, especially the lack of love.) Another reason to prefer the first rendering is that there seems to be a deliberate play on words in the use of 'discriminate, judge between' in 4a and the related expression 'become judges' in 4b (Loh and Hatton). These words come from the same root.

2:4b *that is,* **you are thinking/judging evilly.** The conjunction καί 'and' makes 4b grammatically coordinate with 4a. Thus the οὐ 'negative' goes with both clauses and makes a pair of rhetorical questions, each expecting a positive answer. Thus 4b is a statement in the display, as 4a is.

Most commentators call the genitive in κριταὶ διαλογισμῶν πονηρῶν 'judges of evil reasonings' a genitive of quality, describing the readers as evil-thinking judges. (This same pattern is seen in 1:25, where 'hearers of forgetfulness' means 'forgetful hearers'.) By their acts of favoritism based on social standing, they had become judges with false standards. The communication relation between 4a and 4b is considered to be NUCLEUS-AMPLIFICATION, since the evil thinking and wrong actions are intricately linked.

2:5a Listen *to me,* **my fellow believers, whom I love,** This orienter consists of the imperative ἀκούσατε 'listen' and the vocative ἀδελφοί μου ἀγαπητοί 'my beloved brothers'. The two combine to give prominence not only to the following proposition, 5b, but also to the higher-level contrast between 5b-f and 6a-7b (see the note for 6a). The use of the adjective 'beloved' assures the readers that in this strong rebuke James is motivated by love and is concerned for the welfare of the believers.

2:5b God chose poor people whom *unbelievers consider to* **have nothing of value** The initial οὐχ 'not' in this rhetorical question expects an affirmative answer, hence its expression as a positive statement. The noun θεός 'God' occurs immediately after the negative and is thereby a highlighted topic (Levinsohn, p. 88). The adjective πτωχούς 'poor' is the usual word for those who are lacking in material possessions in contrast with the rich. In 2:1-4 James rebuked the believers for showing partiality to the rich and declared that this is a wrong judgment. Such favoritism is inconsistent with God's attitude, since he has chosen the poor.

The word 'poor' is qualified by the phrase τῷ κόσμῳ 'in/to the world'. Some commentators (e.g., Alford, Moo) interpret this as meaning simply that they are poor in material things. While this is certainly possible, many others (e.g., Tasker, Ropes, Martin) think it is an ethical dative or dative of interest: 'poor in the eyes of unbelievers' or 'in regard to what the world considers wealth'. The latter interpretation seems preferable in this context because the theme of the entire paragraph has to do with the necessity of conforming to God's standards rather than to human standards. The words supplied in the display bring out the contrast between their poverty in the eyes of unbelievers and their riches as seen from God's viewpoint (see 2:5c).

2:5c-d *in order that he might bless them* **abundantly** *because* **they trust** *in him* The phrase πλουσίους ἐν πίστει 'rich in faith' means that they are "rich in the sphere of faith . . . i.e. rich when judged by God's standards" (Ropes). There are two main interpretations of the relation between 'rich in faith' in 5c-d and 'poor in the world' in 5b: (1) Some commentators (e.g., Lenski, Burdick) consider 'rich' to be in apposition to 'the poor', sometimes described as a predicative accusative, functioning as a description of 'the poor': 'God has chosen the poor, who are rich in faith and are heirs of the kingdom'. (2) Many other commentators (e.g., Laws, Martin, Johnson) say that there is an ellipsis of the infinitive εἶναι here with 'rich in faith' completing the verb ἐξελέξατο 'chose', stating what

God intends for the poor. Most versions translate it this way. TEV, for example, has "God chose the poor people of this world to be rich in faith and to possess the kingdom. . . ." Both interpretations are valid, but the display follows the second one, since the concepts in 5c–f effectively express the purpose of God's choice of the poor. The communication relation between 5b and 5c–d is MEANS-purpose.

There is a significant play on words in the contrast between 'the poor' and 'rich in faith'. Although 'the poor' is nonfigurative and qualifies people, 'rich' is figurative and relates grammatically to the prepositional phrase 'in faith', faith being the event of believing or trusting. The wealth is not their faith but rather all the blessings that accompany salvation, which they receive in the sphere or realm of faith (Hiebert). This concept is supplied in 5c–d.

The relation between 5c and 5d is RESULT-REASON. Dana and Mantey (p. 105) list a number of occurrences of the preposition ἐν where its meaning is 'because of', as here, including Gal. 1:24 and Col. 1:21. But it should be noted that there is also merit in the alternative interpretation preferred by Loh and Hatton:

> . . . it is probably best to take it as contrasting with "in the eyes of the world" or "by the world's standard," and having the sense of being "rich in the realm of faith," that is, spiritually wealthy when judged by God's standards.

This view would be difficult to express in translation if one wishes to retain the concept of faith.

Since the "value of faith is placed in uncompromised opposition to the value of riches by the transferring of the very term *plousioi* to the believing poor" (Stulac, p. 96), REASON is in capital letters in the display just as RESULT is. This does not imply that all poor people are rich in faith nor that no rich people will be saved.

2:5e and *in order that* they will become part of the community over which he will rule, The noun βασιλεία 'kingdom' speaks of a second purpose for which God chose the poor. It has to do with their future. The meaning components of 'kingdom' are God's ruling and also the realm over which he rules. This is the only mention of the kingdom in the epistle, but the concept would be familiar to the readers, who had either personally heard the teaching of Jesus about the kingdom of God or had received it by oral tradition. Commentators consider that 'kingdom' here refers to the future manifestation of God's kingdom. The noun κληρονόμος 'heir' reinforces this view.

2:5f *since* that is what he promised to those who love him. The aorist tense of the verb ἐπηγγείλατο 'promised' indicates that God made this promise to believers at some point in the past. This is the same phrase used in 1:12, where those who have faith that is approved by testing are promised a reward from God; thus the 'crown of life' and the coming kingdom are practically synonymous. It is significant that in both contexts 'faith' is equated with 'loving God'. Regarding the twofold purpose for which God chose the poor (2:5c–f), Tasker says, "He has both exalted them in the present circumstances of their life and given them hope for the future. . . ."

2:6a But you dishonor the poor people, The conjunction δέ 'but' along with the fronted pronoun ὑμεῖς 'you' marks the switch of topic from God's treatment of the poor (in 2:5b) to how the addressees treat them. Verses 5a–7b function as the second *basis* for the APPEAL in 2:1. The most prominent proposition in 5a–7b is 6a: their action is wrong because it is the opposite of God's standard. Hence 6a is labeled as NUCLEUS of the second *basis*.

2:6b *even though* it is the rich people, *not the poor people*, who are oppressing you, The words 'even though' are supplied in this and the following two propositions to make it clear that 6b, 6c, and 7a are in the communication relation of concession to the 6a CONTRAEXPECTATION. One would have expected the readers to dishonor those who were oppressing them.

The initial οὐκ 'not' in the rhetorical question means that an affirmative answer is expected, so the question is rephrased as a positive statement. There is an abrupt change of topic here from the poor to the rich although no transitional particle marks it. In the display the transition to 'the rich' as the new topic is made smooth by supplying the idea that it was not the poor who were the oppressors. The compound verb καταδυναστεύω 'oppress' pictures a potentate exercising his power in an oppressive manner. This refers primarily to social and economic mistreatment (Hiebert).

2:6c and *even though* they forcibly arrest you *to accuse you* in front of judges The free pronoun αὐτοί 'they themselves' is fronted for emphasis, laying stress on the fact that the rich are the very ones they were favoring. This is a court scene and the verb ἕλκω 'drag' indicates that they were forcibly taken against their will. This need not be translated literally but should be the culturally accepted equivalent. Although the mistreatment was probably motivated by financial interest, it may have been combined with scorn for their faith (Moo).

2:7a and *even though* they speak evil against *Jesus Christ*, This is the third concession to the 6a CONTRAEXPECTATION. The free pronoun αὐτοί 'they' is again fronted for emphasis. The verb phrase βλασφημοῦσιν τὸ καλὸν ὄνομα 'blaspheme the good name' indicates bitter religious hostility on the part of the rich, who were probably wealthy Christ-rejecting Jews (Mayor). The 'good name' is surely the name Jesus or Jesus Christ, since it is clear from 2:1 that the readers are Christians. In the display Jesus Christ is given, since this title is used elsewhere in the book, but either name would be sufficient to identify the referent. Moo says, "How incongruous that those who blaspheme that 'honourable name' should be accorded preferential treatment in the church!"

2:7b the very good one to whom you belong. The expression ἐπικληθὲν ἐφ' ὑμᾶς 'called on you' is a Hebraism denoting that they belong to the one whose name they bear (Deut. 28:10; Jer. 14:9). Some commentators think that the aorist tense of this participle may suggest an allusion to a specific time, which probably would be the time of their confession at baptism (Laws), but this is not in focus here.

2:8a *God* has commanded *you* in the Scripture In 8a the topic of discussion in vv. 8–11 is introduced; it centers around the noun νόμος 'law'. To a Jew 'the law' was not a generic term but a technical religious term meaning commandments from God given to people in the sacred writings that they were obligated to obey. To understand the rest of this passage it is necessary to make this implicit information clear at the beginning of 2:8-11, since in many languages the topic under discussion is obligatorily introduced first. The whole of 2:8-11 functions as the third *basis* for the *APPEAL* in 2:1—showing favoritism is condemned by God in his commandments and is therefore sin.

2:8b that each of you must love other people as you(sg) love yourself. James states in a quotation the content of the particular aspect of the law that is under focus here. Most commentators says it is a quotation of Lev. 19:18. In the quotation the second person singular is used instead of the usual plural found in most exhortations. The singular verb marks this as an individual duty. The object of the verb is τὸν πλησίον σου 'your neighbor', which for a Jew would be limited to one of their own people, but Jesus expanded the term to include foreigners (Luke 10:25-37) and enemies (Matt. 5:44). James makes it clear that every person has the obligation to love all people without limitation. In some languages the idea of love, especially of oneself, is difficult to translate. It might be expressed as 'be concerned for others as you are concerned for yourselves'. The concept of loyalty rather than affection is foremost (Loh and Hatton). Also, it should be noted that in some languages a general principle like this is more commonly expressed in the first person plural inclusive: 'God has commanded us in the Scripture that each of us must love other people as we love ourselves'.

2:8c That commandment is most important (*or*, is *the one Jesus our* King *commanded us to do*). When James refers to the Old Testament law, or one of its commandments, he simply uses νόμος 'law', but when he is referring to the Christian understanding of 'law', he qualifies νόμος in some way. For example, in 1:25 and 2:12 it occurs with the noun ἐλευθερίας 'of freedom'. In 2:8c νόμον is used without an article, probably to stress the quality of the law, and is qualified by the adjective βασιλικόν 'royal'. What James is implying is that obedience to the commandment to love fulfills the entire will of God, especially as revealed in the teaching of Jesus (Martin).

There are two main views as to what 'royal law' means: (1) It is the highest (supreme) law, summing up all other laws (Alford, Hiebert). According to this view, 'royal' is a metonymy, a king being the most important official; hence 'royal' signifies 'most important'. (2) It is the royal law because it was given by the King, God or Jesus Christ (Davids 1982, Adamson). In the display both views of 'royal' are presented as acceptable alternatives. The first is the preferred one because it preserves the focus better, but the second has merit, especially considering the reference to the 'kingdom' in v. 5.

It would be possible to combine these two alternatives if one agrees with Tasker, who says,

This law is called *royal*, partly because it is the law of the kingdom of God, given by the supreme King Himself, and partly because, in its very comprehensiveness, it is the law that governs all other laws concerning human relationships.

Combining both ideas would give 'That commandment is the most important, *since our* King (*or, Jesus our* King) *has commanded us to do that*'.

2:8d–e If you really are loving others, you are doing right. This conditional clause occurs at the beginning of v. 8, but because of the grammatical and semantic mismatch it is best in English to put it adjacent to the apodosis or conclusion of the sentence. The words νόμον τελεῖτε 'you fulfill the law' are best expressed in terms of that law's specific content. The conjunction εἰ 'if' used with the indicative indicates a condition that actually existed; some commentators (e.g., Ropes) therefore interpret this verse as a response to those who would excuse their treatment of the rich as an expression of love for them. However, it is better to understand it as simply acknowledging that some of them were not guilty of showing favoritism (Hiebert, Laws).

The particle μέντοι 'indeed', which introduces this clause, may be adversative, with the sense 'however'. If understood this way (so Mayor, Alford), v. 8 introduces a contrast with the preceding context, probably 6a. But most commentators (e.g., Martin, Kistemaker) take μέντοι here as a particle of affirmation, 'indeed, really'. Louw and Nida (p. 795, 89.136) point out that "μέντοι . . . δέ" is a marker of "sets of items in contrast with one another"; they cite James 2:8-9 as an example. This would make 2:8d-e the beginning of a contrast that extends through 9b: 'if indeed on the one hand you fulfill the royal law . . . but if on the other hand you show partiality'. In this context the contrast between v. 8 and v. 9 is more prominent than any connection to the previous statements. REB reflects the adversative view with "however," but most of the versions consider the particle affirmative. Some use "really," as in the display.

2:9a But if *on the other hand* you honor some people more than others, Propositions 9a and b form the NUCLEUS of the contrast that began in 8d–e. A strong contrast is signaled here by the conjunction δέ 'but' and the switch to εἰ προσωπολημπτεῖτε 'if you respect persons'. Again, the conjunction εἰ 'if' used with the indicative shows that James considers this to be a real-life situation, not simply a hypothetical possibility.

2:9b you are doing wrong (*or,* sinning). The strong verb phrase ἁμαρτίαν ἐργάζεσθε 'sin you are working' implies intentional action (Oesterley). Furthermore, the fronting of the object parallels the structure of the positive statement at the end of v. 8 and gives prominence to the contrast between 'well you are doing' in 8e and 'sin you are working' in 9b.

2:9c-d *Because* you have not done what *God* commanded *us* to do, he condemns you as persons who break/violate the law, The participial phrase ἐλεγχόμενοι ὑπὸ τοῦ νόμου ὡς παραβάται 'being reproved by the law as transgressors' is in apposition to the preceding clause, and it functions as an amplification of that strong accusation. Here 'the law' is personified as a witness that convicts them of sin every time they are partial to the rich. It is not James who condemns them but the law. "Whether the reference is to the law of God as a whole or to the law of love in particular, in either case they stand condemned," says Hiebert. This personification, which is not possible in many languages, is restated in the display: God, who gave the law, is the one who condemns. The communication relation between 9c and 9d is reason-RESULT, expressed here by 'Because'.

2:10a since if a person obeys all the *other* commands, The conjunction γάρ 'for' introduces vv. 10 and 11, which are James' grounds proving his claim that the person who does not love his neighbor is a lawbreaker. The phrase ὅλον τὸν νόμον 'the whole law' is fronted for emphasis and the use of the singular noun for 'law' indicates that it refers to the law as a whole (Alford), except, of course, for the one point in which he stumbles. The use of the subjunctive as in this clause and in 10b often indicates a hypothetical situation, but the omission of the particle ἄν indicates that James considers this a real possibility, implying that he thinks some of them were probably guilty (Hiebert). The ὅστις 'whoever' construction is a type of conditional translatable by 'if anyone' or 'if a person'; the latter is used in the display.

yet he doesn't obey just one command, The conjunction δέ 'but' marks a concession-CONTRA-EXPECTATION relation between the two clauses in 10a. This is expressed in the display by translating δέ as 'yet'. The verb πταίω means 'stumble' and is used here figuratively. Its meaning is to make a mistake or commit a sin.

2:10b he has disobeyed *God* and *God* condemns him. The verb phrase γέγονεν πάντων ἔνοχος 'he has become guilty of all' in the context of the law given by God would mean to any Jew that the person had disobeyed what God had commanded and therefore was subject to punishment by God.

The word πάντων 'of all' is interpreted in different ways. (1) A few would say it was meant literally. Very few commentators hold this view; even so, πάντων is translated literally in most versions. NIV, for example, has "is guilty of breaking all of it." (2) The vast majority of commentators say that the breaking of even one commandment incurs guilt in respect to the law as a whole, since the law is fundamentally a unity, being an expression of the will of one Lawgiver (Tasker). (3) Another view is that the breaking of one point of the law reveals a nature that will break the law in other points when there is an opportunity (Bennett, p. 159, quoted by Hiebert). Although there is merit in the third view, the second view is to be preferred, since any violation of the law is an offense against God, who gave the law.

Several commentators mention the fact that though strict rabbis taught the unity of the law, some of them held that obedience to certain specific laws was as good as obedience to the whole (Adamson). James may have had this in mind as he wrote 10b. What should be clear in any translation is that obedience cannot be on a selective basis. JBP's rendering is good: "is none the less a lawbreaker." In many languages a literal rendering would be understood as the person having actually violated all of the other parts of the law. But the focus should be on disobedience to the Lawgiver and the consequence of such disobedience, in the rendering in the display.

2:11a Indeed, God who said, "Don't commit adultery," also said, "Don't murder." The conjunction γάρ 'for' introduces this illustration of the principle stated in 10a-b. This is an axiomatic grounds because it appeals to a self-evident truth. The phrase ὁ ... εἰπών 'the one who said' is a typical Jewish way to avoid using the name of God. It centers attention not on the individual commands but on the fact that the same God gave both. This should be reflected in the translation.

There are many different opinions as to why James uses these two particular commandments for his illustration. They are the first two of the second table of the Decalogue, which has to do with relations with one's neighbors. These two laws were commonly used by the Jews as examples of the requirements of the law (Moo). Others point out that breaking either of them violates the law of love, which is very much in focus in this unit. Songer (p. 116) suggests that the selection of these two commands enables James "to deepen the blackness of the sin of partiality by associating it with adultery and murder" (quoted by Hiebert). What they were viewing as a trivial matter James says is a very serious breach of God's will for their lives. These are interesting speculations but will not affect the translation. Most commentators point out that the order here reverses the sixth and seventh commandments. However, this same order is found in the Codex Vaticanus manuscript of the Septuagint as well as in Luke 18:20 and Rom. 13:9. So there is probably no subtle significance in the order here.

2:11b-c If you(sg) do not commit adultery but you(sg) murder, you(sg) have become a person who breaks/violates the law. This conclusion of the illustration is a restatement of the conclusion made in 9c-d. From the generalized ὅστις 'whoever' of 2:10, James now moves to the definite singular 'you' in the verb γέγονας 'you have become', indicating individual guilt, although this idea may already be present by virtue of the second person singular in the commandments quoted here. The perfect tense indicates a state, the state of being a transgressor. The significance of this argument is that because they have broken a commandment of God by honoring some people more than others, they are convicted as transgressors of the law. The communication relation between 9c-10b and 11a-c is that of NUCLEUS-amplification.

BOUNDARIES AND COHERENCE

The initial boundary of 2:1-11 was discussed under 1:21-27. The beginning of the next unit at 2:12 is marked by a switch of topic: from condemning partiality, which is to break God's law, to the need for a positive response of mercy toward all people in order to avoid God's judgment. The introductory οὕτως 'so' in 2:12 points forward to the ὡς 'as' clause rather than to what has gone before (Alford). Furthermore, the *APPEAL-basis* macrostructure pattern throughout the epistle supports this break. In v. 12 there is a generic summary of the 2:1-11 paragraph, and in v. 13 there is an axiomatic statement characteristic of these generic *bases*.

Some commentators and versions make a paragraph break following 2:4 (Blue, Davids 1982, Kistemaker, Hiebert; TEV, NIV, CEV, NCV); others, following 2:7 (Ropes, Mitton, Lenski, Tasker; TEV, NIV) or 2:9 (Blue; CEV, JB). Laws also makes a break after 2:9, saying that James moves from the topic of keeping one major precept to keeping the whole law. She feels this introduces a new idea, though she adds, "but it is probably intended to add further seriousness to his previous warning." Still, the theme of partiality runs through the whole of 2:1-11, and for this reason these breaks at 4, 7, and 9 are considered to be between lower-level units that function as the *bases* of the *APPEAL* in v. 1. But even though 2:1-11 is one coherent discourse-level paragraph, it may be wise to mark these lower-level units with paragraph breaks in a translation in order to facilitate reading and comprehension. Most English versions do this.

The semantic coherence of 2:1-11 is shown by the use of the noun προσωπολημψία 'partiality' in vv. 2 and 9 and verbs in the same semantic domain, διακρίνω 'discriminate' in v. 4 and ἀτιμάζω 'dishonor' in v. 6, as well as the illustration of partiality in vv. 2-3. Coherence is also shown by the contrast between terms for the rich and poor, πτωχός 'poor (man)' in vv. 2, 3, 5, and 6 and πλούσιος 'rich (man)' in v. 6, as well as the reference to the rich as 'the one wearing fine clothing' in vv. 2 and 3 and the figurative use of πλούσιος in the expression 'rich in faith' in v. 5. Further coherence comes from ἀγαπάω '(to) love' in relation to God in v. 5 and in relation to people in v. 8.

Referential coherence is seen in the contrast between God's character and actions and the people's actions. This is highlighted by the use of the forefronted subject θεός 'God' in v. 5 and the emphatic ὑμεῖς δέ 'but you' in v. 6.

PROMINENCE AND THEME

The theme of the 2:1-11 paragraph is taken from the *APPEAL* and a brief condensation of the *bases*, these being integral parts of a hortatory paragraph pattern.

SECTION CONSTITUENT 2:12–13
(Hortatory Paragraph: Motivational Basis of 2:1–11)

THEME: Continually act mercifully toward others, since God will not act mercifully to those who do not act mercifully toward others.

¶ PTRN	RELATIONAL STRUCTURE	CONTENTS
APPEAL	CONGRUENCE	2:12a Continually speak and act in such a way (*or, mercifully*) toward others
	standard — 'law'	2:12b *as people should whom God* will judge by the law
	identification	2:12c that sets *us* free *from the penalty of sin*. †
BASIS	circumstance	2:13a *Speak and act like this,* since when *God* judges *us,*
	NUCLEUS	2:13b he will not act mercifully toward those who do not act mercifully *toward others.*
	AMPLIFICATION	2:13c When anyone acts mercifully *toward others*, he can rejoice since it is evident that God has mercifully saved him from being judged (*or, he can rejoice because God will* judge *him mercifully*).

INTENT AND PARAGRAPH PATTERN

James' purpose in the 2:12–13 unit is to motivate the readers to deal mercifully with the poor as well as with the rich based on God's having dealt mercifully with them (see "Intent and Macrostructure" of 2:1–13). The paragraph is structurally hortatory, since it contains an *APPEAL* in v. 12 (see "Intent and Macrostructure" of 2:1–13 for the function of the v. 12 *APPEAL*).

The unit's most prominent constituent is the *BASIS* in v. 13, hence the label in upper-case letters. This prominence derives from the fact that the motivational material is found primarily in that verse. God's judgment of the readers depends on the way they treat other people, so they would do well to heed the *APPEAL* in 2:1.

NOTES

2:12a Continually speak and act in such a way (*or, mercifully*) toward others The 2:12a *APPEAL* provides the positive prescribed implementation of the main *APPEAL* in 2:1, which is negative. In making this *APPEAL*, James uses two verbs, both of which have been used before, λαλέω 'speak' in 1:19 and ποιέω 'do, act' (in cognate noun form) in 1:22, 23, and 25. These two verbs include all of a person's conduct; the present imperative indicates that the actions should be habitual. Both verbs are immediately preceded by the adverb of manner οὕτως 'so/thus'; this gives equal prominence to each verb. This adverb functions in combination with ὡς 'as' (in 12b) to designate the manner of conduct. (The same combination is used in 1 Cor. 9:26.) Since in many languages a generic translation of the adverb 'so, in such a way' would not be clear, a more specific rendering, 'mercifully', inferred from the immediate context, is given in the display as a valid alternative. By showing mercy to others, they exhibit the character of God (Davids 1994).

2:12b as *people should whom God* will judge by the law The subordinating conjunction ὡς 'as' introduces the manner of speaking and acting properly. The participial phrase μέλλοντες κρίνεσθαι 'being about to be judged' does not so much indicate the nearness of judgment as its certainty (Davids 1982). The standard of judgment is stated in the prepositional phrase διὰ νόμου ἐλευθερίας 'through a law of freedom'. As believers, they will want to be pleasing to the Lord, James assumes. The absence of the article before both nouns in this phrase gives prominence to the character of the law that will be the standard of God's judgment (Mayor). The adverb οὕτως 'so, thus' in 12a is paired with the conjunction ὡς 'as' here to form a relation of CONGRUENCE-standard between 12a and 12b–c.

2:12c that sets *us* free *from the penalty of sin*. The expression νόμου ἐλευθερίας 'law of freedom' occurs in the New Testament only here and in James 1:25. Hiebert says of it, "The designation is James's way of distinguishing this law from the Mosaic law, especially as interpreted by the rabbis." That there is a difference is clear. When the law is internalized in the new covenant (see Jer. 31:31–36), it becomes "implanted" in the heart (James 1:21). There are two basic aspects of this freedom, being freed from the penalty of sin and also being given the power to obey God's will (Moo). In 1:25 it is this latter concept that is in focus, since the context is the importance of obedience. Here, in the context of the need for mercy toward others, the manifestation of God's mercy in freeing us from the penalty of sin is in focus, and that is supplied in the display. If a translator prefers to render both occurrences the same, a valid alternative would be 'that enables *us* to do *what God wants us to do*'.

2:13a–b *Speak and act like this,* **since when *God judges us,* he will not act mercifully toward those who do not act mercifully** *toward others.* The conjunction γάρ 'for' introduces this verse as the *BASIS* of the *APPEAL* in v. 12. Here James adds to the idea of judgment that of mercy in two statements that seem to be proverbial sayings. The change from second person in v. 12 to third person in v. 13 suggests that what is given is a general principle (Laws).

2:13c When anyone acts mercifully *toward others,* **he can rejoice** *since it is evident that God has mercifully saved him from* **being judged (*or,* he can rejoice because *God will judge him mercifully*).** Commentators differ in their interpretation of the clause κατακαυχᾶται ἔλεος κρίσεως 'mercy triumphs over judgment'. A number (e.g., Ropes, Tasker) state that it represents the converse of the previous sentence, but, as Laws points out, there is no conjunction between the two to show their relation. The topics of judgment and mercy are clearly continued, but there are different views as to whose mercy and judgment are referred to. Some (e.g., Motyer, Manton) hold that the reference is primarily to two attributes of God. However, the majority (e.g., Laws, Hiebert) feel that the focus is on the believers' mercy toward others, which should be a response to, or reflection of, God's mercy on them, even though they agree that the judgment is God's.

The verb κατακαυχάομαι occurs only three times in the New Testament. In James 3:14 and Rom. 11:18 it has the meaning of 'boast, exult over'. But for James 2:13 BAGD (411.2) gives its meaning as "triumph over," and Louw and Nida (74.11) as "to have greater power" (i.e., mercy is more powerful than judgment). The difficulty of rendering this is compounded by both the subject and object of the action being personifications. Moreover, they are noun forms that refer to event concepts and must therefore be restated as verbs.

If this clause is taken as a simple converse of the previous sentence, as many do take it, the meaning is that those who show mercy need not fear the judgment, since mercy cancels out judgment (Alford). However, this implies that one may earn salvation by showing mercy to others.

Another view is that our merciful attitude and actions will count as evidence of God's work in our lives, which is the grounds of our confidence in the Day of Judgment (Moo). Hiebert says,

> The practice of mercy toward others is the evidence that God's grace has produced a transformation in a person.... By his conduct the merciless man reveals that he has never vitally apprehended God's mercy himself (Matt. 18:23–25).

This view underlies the words supplied in the display. It is the preferred interpretation, since the tone of Scripture is that a merciful attitude is the result of salvation rather than its cause. The first view is a valid alternative, however, since many commentators hold it. In both of these views, the basic idea is that because God has been merciful to us, we must be merciful to others. This truth functions as the *BASIS* for the *APPEAL* to be merciful in 12a–c.

BOUNDARIES AND COHERENCE

The opening boundary of 2:12–13 was discussed under 2:1–11, the final boundary under 2:1–13. Lexical coherence is shown by the use of the cognates κρίνω '(to) judge' in v. 12 and κρίσις 'judgment' in v. 13 (twice). The conjunction γάρ in v. 13 ties vv. 12 and 13 together as a unit.

PROMINENCE AND THEME

Both the *APPEAL* and *BASIS* are represented in the theme of 2:12–13, which is the norm for a hortatory paragraph.

DIVISION CONSTITUENT 2:14–26
(Expository Section: Basis of 1:21–2:13 and 3:1–5:11)

THEME: Only by doing good to others can a person prove that he truly trusts in God, since it is useless for one to say that he trusts in God if he does not do what God commands.

MACROSTRUCTURE	CONTENTS
CLAIM	2:14–25 Anyone who says he trusts in Jesus Christ but does not act compassionately to others is not truly trusting in him. Only by obeying God and doing good to others can a person prove that he trusts in him.
justification	2:26 It is useless for one to say that he trusts in God if he does not do what God commands.

INTENT AND MACROSTRUCTURE

The 2:14–26 section consists of two parts, a CLAIM (2:14–25) and a *justification* (2:26), and is thus expository. James' purpose is to clarify the readers' understanding of the true nature of faith in order to provide motivation for obeying all of the exhortations in the entire division. In the 2:14–25 CLAIM he discusses faith and works and their interrelationship. In the 2:26 *justification* he recapitulates the truth that without good deeds there is no real faith. As Hiebert (p. 157) says, "James insists that a living faith will authenticate itself in the production of works."

The 2:14–26 section is unusually prominent for the following reasons:

1. The genre is distinctive. In a book with predominantly hortatory units (77 of the 108 verses are in hortatory units), this section is by far the longest expository one, consisting of thirteen verses. In chapter 1 there are only three expository units (one paragraph and two propositional clusters), with a total of four verses. In chapters 3–5 there are four short expository units, with a total of fourteen verses.

2. In 2:14–26 James changes the pace of the discourse with a predominance of features characteristic of the diatribe style (see Ropes, pp. 12–16, for his treatment of this). He opens with two rhetorical questions in v. 14 and follows with others in vv. 16, 20, 21, and 25. In v. 18 there is a truncated dialogue with an imaginary interlocutor. The argumentative style is marked by such expressions as θέλεις δὲ γνῶναι 'but are you willing to know' (v. 20), βλέπεις 'you see' (v. 22), and ὁρᾶτε 'you see' (v. 24). The examples of Abraham and Rahab in vv. 21–25 are also characteristic of the diatribe.

3. The function of this section within the higher-layered structure of the epistle is another indication of its being a peak (see Longacre, pp. 20–25). It functions as the BASIS for all the SPECIFIC APPEALS (1:21–27, 2:1–13, 3:1–18, 4:1–17, and 5:1–11), as explained in "Intent and Macrostructure" under the 1:19–5:11 division, and is therefore the expository peak of 1:19–5:11, showing how godly conduct is a vital and integral part of genuine faith.

BOUNDARIES AND COHERENCE

The initial boundary of 2:14–26 was discussed under 2:1–13. The beginning of the next unit at 3:1 is marked by the vocative ἀδελφοί μου 'my brothers' and by a change of topic: from the nature of true faith to the need for restraint in speech. There is also a change of genre: from expository to hortatory.

Lexical coherence in 2:14–26 is shown by the prominent use of πίστις 'faith' in vv. 14, 17, 18 (three times), 20, 22 (two times), 24, and 26, contrasted with ἔργα 'deeds' in the same verses. This usage occurs nowhere else in the letter. The adjective νεκρός 'dead' in vv. 17 and 26 and another adjective in the same semantic domain, ἀργός 'barren' in v. 20, also add coherence.

PROMINENCE AND THEME

In a CLAIM-*justification* unit both constituents are integral to the theme; therefore, the theme of the 2:14–26 section is drawn from both its CLAIM and *justification*, focusing on the fact that faith and good deeds are two inseparable elements of salvation.

SECTION CONSTITUENT 2:14–25 (Expository Subsection: Claim of 2:14–26)

THEME: Anyone who says he trusts in Jesus Christ but does not act compassionately to others is not truly trusting in him. Only by obeying God and doing good to others can a person prove that he trusts in him.

MACROSTRUCTURE	CONTENTS
NUCLEUS$_1$ ———————	2:14–17 Anyone who says he trusts in Jesus Christ but does not act compassionately toward others is not truly trusting in him.
NUCLEUS$_2$ ———————	2:18–25 But someone may claim that one person is saved because he trusts in God and another person is saved because he does good to others. In answer to that, the inadequacy of faith without good deeds is demonstrated by the example of demons. From the examples of Abraham and Rahab we can see that only by obeying God and doing good to others can a person prove that he truly trusts in him.

INTENT AND MACROSTRUCTURE

In the 2:14–25 subsection James proceeds to enlarge on the nature of faith with the ultimate purpose of affecting the readers' behavior by giving them a better understanding of what is a bedrock principle of Christian living: genuine faith always produces good deeds. In the first paragraph (2:14–17) he vividly illustrates the uselessness of a faith unaccompanied by compassionate actions. In the second paragraph (2:18–25) he presents an *objection* to his teaching followed by two effective REFUTATIONS with examples from Scripture to prove that real faith can be verified only by acts of obedience and compassion.

BOUNDARIES AND COHERENCE

The initial boundary of 2:14–25 was discussed under 2:1–13. The beginning of the next unit at 2:26 is marked by γάρ 'for', which introduces a sentence that acts as the *justification* of the entire preceding unit (2:14–25) and not just of the previous clause. There is also a change of topic: from the historical illustration of Rahab to a generic statement about the nature of faith. The simile in 2:26 that compares faith without works to a body without life is in fact a summary of the truth presented in vv. 14–25.

Structural coherence between the two paragraphs of 2:14–25 is seen in their parallel construction, each with CLAIMS and *justifications*. In the 2:14–17 paragraph, the CLAIM (14a–d) is followed by its *justification* (15–16d) with a *restatement* of the CLAIM (17a–d). In the 2:18–25 paragraph, the first CLAIM (18c–f) is followed by its *justification* (19a–c) and the second CLAIM (24a–e) is verified by two *justifications* (20a–23d and 25a–c). These structural features along with the repeated occurrences of πίστις 'faith' and ἔργα 'deeds' (discussed in "Boundaries and Coherence" under 2:14–26) provide strong coherence in 2:14–25.

PROMINENCE AND THEME

The two NUCLEI of 2:14–25 are in a conjoined relation and both deal with the CLAIM made by James regarding the necessity of acts of obedience and compassion as proof of genuine faith. Since both are naturally prominent, the theme is drawn from both of them.

SUBSECTION CONSTITUENT 2:14–17
(Expository Paragraph: Nucleus₁ of 2:14–25)

THEME: Anyone who says he trusts in Jesus Christ but does not act compassionately toward others is not truly trusting in him.

¶ PTRN	RELATIONAL STRUCTURE	CONTENTS
CLAIM	CONSEQUENCE — condition — NUCLEUS — contrast	2:14a My fellow believers, if any person says, "I trust *in the Lord Jesus Christ*,"
	— NUCLEUS	2:14b but he does not do good *to other people*,
	CONSEQUENCE — NUCLEUS	2:14c what he says will not benefit *him*. [RHQ]
	— amplification	2:14d *God* will certainly not save the person who believes like that. [RHQ]
justification	— condition₁	2:15 *To illustrate*, if (*or*, Suppose) a fellow believer, either a man or a woman, is consistently lacking clothing or food for each day
	condition₂ — NUCLEUS — contrast	2:16a and if one of you says to them, "May *God* bless you and supply the clothing and food that you need,"
	— NUCLEUS	2:16b but you don't give them the things they need in order to live,
	CONSEQUENCE — CONTRAEXPECTATION — concession	2:16c *even though you have spoken well to them,*
		2:16d you have spoken in vain; *you have not helped them or yourselves*. [RHQ]
restatement of CLAIM	— condition	2:17a In the same way, *if a person* does not do good *to others*,
	CONSEQUENCE — NUCLEUS — NUCLEUS	2:17b *what he has said about* his trusting *in Christ is as useless*
	— comparison	2:17c *as* a dead person *is useless*; [MET]
	— amplification	2:17d he does not really trust *in Christ*.

INTENT AND PARAGRAPH PATTERN

In the 2:14–17 paragraph James goes on to the topic of the care of the poor, focusing on good deeds and their relevance to faith. The paragraph comprises a CLAIM regarding the uselessness of faith without corresponding deeds (2:14) and the *justification* for that CLAIM (2:15-16). It concludes with a *restatement* (2:17) of the CLAIM in v. 14, hence is expository, functioning within a unit (2:14–26) that is also expository.

NOTES

2:14a-b My fellow believers, if any person says, "I trust *in the Lord Jesus Christ*," but he does not do good *to other people*, The vocative ἀδελφοί μου 'my brothers' marks the beginning of a new paragraph. In this particular context it has a special significance because the illustration that follows focuses upon the needs of another brother or sister.

The noun πίστις 'faith' is forefronted, making it the focal concern. Here James addresses the nature of faith, especially its relationship with ἔργα 'works, deeds'. Since both of these nouns are event concepts, they are restated as verbs in propositions. In the display the object of 'trust' is 'the Lord Jesus Christ', based on 2:1. The context further shows that works consist in good deeds done to other people; hence 'to other people' is supplied in the display.

A conditional with the present subjunctive implies a continuing claim to have faith but a continual lack of deeds (Martin). It is said that this person claims to have faith, not that he has faith. The hypothetical form does not imply hypocrisy; rather, as the context shows, the person making the claim lacks an understanding of what real faith means.

2:14c what he says will not benefit *him*. The phrase τί τὸ ὄφελος 'what (is) the profit' occurs first in the verse, but since it is the apodosis of the conditional sentence, the display states it in the natural order of English. This is a rhetorical question to which the implied response is that there is no benefit. The profit is before God and relates to salvation, as shown by the following rhetorical question in 14d.

2:14d God will certainly not save the person who believes like that. The initial μή 'not' in this second rhetorical question implies a negative response. The noun πίστις 'faith' is an event concept, here personified. Grammatically, 'faith' is the subject of the verb phrase δύναται . . . σῶσαι 'can save', but semantically the agent of the action is God. The rendering in the display is based on the analysis that 'God' is agent and 'faith' is the characteristic of the person who is the object of the action. Most commentators (e.g., Moo, Davids 1982) say that the aorist infinitive σῶσαι 'to save' refers to the future, the coming judgment. It is significant that 'faith' occurs with the article here, which is the article of previous reference, indicating that James is not denying the efficacy of faith in salvation but rather the kind of faith previously described.

Virtually all commentators refer to a tension between James and Paul in their teaching regarding the relationship of 'faith' and 'works, deeds' in salvation. Some try to resolve the problem by saying that James and Paul use the terms in a different sense. They propose that James used 'works' to refer to deeds of love and mercy, whereas Paul combats an insistence on 'works of the law', that is, the legalistic observance of the Mosaic law (Rakestraw). This is partially true, but what Paul and James mean by 'works', as Moo points out, is basically the same thing: actions done in obedience to God. The main difference between them is that they were addressing different situations (see the note on 2:21b). A careful translation of these terms, especially in 14d, will help to avoid the apparent conflict.

2:15 *To illustrate,* if (*or,* Suppose) a fellow believer, either a man or a woman, is consistently lacking clothing or food for each day No special marker is here to indicate that this is an illustration, but any appropriate means of signaling that it is should be used in translating this. (For a fuller discussion, see the note on 2:2a.)

The conjunction ἐάν 'if' introduces a hypothetical situation; however, the details remind us of the poverty in the early church described in the Book of Acts, no doubt a situation still common among the readers. The adjective γυμνός 'naked' probably means the lack of proper clothing or the lack of an outer garment. The use of the verb ὑπάρχω 'be, exist' instead of the usual verb εἰμί suggests that the need was a past condition extending into the present (Adamson). Although some feel that the situation was one of extreme destitution, Laws suggests that it was more likely a degree of poverty that might not seem to require emergency action but could be dismissed with hopeful wishes.

2:16a and if one of you says to them, "May God bless you The verbs in the response ('go', 'be warmed', 'be fed') are all in the imperative, and they may represent a pious wish or prayer. The verb phrase ὑπάγετε ἐν εἰρήνῃ 'go in peace' in 16a is a familiar Jewish form of dismissal (Moo). In English versions it is rendered by various forms of beneficent response to the situation: "God bless you" (TEV, NLT), "I wish you well" (NIV, JB), "Good luck to you" (REB, JBP). The first of these is reflected in the display, since the context indicates that this is a kind of prayer in which God is the implicit actor.

and supply the clothing and food that you need," Some commentators (e.g., Huther, Kistemaker, Moffatt) say, and most of the versions imply, that the two imperatives 'warm yourselves and eat well' are in the middle voice, which would mean that these poor people should take care of their own needs. Others (e.g., Ropes, Adamson, Laws) say that the context requires that the imperatives be interpreted as passives, 'be warmed and well fed', which would imply an outside source of supply. Davids (1994) says this is the equivalent of "God will provide." Either interpretation would be valid, but in the context the latter is preferable, especially if it is considered a prayer. The most significant implication is that the speaker fails to take responsibility to meet the obvious needs.

2:16b but you don't give them the things they need in order to live, The conjunction δέ 'but' following the verb phrase μὴ δῶτε 'you do not give' points up the inconsistency between the words and the lack of action.

2:16c-d *even though you have spoken well to them,* you have spoken in vain; *you have not helped them or yourselves.* The question τί τὸ ὄφελος 'what (is) the profit' is rhetorical and implies a negative answer. It is the apodosis of the conditions in vv. 15 and 16. Grammatically 16d is the CONSEQUENCE of the conditions in 15–16b, and semantically there is a concession-CONTRA-EXPECTATION relation. The elided 16c concession is supplied from the context. These two verses, 15 and 16, are an illustrative explanation of the CLAIM made in v. 14, and they function as a *justification* for it.

In Greek 16d is grammatically parallel to 14c and they both use the expression τί τὸ ὄφελος 'what (is) the profit?'. The uselessness referred to in v. 14 is explicitly stated in 14d; but in 16d it is necessary to supply this implicit information from the context, hence '*you have not helped them or yourselves*'. As Moo remarks, "Not only do the empty words of this 'believer' do no good for these others; they bring no spiritual 'profit' to himself either."

2:17a–b In the same way, *if a person* does not do good *to others*, *what he has said about* his trusting *in Christ* is *as useless* James now draws his conclusion from the case illustrated. The adverb οὕτως 'thus, so', followed by the conjunction καί 'also, indeed', is his usual way of applying an illustration or example, as seen in 1:11, 2:26, and 3:5 (Martin).

As earlier, 'faith' and 'works, deeds' are rendered as verbs, with the particular aspect of works in focus as the context indicates.

The adjective νεκρός 'dead' (17c) is used metaphorically, the point of similarity being something ineffectual or useless. There are two opposites in view: a living faith and a dead, useless faith. (Note that it is not faith and deeds.) While the word 'dead' might be taken as a dead metaphor, since it is used elsewhere in Scripture with a similar meaning (see BAGD, 534.1b), its use in a simile in 2:26 involving physical as well as figurative death encourages us to consider it a live metaphor here. As a dead metaphor it would be rendered 'what he has said about trusting Christ is completely useless'. In the display it is rendered as a live metaphor, with the point of similarity in 17b and the image in 17c.

2:17c *as* a dead person *is useless*; A profession of faith by one who does not manifest it by what he does is here compared to a dead person. Both are useless. See the previous note on νεκρός.

2:17d he does not really trust *in Christ*. Commentators differ in their interpretation of the prepositional phrase καθ' ἑαυτήν 'by itself', especially about which noun it modifies. Some (e.g., Adamson, Davids 1982, and most versions) feel that it modifies πίστις 'faith' (in 17b), with the meaning that faith by itself, not having good deeds, is dead. Others (e.g., Huther, Laws; JB, JBP) say that it modifies νεκρά 'dead' (in 17c), thus strengthening or intensifying that adjective. (Both JB and JBP translate it as "quite dead.") The first interpretation seems preferable, since the focus of the passage is on effective faith and is brought out by the rendering here: 'he does not really trust *in Christ*'. In the Greek 'by itself' is at the end of the clause, which communicates the emphasis that the metaphorical 'dead' conveys. Such faith is inoperative. Tasker concludes it "is not faith at all."

BOUNDARIES AND COHERENCE

The initial boundary of 2:14–17 was discussed under 2:14–26. The beginning of the next unit at 2:18 is marked by a change of focus from useless faith to evidences of genuine faith as well as by dialogue with a new actor, τις 'someone', representing those who object to James' insistence on the necessity of deeds that give evidence of genuine faith. Coherence is seen in the use of ὄφελος 'profit' in v. 14 and v. 16 and by the illustration of the absence of love and concern for the poor in vv. 15–16.

PROMINENCE AND THEME

The 2:14–17 paragraph consists of a CLAIM, a *justification,* and a *restatement* of the CLAIM. In a CLAIM-*justification* paragraph, both components are integral to the expository paragraph pattern, so both are included in the theme statement.

SUBSECTION CONSTITUENT 2:18–25
(Expository Paragraph: Nucleus₂ of 2:14–25)

THEME: But someone may claim that one person is saved because he trusts in God and another person is saved because he does good to others. In answer to that, the inadequacy of faith without good deeds is demonstrated by the example of demons. From the examples of Abraham and Rahab we can see that only by obeying God and doing good to others can a person prove that he truly trusts in him.

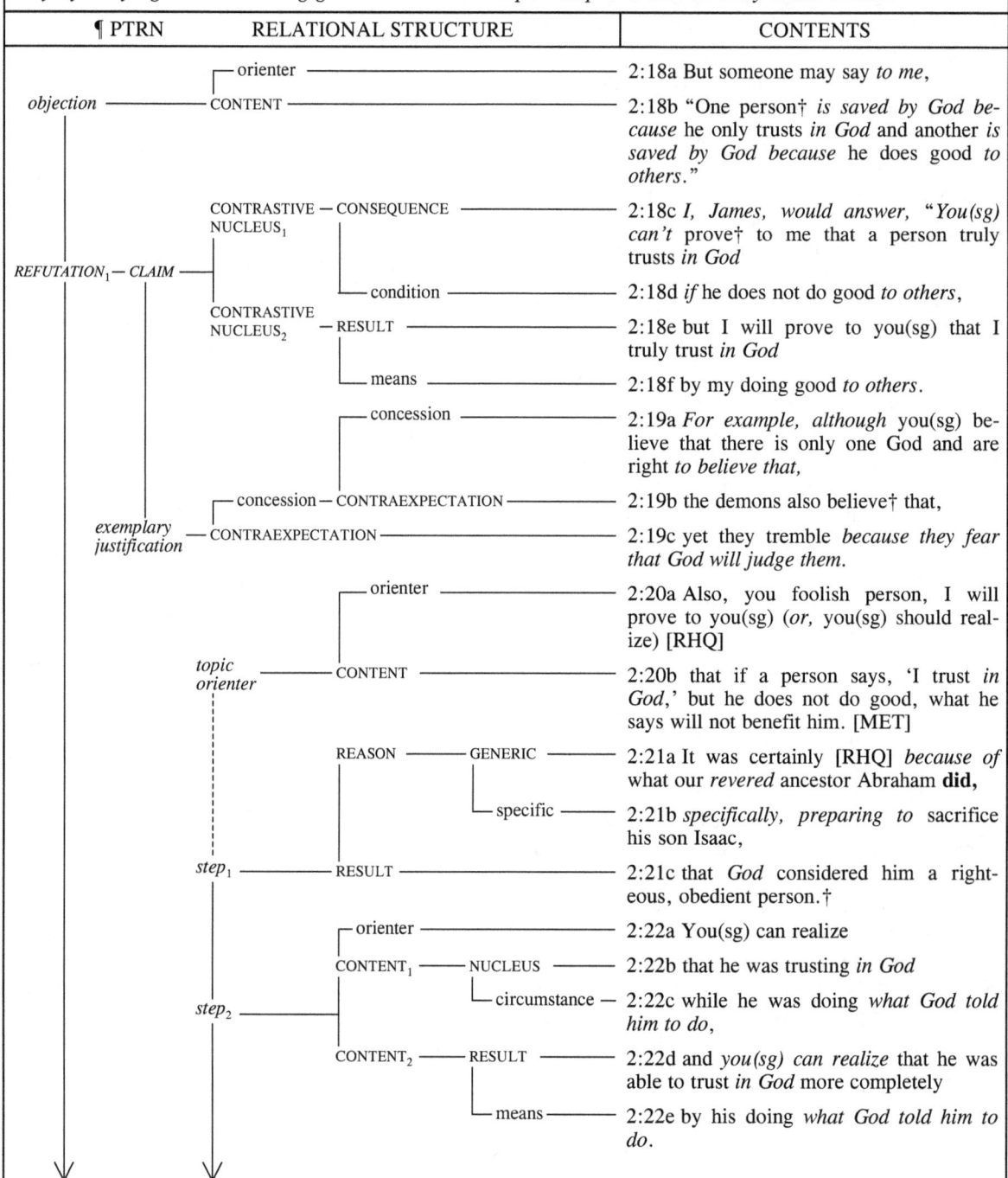

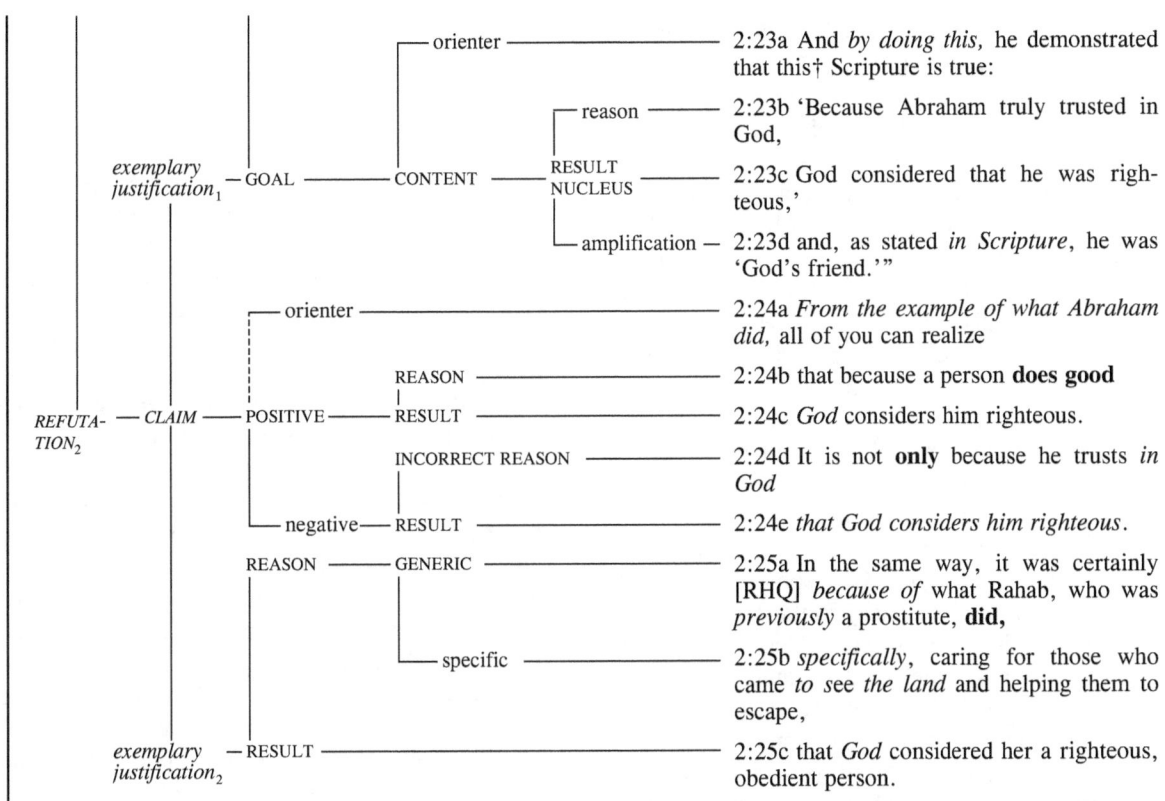

INTENT AND PARAGRAPH PATTERN

In 2:18-25 James reaches a point where he now anticipates an objection to his teaching regarding faith and good deeds and gives counter-arguments to answer this objection. This is a style that many writers equate with the diatribe form of argumentation (see p. 7).

There are two levels of paragraph pattern relations in 2:18-25. On the higher level are an *objection* (18a-b) and two REFUTATIONS (18c-19c and 20a-25c). At the lower level the CLAIM in 18c-f about the proof of real faith is followed by its *justification* (19a-c), which shows the uselessness of bogus faith. The CLAIM in 24a-e about the necessity of both faith and works has two exemplary *justifications*, the first about Abraham (20a-23d) and the second about Rahab (25a-c). Both are positive examples of the effectiveness of genuine faith. The ultimate intent is to influence behavior through the proper understanding of the nature of faith.

NOTES

2:18a-b But someone may say *to me*, Moving now to another stage in his argument, James introduces another person by means of the indefinite pronoun τις 'someone'. This is a person who raises an objection to what he has been saying.

2:18b "One person *is saved by God because* he only trusts *in God* and another *is saved by God because* he does good *to others*." The Greek is σὺ πίστιν ἔχεις κἀγὼ ἔργα ἔχω 'you have faith and I have works'. This statement is very complex and subject to many different interpretations. Among the points of uncertainty are (1) how much is included in the objector's direct discourse, (2) who the speaker is, and (3) who the personal pronouns σύ 'you' and κἀγώ 'and I' refer to. As to the first of these problems, a few commentators believe that the objector's direct discourse continues through to the end of v. 18 (e.g., Alford) or v. 19 (e.g., Martin, Adamson); however, most (e.g., Ropes, Hiebert, Huther) believe that it ends in the middle of v. 18 with ἔχω 'I have'. The context seems to support the majority opinion, since 18c is clearly a challenge in reply to the objection.

The other two problems (i.e., the identity of the speaker and the pronoun referents) are interrelated. There are three main views of the identity of the speaker:

1. In view of the personal pronouns in 18b, some commentators (e.g., Adamson, Mayor)

consider this speaker an ally of James since he claims good deeds, as seems to be James' emphasis. But one of the main difficulties with this view is the opening clause of 18a, ἀλλ' ἐρεῖ τις 'but someone will say', which is the standard way of introducing an objection in an argument in Greek. Moreover, there would seem to be no reason to introduce a third person ally, since James has been freely expressing his views in the preceding verses.

2. Other commentators (e.g., Martin, Hiebert) consider the speaker to be an objector to James' view. In this case, the introductory clause would have its usual function, but the difficulty is that the personal pronouns cannot be interpreted naturally in 18b, since James was certainly not emphasizing faith to the exclusion of actions. One solution to handle this apparent discrepancy in the pronouns is to consider the direct speech ended with the first three words, questioning James' faith (as Westcott and Hort suggest in the margin, using a question form: "Do you have faith?"). Moffatt renders it "And you claim to have faith! Yes, and I claim to have deeds as well...." However, this neglects the obvious parallelism of σὺ πίστιν ἔχεις κἀγὼ ἔργα ἔχω 'you have faith and I have works'. Another solution is to take vv. 18–19 as all from the objector and James' answer as beginning at v. 20. However, the latter part of v. 18 is clearly a challenge to the objector and is best taken as James' reply.

3. The third view, which is the best solution, is the one held by the majority of commentators (e.g., Ropes, Moo, Laws, Cranfield 1965a, Loh and Hatton). In this view the speaker is an objector but the pronouns do not refer to James and the one objecting—they simply distinguish two different individuals. In other words, 'you' and 'I' are viewed as essentially equivalent to 'one' and 'another', as the NEB has it: "Here is one who claims to have faith and another who points to his deeds." It is quite true that interpreting the personal pronouns in this way is unusual and that there are more natural ways in Greek to express this concept, such as the more straightforward ἄλλος ... ἄλλος 'one ... another'. Even so, this interpretation is the preferred one, considering all the difficulties presented by the other two views. Thus it is the one reflected in the rendering in the display. Laws says, "This solution to the difficulty is adopted because it seems to make the best sense in context, not because it is entirely satisfactory."

An alternative way of handling the difficulty of the pronoun references would be to postulate yet another person as the objector's addressee: 'But someone may say *to another person,* "You *are saved by God because* you trust *in him* and I *am saved by God because* I do good *to others.*"' This is a valid alternative and seems closer to the text. However, the alternative given in the display was chosen because it is a clearer presentation of the argument and avoids the complication of introducing a third person who appears and then is not mentioned again.

As to the meaning of 'faith' and 'works' in this context, some (e.g., Laws) say that the objector equates these two with diversities of gifts, claiming that faith and deeds are two distinct virtues of equal worth. This would mean that the objector sees faith and deeds as independent of each other, *both* being acceptable with God. James refutes this in vv. 20–24, showing that faith and deeds are not independent of each other—they are interrelated.

The words 'is saved' are supplied from the context: it is clear, from ' save' in v. 14 and 'justified' in vv. 21–24 that this idea is implicit. The passive voice is used in order to keep the focus on the individuals involved in the argument. However, in some languages it will be necessary to state this in the active, with 'God' as the agent.

2:18c I, James, would answer, "You(sg) can't prove to me that a person truly trusts *in God*

Although a few commentators (e.g., Martin, Adamson) claim that the objector is still speaking here, the majority (e.g., Ropes, Laws, Huther) consider this to be the beginning of James' response to the objection, since the initial clause in 18c, δεῖξόν μοι τὴν πίστιν σου 'show me your faith', gives a challenge in reply to the objection. This is made clear in the rendering here by supplying the needed words in italics. James makes this statement to refute the viewpoint of the person who says he has faith but does not have deeds (2:14a–b); therefore in his response he focuses on the one who falsely holds this view. The content of James' response begins with 18c and goes through 23d, as the quotation marks show.

In the Greek δεῖξόν μοι 'show me' is imperative and is used as a rhetorical device in which an impossible demand is made to prove that the point of the objector is absurd (Laws). It is rendered here as a negative statement that reflects the underlying meaning of the imperative clause. Other possible renderings would be '*You falsely think that* you can show me' or 'Show me . . . *if you can*'.

2:18d *if* he does not do good *to others*, The phrase χωρὶς τῶν ἔργων 'without the works' represents an event and so is restated here as a verb. The communication relation between 18c and 18d is CONSEQUENCE-condition. The meaning of 'works', already given in vv. 15–17 (i.e., doing good to those in need), is supplied in the rendering here.

If the alternative rendering suggested in the note on 2:18b, which postulates another person as the objector's addressee, is used, 18c–d would read as follows: '*I James say to the one who claims that he only trusts in God, "You can't prove to me that you trust in God if you do not do good to others."*'

2:18e but I will prove to you(sg) that I truly trust *in God* The conjunction and pronoun combination κἀγώ 'and/but I' introduces a clause that semantically is a contrast to the one in 18c–d (Levinsohn, p. 79); hence καί is an adversative here, rendered 'but' in the display.

2:18f by my doing good *to others*. James here contends that good deeds demonstrate true faith. The chiastic form of 18c–f is vivid:

A δεῖξόν μοι τὴν πίστιν σου 'show me the faith of you'
  B χωρὶς τῶν ἔργων 'without the works'
  B' κἀγώ σοι δείξω ἐκ τῶν ἔργων μου 'and I to you will show by my works'
A' τὴν πίστιν 'the faith'

2:19a *For example, although* you(sg) believe that there is only one God In 2:19a–c James is justifying the 2:18 CLAIM by showing the inadequacy of barren faith. He points to demons (19b) as an example of such "faith," comparing a person who has an intellectual belief in a creed but who fails to do good to others with the demons. Demons also believe in the reality of God. But their response is fear, because they know their judgment is certain. That this is an example is made clear in the rendering by supplying the introductory phrase 'For example'.

There are textual variants in 19a, mainly the presence or absence of the article and also word order variants. The reading used in the GNT is εἷς ἐστιν ὁ θεός 'one is God', which stresses the unity of God. A second important reading is εἷς θεός ἐστιν 'there is one God', which focuses on the uniqueness of God. The first reading is given a B rating by the UBS committee, indicating their belief that this reading is almost certain. In any case, there is no crucial difference in the meaning of these readings (Davids 1982): both express the opening line of the Jewish confession of faith, the Shema, with its emphasis upon monotheism. Most versions translate it "there is one God," as here also. Some commentators (e.g., Laws, Martin) consider this a question, but most (e.g., Alford, Mayor, Huther) consider it a statement. (The difference is not significant. If it *is* a question, it is a rhetorical one, expecting a positive answer.)

and are right *to believe that*, The phrase καλῶς ποιεῖς 'you do well' is considered by some to be ironic, since καλῶς is certainly used ironically in Mark 7:9. But it is more likely to be a favorable comment, probably with a touch of irony, especially in the light of the rest of the verse (Ropes). Such belief is necessary, but it is not enough for salvation.

2:19b the demons also believe that, It is important to recognize that the verb πιστεύω 'believe' is used in different senses, one of which is 'to know to be true' and another 'to trust'. It is the former that is the meaning here. James is referring to an intellectual assent to a creed rather than to a personal commitment, which would include obedience. In another language the term for such bogus faith may be quite different from the one used for saving faith. It may be necessary to render it as 'the demons also say that God exists'. The meaning is that the demons assent to the same doctrine.

2:19c yet they tremble *because they fear that God will judge them*. Most commentators point out that the verb φρίσσω 'shudder' implies fear before the one God because the demons know that he will not save but rather judge them. This reason is supplied in the display. The communication relation between 19b and 19c is concession-CONTRAEXPECTATION, and is expressed by 'yet' in the display. Despite an intellectual assent of faith, the response to God is one of fear of judgment. As Adamson says, "The point James is now driving home is that a Christian creed without corresponding Christian conduct will save neither devil nor man."

2:20a Also, you foolish person, I will prove to you(sg) (*or*, you(sg) should realize) The conjunction δέ 'but/and' is not contrastive here. Rather, it introduces a continuation of the argument. Martin suggests it may well be a sign of stepping up the attack. James continues to address the objector of 18a using the vocative ὦ ἄνθρωπε κενέ 'O vain man'. The adjective 'vain' basically means 'empty'. It is used figuratively here to refer to a lack in spiritual understanding. The use of ὦ initially in the direct address strengthens the reproof.

The verb phrase θέλεις ... γνῶναι 'are you willing to know' is a rhetorical question interpreted by some as equivalent to a conditional clause (Mayor, Moo): 'if you wish to have proof'. Others consider it a continuation of the reproof (Kistemaker): 'do you want evidence?' The meaning would be best represented in the display as a statement such as 'I will now prove to you' (Bratcher), since the rhetorical question is the author's way of introducing scriptural evidence to prove his claim that faith without good deeds is useless. This was originally stated in 14 and restated in 17, 18c–f, and again here in 20. A good alternative is 'you should realize', since the context implies that the knowledge is clear and can be rejected only by an unwillingness to face the issue.

2:20b that if a person says, 'I trust *in* God,' but he does not do good, what he says will not benefit him. In this verse both πίστις 'faith' and ἔργα 'works, deeds' occur with the article, which points back to the nature of these topics under discussion. Instead of the adjective ἀργή 'barren, ineffective', some manuscripts have νεκρά 'dead', but the GNT reads ἀργή with a B rating, indicating that the UBS committee considers this reading almost certain. This reading may involve a subtle play on words between ἔργων 'works' and ἀργή 'workless' (Ropes, Martin). The word 'workless' means 'ineffective' and, in this context, 'unproductive of salvation' (see v. 14).

2:21a It was certainly *because of* what our *revered* ancestor Abraham did, Verse 21 is another rhetorical question that implies a positive answer. It is restated as an affirmative statement in the display. James is appealing to the Old Testament for proof of his claim that a saving faith manifests itself in the production of good deeds. He chooses to cite Abraham, who was considered by all Jews and Christians as the supreme example of faith. This implicit information is supplied in the display: 'revered'.

The prepositional phrase ἐξ ἔργων 'by/from works' is highlighted by virtue of its being forefronted and separating the negative from the verb (Levinsohn, p. 88). Some versions translate the preposition as 'by', implying means (JB, REB, RSV). But the semantic concept of means requires that the agent be the same as that of the main verb; and here, as all agree, God is the one who justifies. Therefore it is here interpreted as reason. Some commentators, Lenski and Huther, for example, as well as the NIV and NLT, also interpret it as reason. Heibert says reason or source.

The communication relation of 21a–b with 21c is REASON-RESULT, expressed in the display as 'because'. Since 21a has marked prominence due to the forefronting of 'by works', the REASON label is in upper-case letters.

The noun 'works' expresses an event concept and is therefore restated in the display as a clause. Several commentators note that it is a plural noun. It is a plural of category, referring to Abraham's conduct.

2:21b *specifically, preparing to* sacrifice his son Isaac, The aorist tense of the verb ἀναφέρω 'offer' (which is a technical term for sacrifice) indicates a completed act in Abraham's intention (Hiebert). The offering was an act of faith, completed faith (Burns). Since the original readers would have known that Isaac was not actually slain on the altar, James did not make that explicit, but in many languages it may be necessary to make it explicit, hence 'preparing to'.

2:21c that *God* considered him a righteous, obedient person. The verb δικαιόω 'justify' is used here in the passive voice with 'God' the implicit agent. There are three main interpretations of the term 'justify' (the difference being shown in italics): (1) He was *considered* righteous or *declared* righteous because of what he did (Alford, Huther, Moo; NIV, NLT, WEY). (2) He was *shown* to be righteous by his deed (Tasker, Adamson, Johnson; CBW); that is, his works were the means of demonstrating that he was righteous. (3) He was *put right with God* through his actions (Laws; TEV, TNT). The third view implies that a person can earn his own salvation and is therefore rejected. Beyond that, the interpretation of 'justify' here is not an easy decision. Obviously it does not refer to Abraham's initial declaration of his faith. He had had a relationship with God for a long time before the incident referred to here. James' meaning is clarified by recalling the Gen. 22:12 context: God's words were "Now I know that you fear God." "Now I know" was the declaration that Abraham was, in God's sight, indeed righteous. Thus the rendering in the display reflects the first view. The words 'righteous' and 'obedient' in the display reflect the moral focus of the term 'justify' here—it is not intended in a legal sense (Loh and Hatton). The following verses (vv. 22-23) also clarify the meaning of 'justify' in this passage.

Since the focus of 2:14-26 is on the necessity of good deeds to prove faith, an acceptable rendering would be 'It was certainly what Abraham did that demonstrated that he was righteous'. This reflects the second interpretation of the verb 'justify'. Actually, the first and second interpretations are not necessarily mutually exclusive. The first emphasizes God's perspective, the second man's. In a more general sense 'justify' can mean 'to accept as righteous'. In some languages it can be translated as 'approve' (Bratcher). In choosing the most appropriate term for 'justify' it is important that it not imply that salvation is achieved by works. The context makes the place of works clear: it is not an alternative for faith, but a necessary part of genuine faith.

Much has been said about the apparent conflict between James and Paul. Paul says in Rom. 3:28, "we reckon that a man is justified by faith without works"; James, on the other hand, here says, "you see, then, that a man is justified by works and not by faith alone" (2:24). This apparent contradiction may be resolved partly by noting the context: Paul refers to works in obedience to the Jewish law, whereas James uses the term to refer to more general acts, especially deeds of charity. Paul is focusing on the initial experience of acceptance by God, and James on the continuing life of faith. As Ropes says, "James' real contention in vv. 20-22 is not so much of the necessity of works as of the inseparability of vital faith and works."

2:22a You(sg) can realize Although a few versions (KJV, TEV) consider this verse a question, the majority of commentators and most versions interpret it as a statement. It states the logical deduction from the example. The singular verb βλέπεις 'you see' shows that James is calling this evidence to the objector's attention.

2:22b that he was trusting *in God* Moo points out that "it is the nature of Abraham's faith, a faith that is not 'barren' (v. 20), that James wants to illustrate. Moreover, Genesis 15:6, with its stress on Abraham's faith, has probably been in James' mind all along." In the noun phrase ἡ πίστις 'the faith' the definite article is a reference to Abraham's faith, which was assumed to be present in v. 21.

2:22c while he was doing *what God told him to do,* The Greek is συνήργει τοῖς ἔργοις αὐτοῦ '(faith) was working together with his works'. This proposition indicates the close connection between Abraham's faith and his deeds. The abstract nouns 'faith' and 'works' are difficult to translate because they are event concepts that need to be rendered as clauses; this is further complicated by their being personified. The meaning here is that faith and action are never separated, the one flows naturally from the other. The imperfect tense of the verb 'work together' suggests that this working union of faith and works was characteristic of Abraham's life.

The noun ἔργα 'works, deeds' is here rendered 'what God told him to do', although more often it is rendered 'by doing good to others'. The broader rendering here more accurately reflects the meaning of ἔργα in the illustration about Abraham. (It is rendered similarly in 2:26c.)

2:22d-e and *you(sg) can realize* that he was able to trust *in God* more completely by his doing *what God told him to do.* The verb τελειόω '(to) perfect/complete' when used in connection with πίστις 'faith' does not imply that Abraham had previously had a weak or defective faith but that faith is brought to maturity through actions. Only when faith produces works does it become "ever more completely that which it should be according to its nature and destination" (Huther).

The prepositional phrase ἐκ τῶν ἔργων 'by works' indicates the means of the perfection of his faith. The majority of versions have "by his works" and the rendering in the display is based on this. This correlates with the interpretation of the same phrase in 2:18.

2:23a And *by doing this,* he demonstrated that this Scripture is true: The initial conjunction καί 'and' connects the thoughts of the two preceding verses (21 and 22) to v. 23, showing how what James has just said about Abraham is supported by Scripture.

The verb πληρόω 'fulfill' has been variously interpreted in this passage. If Gen. 15:6 is taken as prophetic, then Abraham's conduct set forth in

Genesis 22 fulfilled this prophecy (Ropes, Huther). The majority of versions use the word "fulfill," implying such a view. However, 'fulfill' can also mean 'to complete' in the sense of finding its ultimate significance and meaning (Moo, Martin). This is reflected in the NCV: "This shows the full meaning of the Scripture that says. . . ." Hiebert says that "it demonstrated what was latent in that earlier justification," adding that it was "the logical fulfillment of the statement in Genesis 15:6." This view is the preferable one, since James wants to show that Abraham's faith was active and that God's verdict was reconfirmed on the basis of what he did (Moo).

If it is not possible in the target language to refer to a Scripture before it is quoted, 23a–c could be rendered 'In the Scripture it was stated: "Because Abraham trusted in God, God considered that he was righteous." By what he did Abraham demonstrated that the Scripture is true.'

2:23b–c 'Because Abraham truly trusted in God, God considered that he was righteous,' The communication relation between 21–22 and 23 is step-GOAL. The first step (v. 21) states the action being focused on, whereas the second step (v. 22) indicates the relationship of that action to Abraham's faith. Then, in v. 23, the GOAL is reached, wherein James shows how this corresponds to the Old Testament Scripture.

2:23d and, as stated *in Scripture*, he was 'God's friend.'" The phrase φίλος θεοῦ 'friend of God' comes from 2 Chron. 20:7 and Isa. 41:8. This is a second indication from the Old Testament of God's special relationship with Abraham. The relation is labeled amplification, linking it with the preceding proposition.

2:24a *From the example of what Abraham did*, all of you can realize The verb ὁράω 'see' is plural, indicating that James is turning from the opponent back to the readers. He now formulates a theological principle drawn from Abraham's life, and this intention is supplied in the display.

2:24b that because a person does good The emphasis on the prepositional phrase ἐξ ἔργων 'by/ from works' is shown by its being fronted.

2:24c *God* considers him righteous. The verb δικαιόω 'justify' is used in the passive voice, as in 21c, with 'God' as the implicit agent (see the note on 21c). Here the verb is in the present tense rather than aorist; thus it speaks of God's standing practice (Hiebert). The communication relation between 24b and 24c is REASON-RESULT. The forefronting of the prepositional phrase 'by works' gives the 24b proposition marked prominence and its label, REASON, is in upper-case letters.

2:24d–e It is not only because he trusts *in God* that God considers him righteous. The adverb μόνον 'only' is emphatic because it occurs at the end of the sentence. James is refuting the position that only faith is necessary; he is not belittling the importance of faith. His use of 'only' demonstrates that faith is an essential part of salvation, but his point is that God will not approve a person just because he professes faith. Proposition 24d is labeled INCORRECT REASON since this is a reason that does not result in God's declaring a person righteous.

2:25a In the same way, it was certainly *because of* what Rahab, James now adds to the example of Abraham that of Rahab. The form of v. 25 is similar to v. 21. The adverb ὁμοίως 'likewise' marks this similarity; δὲ καί 'and also' signals that this is a second example. Some suggest that James chose Abraham and Rahab as examples because they both showed hospitality, or because they both had pagan backgrounds, but neither of these characteristics is in focus here. A more plausible explanation is that whereas Abraham was the most revered of the Hebrew race, Rahab was a Gentile, a woman, and a prostitute, showing the universal applicability of the truth James has been proclaiming (Tasker).

who was *previously* a prostitute, In some languages it may be necessary to supply the fact that she had been a prostitute previous to responding in obedience to God, hence 'previously' in the display. The translator should avoid any possible implication that God condones prostitution.

did, The prepositional phrase ἐξ ἔργων 'by works' is again fronted for emphasis.

2:25b *specifically*, caring for those who came *to see the land* and helping them to escape, In this context the noun ἄγγελος 'messenger' refers to those who came secretly to explore the land rather than to bear a particular message (Loh and Hatton). The verb ὑποδέχομαι 'welcome/entertain' implies accepting the messengers as welcome guests and caring for their needs. The phrase καὶ ἑτέρᾳ ὁδῷ ἐκβαλοῦσα 'and sent them out by a different way' means that she helped them to escape.

2:25c that God considered her a righteous, obedient person. The verb here is δικαιόω 'justify' (see the note on 21c). It was because of her actions that God considered Rahab righteous. Rahab's faith is not mentioned here but it is clear from the argument that James assumes it, and in some translations this may need to be made explicit for correct understanding.

BOUNDARIES AND COHERENCE

The initial boundary of 2:18–25 was discussed under 2:14–17, the final one under 2:14–25. Some versions and commentaries divide the unit between v. 19 and v. 20 (Kistemaker; NIV, NCV, CEV), others between v. 20 and v. 21 (Hiebert, Lenski, Blue; NLT), still others between v. 24 and v. 25 (Kistemaker, Lenski; NIV, TEV, NCV). However, the theme of evidence of genuine faith runs throughout vv. 18–25, and for this reason these breaks are considered simply breaks between lower-level units.

Lexical coherence in the 2:18–25 paragraph is provided by ἐκ τῶν ἔργων or ἐξ ἔργων 'by works' in vv. 18, 21, 22, 24, and 25 and its contrast with ἐκ πίστεως 'by faith' in v. 24. Coherence is added also by the verb δικαιόω 'justify' in vv. 21, 24, and 25 along with the verb phrase λογίζομαι εἰς δικαιοσύνην 'reckon for righteousness' in the same semantic domain in v. 23. Further coherence is shown by two occurrences of δείκνυμι 'show/prove' in v. 18 followed by the biblical illustrations in vv. 21–25 that are the evidence referred to by that verb.

PROMINENCE AND THEME

The theme of 2:18–25 is drawn from the *objection* and both REFUTATIONS. Included are condensed statements of the 18c–f and 24a–e CLAIMS and the three *justifications* (19a–c, 20a–23d, and 25a–c). In each case, the condensed statements are either the most naturally prominent segments of these units or are integral components of the paragraph pattern.

SECTION CONSTITUENT 2:26
(Expository Propositional Cluster: Axiomatic Justification of 2:14–25)

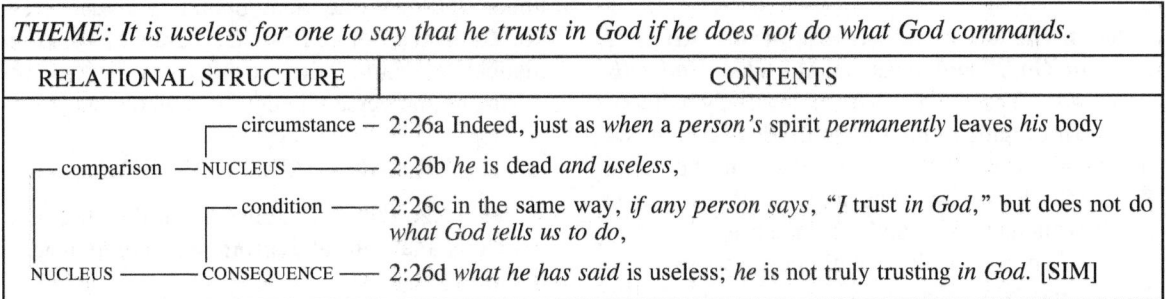

INTENT AND STRUCTURE

The 2:26 propositional cluster is a simile. It consists of a comparison of useless faith (26c–d) to a dead, spiritless body (26a–b). Since it functions as the *axiomatic justification* for the 2:14–25 CLAIM, it is expository. The author's intent is to clarify the readers' understanding of the nature of genuine faith so that their conduct will manifest the faith they profess.

NOTES

2:26a Indeed, James concludes his discussion of the relationship of faith and works with a striking analogy. The conjunction γάρ 'for' relates this verse to what precedes. Some commentators (Alford, Huther) say that it refers primarily to the illustration of Rahab in the previous verse and to the same general principle in v. 24, but the majority (e.g., Hiebert, Davids 1982) agree that it goes further back and is the general conclusion to the whole argument (see "Intent and Macrostructure" for 2:14–26). In the display the transitional adverb 'indeed' is used to show the relation of this verse to the whole 2:14-25 unit. This is better than 'for', which usually is a link to the immediately preceding proposition.

just as *when* a *person's* spirit *permanently* leaves *his* body The conjunction ὥσπερ 'as, just as', in correlation with οὕτως 'so, in the same way', introduces the comparison (see the note on 26c). The translator should use whatever term is appropriate for a comparison here. In some languages it is natural to have an introducer like 'just as', whereas in others the phrase 'in the same way' at the beginning of 26c-d is adequate in itself and more natural.

Commentators agree that the noun σῶμα 'body' here refers to the material human body, but there are different views regarding the noun πνεῦμα 'spirit'. The majority of commentators and versions take it to mean the inner being, the human spirit or soul, though a few translate it "breath" (e.g., Martin, Oesterley; NAB, REB). It is true that the normal term for the human spirit is ψυχή 'soul', but πνεῦμα, when contrasted with the body as here, means that vital principle that imparts life to the body. Thus 'spirit' is the preferred rendering.

2:26b *he* **is dead** *and useless,* All of v. 26 is a simile explicitly comparing faith without works to a body without the spirit (see the notes on 2:17b and c).

2:26c in the same way, *if any person says, "I trust in God,"* **but does not do** *what God tells us to do,* The comparison of the body without the spirit to faith without good deeds is completed in 26c-d. The adverb οὕτως 'so, in the same way' introduces 26c. The topic of the simile is 'faith without works' and the image is 'the body without spirit', with 'faith' corresponding to 'body' and 'works' corresponding to 'spirit'. We might normally expect that 'works' would correspond to 'body', and 'faith' to 'spirit'. However, the main point of the analogy is that the absence of 'works', like the absence of 'spirit', means death. James is concerned that they possess the right kind of faith. The presence of the definite article with the first member of each pair in the comparison signals that both are generic while the absence of the article with the second member makes 'spirit' and 'deeds' qualitative, emphasizing their essentialness (Hiebert). Although the phrase 'by doing good to others' has been generally used to render the noun ἔργα 'works, deeds', here it is rendered by 'doing what God tells us to do'. This is much broader and more accurately reflects the meaning of ἔργα in the illustration of Abraham in 2:22-24.

2:26d *what he has said* **is useless;** *he* **is not truly trusting** *in God.* The Greek is ἡ πίστις χωρὶς ἔργων νεκρά ἐστιν 'faith without works is dead'. In the display the metaphorical 'dead' is rendered nonfiguratively as 'useless'. Without deeds the faith that a person may profess is futile and useless. Tasker concludes that "if it is unproductive of good deeds, it is not really faith at all."

BOUNDARIES AND COHERENCE

The initial boundary of 2:26 was discussed under 2:14-25, the final boundary under 2:14-26. Coherence in v. 26 is the result of its grammatical structure: the correlatives ὥσπερ and οὕτως tie the verse together as a whole.

PROMINENCE AND THEME

The 2:26 theme is drawn from the NUCLEUS, which is the naturally prominent component of the unit.

DIVISION CONSTITUENT 3:1–18 (Hortatory Section: Appeal₃ of 1:19–5:11)

> *THEME: You should all strive to speak rightly, since what you say has a powerful effect on others. So don't boast that you are wise if you are jealous of others and self-seeking. Those who act peaceably toward others will cause the whole community to act righteously.*

MACROSTRUCTURE	CONTENTS
APPEAL	3:1–17 Not many of you should become ones who habitually teach, since God will judge teachers with greater scrutiny than others. You should all strive to speak rightly, since what you say has a powerful effect on others, often destructive. So don't boast that you are wise if you are jealous of others and self-seeking.
motivational basis	3:18 Those who act peaceably toward others will cause the whole community to act righteously.

INTENT AND MACROSTRUCTURE

The 3:1–18 section is composed of an APPEAL (3:1–17) and a *motivational basis* (3:18). It is a hortatory unit: imperatives are in vv. 1, 13, and 14 and mitigated appeals in 2 and 10. James' intent here is to affect the readers' actions, especially their speech. In the APPEAL (3:1–17) he presents the devastating potential of an uncontrolled tongue, which is the evidence of an evil heart and results in all kinds of evil in the lives of believers. He wants to stimulate pure speech that has its source in godly wisdom. The *motivational basis* in 3:18 provides the incentive for obeying the 3:1–17 exhortations, that they might achieve peace and righteousness in the community.

Some commentators (e.g., Ropes) say that the primary focus of this whole section is the church teachers. Martin (p. 104) claims that the main cause of the dissension and division was the teachers. Proponents of this view consider that James' intent in chapter 3 is to affect these leaders' actions and words so as to bring harmony in the church. However, even though it is true that the teachers played an important role in the church, the audience addressed in this unit is much broader (see "Intent and Paragraph Pattern" under 3:1–12 and also the note on 3:2a).

BOUNDARIES AND COHERENCE

The initial boundary of the 3:1–18 section was discussed under 2:14–26. The beginning of the next unit at 4:1 is marked by a change of topic: from wisdom to worldly desires and conduct. There is also a distinct change of style, with a series of rhetorical questions as in a diatribe and a sterner tone of direct confrontation without the familiar affectionate vocative 'my brothers'.

Some commentators (e.g., Davids 1982 and Moo) see 3:1–4:12 as one high-level unit instead of breaking it into two separate units, 3:1–18 and 4:1–17, as we propose. In answer to Davids, Martin (p. ci) points out that 3:1–4:12 "has a number of subthemes (as in 4:6) that should be brought out and not subsumed under a general heading of the 'Demand for Pure Speech'." The distinct change of topic at the end of chapter 3, from wisdom and peace to 'wars and fights' also supports a break before 4:1. Furthermore, 3:18 as a proverb functioning as the *basis* for 3:1–17 marks the end of one section and the rhetorical questions in 4:1 signal a new beginning. Even more importantly, chapter 4 reaches a new height. The mounting tension in 4:1–6 concerning the deplorable spiritual condition of the readers culminates in 4:7–10 with the proposed solution to their problems: repentance and restoration (see "Intent and Macrostructure" under 4:1–17).

Johnson proposes a similar analysis, seeing 3:13–4:10 as a coherent unit. He points out stylistic similarities characteristic of the diatribe between 3:13–18 and 4:1–10. (However, this is not significant since the same style also occurs in 2:14–26—diatribe is a characteristic of James' style overall.) Johnson also unites these two units on the basis of a common theme, envy: ζῆλον πικρόν 'bitter jealousy' in 3:14, ζῆλος καὶ ἐριθεία 'jealousy and rivalry' in 3:16, ζηλοῦτε 'you are jealous' in 4:2, and φθόνον 'envy' in 4:5. Although there is some validity to this, note that most commentators interpret 'envy' in 4:5 as God's attitude toward man rather than human envy. Furthermore, since chapter 4 is a condemnation of all wrongdoing that has gone before, some overlap of terms is to be expected.

That there is a sharp break between 3:18 and 4:1 is substantiated semantically and stylistically. Semantically, 3:13–18 is more closely related to what precedes it than to what follows. The 3:13-17 unit continues the theme of 3:1-12. There are significant links between the two, such as πικρόν 'bitter' in 3:11 and 3:14, as well as ἀκατάστατον 'unruly' in 3:8 and ἀκαταστασία 'tumult' in 3:16. Also, the term σοφός 'wise', which occurs at the beginning of the 3:13-17 unit, was at times used in Jewish literature as a title for teachers (διδάσκαλος), mentioned at the beginning of the 3:1-12 unit. Furthermore, there is a distinct change of style between 3:13-18 and 4:1-6.

The semantic coherence of 3:1-18 consists in the correlation between references in 3:1-17 to 'the perfect man' (3:2) and 'good conduct' (3:13) and references to 'righteousness' and 'peacemakers' in 3:18. There is also lexical coherence: the adjective εἰρηνικός 'peaceable' (3:17) corresponds to the noun εἰρήνη 'peace' in (3:18).

PROMINENCE AND THEME

The 3:1-18 section, which is hortatory, comprises an *APPEAL* and its *basis*. In a hortatory unit both of these constituents are essential; therefore, significant parts of the theme of each are included in the theme statement of 3:1-18.

SECTION CONSTITUENT 3:1–17 (Hortatory Subsection: Appeal of 3:1–18)

THEME: Not many of you should become ones who habitually teach, since God will judge teachers with greater scrutiny than others. You should all strive to speak rightly, since what you say has a powerful effect on others, often destructive. So don't boast that you are wise if you are jealous of others and self-seeking.

MACROSTRUCTURE	CONTENTS
APPEAL$_1$	3:1–12 Not many of you should become ones who habitually teach, since God will judge teachers with greater scrutiny than he will judge others. You should all strive to speak rightly, since what you say has a powerful effect on others, often destructive and hypocritical.
APPEAL$_2$	3:13–17 Don't boast that you are wise if you are jealous of others and self-seeking. Rather, do good to demonstrate that you are truly wise, acting peaceably and compassionately toward others.

INTENT AND MACROSTRUCTURE

The 3:1–17 subsection is hortatory and consists of two *APPEALS* in a conjoined relation. In the first (3:1–12) the dangers inherent in the tongue and the need for purity in speech are presented. In the second (3:13–17) James moves from speech to the underlying attitude of the heart. Wisdom should dwell there in order to express itself by what one says and does. As Blue points out, "Winsome speech demands a wise source. Both controlled talk and cultivated thought are necessary." For James' intent in 3:1–17 see the discussion under 3:1–18.

BOUNDARIES AND COHERENCE

The initial boundary of 3:1–17 was discussed under 2:14–26. The beginning of the next unit at 3:18 is marked by a switch of topic: from the nature of godly wisdom to its effect, peace and righteousness. There is also a change of genre from hortatory to expository.

The semantic coherence between the two paragraphs of this subsection (3:1–12 and 3:13–17) consists in wisdom's being the answer to the problem of control of the tongue. In other words, the topic of the second paragraph is the answer to the topic of the first paragraph.

There are also lexical parallels: the verbs αὐχέω 'boast' (3:5) in the first paragraph and κατακαυχάομαι 'brag' (3:14) in the second; the noun phrases ἀκατάστατον κακόν 'restless evil' (3:8) in the first paragraph and ζῆλον πικρὸν . . . καὶ ἐριθείαν 'bitter jealousy . . . and rivalry' (3:14) in the second; ἰοῦ θανατηφόρου 'death-bearing poison' (3:8) in the first paragraph and δαιμονιώδης 'demonic' (3:15) in the second; and the adjectives τέλειος 'perfect' (3:2) in the first paragraph and ἁγνή 'pure' (3:17) in the second.

PROMINENCE AND THEME

Since the two paragraphs of 3:1–17 are conjoined and thus both naturally prominent, the theme of the 3:1–17 subsection is drawn from the theme of each paragraph.

SUBSECTION CONSTITUENT 3:1–12
(Hortatory Paragraph: Nucleus₁ of 3:1–17)

THEME: Not many of you should become ones who habitually teach, since God will judge teachers with greater scrutiny than he will judge others. You should all strive to speak rightly, since what you say has a powerful effect on others, often destructive and hypocritical.

¶ PTRN	RELATIONAL STRUCTURE	CONTENTS
APPEAL₁		3:1a My fellow believers, not many of you should desire to become ones who habitually teach/counsel *others*,
	orienter	3:1b *since* you know
	circumstance	3:1c *that when we(exc) teach/counsel others that they should do right,*
basis — CONTENT — NUCLEUS		3:1d *God* will judge†/examine us(exc) with greater scrutiny *than he will judge/examine others who do not know what is right.*
topic orienter (transitional)		3:2a After all, we **all** in many ways do wrong. [MET]
APPEAL₂ (mitigated)		3:2b *However, we should all strive to speak rightly*,
	condition	3:2c *since* if anyone always speaks rightly, [LIT]
basis (motivational) — CLAIM — CONSEQUENCE NUCLEUS		3:2d *he* will be all God intended him to be;
	amplification	3:2e *he will be* able to control all his actions. [MET, MTY]
	condition - MEANS	3:3a *To illustrate*, if we put bits into the mouths of horses
	purpose	3:3b in order to cause them to obey us,
ILLUSTRATION₁ — CONSEQUENCE		3:3c we can direct them. [MTY]
	orienter	3:4a Think also about ships.
	concession₁	3:4b *Although* they are very large
	concession₂	3:4c and *although* strong winds can move them,
	means	3:4d by means of *using* a very small rudder
ILLUSTRATION₂ — CONTRAEXPECTATION — RESULT		3:4e a person can direct them wherever he wants them to go.
	concession	3:5a In the same way as that [3:3–4], *although* the tongue/mouth is very small,
justification₁ — NUCLEUS — CONTRAEXPECTATION		3:5b we [PRS] affect/harm **many** people by what we proudly say.
	ILLUSTRATION	3:5c Think *also* about how a **small flame** may set on fire a **large forest** (or, **area of brushwood**).

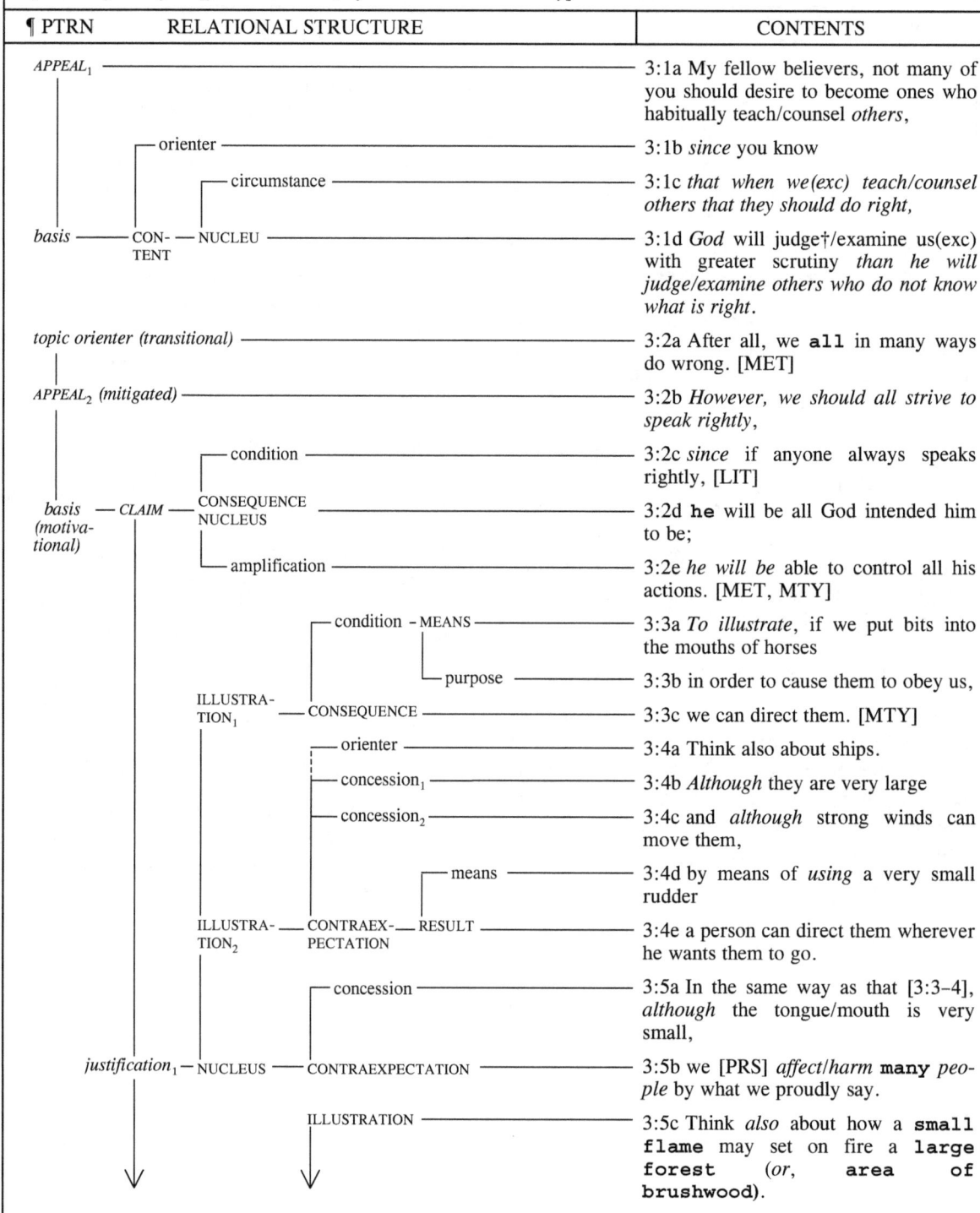

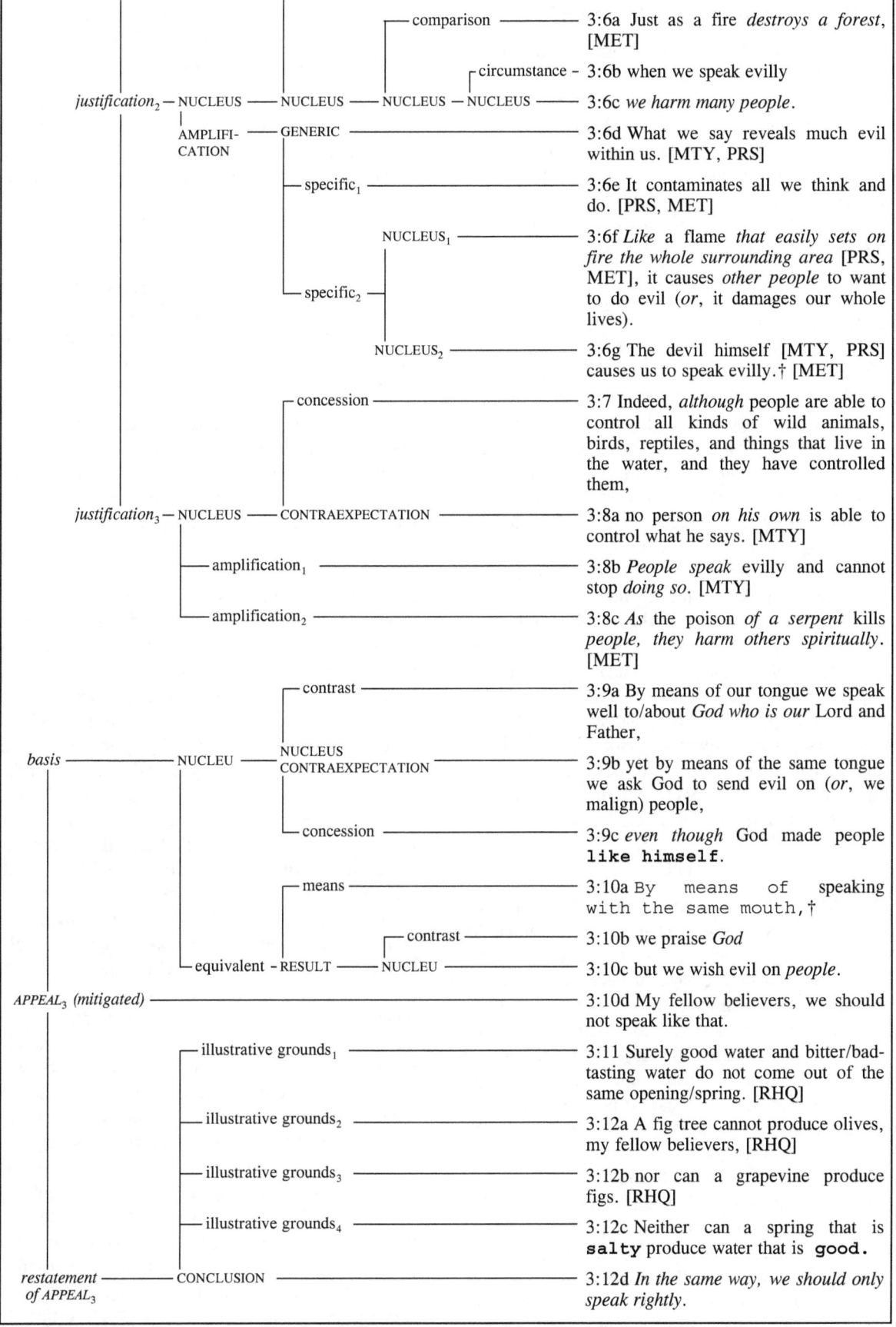

INTENT AND PARAGRAPH PATTERN

In the 3:1-12 hortatory paragraph James takes up the warning of 1:19, 26, and 2:12 about restraint in speaking, insisting that true faith results in proper control of the tongue. James relates this need first to the church teachers (v. 1) and then to the believers generally (vv. 2-12). His intent is to affect the speech of the readers through an understanding of the real problems underlying impure speech. He wants them to be aware of the dangers of an uncontrolled tongue.

The unit consists of three APPEALS, each with at least one *basis*. The first APPEAL (indicated by an imperative in 1a) addresses those aspiring to be teachers and has as its *basis* a warning of greater scrutiny than others will receive (1b-d). The second APPEAL (2b) is implicit; it functions as a mitigated appeal (see the note on 2b). In the *basis* there are three illustrations showing the power and destructive effect of speech. The *basis* consists of an embedded expository paragraph pattern in which 2c-e is a CLAIM followed by three *justifications* (3a-5b, 5c-6g, 7-8c). The third APPEAL (10d), also mitigated, is preceded by its *basis* (9a-10c), which deplores the inconsistency of their speech. This is followed by examples of consistency taken from nature (spring water, fig tree, etc.). The examples are illustrative grounds for James' point that believers should always speak rightly. These illustrative grounds are seen as supporting an implied restatement (3:12d) of the third APPEAL, expressed in more precise, positive terms.

NOTES

3:1a My fellow believers, not many of you should desire to become ones who habitually teach/counsel *others*, James introduces the subject of speech by focusing on teachers. Teachers played a prominent part in the life of the early church. The status given to teachers prompted some believers to seek this ministry for the wrong reasons and without proper qualifications. Fully aware of a teacher's great responsibility, James gives a strong warning by means of the introductory verb phrase μὴ πολλοὶ διδάσκαλοι γίνεσθε 'let not many become teachers'. The negative with the present imperative implies that there was a movement on the part of many to become teachers and this movement should be restrained (Hiebert). This was not meant to discourage people from becoming teachers but rather point out the special dangers and responsibilities involved in the task. Some have suggested that James is opposing false teachers, but there is nothing in the context to indicate that.

3:1b *since* you know The participle εἰδότες 'knowing' implies that it was widely recognized that teachers were to be held strictly accountable. A participle following a main clause may signal reason or grounds. In this case 1b-d functions as the *basis* of the APPEAL in 1a. This function is expressed in the display as 'since'.

3:1c *that when we(exc) teach/counsel others that they should do right,* This implicit proposition is a necessary part of the argument. The content of the teaching itself is supplied from the context as moral instruction.

3:1d *God* will judge/examine us(exc) The verb phrase κρίμα λημψόμεθα 'judgment we will receive' expresses the event of being judged, with 'God' the implied agent of the judging. In using the first person plural, James includes himself as one who teaches, showing that he feels the weight of this responsibility. He is "referring only to the teachers," Loh and Hatton say, pointing out that "for languages where there is a difference between the inclusive and exclusive 'we,' the exclusive one should be used here." The noun 'judgment' refers to the general process of judging and also the judicial verdict. If in the receptor language the term for 'judge' implies condemnation, it may be necessary to add the qualifying clause 'if we do not do right'. Tasker affirms that they "will receive greater condemnation than the rest of men if they have failed to walk in that way themselves." But the translation should not imply that it is wrong to become a teacher.

with greater scrutiny *than he will judge/examine others who do not know what is right.* The adjective μεῖζον 'greater' implies a comparison. In many languages it must be made explicit what the comparison is to. Laws points out that although the term κρίμα 'judgment' generally carries the sense of condemnation when used with λαμβάνω, as here, it seems unlikely that James means that teachers will be subject to greater punishment. Rather, he is referring to rigorous scrutiny at the final judgment. Ropes comments, "having, or professing to have, clear and full knowledge of duty, he is the more bound to obey it. . . ." Hiebert points out that increased influence means increased responsibility. James may be referring to some of the teachings of Jesus on this subject, such as Luke 12:42-48, especially

v. 48: "From everyone who has been given much, much will be demanded; and from the one who has been entrusted with much, much more will be asked."

3:2a After all, The conjunction γάρ 'for' has a twofold function here: It gives the reason for God's closer examination of teachers and is also explanatory. The latter is, in fact, its primary purpose, expanding the reference to all mankind as universally sinners. Many versions even omit 'for' (e.g., TEV, NIV, REB, CEV, NCV). The display follows JB with "after all."

The function of 2a is as a *topic orienter*. It changes the focus from teachers to the topic of speech in general.

we all in many ways do wrong. The adjective πολύς 'many/much', which is in the accusative case here, is used adverbially. It refers either to the number of sins (RSV has "many mistakes") or to the variety of sins (NIV has "in many ways"). The context indicates that the latter is preferable and that speech is *one* of the ways in which we do wrong.

The verb πταίω 'stumble' is figurative: it refers to moral failure or sin. The present tense indicates repeated actions.

The adjective ἅπαντες 'all' is emphatic both in form and by its position at the end of the clause. This emphasis indicates that the dangers of speech apply not only to teachers, but to all people (Hiebert).

3:2b However, we should all strive to speak rightly, This second APPEAL is supplied because it is a necessary part of the argument. In Sherman and Tuggy's SSA of 1 John (p. 2), Tuggy describes degrees of mitigated appeals, saying that in Greek "the greatest degree of mitigation is expressed by a conditional clause attached to an independent clause whose meaning content is of positive value to the reader." By supplying 3:2b and placing it before the condition-CONSEQUENCE, the 3:2c conditional clause is not left as the only expression of the appeal. The condition-CONSEQUENCE construction then functions as the *motivational basis* for this APPEAL. An option would be to put the 2b APPEAL after 2e, that is, after the condition-CONSEQUENCE construction and the amplification of the CONSEQUENCE. This would be the same reasoning order as in the Greek text, where the APPEAL is only implicit. The order presented in the display, however, is more helpful for the translator.

3:2c since The paragraph pattern formed by 2b and 2c–8c is APPEAL–*motivational basis*. This is expressed by 'since'.

if The conjunction εἰ 'if' introduces a first-class conditional clause—one that assumes the truth of the protasis, here used for the sake of argument regardless of its real truth or falsity (Martin).

anyone always speaks rightly, The verb πταίω 'stumble' is again used figuratively here to refer to moral failure. It is a litotes. While it would be possible to retain the statement in the negative, it seems more forceful when stated in positive terms in correlation with the positive consequence in 2d.

3:2d he The demonstrative pronoun οὗτος 'this one' begins the apodosis. Levinsohn (p. 95) says that here οὗτος is "preposed for emphasis."

will be all God intended him to be; The adjective τέλειος 'perfect' reiterates the thought of 1:4: spiritual maturity, not sinlessness (see the note on 1:4b). This proposition is the CLAIM James makes, following it with three *justifications* (3a–5b, 5c–6g, 7–8c). That is, he first asserts that speech is a vital force in spiritual maturity, then confirms this assertion by showing (1) the relationship of speech to the ability to control one's actions and (2) how destructive speech can be and (3) how difficult it is to control one's tongue.

3:2e he will be able to control all his actions. The verb χαλιναγωγέω '(to) bridle' is considered to be a live metaphor, since James goes on to talk about the bits of horses in v. 3. However, in all versions consulted, except for KJV and RSV, it is translated as a dead metaphor. In 1:26 the same verb is used of controlling the tongue. Here, the author amplifies the idea with the direct object ὅλον τὸ σῶμα 'all the body'. Many commentators and versions (e.g., Adamson, Tasker; NIV, REB, RSV, NRSV) translate this literally: 'whole body'. However, it is better to take it as a synecdoche or metonymy signifying 'himself' or 'his actions' (Ropes), especially since the entire preceding section (2:14–26) is about the importance of actions. Martin suggests that there could be a secondary reference to the entire congregation, pointing out not only its frequent use in vv. 2, 3, and 6, but also the way the argument proceeds, especially in the details of the illustrations (see the note on 3c evaluating this interpretation).

The adjective phrase δυνατὸς χαλιναγωγῆσαι καὶ ὅλον τὸ σῶμα 'able also to bridle all the body' could be interpreted as suggesting that the person who is master of his speech is by that very fact in total control of himself (Laws). The illustration of the horse and bit, which follows in v. 3, would seem to support this interpretation. However, the whole argument, especially in vv. 7–8, rules this out. Most commentators agree with Adamson: "But James does not mean to say that we can control our body by controlling our tongue; he means that if we can do the latter, we shall be able to do the former, which is easier."

3:3a *To illustrate,* if With this verse James begins a series of illustrations that show the power and danger of the tongue (vv. 3–6). All three illustrations involve the contrast between the small size of the item and the magnitude of its effect. The reference to χαλινός 'bit/bridle' in v. 3 links the first illustration with v. 2, which has the cognate verb χαλιναγωγέω '(to) bridle'.

There is a textual variant at the beginning of v. 3. Instead of εἰ δέ 'now if', some manuscripts have ἴδε 'behold', variously spelled in different manuscripts. One important manuscript reads ἴδε γάρ 'for behold'. GNT has εἰ δέ with a C rating, indicating difficulty in deciding which variant to use in the text. Commentators and versions differ. Some (e.g., Hiebert, Huther, Martin, and all versions except KJV) favor εἰ δέ, whereas others (e.g., Ropes, Laws, Tasker) favor ἴδε. External evidence favors εἰ δέ, but proponents of ἴδε say that the internal evidence, namely the use of ἰδοὺ καί 'behold also' in v. 4, favors ἴδε. The rendering in the display reflects εἰ δέ, based on its being the more difficult reading to explain—ἴδε is considered an attempt to harmonize.

The conjunction εἰ 'if' introduces a first-class conditional clause—it does not imply doubt but is simply argumentative (Hiebert). In fact, the majority of versions do not translate this εἰ as 'if', although RSV and NEB do. The NIV, NCV, and REB translate it "when." In the display the communication relation between 3a–b and 3c is shown to be condition-CONSEQUENCE.

The initial conjunction δέ 'but' is transitional: it introduces an illustration and distinguishes the illustration from the principle stated in v. 2 (Huther). In the display this function is brought out by the introducer 'to illustrate', alerting the translator to the need to signal the illustration in whatever way is appropriate.

we put bits into the mouths of horses The genitive ἵππων 'of horses' is fronted, indicating a new topic. James turns now from people to an illustration involving horses (Levinsohn, p. 94). The use of the article and the plural makes this a reference to horses in general. The first person plural 'we' and the present (iterative) tense of the verb βάλλω 'put' (as well as of the verb μετάγω 'direct' in 3c) confirm that this is a generic statement. In the receptor language the preferred way of stating a general truth should be used. It may be better to speak of 'a horse' as in TEV, JB, and JBP, rather than 'horses'.

The noun χαλινός can refer either to the whole bridle or to the bit that is placed into the horse's mouth. Technically, 'bridle' is more accurate, since a whole bridle is needed for control. However, since 'bit' was the part put into the mouth, either term would be acceptable. All English versions have "bit." In some languages a cultural equivalent may be needed or a descriptive phrase such as 'a small piece of metal'. The significant element in focus is the ability to control a large animal.

3:3b in order to cause them to obey us, The verb phrase εἰς τὸ πείθεσθαι αὐτοὺς ἡμῖν 'to make them obey us' shows that the aim in bridling the horse is to secure the obedience of the whole horse, not just its mouth.

3:3c we can direct them. The verb μετάγω 'direct' at the end of v. 3 means having the horse under control so that he may be steered. The object of the verb, ὅλον τὸ σῶμα αὐτῶν 'their whole body', puts emphasis on the size of the animal. In this illustration the point of similarity between a bit and the tongue is that they are both small yet can control something that is large. Although James does not specifically mention the small size of the bit, he probably intended this to be inferred, since he does stress that a bit enables a horse's whole body to be controlled. JBP expresses this contrast explicitly: "Men control the movements of a large animal like the horse with a tiny bit placed in its mouth." In some languages 'the whole body' or even 'the whole animal' would sound awkward or unnatural. It seems preferable to refer simply to the animal itself, as in TEV and CEV. If in the receptor term used for 'bit' the concept of smallness is not evident, it would be good to say 'a large horse', as in JBP and NLT, since this puts the emphasis on the size of the animal rather than the completeness of the control. In the ship illustration that follows (v. 4), it is the size of the ship that is emphasized and not how much of the ship can be controlled.

Some commentators (e.g., Martin, Reicke) see in the noun 'body' a strong secondary reference to the church: a church leader who regulates the preaching controls the whole group of believers thereby. This is an interesting application but, as Plummer says, "such symbolism is read into the text, not extracted from it."

3:4a Think also about ships. The opening words ἰδοὺ καί 'behold also' direct attention to a further illustration. Some commentators (Alford, Hiebert) say that ἰδού is an exclamatory particle that adds vividness to the illustration; others (e.g., Laws, Mitton) treat it as a verb. (The particle is distinguishable from the imperative ἰδοῦ 'look at' only by the type of accent on the final vowel.) Although ἰδού is a particle, it is translated here as a verb, one that functions as an orienter to draw attention to the illustration about ships. Most versions translate it in a similar fashion (TEV, NIV, REB, JB) or omit it entirely (CEV, NCV, JBP, NLT). The conjunction καί connects this illustration with the previous one.

3:4b-c *Although* they are very large and *although* strong winds can move them, The relation between 4b-c and 4d-e is concession-CONTRAEXPECTATION, which in the display is expressed by the word 'although'. The two participial phrases τηλικαῦτα ὄντα 'being so great' and ὑπὸ ἀνέμων σκληρῶν ἐλαυνόμενα 'being driven by strong winds' are coordinate, since they are connected by καί 'and' and there is nothing in the context to suggest a different meaning of καί here. Both phrases point out the difficulty of guiding the ship in order to cause the power of the small rudder to be emphasized.

3:4d-e by means of *using* a very small rudder a person can direct them wherever he wants them to go. The parallelism of the two illustrations about horses and ships is brought out by the repetition of the verb μετάγω 'direct'. The superlative form of the adjective ἐλάχιστος 'very little' emphasizes the smallness of the rudder compared with the large size of a ship.

Commentators differ in their understanding of the noun ὁρμή 'impulse' in James' statement that a ship's direction is not determined by the strong wind but by the impulse of the one steering it. Some (e.g., Mayor, Lenski) say it refers to the physical pressure exerted on the tiller by the helmsman, but the majority (e.g., Huther, Alford) believe that it indicates his own personal desire. In Acts 14:5, the only other place in the New Testament where the word is used, it refers to the strong desire of the opponents to use violence. The second sense is probably most basic, but both senses are in view. Hiebert says, "His inner desire must find expression in positive action to achieve the necessary control."

3:5a In the same way as that [3:3-4], *although* the tongue/mouth is very small, Before his third illustration in 5c (a flame), James makes an application here regarding the tongue. The initial adverb οὕτως 'thus' asserts the comparison between the two illustrations in vv. 3-4 and the tongue. Note that the word 'tongue' in v. 5 is used literally, meaning the physical tongue, though later in this paragraph, in vv. 6 and 8, 'tongue' is a metonymy for speech.

The literal 'tongue' (in some languages 'mouth') needs to be retained in translating v. 5 in order for the comparison of size to be understood. In vv. 6 and 8, however, a verb expression referring to the act of speaking may be needed.

3:5b we *affect/harm* <u>many</u> people by what we proudly say. The focus of 5b is on the great power of speech to affect people. Here 'tongue' is personified as the subject of the verb αὐχέω 'boast' but is rendered nonfiguratively in the display: 'we . . . by what we proudly say'.

The forefronted adjectival pronoun μεγάλα 'great things', which is rendered here as 'many people', brings out the contrast between the tongue's small size and its tremendous effect. Some commentators (e.g., Davids 1982) say that αὐχέω 'boast' is used here in a derogatory sense. Others (e.g., Ropes, Lenski, Mayor) say that μεγάλα αὐχεῖ, whether written as two words or as one, suggests only the possibility of evil and that James reserves the damage done by our speech for a separate treatment in the following illustration (5c-6c). Based on this latter view, the rendering in the display is worded in a neutral way. The damaging effect itself is reserved for the following propositions.

In some languages it might be difficult to find a neutral term for 'affect'. In such cases, it would be acceptable in this context to translate it 'we harm many people by what we proudly say'. Such a translation would anticipate the illustration of fire in 5c-6c.

3:5c Think *also* about how a <u>small</u> <u>flame</u> may set on fire a <u>large</u> <u>forest</u> (*or*, <u>area of brushwood</u>). In this third illustration there is again a contrast of size, as in the other two, but there is an additional component as well. In one sense the three illustrations have a unity, reflecting lexical and even semantic shifts in thought. But in the broader context the third illustration involves a new step in the argument. Beginning in 5c, which is the beginning of the second *justification* for the CLAIM in 2c, the idea of control gives way to that of destructive power.

As in v. 4, the particle ἰδού 'look' introduces and calls attention to the illustration that follows. The adjective ἡλίκος, 'how much' can mean 'how great' or 'how small' depending upon the context. Here it occurs before both πῦρ 'fire' and ὕλη 'forest' and the resultant phrases are forefronted, emphasizing the great contrast between a tiny spark and the large area it can affect. The noun ὕλη 'wood' could mean a standing forest or a stack of lumber. Almost all commentators and versions say 'forest', but several point out that, in view of the nature of the Palestinian landscape, uncultivated brushwood or scrub is what James had in mind. In languages of the tropical rain forests, the illustration would be incongruous if the receptor word for 'forest' were used.

The verb ἀνάπτω 'kindle' means the setting of the fire. The illustration is of a spreading destruction that is devastating because it is not controlled (Hiebert).

3:6a–c Just as a fire *destroys a forest,* when we speak evilly *we harm many people*. The initial conjunction καί 'and' in 6a connects this metaphorical description of an uncontrolled tongue with the illustration in 5c. This is an apt metaphor for the tongue's destructive potential. The topic is the tongue, the image is fire, and the point of similarity is the power to destroy. Note that the impact of this statement in 6a–c might be diminished if 'harm', the second alternative in 5b, is used (see the note on 5b, especially the final paragraph).

3:6d–g The Greek here is ὁ κόσμος τῆς ἀδικίας, ἡ γλῶσσα καθίσταται ἐν τοῖς μέλεσιν ἡμῶν, ἡ σπιλοῦσα ὅλον τὸ σῶμα καὶ φλογίζουσα τὸν τροχὸν τῆς γενέσεως καὶ φλογιζομένη ὑπὸ τῆς γεέννης 'the world of iniquity, the tongue is set among our members, spotting all the body and inflaming the course of nature and being inflamed by *gehenna*'. This is extremely complex and difficult. As Hiebert says, "The structure and intended meaning of the remainder of verse 6 is beset with difficulty. There are five expressions in the nominative case with only one verb in the indicative. Different punctuations are possible." This complexity is compounded by the preponderance of personification, the central topic's being a metonymy for speech, and the ambiguity concerning whether the destructive effect is internal (within ourselves) or external (in our relationships with other people).

The 5c–6c comparison of an uncontrolled tongue to a destructive fire is further developed in 6d–g, so the communication relation between these two units is NUCLEUS-AMPLIFICATION. The extensive and graphic descriptions of the tongue in 6d–g give unusual prominence to the AMPLIFICATION, hence the upper-case letters.

3:6d What we say reveals much evil within us. Much has been written about the phrase ὁ κόσμος τῆς ἀδικίας 'the world of unrighteousness'. The first problem is deciding what it is grammatically connected with. Some commentators (e.g., Alford, Adamson) believe that it is connected with what precedes, either as appositive to the noun πῦρ 'fire' in 6a or as descriptive of 'the tongue' in 6b. However, most (e.g., Hiebert, Mayor, Martin) say that it is connected with what follows: 'as a world of unrighteousness the tongue is set among our members'. According to this view, it functions as a predicate nominative, fronted for emphasis. This view is better for the following reasons:

1. The grammar is clearer if there is a break after πῦρ.
2. The article with 'world' gives it a prominence that would be more fitting as a part of the following sentence.
3. This view best explains the function of the second ἡ γλῶσσα 'the tongue' in v. 6.
4. It also best explains the feminine participle ἡ σπιλοῦσα 'that which stains', which functions as a modifier of 'tongue' in 6d rather than as a predicate following the verb καθίσταται 'is appointed'.

The next problem is the meaning of ὁ κόσμος 'the world'. There are three main views: (1) Since 'world' has the root meaning of adornment, some take the tongue to be 'the ornament' of wickedness, that which makes evil attractive. (2) Another view is that 'world' means 'sum total' as suggested by the Vulgate rendering: 'the tongue becomes (or proves to be) the sum total of iniquity'. (3) The third view is that it means 'the wicked world' (a genitive of quality), a vast system hostile to God. The first view can be ruled out as not fitting the context. The second is defended by Huther, who sees it as referring to a fullness of unrighteousness that pervades the other parts of the body, but in this view a different sense is given to κόσμος from its usage in the rest of the book (e.g., 1:27, 4:4). The third view is therefore the preferable one, since 'world' is the more usual meaning of κόσμος. Also, the presence of the article with both nouns in the construction indicates a specific reference, as would be best reflected in the third view (Moo).

The verb καθίσταται 'is appointed/constituted' can be rendered with reflexive force here (also in 4:4). When so rendered, γλῶσσα 'tongue' in 6d (the second 'tongue' in v. 6) is the subject of the reflexive verb, and 'the world of unrighteousness' is the second goal of the 'appointing', the other goal being 'itself': 'the tongue appoints itself as the wicked world among our members (ἐν τοῖς μέλεσιν ἡμῶν)'. Since 'among our members' is a metonymy, it might well be recast as 'within us': 'the tongue appoints itself as the spokesman for the wicked world within us'. Of course, this is a personification of 'tongue'. Moreover, both 'tongue' and 'wicked world are metonymies, a figure unknown in many languages, and it is best to recast them nonfiguratively, as in the display. James may have had Matt. 15:18–19 in mind here: words express the attitudes of the heart, in which are found evil thoughts, slander, immorality, and other vices.

3:6e It contaminates The remainder of v. 6 continues the description of the destructive nature of evil speech. The participial phrases here modify the clause ὁ κόσμος . . . μέλεσιν ἡμῶν 'the world of iniquity, the tongue is set among our members'. There are three participles in the nominative case linked by καί 'and' between each of them. Only the first one has the definite article and some commentators (e.g., Hiebert, Lenski) feel that the other two are therefore subordinate to the first one, ἡ σπιλοῦσα 'the one staining': 'it stains the whole body, both setting on fire . . . and being set on fire'. However, the majority (e.g., Huther, Martin, Adamson) consider the three to be parallel descriptions of the tongue: 'it stains the whole body and sets on fire . . . and is set on fire'. The majority view is preferable. In the display 6e and 6f–g are shown as specifics of the more generic 6d. Grammatically, the three participial phrases are subordinate; semantically, they delineate particular effects of the 'world of iniquity' within.

all we think and do. The noun phrase ὅλον τὸ σῶμα 'all the body' refers not to the physical body but to the entire personality or inner character. Martin continues to see this figure as applying to the church; he stresses the contaminating influence of the "irresponsible speech of errant teachers" on the whole church, but this limits the meaning too much, though it may be a valid application.

3:6f *Like* a flame *that easily sets on fire the whole surrounding area,* it causes *other people to want to do evil (or, it damages our whole lives).* The present active participle φλογίζουσα 'inflaming' returns to the figure of fire, which in the Greek is a live metaphor. The topic of the metaphor beginning in 5c is speech. The image is a flame and the point of similarity is the instant destructive cause-effect dynamic of fire and the bad things we say. If in a given language the use of the metaphor obscures the meaning or distorts the focus, it would be better to render this nonfiguratively.

The direct object of 'inflaming' is the noun phrase τὸν τροχὸν τῆς γενέσεως 'the course of nature', the meaning of which is unclear. (Both nouns in this phrase have more than one meaning.) Many commentators think James is referring to the course of an individual's life with its varied relationships from beginning to end. But others imply that he also has in view the effect of the tongue on others, as is especially brought to the fore in 6f: "this expression seems intended to set forth the wider social impact of the uncontrolled tongue" (Hiebert). Ropes is similar: "what is actually enkindled by the tongue is mankind and human society . . ." (see also Kistemaker, pp. 110–11, and Lenski, pp. 606–7). The entire context of this chapter shows that James is concerned about the effect of speech in human relationships. If the effect is limited to the individual's life, it would be essentially a repetition of proposition 6e, but including the effect on others here is typical of the pattern used throughout the book. However, both views are valid, and both are given as alternatives in the display.

3:6g The devil himself causes us to speak evilly. The same verb that was used in 6f is used here, but here it is a present passive participle, φλογιζομένη 'being inflamed'. The agent is expressed by the prepositional phrase ὑπὸ τῆς γεέννης 'by *gehenna*', which is the place of final judgment, a metonymy referring to the devil. Moo says, "The power of Satan himself, the chief denizen of hell, gives to the tongue its great destructive potential." Although structurally this participial phrase (6g) is parallel to the two preceding ones (6e and 6f), semantically there may well be a closer relation between 6f and 6g, since the same verb is used in both of them. TEV combines the two: "It sets on fire the entire course of our existence with the fire that comes to it from hell itself." NLT reflects a RESULT-reason relation: "It can turn the entire course of your life into a blazing flame of destruction, for it is set on fire by hell itself." If the receptor language uses metaphors, this could be rendered as a live metaphor with the point of similarity between the topic and the image being their destructive effect: 'the devil himself causes us to speak evilly, *as if he were using* the fires of hell *to harm people*'. However, one must be sure that the inclusion of such a figure does not obscure the meaning or distort the focus.

3:7 Indeed, There are two possible interpretations of the function of the initial conjunction γάρ 'for'. One view is that it introduces vv. 7-8, which provide the grounds for what was said in v. 6. Of those who hold this view, some (e.g., Moo, Mayor) limit such grounds to substantiating the assertion that the tongue receives its power from hell; others (e.g., Ropes, Martin) believe that the grounds substantiate all the strong terms used about "the mischief of the tongue" (Alford) in v. 6. This is certainly a possible interpretation. However, Stulac, Pope, and others view vv. 7-8 as a further description of the tongue: not only is it powerful and destructive, it is also humanly uncontrollable. Most versions (NIV, TEV, JB, REB, CEV, NCV, NLT, JBP, WEY) omit 'for', which is perhaps a clue to the fact that γάρ is moving the supportive argument (3:3-8) along as a whole rather than introducing a reason for the preceding verse. We take vv. 7-8 as the third *justification* for the CLAIM in 2c-e, so that γάρ is translated 'indeed' rather than 'for'. The idea of control is central in this CLAIM (see the note on 3:2e), so these two verses should not be viewed merely as subordinate to v. 6 but rather as a further step in the devastating picture of the tongue. (Even if 7-8 is viewed as grounds for 6d-g, γάρ would be best translated as 'indeed' in order to show that there is a connection with more than what immediately precedes it.)

***although* people are able to control all kinds of wild animals, birds, reptiles, and things that live in the water, and they have controlled them,** The noun φύσις 'kind, class' is a generic term that can be applied to both animals and mankind. In its first occurrence in v. 7 it refers to animals and is followed by a fourfold classification of animals (similar to the list in Gen. 1:26, where man is given control over the created beings). At the end of v. 7 φύσις occurs again, this time referring to man, 'the human species', where it serves to highlight the contrast between the animal and the human kingdom.

The verb δαμάζω 'tame, control' also occurs twice in v. 7, the first time as a present passive and the second time as perfect passive. A few (e.g., Dibelius) say the twofold use is purely rhetorical for emphasis. However, the majority think the present tense means that the animals are habitually tamed, while the perfect tense has the historical perspective: it was granted to mankind to tame them from the beginning. Although some (e.g., Laws) say that the noun phrase τῇ φύσει τῇ ἀνθρωπίνῃ 'by/to mankind' is a dative of advantage, the majority (e.g., Martin, Mayor) say that it expresses instrumentality or functions as the agent of the passive verb (Moulton, p. 240.j). The latter is preferable in this context.

3:8a no person *on his own* is able to control what he says. The particle δέ in this context indicates a contrast between v. 7 and v. 8, hence the concession-CONTRAEXPECTATION relation in the display. All versions express this contrast by an initial 'but' in v. 8. The noun γλῶσσα 'tongue' is forefronted, topicalizing it and putting it in focus. The noun ἀνθρώπων 'of men' is also in an emphatic position: clause-final. Some (Ropes) contend that this is simply a strong way of saying that complete control is not to be expected, but a number of commentators (e.g., Mayor, Hiebert) agree with Augustine that man by himself cannot achieve this control, implying that without God's help this is impossible. This idea is supplied in the display as 'on his own'.

3:8b *People speak* evilly and cannot stop *doing so*. The Greek is ἀκατάστατον κακόν 'an unstable evil'. The neuter noun κακόν is grammatically ambiguous; that is, it could be either nominative or accusative. If taken as an accusative, it would be in apposition to the τὴν γλῶσσαν 'the tongue' in 8a, which is accusative. But it is more likely nominative, since it is parallel with the clearly nominative μεστή 'full' in 8c. Some (e.g., Lenski, Hiebert) prefer to regard this phrase as simply an exclamation of moral indignation, but most regard it as a predicate nominative with 'it is' understood: '*It is* an unstable evil'. Our rendering is based on this view.

Although all commentators and versions refer to 'the tongue' as a thing ('it'), it is important to remember that 'the tongue' is metonymy, signifying the event of speech. Thus in the display 'unstable evil' is rendered with verb phrases, and the agent 'people' is supplied.

There is a textual variant for the adjective in this phrase. Instead of ἀκατάστατον 'unstable' some manuscripts have ἀκατάσχετον 'unruly'. The GNT chooses 'unstable' with a B rating, indicating that the text is almost certain. We accept this as the better reading.

3:8c As the poison *of a serpent* kills *people, they harm others spiritually.* The adjective phrase μεστὴ ἰοῦ θανατηφόρου 'full of death-bearing poison' is grammatically parallel with 8b, the preceding proposition. Many commentators regard this as a metaphor referring to the bite of a poisonous snake. The rendering in the display is based on this. The harm is spiritual or emotional, not physical.

3:9a By means of our tongue The absence of any connecting particle at 9a marks vv. 9–12 as a new aspect in the discussion: the inconsistencies in the way people speak. The prepositional phrase ἐν αὐτῇ 'by it' puts emphasis on the instrument of speech. The same phrase is repeated in 9b, intensifying the emphasis. In another language the appropriate term for speech in an instrumental sense should be used.

we speak well to/about *God who is our* Lord and Father, The essential meaning of the verb εὐλογέω 'bless, praise', although it may refer to worship or prayer, is to speak well in relation to God, either addressed to God or about God. The noun phrase τὸν κύριον καὶ πατέρα 'the Lord and Father' is the object of εὐλογοῦμεν 'we praise'. This is an unusual phrase for 'God'; the more commonly used one is 'God and Father', as in 1:27. Some manuscripts have θεόν 'God' rather than 'Lord'; however, the GNT chooses 'Lord' with an A rating, indicating that their editors consider the text certain. The first term, 'Lord', refers to God's power or authority; the second, 'Father', refers to God's love for humankind, which, in the context, would add force to the rebuke in 9b-c. In the display the word 'God' is supplied before 'Lord' in order to emphasize the authority of God and because this expression is such an unusual way of referring to God.

Commentators differ as to the significance of the first person plural in the verb 'bless'. Some (e.g., Alford) say it means humankind in general; others (e.g., Huther, Davids 1982) believe that the primary reference is to Christians. The latter is preferable, since James' focus throughout the book is on the conduct of believers. As in 3:3a, he is referring to believers as a class. That would include himself but certainly not indicate any personal guilt. The present tense of this verb indicates habitual actions.

3:9b yet by means of the same tongue we ask God to send evil on (*or*, we malign) people, The instrumental phrase ἐν αὐτῇ 'by it' of 9a is repeated here (see the note on 9a regarding this as well as the person and tense of the verb). The verb here is καταράομαι 'curse', which may refer to personal abuse resulting, for example, from losing one's temper in controversy (Oesterley), or it may mean actually calling down curses on someone. It is the opposite of 'bless' in 9a. Several commentators (e.g., Adamson, Hiebert) see this as a reference to the angry disputes and slanderous remarks within the community described in 4:1-2 and 11-12. But Moo goes so far as to say "to curse someone is not just to swear at them; it is to desire that they be cut off from God and experience eternal punishment." Both alternatives are acceptable.

The direct object τοὺς ἀνθρώπους is a generic term referring to humankind in general.

3:9c *even though* God made people like himself. The phrase καθ' ὁμοίωσιν θεοῦ 'according to God's likeness' is forefronted for emphasis, focusing on the fact that they were created in God's image. It should be rendered so as to show this prominence in the way that is appropriate in the receptor language.

The perfect active participle γεγονότας 'having become' implies that God's image remains in mankind and has not been totally effaced by sin. To curse a man is an offense to God who made him. In effect, the one cursing man is cursing God himself (Tasker).

3:10a By means of speaking with the same mouth, The noun στόμα 'mouth' along with the verb ἐξέρχομαι 'come/go out' recalls Jesus' teaching in Matt. 15:11 and 17-20: speech reveals what is in the heart. If in another language it is not natural to refer to speech as instrument, 'the same mouth' could be considered a synecdoche, so that 10a-c would be rendered 'the same person praises God but wishes evil on people'.

3:10b-c we praise *God* but we wish evil on *people*. The topic addressed in v. 9 is continued in v. 10, with the cognate nouns εὐλογία 'blessing' and κατάρα 'cursing' instead of the verbs. This repetition, along with the adjective αὐτοῦ 'same', sets the stage for the rebuke in 10d. The communication relation between 9a-c and 10a-c is NUCLEUS-equivalent, since the two are semantically identical except for 9c. The restatement further emphasizes the inconsistency of their speech.

3:10d My fellow believers, we should not speak like that. The verb phrase οὐ χρή 'it is not fitting' is very strong and is translated as 'ought not' or 'should not' in virtually all versions. TEV has "This should not happen!" The adverb οὕτως 'thus' refers to the inconsistent way of speaking. (Obviously it does not mean that if there were only cursing James would approve.)

The vocative ἀδελφοί μου 'my brothers' indicates that though James is censuring their actions, he is speaking gently and with affection. This rebuke is a CLAIM that functions as a mitigated APPEAL; 9a-10c is the *justification* for this CLAIM and functions as the *basis* of the APPEAL.

3:11 Surely good water and bitter/bad-tasting water do not come out of the same opening/spring. James concludes his argument with two rhetorical questions, again illustrating his point from nature. The particle μήτι 'not' at the beginning of v. 11 indicates that an emphatic negative response is expected.

The noun πηγή 'spring' is the subject of the verb βρύει 'pour out'. The phrase τὸ γλυκὺ καὶ τὸ πικρόν 'the sweet and the bitter (water)' functions as the object of the verb. In the prepositional phrase ἐκ τῆς αὐτῆς ὀπῆς 'from the same opening' the adjective 'same' refers to nature's consistency. (The initial particle 'not' indicates the contrast between the consistency of nature and the inconsistency of speech.) In rendering this, it may be more natural in many languages to talk about water flowing from an opening or a spring, as in the display, rather than being sent forth by the spring.

The adjective πικρός 'bitter' is not the usual word for salty water, but most commentators define it either as 'salty' or 'brackish'. The significant point is that it is undrinkable. It may be that James chose 'bitter' here in anticipation of the same adjective in v. 14, where it describes the jealousy in their hearts.

3:12a-b A fig tree cannot produce olives, my fellow believers, nor can a grapevine produce figs. This is the second of the two rhetorical questions. The verb δύναται 'can' emphasizes nature's consistency: each plant produces according to its own nature. The vocative ἀδελφοί μου 'my brothers', which usually marks a transition to a new topic, is used here for emphasis and to show James' affectionate concern to drive home this point (Hiebert).

3:12c Neither can a spring that is salty produce water that is good. In concluding his argument James here reverts to the example of water in v. 11. The Greek is οὔτε ἁλυκὸν γλυκὺ ποιῆσαι ὕδωρ 'neither salt make water sweet'. The verb 'can' is understood from the previous proposition. The adjectives 'salty' and 'sweet' are sequential and fronted before the verb, and the noun 'water' is sentence final. This word order emphasizes the contrast between 'salty' and 'sweet'. Some manuscripts have οὕτως 'thus' before οὔτε, but GNT accepts the shorter reading with a B rating, "almost certain."

Tasker observes, "Hort may be right in supposing that 'the last illustration implies that not the verbal blessing of God but the cursing of men is a true index to what lies within'."

3:12d *In the same way, we should only speak rightly*. This proposition is supplied because it is a necessary part of the argument. It is the conclusion drawn from the preceding illustrations (Davids 1994). The discourse structure of many languages requires that in a logical argument after a series of premises a conclusion must be drawn.

BOUNDARIES AND COHERENCE

The initial boundary of 3:1-12 was discussed under 2:14-26. The final boundary at 3:13 is marked by a change of topic: from the control of speech to true wisdom. Lexical coherence is shown by the nouns γλῶσσα 'tongue' in vv. 5, 6 (twice), and 8; λόγος 'word' in v. 2; διδάσκαλοι 'teachers' in v. 1; and the verbs of speech εὐλογέω 'bless' and καταράομαι 'curse' in v. 9 with their cognate nouns in v. 10. There are also nouns that are related to 'tongue' semantically: σῶμα 'body' in vv. 2, 3, and 6; μέλος 'parts of the body' in vv. 5 and 6; and στόμα 'mouth' in vv. 3 and 10. Verbs of control give further semantic coherence: χαλιναγωγέω '(to) bridle' in v. 2 together with the cognate noun χαλινός 'bits' in v. 3; μετάγω 'direct, control' in v. 4; and δαμάζω 'tame, control' in v. 7 (twice) and v. 8. None of these words occur in 3:13–18.

Relational coherence is shown by the particle ἰδού 'behold', which introduces the illustrations in vv. 4 and 5. (If the textual variant ἴδε is accepted as introducing the illustration in v. 3, this would provide further coherence.)

Some (Adamson, Mayor; JB, NLT, JBP) divide the unit between v. 1 and v. 2, making a separate paragraph with the topic of the teacher's responsibility. Davids (1982) and Stulac both divide the unit after the first clause of v. 2. Tasker divides it in the middle of v. 5, separating the advice to teachers from the rest of the chapter. But while it is true that the teachers are directly addressed at the beginning of chapter 3, we consider this topic as primarily a means of introducing the problem of the uncontrolled tongue; hence we make no division at all, considering 3:1–12 to be one paragraph.

There are others who propose paragraph breaks within 3:1–12 based on criteria other than the topic of teachers: between vv. 2 and 3 (Hiebert, Kistemaker; NIV, CEV); between 5b and 5c (Stulac; TEV, REB, NCV); between 5 and 6 (Blue, Mitton; RSV, WEY); between 6 and 7 (Hiebert; NIV, NLT, JBP); and between 8 and 9 (Hiebert, Kistemaker, Blue; NIV, CEV). However, the theme of the tongue runs through the entire 1–12 unit. It is mainly for this reason that we consider these breaks simply as indicators of lower-level constituents. Others who, like us, do not divide 3:1–12 at all include Martin, Laws, Lenski, Bratcher, Loh and Hatton, and Williams (CBW).

Translators should remember that in the layout of a translation it may be wise to make paragraph breaks at the lower-level units, even if 3:1–12 *is* a coherent discourse-level paragraph. Such breaks facilitate reading and comprehension, and most English versions do this.

PROMINENCE AND THEME

In a hortatory paragraph both *APPEAL* and *basis* are thematic since they are integral parts of a hortatory paragraph pattern. The theme for the 3:1–12 paragraph is therefore based on the three *APPEALS* and their *bases*, although because of the similarity of the second and third *APPEALS* they appear in the theme as one: "You should all strive to speak rightly." In the Greek this statement is in the first person plural; however, the second person plural is used in the theme statement in order to harmonize with the other themes.

SUBSECTION CONSTITUENT 3:13–17
(Hortatory Paragraph: Nucleus₂ of 3:1–17)

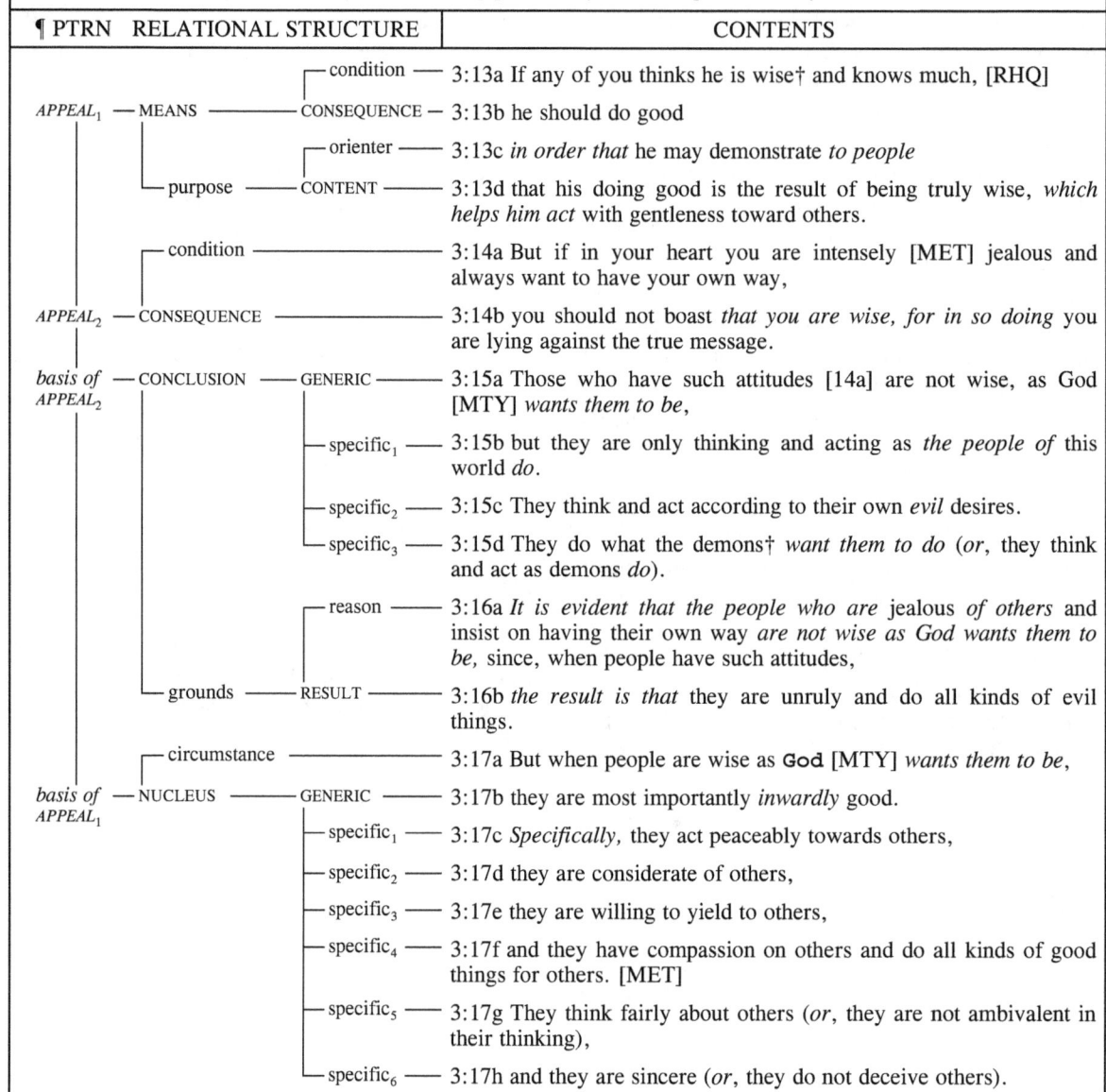

INTENT AND PARAGRAPH PATTERN

James' intent in the 3:13–17 unit is to stimulate good conduct that will demonstrate godly wisdom. This hortatory unit is composed of two *APPEALS*, one expressed by the third person imperative in 13b, δειξάτω 'let him show', and the other by the imperatives μὴ κατακαυχᾶσθε καὶ ψεύδεσθε 'do not boast and lie' in 14b. Each has its own *basis* (17a–h and 15a–16b respectively).

The unit is structured as a chiasm, contrasting wisdom that is from God with a false wisdom of human, and ultimately demonic, origin:

A He should do good to demonstrate that he is wise. (3:13)

   B Don't boast that you are wise if you are jealous and self-seeking. (3:14)

   B' Those who have such attitudes [14a] are not being wise as God wants them to be. (3:15–16)

A' When people are wise as God wants them to be, they are most importantly inwardly good. (3:17)

Verses 15 and 16 function as the *basis* for the second APPEAL (v. 14). This basis shows that the wisdom these people profess does not have its source in God and is not the kind of wisdom that pleases God. Verse 17 functions as the *basis* for the first APPEAL (13a–d) and in contrast to the other *basis* shows the nature of true godly wisdom.

NOTES

3:13a If any of you thinks he is wise and knows much, The rhetorical question at the beginning of this paragraph is a characteristic of the diatribe style. James frequently uses such a question to get the attention of the readers. Here his question targets those who are assuming that they are wise. He challenges them to examine their lives in order to ascertain the truth. Some commentators (Hiebert, Tasker) point out that this could be expressed in a conditional clause. In the display the conditional is used since in many languages it is more natural, and the communication relation between 13a and 13b is condition-CONSEQUENCE. However, if in a given language rhetorical questions are used to challenge or express reproach, a rhetorical question would be very forceful here.

There is a difference of opinion about the audience James is addressing in 3:13–17. A number of commentators (e.g., Ropes, Davids 1982, Alford) see a strong connection with 3:1, which was addressed to teachers, so they consider the entire 3:1–18 section primarily for teachers. Ross, who holds this view, points out that the adjective σοφός 'wise' was used in noun form as a technical term for teachers. But other commentators (e.g., Martin, Moo, Laws), while acknowledging an application to teachers, say that the message is to all believers, since wisdom is a virtue available to all (cf. 1:5). This latter view is preferable and is reflected in the display. (Martin does concede that "The opening words are . . . a challenge to those whose business was with words spoken and intended to be received as authoritative.")

Moore (p. 60) says that the adjectives σοφός 'wise' and ἐπιστήμων 'intelligent' are a near-synonymous doublet. In this case, it would be acceptable to translate them as 'truly wise' (Bratcher). Alternatively, the first term could be considered a moral quality and the second an intellectual one, as in the display.

3:13b–c he should do good *in order that* he may demonstrate *to people* The imperative δειξάτω 'let him show' in the aorist tense calls for an effective demonstration (Hiebert). This verb is followed by the prepositional phrase ἐκ τῆς καλῆς ἀναστροφῆς 'by good conduct', which indicates the general source from which the proof is to be drawn. There is a mismatch between the grammatical and semantic structure in these two propositions. Although grammatically the imperative is 'demonstrate', semantically the APPEAL is to good conduct, conduct that will demonstrate true wisdom, hence a MEANS-purpose communication relation between 13b and 13c–d. James' challenge here is similar to the one in 2:18 in which faith is to be demonstrated by good deeds.

3:13d that his doing good The noun phrase τὰ ἔργα αὐτοῦ 'his works' is the object of the verb δειξάτω 'let him show'.

is the result of being truly wise, *which helps him act* with gentleness toward others. The prepositional phrase ἐν πραΰτητι σοφίας 'in the meekness of wisdom' could be seen as attached to the verb 'let him show' as the previous prepositional phrase is (in 13b). Semantically, however, it is more closely attached to the object, 'his works': his deeds are to be done in the meekness (gentleness) that comes from wisdom.

Since the phrase 'in the meekness of wisdom' is a Hebrew idiom, the relation between the two nouns is not clear. But the focus of the paragraph is on wisdom, and gentleness is a characteristic of true wisdom, so it can be said that by such conduct one shows that he is truly wise. Only by such an attitude is true wisdom shown. Thus we interpret the phrase as 'the gentleness that characterizes wisdom' or 'the gentleness that springs from wisdom'. Hiebert declares, "It is that attitude of heart that produces gentleness and mildness in dealing with others—not weakness (Matt. 11:29) but power under control." There is certainly also an emphasis on humility, the opposite of arrogant self-assertiveness. Ropes says that it is gentleness, not wisdom, that is to be demonstrated; but most (e.g., Adamson, Mayor) say that gentleness shows that one is wise. In translating this, a term that is the opposite of bitter jealousy and rivalry would be appropriate, since this is the contrast presented in vv. 13–14.

3:14a But if in your heart you are intensely jealous The particle δέ 'but/and' here marks a contrast between the godly conduct described in v. 13 and the self-centered aggressiveness in v. 14. The fronting of the phrase ζῆλον πικρόν 'bitter jealousy' along with δέ marks a change of topic.

Although in the Greek the prepositional phrase ἐν τῇ καρδίᾳ ὑμῶν 'in your heart' follows ἐριθεία 'selfish ambition', this phrase is placed at the beginning of the proposition because it relates to both 'jealousy' and 'selfish ambition'. Note that 'heart' could be considered a synecdoche signifying the whole person (i.e., 'you'). Indeed, if the words in the receptor language for 'jealousy' and 'self-seeking' are inner attitudes, it might be unnatural to translate 'in your heart' literally.

The primary meaning of the noun ζῆλος 'jealousy' is 'zeal'. It is a term that may be used in a good sense, but here it is used in a bad sense, as the context shows and as its modifier, πικρός 'bitter', also shows. This modifier is figurative—it refers to resentful feelings (Louw and Nida, 88.170). In the Greek it ties v. 14 to v. 11, where πικρός is used in its literal sense to describe bitter water. Bratcher suggests that this adjective functions here to intensify 'jealousy'; and since in many languages 'bitter' does not collocate with 'jealousy', it is rendered 'intensely jealous' in the display.

and always want to have your own way, The noun ἐριθεία 'selfish ambition' refers to unethical self-seeking to gain personal advantage (Hiebert). Since this is an abstract noun and refers to an event, it is rendered with a verb phrase here.

3:14b This proposition involves two imperative verbs, κατακαυχᾶσθε 'boast' and ψεύδεσθε 'lie', and a prepositional phrase, κατὰ τῆς ἀληθείας 'against the truth'. It is not clear whether the phrase is connected with both of the verbs or only the second one. Some (e.g., Alford, Huther) say that it is connected with both: 'don't boast against the truth and lie against it'. Others (e.g., Ropes, Mayor) say that it is connected only with the second verb: 'don't lie against the truth'. The latter is preferable, since the boast is about wisdom and not about truth. Also, this interpretation avoids a measure of tautology.

you should not boast *that you are wise*, The present imperative κατακαυχᾶσθε 'boast' occurs with μή, which could imply that they should stop an action that was going on. However, since this imperative is functioning as a negative APPEAL in contrast to the positive APPEAL in v. 13, it is more likely that this is a general principle: they should not boast of being wise if their lives were not characterized by the humility that comes from true wisdom. In many languages it is necessary to supply the content of the boast. It is supplied here based on the context.

***for in so doing* you are lying against the true message.** The second verb, ψεύδεσθε 'lie', is connected to the first verb by καί 'and' and is also a present imperative. Commentators differ as to the relationship between the two verbs. Some (e.g., Laws, Huther) consider them parallel or alternatives, as in NIV's "do not boast about it or deny the truth." Others (e.g., Martin, Mayor) say that there is a closer relationship, cause and effect, for example, as in NASB's "do not be arrogant and *so* lie against the truth." The latter view is preferable since the second verb seems to be an evaluation of the first, even though both verbs refer to the same situation. (Adamson considers the entire construction a hendiadys: he translates μὴ κατακαυχᾶσθε ... ἀληθείας as "glory not in your lies against the truth.") Moreover, it is apparent that semantically there is a causal relationship here, even though, grammatically, coordination appears to be signaled by καί. Zerwick (pp. 152–54) in his discussion of the particle καί calls this "the 'neutral use' of simple καί," citing examples such as Matt. 5:15, "they light a candle and set it ... on a candlestick καί it lights all," pointing out that "so that" would express the meaning of καί better in such a use. The rendering in the display reflects his view: these are not separate concepts but interrelated, and therefore rendered 'for in so doing' followed by an indicative rather than a second imperative. A rendering like the one in TEV is equally acceptable: 'don't lie against the truth by boasting that you are wise'. The 'truth' here refers to the true message, as occurs in 1:18 and 5:19.

3:15a Those who have such attitudes [14a] are not wise, as God *wants them to be*, The noun phrase αὕτη ἡ σοφία 'this wisdom' is anaphoric, referring to the attitudes of jealousy and rivalry described in v. 14. Much has been written about the subject of the verb ἔστιν 'is'. Some (e.g., Huther) say that it is 'this wisdom'; others (e.g., Laws) say that 'this' is the subject and 'wisdom' the predicate nominative. According to the first view the participial phrase ἄνωθεν κατερχομένη 'coming down from above' functions in the predicate as an indefinite attributive: 'this wisdom is not one coming down from above'. According to the second view the participial phrase modifies 'wisdom': 'this is not the wisdom coming down from above'. Of course, this may be an important distinction grammatically, but there is little difference semantically: the emphasis is upon the source in both views—it is wisdom that is not from above, not God-given. In the NIV quotation marks are used to indicate that it is counterfeit wisdom. Such "wisdom" is contrasted with true wisdom from God as described in v. 17.

The noun 'wisdom' is an abstract noun, 'the quality of being wise or acting wisely'. This is an attributive and so is rendered in the display by the copula 'are' plus the adjective 'wise'.

3:15b but they are only thinking and acting as *the people of* this world *do*. The adversative ἀλλά 'but' marks the contrast between a generic statement describing what this false wisdom is not (15a) and three specific adjectives describing what it actually is, a false wisdom (15b–d). A number of commentators (e.g., Martin, Hiebert) point out that these three adjectives form a climax: each expresses increasing alienation from God. The first of the three, ἐπίγειος 'earthly', expresses a strong contrast with ἄνωθεν 'from above'. It refers to earthly motives and reflects the attitude of those who do not even consider God in their thoughts or actions.

The communication relation between 15a and 15b–d could be considered NEGATIVE-positive with the latter composed of three nuclei (15b, c, d). However, although it is true that 15b–d state the characteristics of those who act unwisely in positive grammatical form in contrast to the negative form of 15a, these are clearly negative concepts. Therefore 15a and b–d are considered GENERIC-specific to parallel the GENERIC-specific pattern within the *basis* for the positive APPEAL (3:17b being GENERIC and 17c–h specifics). The semantic content of 15a and b–d also shows the GENERIC-specific relation.

3:15c They think and act according to their own *evil* desires. The adjective ψυχική 'natural, unspiritual' is derived from ψυχή 'soul', which always has a negative connotation in the New Testament. That is, it relates to the sinful human nature. Hiebert says that "the term here describes a wisdom that springs from the mental and emotional impulses of fallen humanity and is marked by its depraved concepts, desires, and aspirations."

3:15d They do what the demons *want them to do (or,* they think and act as demons *do).* The adjective δαιμονιώδης 'demonic' is the climax of the description of those who were falsely claiming to be wise. The implication here is either that this so-called wisdom originates with demons or is similar to the way demons act. According to most commentators (e.g., Martin, Adamson, Johnson) the meaning is that their behavior was instigated by the demons themselves. This may be preferable, but the display presents both alternatives. Technically speaking, the term 'demonic' refers to demons, not to the devil only. However, the important issue is the contrast between wisdom from above and wisdom from an ungodly source. If in the receptor language the best contrast would be between God and the devil, it would be better to use 'of the devil' instead of 'demonic', as Adamson and many versions do (NIV, RSV, JBP, JB, CEV).

3:16a *It is evident that the people who are* jealous *of others* and insist on having their own way *are not wise as God wants them to be*, The conjunction γάρ 'for' introduces the grounds for the strong condemnation of ungodly wisdom in v. 15. James refers back to the attitudes of those who falsely claim to be wise, using the same nouns, ζῆλος 'jealousy' and ἐριθεία 'selfish ambition', that are in v. 14. His judgment is justified because of the disastrous results of these attitudes and consequent actions that we see in 16b.

since, when people have such attitudes, The initial conjunction ὅπου 'where' may be a marker of either cause or reason (Louw and Nida, 89.35), as in 1 Cor. 3:3. In the display, 'when' is used, but the reason-RESULT relation is more in focus than circumstance-NUCLEUS, so the communication relation between 16a and 16b is labeled reason-RESULT.

3:16b *the result is that* they are unruly The noun ἀκαταστασία 'disorder' refers to turmoil in the church. In 1:8 James uses the adjective form of this noun to characterize a 'double-minded man' and in 3:8 to describe the uncontrolled tongue.

and do all kinds of evil things. The noun phrase πᾶν φαῦλον πρᾶγμα 'every evil practice' concludes the discussion of false wisdom. The adjective φαῦλος 'evil' also means 'worthless', a description of deeds that are bad because no good results come from them. But its primary meaning in the New Testament is the opposite of good. Davids (1982) says, "Rivalry and party spirit destroy the cohesiveness of the Christian community, which is built on unity and love."

3:17a But when people are wise as God *wants them to be*, Verse 17 is the last segment of a chiastic structure (see "Intent and Paragraph Pattern" under the display of 3:13–17). Here James presents the characteristics of true godly wisdom, not as an intellectual concept but rather as the kinds of behavior such wisdom produces. The verse begins with the conjunction δέ 'but', marking the beginning of the *basis* for the APPEAL in v. 13. This conjunction, along with the fronted noun clause ἡ . . . ἄνωθεν σοφία 'the from above wisdom', also marks a switch of topic: from the wisdom that is *not* from above to the wisdom that *is* from above. The adverb 'from above' that precedes 'wisdom' emphasizes it. This same adverb is used in 1:17 to indicate divine origin. In both places it is a metonymy for 'God'.

3:17b they are most importantly *inwardly good*. The first adjective in the list of wise behaviors is ἁγνή 'pure'. It is preceded by the particles πρῶτον μέν 'firstly', which expression not only distinguishes ἁγνή from the rest of the adjectives but also makes prominent the fact that the very nature of godly wisdom is purity. Hiebert says, "This virtue stands first, not in the matters of time but in importance. It is the source and key to all the following qualities." Commentators agree that purity is primarily an inner quality closely associated with the concept of holiness, since it comes from the same root as the adjective ἅγιος 'holy'. The term is generic, hence rendered 'good' here. Stulac points out that the "foremost reason for valuing wisdom is that it will lead people to do what is morally right."

3:17c *Specifically*, they act peaceably toward others, The adverb ἔπειτα 'then' introduces the rest of the adjectives describing godly wisdom. The communication relation between the first adjective in 17b and this list in 17c–h is best described as GENERIC-specific, since all of these are specific kinds of behavior that flow from the inner purity of this wisdom. The first three of these specific traits are in strong contrast to ζῆλος 'jealousy' and ἐριθεία 'selfish ambition', the characteristics of false wisdom in vv. 14 and 16. The adjective εἰρηνική 'peaceable' in this context refers to desiring peace and working to bring it about among others.

3:17d they are considerate of others, The next adjective ἐπιεικής 'gentle' includes the thought of respect for the feelings of others and not insisting on one's own rights. Semantically it is closely related to the noun πραΰτης 'gentleness' in 13c, the distinguishing characteristic of true wisdom.

3:17e they are willing to yield to others, The adjective εὐπειθής 'compliant' indicates a willingness to listen to others and defer to them if no moral principle is involved (Moo). It is a difficult term to define precisely and is variously translated as "submissive" (NIV), "considerate" (JB), "approachable" (JBP), and "willing to yield to others" (NLT). The display follows the NLT rendering, which clearly indicates the opposite of the self-seeking decried in 14a.

3:17f and they have compassion on others and do all kinds of good things for others. The adjective phrase μεστὴ ἐλέους καὶ καρπῶν ἀγαθῶν 'full of mercy and good fruits' is the only compound phrase in the 17c–h list. It links two characteristics closely together. Both are practical demonstrations of love and stand in contrast with πᾶν φαῦλον πρᾶγμα 'every evil practice' in v. 16. These concepts parallel 1:27, where 'true religion' is evidenced by acts of kindness. The very phrase 'good fruits' indicates the expectancy of results in the lives of those who have true wisdom, with the plural indicating a variety of good works.

3:17g They think fairly about others (*or*, they are not ambivalent in their thinking), The adjective ἀδιάκριτος 'impartial/unwavering' is formed from the verb διακρίνω, which basically means 'divide', prefixed by α, which is a negativizer. Literally it means 'undivided in mind'. It may be interpreted in two different ways: (1) Some commentators and versions (e.g., Moo, Martin; NIV, TEV, NJB, NAB, NLT) favor the active sense, with the meaning of 'impartial', based on the use of the verb διακρίνω 'discriminate' in an active sense in 2:4. Seen this way, this statement is an attempt to counteract the disunity in the church (Laws). (2) Others (e.g., Davids 1982, Tasker; RSV, WEY, JBP, NASB, REB) take it as a passive, with the meaning of 'unwavering', based on the use of the same verb in the passive sense of 'doubt' in 1:6. Davids (1982) says that this view fits better with the final adjective (17h). Since both interpretations are acceptable, both are presented in the display.

3:17h and they are sincere (or, they do not deceive others). The adjective ἀνυπόκριτος 'sincere, without hypocrisy', like all the adjectives in 17c–h, modifies 'the wisdom from above'. It means free from all pretense (Hiebert) and like the other adjectives is considered a description of the behavior of those who possess such wisdom. Most commentators and versions (e.g., Davids 1982, Mayor, Moo; NIV, REB, NLT, RSV, CEV) say or imply that this is an inner quality of a person that would facilitate honest relationships (Martin). Such individuals are what they claim to be. Tasker gives the meaning as "*without hypocrisy* in all human relationships." Since the context largely focuses on conduct toward others, this idea is given as a valid alternative. In some languages 'sincere' may also be best expressed in relation to others.

BOUNDARIES AND COHERENCE

The initial boundary for the 3:13–17 unit was discussed under 3:1–12 and the final boundary under 3:1–17.

Lexical coherence is shown by the noun σοφία in vv. 13, 15, and 17 and the cognate adjective σοφός 'wise' in v. 13. The noun phrases καλῆς ἀναστροφῆς '(by) good conduct' in v. 13 and καρπῶν ἀγαθῶν 'of good fruit/deeds' in v. 17 add further coherence.

Semantic coherence is shown by the concept of 'wisdom not from above' in vv. 15–16 contrasted with 'wisdom from above' in v. 17. Godly wisdom is demonstrated by good deeds and attitudes; wisdom not from God, by attitudes expressed by the nouns ζῆλος jealousy and ἐριθεία 'selfish ambition' in vv. 14 and 16.

The relational coherence of 3:13–17 is seen in its chiastic structure (see "Intent and Paragraph Pattern" for this unit). In the ABB'A' chiastic ordering, δέ occurs at the switches from A to B (14a) and from B' to A' (17a).

A few commentators (Hiebert, Kistemaker, Adamson) and versions (NIV, NLT) divide the unit between v. 16 and v. 17, since vv. 14–15 describe worldly wisdom and v. 16, in contrast, presents true wisdom. However, the topic of wisdom runs throughout, so we consider this a break between lower-level constituents.

PROMINENCE AND THEME

In the 3:13–17 paragraph there are two *APPEALS* and two *bases*. Because these are integral to the hortatory paragraph pattern, the theme statement is drawn from all four. However, in the theme the negative *APPEAL* (the second *APPEAL*) and its *basis* are placed before the positive *APPEAL* (the first *APPEAL*) and its *basis* since the proper emphasis is best achieved in that order. Actually, 14a functions as a partial summary of the *basis* for the second *APPEAL* (15a–16b).

SECTION CONSTITUENT 3:18
(Expository Propositional Cluster: Axiomatic Basis of 3:1-17)

THEME: Those who act peaceably toward others will cause the whole community to act righteously.	
RELATIONAL STRUCTURE	CONTENTS
┌─ REASON ───────	3:18a Those who act **peaceably** toward others cause others to act peaceably
└─ RESULT ───────	3:18b with the result that they all live together doing good. [MET]

INTENT AND STRUCTURE

The 3:18 propositional cluster forms the *axiomatic basis* for the 3:1–17 subsection. Since its only finite verb is indicative, this is an expository unit. There is no paragraph pattern since it is not a paragraph. Rather, it is a reason-RESULT construction that motivates the readers to correct attitudes and actions. James' intent is to reinforce the message of 3:1–17 regarding the need for conduct pleasing to God and thus affect the behavior of the readers by stimulating them to peaceful relationships and righteousness.

NOTES

3:18a Those who act <u>peaceably</u> toward others
The v. 18 proverb functions as the emphatic conclusion to the 3:1–17 unit (Martin). Its predominant theme is the concept of peace introduced in v. 17. This concept is closely associated with the concept of righteousness, which is suggested in v. 17 by 'good fruits' and is carried over in v. 18.

The final noun phrase in v. 18, τοῖς ποιοῦσιν εἰρήνην 'by/for those making peace' is interpreted by many commentators (e.g., Davids 1982, Tasker; NIV, TEV, NJB, NASB) as the agent of the action: 'by those making peace'. Others (e.g., Mayor, Huther; NAB, NRSV) say that though the dative may be used for agency, the more natural usage is dative of advantage: 'for those making peace'. Still others (e.g., Hiebert, Adamson) say that it indicates both the agent and the beneficiaries. The first view is preferable, since there is no other viable agent for the verb. Almost all versions (NIV, TEV, JB, JBP, CEV, NCV) translate this phrase as the subject of an active verb.

cause others to act peaceably The noun phrase καρπὸς ... δικαιοσύνης 'the fruit of righteousness' is the subject of the passive verb σπείρεται 'is sown'. This verb is in the present tense, which indicates customary action. Only NRSV, RSV, and KJV retain the passive construction.

The prepositional phrase ἐν εἰρήνῃ 'in peace' appears redundant, but it was undoubtedly used to emphasize the concept of peace. The phrase itself is fronted for emphasis. It may indicate the manner of the sowing (Davids 1982), the circumstances in which the seed is sown (Hiebert), or what is sown (Blue). The significant fact is that peace is necessary to produce righteousness. In the display 'is sown in peace' is rendered 'cause others to act peaceably'.

3:18b with the result that they all live together doing good. The noun phrase καρπὸς ... δικαιοσύνης 'fruit of righteousness' may be understood in one of two ways. Most commentators (e.g., Davids 1982, Alford) take 'of righteousness' as an appositional genitive: 'the fruit that consists of righteousness'. Others (e.g., Ropes, Lenski) take it as a subjective genitive: 'the fruit that righteousness produces', based on verses such as Isa. 32:17 and Luke 3:8. The former view is preferable in this context. Strictly speaking, it is seed rather than fruit that is sown, as brought out in the NASB, "the seed whose fruit is righteousness," and the TEV, "Goodness is the harvest that is produced from the seed the peacemakers plant in peace." Notice that although these renderings retain the figure (which is a live metaphor), it is not necessary to retain the image in translating. It is rendered in the display as 'doing good', since the righteousness that is brought about by the peacemakers refers not to justification but to the upright conduct that is pleasing to God. Stulac says,

> James wants peace for the church because peace is the context in which righteousness can flourish. This is the positive side of what James said in 1:20, that human anger does not bring about the righteous life that God desires.

BOUNDARIES AND COHERENCE

The initial boundary of 3:18 was discussed under 3:1–17 and the final one under 3:1–18. It coheres as one Greek sentence.

PROMINENCE AND THEME

The 3:18 unit consists of a REASON and RESULT. Generally, RESULT is more prominent than a reason, but here the reason has marked prominence by virtue of the emphasis upon the concept of peace. Thus both labels are shown in upper-case letters in the display, and the theme statement is drawn from both units.

DIVISION CONSTITUENT 4:1–17 (Hortatory Section: Appeal₄ of 1:19–5:11)

THEME: You are fighting among yourselves because of your evil desires. Be sad because you have sinned, and humble yourselves before God. If anyone knows the right thing that he ought to do yet doesn't do it, he is sinning.

MACROSTRUCTURE	CONTENTS
APPEAL	4:1–16 You are fighting among yourselves because of your evil desires and you have become God's enemies. He opposes the proud but helps those who act humbly. Therefore be sad because you have sinned, and humble yourselves before God. Stop speaking evil against each other and don't boast about what you will do in the future.
axiomatic basis	4:17 Certainly if anyone knows the right thing that he ought to do yet doesn't do it, he is sinning.

INTENT AND MACROSTRUCTURE

In the 4:1–17 unit James addresses the problems in the Christian community that are the result of problems in individual lives. Many of them had been corrupted by envy and selfish ambition; bitter quarrels and strife among believers were the result. James wants them to learn to live together in love and peace with each other. His intent is to affect their behavior and also their attitudes by warning them of their present condition (4:1–16) and the consequences (4:17) if they do not respond to God in obedience by returning to him in repentance and humility. The section comprises an *APPEAL* (4:1–16) and an *axiomatic basis* (4:17) and is therefore hortatory.

This section is the peak of the epistle. It begins with two provocative rhetorical questions in 4:1. After that, the negative-positive declarations in 4:2–3 and the harsh vocative in 4:4, along with two more rhetorical questions (vv. 4–5), seem to move the discourse along to a new height. Then comes the core of the peak (vv. 7–10), which gives unusual rhetorical prominence to the unit by virtue of its frequent imperatives one right after the other (for other prominence markers in 7–10 see "Intent and Paragraph Pattern" under 4:7–10). The sandwich structure in vv. 13–16 also marks this unit as distinct. In addition, the unusual number of words or phrases that are forefronted for emphasis (ten in 4:1–17) further marks this unit as the epistle's hortatory peak.

BOUNDARIES AND COHERENCE

The initial boundary of the 4:1–17 unit was discussed under 3:1–18. The beginning of the next unit at 5:1 is marked by a change of topic: from a need for repentance to retribution for the rich. It is also marked by the vocative οἱ πλούσιοι 'rich men'.

Lexical coherence between the two constituents of this section is shown by the noun phrase ποιητὴς νόμου 'doer of the law' in v. 11 and καλὸν ποιεῖν 'to do good' and μὴ ποιοῦντι 'not doing (it)' in v. 17. Throughout the epistle, James has a very specialized usage of the verb 'do'. In chapter 1 he refers to those who hear the word but are not doers of what they hear (1:23–25). In chapter 2 he tells his readers to speak and do as those who will be judged through a law of freedom (2:12). Here in chapter 4, as elsewhere, James is using 'do' in the sense of correct moral conduct.

Some commentators (e.g., Ropes, Martin) consider 4:1–5:20 as a high-level unit with the general topic of the contrast between worldly conduct and Christian conduct. Hiebert similarly views 4:1–5:12 as faith's reactions to worldly conduct. But we reject such broad macrostructural divisions as too general to adequately reflect the cyclical structure of James. It should be noted, however, that these analysts break down their high-level unit into lower-level units that are remarkably similar to ours.

PROMINENCE AND THEME

Elements of both the *APPEAL* and *axiomatic basis* are represented in the theme statement of the 4:1–17 unit because these are integral parts of a hortatory unit. The desperate need for repentance is reinforced here by the reminder that obedience to the known will of God is necessary if one is to avoid direct sin.

SECTION CONSTITUENT 4:1–16 (Hortatory Subsection: Appeal of 4:1–17)

> *THEME: You are fighting among yourselves because of your evil desires and you have become God's enemies. He opposes the proud but helps those who act humbly. Therefore be sad because you have sinned, and humble yourselves before God. Stop speaking evil against each other and don't boast about what you will do in the future.*

MACROSTRUCTURE	CONTENTS
basis₁	4:1-3 You are fighting among yourselves because of your evil desires and you are never getting what you want because you pray with wrong motives.
basis₂	4:4-6 You are unfaithful to God and are acting as evil people do, so you have become God's enemies, but God wants to help you. He opposes the proud but helps those who act humbly.
GENERIC APPEAL (core of hortatory peak of the epistle)	4:7-10 Therefore submit yourselves to God and resist the devil. Stop doing and thinking wrongly, and be sad because you have sinned. Indeed, humble yourselves before God and he will exalt you spiritually.
specific appeal₁	4:11-12 Stop speaking evil against one another and thus condemning each other. Only God has the right to condemn others.
specific appeal₂	4:13-16 You should not boast about what you will do in the future, since life is transitory; rather, you should plan to do whatever God wants you to do, since boasting about what you want to do, rather than considering the will of God, is sinful.

INTENT AND MACROSTRUCTURE

The 4:1–16 subsection has a blown-up hortatory paragraph pattern. The 4:7–10 GENERIC APPEAL is supported by two *bases*, 4:1–3 and 4:4–6; it is followed by two *specific appeals,* 4:11–12 and 4:13–16. James' purpose here is to stimulate the readers to genuine repentance for the sins alluded to or gently condemned throughout the letter (1:13–15, 19–21; 2:1–4, 14–17; 3:9–12, 14–16) and here severely censored (4:1–6). The *basis* units are expository. They state clearly the need for repentance. The GENERIC APPEAL is introduced by οὖν 'therefore' and is the core of the epistle's hortatory peak (4:1–17). Here in the core James gives the solution to the great problems within the Christian community (see "Intent and Paragraph Pattern" of 4:7–10). "By drawing out the ultimate consequences of worldly behaviour in this way, James seeks to prick the consciences of his readers and to stimulate their repentance" (Moo, p. 144). Basic to the concept of repentance is the attitude of humility, that is, acknowledging one's total dependence upon God, and this is reflected in vv. 7 and 10.

The two paragraphs following the GENERIC APPEALS are specific applications to situations faced by the believers in their lives. The first (4:11–12) addresses their lack of humility in their judgmental relations with other believers, whereas the second (4:13–16) addresses their self-confident arrogance of reckoning without God. In each of these, James' intent is to cause them to recognize and submit to God's authority.

BOUNDARIES AND COHERENCE

The initial boundary of the 4:1–16 unit was discussed under 3:1–18. The beginning of the next unit at 4:17 is marked by a change of topic: from evidences of worldliness to a warning to those who willfully disobey. The conjunction οὖν 'therefore' in 4:17 introduces a clause that semantically acts as a summary or *axiomatic basis* of the entire preceding unit (4:1–16) and not just of the previous paragraph (4:13–16). The macrostructural pattern of APPEAL-basis throughout the epistle reinforces this break.

There is lexical and semantic coherence between 4:4–6 and 4:7–10 by virtue of the noun ταπεινοῖς 'humble ones' in v. 6 and its cognate verb ταπεινώθητε 'be humbled' in v. 10 and also the unusual, harsh vocatives in both paragraphs: μοιχαλίδες 'adulteresses' in v. 4 and ἁμαρτωλοί 'sinners' and δίψυχοι 'two-souled' in v. 8. Referential coherence in the 4:1–16 subsection is seen in the pronouns that reflect interpersonal relationships: ἐν ὑμῖν 'among you' in v. 1 and the reciprocal pronoun ἀλλήλων 'one another' in v. 11.

Some commentators (e.g., Dibelius, Davids 1982) propose that 4:13–5:6a is a high-level unit; others (e.g., Moo) propose 4:13–5:11. They all point to the introductory phrase ἄγε νῦν 'come now' in 4:13 and 5:1 as well as the general topic of arrogance. Johnson (p. 292) defends the slightly broader unit of 4:11–5:6 with the same theme of arrogance: ". . . an identifiable thematic thread can be seen to run through it. Whether those addressed are 'brothers' (4:11), or are 'those who say' (4:13), or are 'the rich' (5:1), their behavior is attacked by the author."

There is admittedly a relation between 4:13–17 and 5:1–6 both in style (the introductory phrase 'come now') and content (the topic of riches). However, the analysis in the display is preferable for the following reasons:

1. There are clear differences between 4:13–17 and 5:1–6. For example, in 5:1–6 there is no call for repentance but only doom for the rich.
2. The introductory phrase 'come now' is an attention getter (Tasker, Blue) rather than a cohesive device. In its occurrences here (in 4:13 and 5:1) it is used in changing the address to a different group of people (Mitton).
3. Verse 4:17 is a maxim characterized by the shift from the second to the third person and from the specific to the general. Although a few (e.g., Johnson) consider such maxims as hinges between units within a larger unit, the majority (e.g., Ropes, Davids 1982, Ekstrom) refer to them as summaries at the conclusion of a unit. As such, 4:17 marks a major break between the 4:1–17 and 5:1–11 sections.
4. The vocative and imperative of 5:1 characterize that verse as beginning a new unit.

PROMINENCE AND THEME

The most prominent constituent of the 4:1–16 subsection is the GENERIC APPEAL. It is therefore the heart of the 4:1–16 theme. The *bases* that precede the GENERIC APPEAL and the *specific appeals* that follow it are also included since they are integral parts of a hortatory paragraph pattern.

SUBSECTION CONSTITUENT 4:1–3 (Expository Paragraph: Basis₁ of 4:7–10)

THEME: You are fighting among yourselves because of your evil desires and you are never getting what you want because you pray with wrong motives.

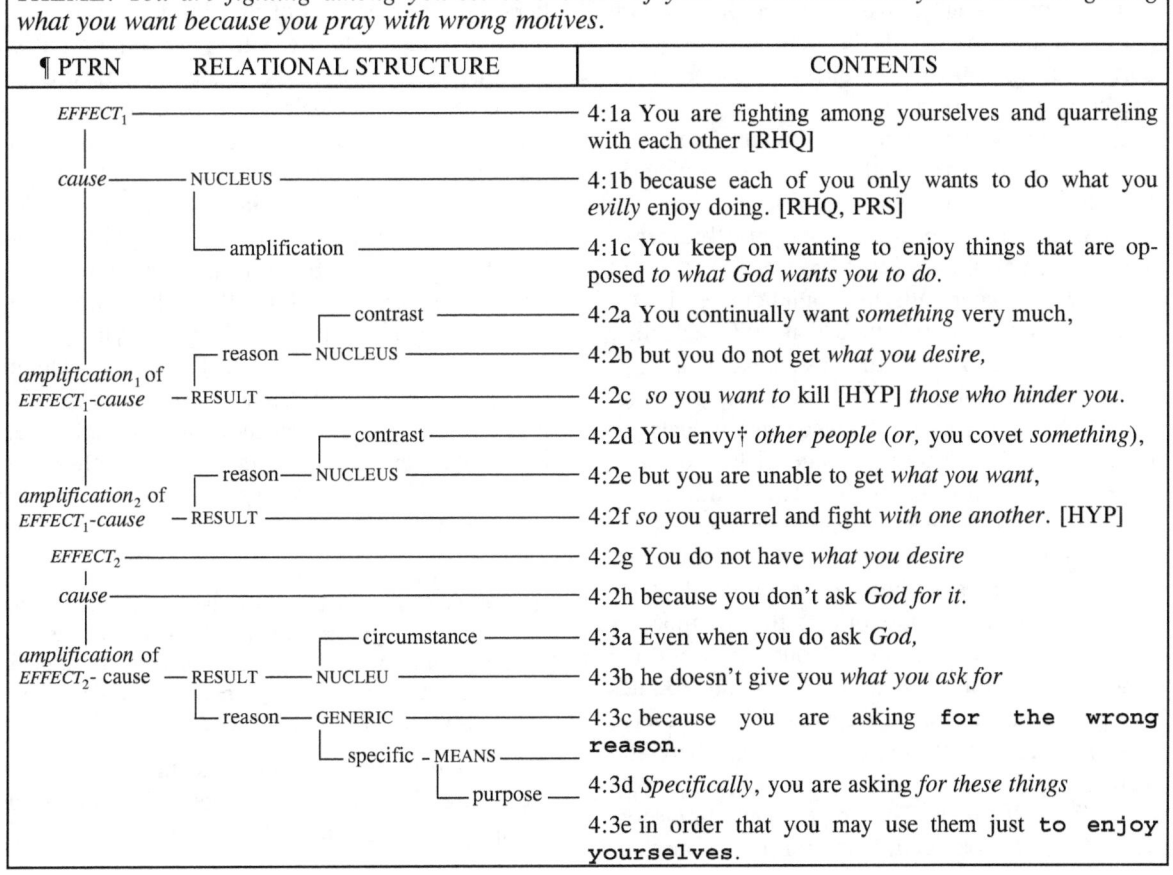

INTENT AND PARAGRAPH PATTERN

In the 4:1-3 paragraph James describes the open hostility among believers in the church. The paragraph comprises an *EFFECT* (1a) followed by a *cause* (1b-c) with two *amplifications* of the *EFFECT-cause* (2a-c and 2d-f), then another *EFFECT* (2g) followed by its *cause* (2h) and an *amplification* of this second *EFFECT-cause* (3a-e). The paragraph is therefore expository. Although there are two *EFFECT-cause* clusters within the unit, the coherence provided by references to frustrated desire for pleasure in both clusters unites them into one paragraph. The first cause of factions within the community is quarrels between individuals, which are due ultimately to their own sinful desire for pleasures. The second cause of frustrated desire is the lack or misuse of prayer. James' intent in this paragraph is to make the readers aware of the real source of the conflicts in the church.

NOTES

4:1a You are fighting among yourselves and quarreling As in 3:13, James uses a rhetorical question without any connecting particle to introduce his next topic. This topic arises naturally from the preceding discussion, since the question points to the source of the conflict so vividly portrayed in 3:14-16. The question is introduced by the interrogative πόθεν 'from where?', which occurs twice in the sentence, showing the depth of James' feeling as he addresses this problem in the church. It is also significant that the commonly used vocative ἀδελφοί 'brothers', which normally marks a paragraph, does not occur. James later calls them adulteresses in 4:4 and sinners and double-minded in 4:8, reflecting his disapproval of their attitudes and actions.

The nouns πόλεμος 'war' and μάχη 'fighting' mean physical conflict between individuals or nations, the first denoting a state of hostility and the second specific outbursts. The plural forms here suggest repeated or continuing conflict. In combination, the terms are virtually synonymous. Moore (p. 60) calls them a figurative doublet. Actually they are metaphorical; the reference is to violent verbal disputes. Doublets are often rendered with only one term, but because James uses these same two concepts in 2f (in reverse order), it seems best to retain both terms here and also in 2f.

with each other The prepositional phrase ἐν ὑμῖν 'among you' could be translated 'in you' and taken to refer to inner feelings of tension and frustration, but the context clearly indicates that the reference is to conflicts within the group.

4:1b because each of you only wants to do what you *evilly* enjoy doing. The second rhetorical question calls for an affirmative response and gives the answer to the first question. The adverb ἐντεῦθεν 'from this' carries on the thought of the preceding πόθεν 'from where?' and emphasizes the cause of the conflict among them. The noun ἡδονή 'pleasure, selfish desire' is the term from which the English word *hedonism* is derived. Often, as here, it has the negative connotation of sinful, self-indulgent pleasure (Moo). As in 1:13-15, James does not blame the devil or any other external force; the source is clearly their own evil impulses.

4:1c You keep on wanting to enjoy things that are opposed to *what God wants you to do*. The participle στρατευομένων 'battling' is a dead warfare metaphor that expresses the concept of opposition. The interpretation of the prepositional phrase ἐν τοῖς μέλεσιν ὑμῶν 'in your members' is essential in understanding the meaning here. Although a few (e.g., Martin) say that the 'members' are the members of the church, the majority of commentators (e.g., Alford, Laws, Adamson) say that the reference is to an internal struggle within each individual, as in 3:6. The latter is preferable because the topic under focus is the source, not the result, of the conflict. The subject of the participle 'battling' is 'your selfish desires', but what is being battled against is not stated. There are two main interpretations of this inner struggle: (1) A few (Burdick, Huther) say that they are battling against everything that stands in the way of their gratification. (2) Others (e.g., Davids 1982, Adamson) essentially say that it is a battle against what they know is right (i.e., their conscience) or against doing right (i.e., righteousness). Tasker summarizes the second view as follows:

> He does not say specifically, as Peter says of lusts (1 Pet. ii:11), that they 'war against the soul', though that is implied; for so long as they have the upper hand man is prevented from doing what he was originally created to do—acknowledge and render obedience to the will of God."

This is the preferable view, and the rendering in the display is based on it in view of the emphasis on upright conduct in 3:18.

4:2 The exegesis of v. 2 is complicated by the difficulty of deciding the relationship of the various verbs in the series—the ancient manuscripts have no punctuation to guide us. One approach is to postulate a series of clauses coming in pairs with contrasting positive and negative verbs, which puts the emphasis on frustrated desires, as in the NIV:

> You want something but don't get it.
> You kill and covet, but you cannot have what you want.
> You quarrel and fight. You do not have, because you do not ask God.

The other approach is represented by the RSV:

> You desire and do not have; so you kill.
> And you covet and cannot obtain; so you fight and wage war.
> You do not have, because you do not ask.

In the second approach the emphasis is placed on frustrated desire's leading to violence. It is preferred because it avoids the anticlimax that 'kill' followed by 'covet' would produce. Also, in this approach the focus is on reason-RESULT, and this focus fits better in the context. (For a full discussion of the two alternatives, see Mayor, pp. 134-37, and Laws, pp. 169-70.)

4:2a You continually want *something* very much, The verb ἐπιθυμέω 'desire greatly' that is used here is a more common and more generic term than ἥδομαι 'desire'. However, it has an evil connotation in this context and refers to the same concept as the noun cognate of ἥδομαι in 1b (Moo). Louw and Nida (25.20) express this negative aspect of desire as "lust," and it is so translated in some versions (KJV, NASB). What these people wanted is not stated but the context indicates that it was things or honors for their own pleasure and self-advancement. The present tense implies continuity, which in the display is expressed by the adverb 'continually'. Although the general term 'something' is supplied as the object in the display, in translation it would be best not to use a term that is limited to material possessions, since the context indicates that positions of power are also involved.

4:2b but you do not get *what you desire*, The verb phrase οὐκ ἔχετε 'have not' shows that their self-seeking was often frustrated. The object is supplied from the context.

4:2c *so* you want to kill *those who hinder you*. Much has been written about the meaning of the verb φονεύω 'kill'. A few commentators (e.g., Adamson, Mayor), finding it too extreme, agree with a conjecture proposed by Erasmus, who read φθονεῖτε 'you envy' for φονεύετε 'you kill', but this has no manuscript support. Others (e.g., Hiebert, Huther) interpret 'kill' figuratively and say it means internal hatred as in Matt. 5:21-22, (equivalent to the figures 'wars' and 'fighting' of v. 1). Davids (1994) says that it probably refers to killing with words rather than literal murder. But there are some (e.g., Martin, Ropes) who say that it should be taken literally, pointing out the activities of the Zealot movement. Moo, among others, adopts a compromise between these latter two views. He regards it as "that extreme to which frustrated desire, if not checked, may lead." For this reason it is rendered in the display as the desire to kill. This may include actual murders, but the focus is kept on the bitter attitude and avoids implying (wrongly) that murder was common in the early church. There is no historical validation of such acts.

The communication relation between 2a-b and 2c is reason-RESULT; so although there is no conjunction between 2b and 2c, the implicit 'so' is supplied here, as also in a number of versions (TEV, JB, REB, NLT, NASB, NRSV). The situation referred to in 2a-c is essentially the same as the situation James deplores in 1a-c; thus it is best seen as an *amplification* of the EFFECT-*cause* in 1a-c and not just of the *cause* in 1b-c.

4:2d You envy *other people* (*or*, you covet *something*), Propositions 2d-f are structurally parallel with 2a-c, each of them expressing a reason-RESULT relation. Both are amplifications of the EFFECT-*cause* relation in 1a-c. Some commentators (e.g., Burdick, Bratcher) imply that the verb ζηλόω 'envy/desire' in 2d repeats the idea already expressed by the verb ἐπιθυμέω 'desire greatly' in 2a. Others (e.g., Tasker, Davids 1989) favor Hort's interpretation, that the two verbs, though having the component of 'desire' in common, are different and that ζηλόω here means 'envy of position/rank/fame'. Mayor contends that the verb used here denotes a feeling toward a person rather than toward a thing in contrast to the verb ἐπιθυμέω 'desire greatly' in 2a. In another language it might be clearer to say 'you envy those who have more authority than you have'. Both views are acceptable, but the latter is preferred (hence first in the display), since the focus of the unit seems to be more on personal relationships than possessions. The prominence of humility in the whole subsection (4:1–16) supports this.

4:2e–f but you are unable to get *what you want,* **so you quarrel and fight** *with one another.* With the verbs μάχομαι '(to) fight' and πολεμέω '(to) war' James returns to the topic he originally introduced in v. 1 about the cause of the friction. (These verbs echo the cognate nouns in v. 1.) Here he shows that the cause of such a state is frustrated desire. Concerning the implicit 'so', see the last paragraph of the note on 4:2c.

4:2g–h You do not have *what you desire* **because you don't ask** *God for it.* Virtually every commentator agrees that the verb αἰτέω 'ask' here refers to prayer. Most versions correctly either supply the implicit 'God' or render it 'pray', implying that the reason they failed to obtain the thing they wanted was a lack of prayer, probably because they were not rightly related to God. The communication relation between 2g and 2h is EFFECT-cause, which is indicated by the preposition διά 'because' in 2h.

4:3a–b Even when you do ask *God***, he doesn't give you** *what you ask for* The verb αἰτεῖτε 'you ask' appears to be contradictory to what James has just said in 2h. One way to resolve this difficulty is to say that some didn't pray whereas others did. A more likely explanation is that although sometimes they failed to pray, at other times they did pray but with the wrong motives. The latter is reflected in the display. CEV has "Yet even when you do pray. . . ." Similar connectives occur in other versions (e.g., TEV, NIV, JBP, REB).

Much has been written about the fact that the verb 'ask', which is in the middle voice in the previous clause (2h), occurs here in the active and in 3c again in the middle voice. Some (e.g., Ropes, Moo) say it is purely stylistic with no difference in meaning. Others (e.g., Hiebert, Lenski) say that the middle implies asking in one's own personal interest. Perhaps James' switch to the active voice from his usual middle may be a deliberate reference to the teaching of Jesus in Matt. 7:7 (Davids 1982). These are possible implications; however, it is probably not necessary to make any of this explicit in translation, since in the context itself it is clearly stated that they asked wrongly for their own pleasures.

4:3c because you are asking **for the wrong reason.** The adverb κακῶς 'wrongly' describes the manner of asking and stands in an emphatic position before the verb. Several versions (TEV, NIV, REB, NASB) translate it as "with wrong motives." The nature of the wrong is explained in the purpose clause in 3e.

4:3d–e *Specifically***, you are asking** *for these things* **in order that you may use them just to enjoy yourselves.** The prepositional phrase ἐν ταῖς ἡδοναῖς ὑμῶν 'in your pleasures' is forefronted, emphasizing the motivation for their prayers, which was to indulge their own evil desires. The communication relation between 3c and 3d–e is GENERIC-specific. As Tasker (p. 88) says, "As long as they allow their lives to be governed by pleasure, real satisfaction, consisting of true peace, full contentment, and solid joy, will always be beyond their reach."

BOUNDARIES AND COHERENCE

The initial boundary of the 4:1–3 unit was discussed under 3:1–18. The beginning of the next unit at 4:4 is marked by the vocative μοιχαλίδες 'adulteresses' and a rhetorical question. There is also a change of topic: from conflicts arising from evil desires to the peril of worldliness.

The lexical coherence of the 4:1–3 unit is shown by the noun ἡδονή 'pleasure, selfish desire' in vv. 1 and 3 and the verb ἐπιθυμέω '(to) desire', which is in the same semantic domain, in v. 2. The metaphor about battling in v. 2 along with the nouns πόλεμος 'war' and μάχη 'fighting' in v. 1 as well as their cognate verbs μάχομαι '(to) fight' and πολεμέω '(to) war' in v. 2 also show coherence. These are presented in a sandwich structure that adds coherence:

A wars and fights among you (1a)
   B you desire and have not (2a–b)
A' you fight and you war (2f)

PROMINENCE AND THEME

The two EFFECT-cause clusters of the 4:1–3 unit are in a conjoined relation. Both deal with the source of the conflict in the church caused by evil desires. Thus both are naturally prominent and the theme is therefore drawn from both.

SUBSECTION CONSTITUENT 4:4–6 (Expository Paragraph: Basis₂ of 4:7–10)

THEME: You are unfaithful to God and are acting as evil people do, so you have become God's enemies, but God wants to help you. He opposes the proud but helps those who act humbly.

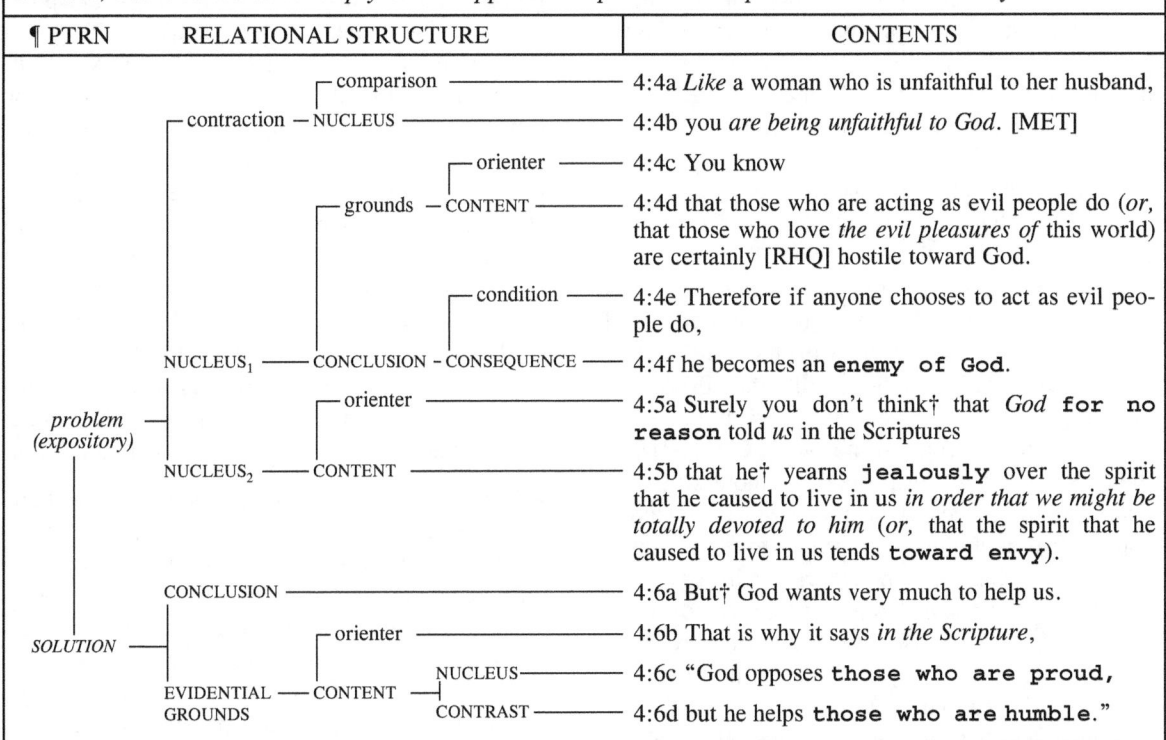

INTENT AND PARAGRAPH PATTERN

The 4:4–6 paragraph consists of an *expository problem* (4:4a–5b) followed by a SOLUTION (4:6a–d) and is thus expository. James' intent is to make the readers aware that they are acting hostilely toward God and that they must choose between worldly pleasures and devotion to God. The initial vocative (4a–b) is a metaphor, a rebuke for abandoning their commitment to God. This rebuke is strengthened by the contrast in 4c–f between friendship with the world and friendship with God. In v. 5 James presents the *problem* from God's perspective: God desires our complete devotion. The SOLUTION, in 6a–d, is the availability of God's grace to help us meet the standards God longs for us to achieve. In fact, he opposes those who proudly choose their own pleasure but helps those who humbly submit to him.

An alternative interpretation is that the *problem* in 5a–b is another picture of man's sinfulness, not God's jealous desire for their devotion. If this interpretation is followed, the SOLUTION in 6a–d is the grace of God, which is able to overcome our evil desires. The alternative rendering of 4:5b is based on this interpretation.

NOTES

4:4a–b Like a woman who is unfaithful to her husband, you *are being unfaithful to God*. The noun μοιχαλίδες 'adulteresses', which is in the feminine case, was undoubtedly interpreted literally by some, since a textual variant with inferior support added the masculine noun μοιχοί 'adulterers' to broaden the application. However, the GNT has the shorter reading with an A rating, indicating that the text is certain. Almost all modern commentators interpret the expression metaphorically, pointing out that in the Old Testament the Israelites' unfaithfulness to God was often compared to that of an unfaithful wife. (Oesterley is one who takes it literally.)

4:4c You know The verb phrase οὐκ οἴδατε 'don't you know' introduces a rhetorical question that implies an affirmative answer. It is rephrased in the display as a positive statement.

**4:4d that those who are acting as evil people do (*or*, that those who love *the evil pleasures of*

this world) The Greek that underlies proposition 4d is an axiom in which abstract nouns express the concepts of friendship and enmity. In some languages it may be difficult, if not impossible, to speak of such concepts in abstract terms, as Louw and Nida (25.33) point out. Frequently it is necessary to relate such emotional attitudes to the individuals who manifest these traits, as in the display.

In the noun phrase ἡ φιλία τοῦ κόσμου 'the friendship of/with the world', τοῦ κόσμου is an objective genitive: "love the world" (TNT). The meaning of the word 'world' is crucial here. It is not the material creation but "unredeemed humanity as an egocentric world-system that is hostile to God" (Hiebert). In the preceding paragraph (3:13–17) about godly wisdom, James speaks of people who are not wise. He describes them as 'earthly, unspiritual, demonlike', and describes their lives as characterized by jealousy and selfish ambition. He refers to these same people here, and the same contrast is brought out. In the first alternative rendering 'the friendship of the world' is expressed as acting like worldly people. As Moo says, "when the believer behaves in a way characteristic of the world, he demonstrates that, at that point, his allegiance is to the world rather than to God." The second alternative is given to reflect the idea of friendship more clearly, in harmony with the 4:1–3 context.

are certainly hostile toward God. The Greek is ἔχθρα τοῦ θεοῦ 'enmity of God'. In some versions this is translated "enmity to/with God" (REB, RSV). The NIV has "hatred toward God." Others have "enemy of God" (JBP, TEV, NLT, JB), although the word here is not ἐχθρός 'enemy', as in 4f. To render it as 'enmity' or 'hostility' is better, since it makes a clearer contrast with the attitude of friendship toward the world. However, 'enemy of God' would be acceptable.

4:4e–f Therefore if anyone chooses to act as evil people do, he becomes an enemy of God. James now restates 4d as a general principle in which is added the verb βούλομαι 'choose': a deliberate choice of conduct must be made. This choice to accept the moral standards of worldly people is an action that sets them against God. The noun phrase ἐχθρὸς τοῦ θεοῦ 'enemy of God' is fronted; this emphasis shows the seriousness of such a decision.

4:5a Surely you don't think that *God* for no reason told *us* in the Scriptures The conjunction ἤ 'or' introduces a rhetorical question that gives further evidence, this time from Scripture, for the point James has been making. Thus it is the orienter of the second NUCLEUS of the *problem*. In the display the conjunction is not rendered 'or', following the NJB, TEV, and other versions. Since the question expects a negative answer, it can be expressed as a statement, as in the display. If in the receptor language a double negative ('don't think . . . for no reason') is not possible or would be misleading, it could be rendered 'You realize that God certainly meant what he said in Scripture'.

The adverb κενῶς 'vainly' is fronted, emphasizing the fact that the message that God caused to be written should have an effect on their lives.

4:5b that he yearns jealously over the spirit that he caused to live in us *in order that we might be totally devoted to him* (*or*, that the spirit that he caused to live in us tends toward envy). The words that James cites are not found in the Old Testament. Most commentators (e.g., Hiebert, Tasker, Martin) say that he was summarizing the truth expressed in several Old Testament passages or that it is a free translation of such passages as Exod. 20:5 (Buth). However, the source of the words does not affect their rendering.

The interpretation itself is very difficult, especially since the ambiguities cannot be solved by studying the Old Testament. The fact that τὸ πνεῦμα 'the spirit' may grammatically be either the subject or object of the verb and may mean either the human spirit or God's Spirit adds to the complexity. Note that the prepositional phrase πρὸς φθόνον 'to envy' is fronted and that the emphasis thus rests on the concept of jealousy. There is furthermore a textual variant in the dependent relative clause. Instead of κατῴκισεν 'he caused to live', some manuscripts have κατῴκησεν 'he/it lived'. But the GNT accepts 'he caused to live' with a B rating, "almost certain." There is also some difference in viewpoint concerning the form of the words, whether this is a question or a statement. It may be read as a question, 'Is the Spirit of God disposed to envy?', which would assume a negative reply with the meaning that the Holy Spirit is not compatible with their sinful yearnings (Motyer). However, the majority hold that it is a statement.

There are three major interpretations, stemming primarily from what the subject is taken to be. The first view (Adamson, Kistemaker; KJV, NIV, NAB, TEV, REB) is that 'the (human) spirit' is the subject of the verb ἐπιποθεῖ 'yearns': 'the spirit that God caused to live in us tends toward envious desires'. Supporters of this view note that this verb is never elsewhere used with 'God' as its subject and also that the noun form of the verb consistently represents a negative concept. They also note that 'the (human) spirit' as the subject of 'yearns' can be construed as fitting into the context (4:1–3). Although this view is not the preferred interpretation, it is represented in the display as an alternative because it is widely accepted.

The second view (Huther, Tasker, Ropes, Barclay; NRSV, TNT) is that 'God' is the subject of the verb and 'the spirit' the object: 'God yearns jealously over the spirit which he caused to live in us'. The apparent collocational difficulty can be resolved by recognizing that in the New Testament there are two terms for envy, the verb phrase used here, πρὸς φθόνον ἐπιποθεῖ 'yearns to jealousy', and the noun ζῆλος 'jealousy, envy'. Sometimes these two are used interchangeably, and sometimes ζῆλος is used of God. Therefore, since James used ζῆλος negatively of human envy in 3:14 and 16, it may be that he chose to use the phrase πρὸς φθόνον ἐπιποθεῖ of God here. From the standpoint of grammar it is more natural that both verbs in the sentence ('yearns' and 'caused to dwell') have the same subject, and 'God' is certainly the understood subject of κατῴκισεν 'caused to dwell'. An emphasis on God's jealousy for us to be devoted wholly to him is completely consistent with the context. In Old Testament imagery, which compares Israel's unfaithfulness to God with a wife's unfaithfulness to her husband, the jealousy of God for his people was part of the picture. Furthermore, ἐπιποθέω is used in a good sense in the New Testament—'to long or yearn for' something or someone. So it is more probable that πρὸς φθόνον can also be taken in a good sense (Miller). For these reasons this second view is the one preferred in the display.

There is yet a third view (Alford, Hiebert, Martin; NCV, NLT, and NBV). In this view 'the Spirit' is the subject: 'the Holy Spirit whom God caused to live in us yearns jealously over us'. The object is here implicit. This could be considered a variant of the second interpretation and also acceptable, since both of these focus upon the divine attitude rather than human frailty. Both fit better into the argument, following v. 4 logically rather than referring back to vv. 1–3.

Martin's interpretation is unusual in that although he has the Holy Spirit as the subject, he sees the verb phrase as addressing human envy: "the Spirit God made to dwell in us opposes envy." He concludes that it is God's jealousy that is described in v. 5, since God is waiting for them to turn from their envy of others back to him. We do not follow this interpretation because the verb 'yearns' always has a positive connotation in the New Testament.

Care must be taken in choosing a term in the receptor language for God's jealousy. Human jealousy has a negative connotation, but divine jealousy desires only the best for the object of God's affection. This implicit concept is supplied in the display by the phrase 'in order that we might be totally devoted to him'.

4:6a But God wants very much to help us. Although δέ functions semantically as an indicator of contrast here, its grammatical function seems to be to indicate some kind of switch. Since μείζονα 'greater' comes before δέ, that switch is from something mentioned previously to something greater, namely from the problem in 4:4a–5b to the solution of God's greater grace made available to mankind (described in 4:6a–d).

The contrast between the statement of God's jealous yearnings for complete devotion to himself in 5b and his grace in 6a is, on the surface, less evident than is the contrast between human sinfulness (the second alternative in 5b) and God's grace in 6a. Still, there is a contrast in the preferred rendering: God's yearnings make rigorous requirements of devotion, but his grace is completely adequate to bring undivided allegiance to those who humbly seek him.

In the noun phrase μείζονα . . . χάριν 'greater grace' the emphasis is upon 'greater', since the adjective is forefronted. Commentators vary as to the completion of the comparative: greater than human deficiencies (Martin), greater than the strength of man's evil desires (Adamson), greater than is needed to meet the requirement of God's jealousy (Ropes). Oesterley suggests that 'greater' is used in the sense of superabundance rather than as a comparative, and Laws concurs with this possibility. The rendering in the display reflects this view.

In translation it may be necessary to supply some link between 5b and 6a, for example, '*This is difficult*, but God wants very much to help us'. TNT renders it "But the grace he gives is even greater than his jealous yearning." Another possibility, suggested by Bratcher, is that the contrast is between v. 4 and v. 6.

4:6b That is why it says *in the Scripture*, The conjunction διό 'wherefore' introduces scriptural evidence of the truth that has just been given and contains both a warning and a promise. The phrase διὸ λέγει is a common formula for introducing a quotation (see Eph. 4:8); it means "that the truth just affirmed has given rise to the sacred utterance to be quoted" (Ropes).

4:6c "God opposes those who are proud, The 6c-d quotation is taken directly from Prov. 3:34 in the Septuagint, except that 'God' is substituted for 'Lord'. James is contrasting people who have distinctly different attitudes, showing that God's favor or disfavor toward a person is determined by that person's inner attitude (Hiebert). The first group he mentions are called ὑπερήφανοι 'arrogant ones', who in this context are those that primarily seek pleasure (3e) and have thereby become enemies of God (4f). As Mayor explains, "The friend of the world is proud because he makes himself his own centre, disowning his dependence upon God. . . ."

4:6d but he helps those who are humble." The second group of people are called ταπεινοί 'humble ones', the ones who have been described in 3:13 and 17 as having true wisdom that comes from God. Both 'arrogant ones' (6c) and 'humble ones' occur without the definite article, which emphasizes the character of these persons. Both are made even more prominent by being fronted.

> The quotation from Prov. 3:34 illustrates and confirms the main position of the preceding passage, vv. 1-5, *viz.*, that God will not yield to Pleasure a part of the allegiance of men's hearts, but that by his grace he enables men to render to him undivided allegiance. (Ropes)

BOUNDARIES AND COHERENCE

The initial boundary of the 4:4-6 unit was discussed under 4:1-3. The beginning of the next paragraph at 4:7 is marked by a change of topic: from worldliness to a call to repentance. There is also a change of genre to hortatory. Semantic coherence in 4:4-6 is shown by striking contrasts: 'friendship' versus 'enmity' in v. 4 and 'arrogant' versus 'humble' as well as 'resists' versus 'gives grace' in v. 6. Verses 4-6 clearly form a unit of some kind, since they deal with one topic, the need to choose between the friendship of the world and devotion to God.

PROMINENCE AND THEME

The theme of the 4:4-6 paragraph is drawn from both the *expository problem* and the *SOLUTION*, since both are integral to the expository problem-solution paragraph pattern. Included in the theme are not only the first NUCLEUS of the *problem* but also the 4a-b contraction, the latter because the initial vocative 'adulteresses' here is different from the usual form of address ('brothers') and conveys a sharp judgment upon the readers, which is significant for the content of this paragraph.

SUBSECTION CONSTITUENT 4:7–10
(Hortatory Paragraph: Generic Appeal of 4:1–16)

THEME: Therefore submit yourselves to God and resist the devil. Stop doing and thinking wrongly, and be sad because you have sinned. Indeed, humble yourselves before God and he will exalt you spiritually.

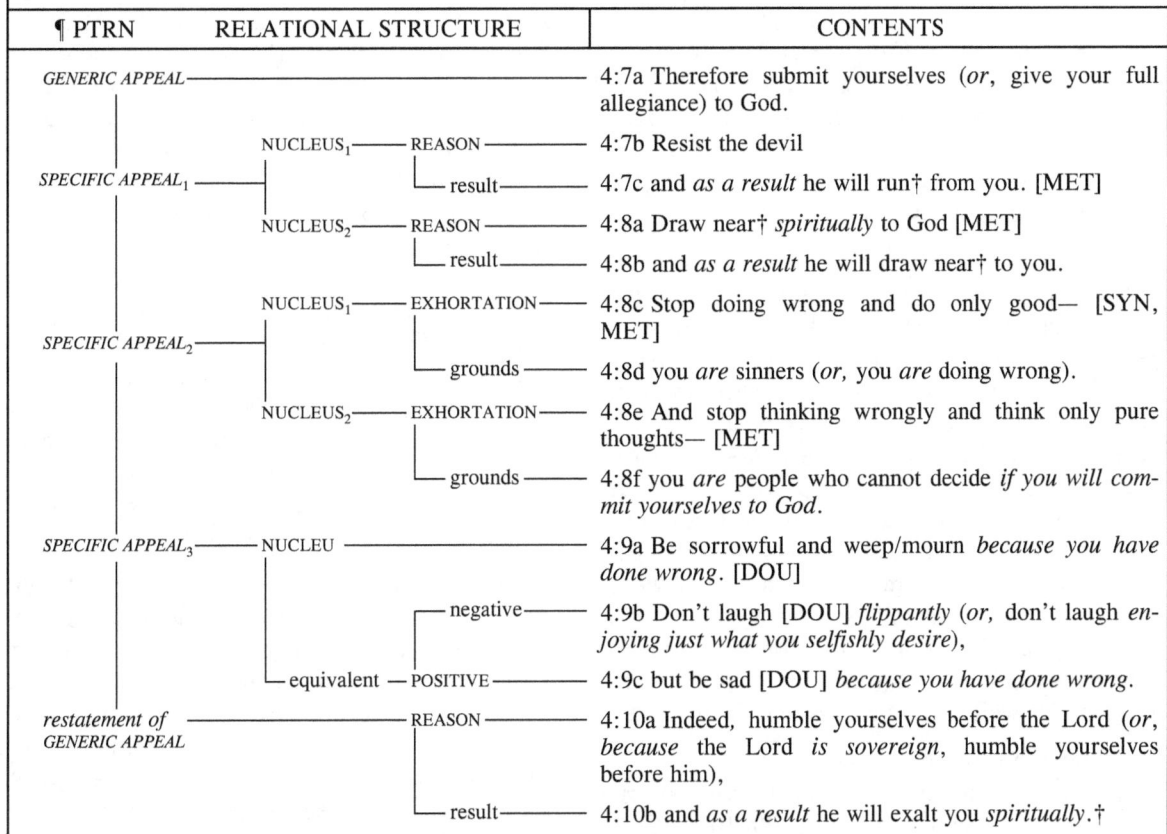

INTENT AND PARAGRAPH PATTERN

In the 4:7–10 paragraph James presents his readers with a passionate appeal. Having accused them of making self-indulgent pleasures the goal of their lives (4:1–3) and deliberately choosing worldly aims and conduct contrary to God's will (4:4–6), he here strongly challenges them to give their allegiance once again to God. By means of a series of exhortations he presents them with the way to renew a right relationship with God. The paragraph is therefore hortatory, consisting of a GENERIC APPEAL (7a) followed by three SPECIFIC APPEALS (7b–8b, 8c–f, 9a–c) and, to conclude, a restatement of the GENERIC APPEAL (10a–b).

The constituents of a hortatory paragraph pattern are normally *basis* and APPEAL, but here there seems to be no *basis*. Note, however, the initial οὖν 'therefore' in 4:7, which points back to the two previous paragraphs, 4:1–3 and 4:4–6. These paragraphs function at the macrostructural level as *bases* for all the APPEALS in 4:7–10. Also, the results of the exhortations in 4:7c, 8b, and 10b are motivational and so a type of grounds or *basis*. In addition, 8d and 8f are labeled as grounds, even though in the Greek text they are vocatives.

This paragraph is seen as the core of the epistle peak for the following reasons:

1. Semantically, it presents the solution to the variety of problems that James addresses throughout the earlier sections: reacting negatively to difficult circumstances (1:13–15), disobeying God's law of love by honoring some people more than others (2:1–11), uncontrolled speech manifesting jealousy and self-seeking (3:1–16), and quarreling and envying others (4:1–6). Only through true repentance, turning from evil, and humbly surrendering to God, as exhorted in 4:7–10,

can there be spiritual restoration and peace in the community.
2. Grammatically, this paragraph contains the greatest concentration of imperatives in the entire book.
3. Emotively, James is moved to great passion and severity here as the two stern vocatives in v. 8 show (ἁμαρτωλοί 'sinners' and δίψυχοι 'double-minded'). These replace the tender ἀδελφοί 'brothers' used in most of the book.
4. The paragraph pattern is unusual for James in that the *bases* for these APPEALS are at the macrostructural level.

A slightly different arrangement of the paragraph pattern could be projected based on the view of those (e.g., Mitton) who join 7b with 7a as the "basic demand" and consider vv. 8–10 as specific elements needed for a renewed spiritual life (Hiebert). Such an analysis would involve five APPEALS (7a–c, 8a–b, 8c–f, 9a–c, 10a–b). The view presented in the display, however, is preferred by a number of commentators (e.g., Davids 1982, Martin, Stulac). We prefer it because 7b–c and 8a–b are parallel in construction: both are imperatives followed by promises, and they are lexically contrastive. Moreover, 10a–b, which most commentators call a summary or conclusion, fits well with 7a as a sandwich structure.

   A Submit yourselves to God. (7a)
      B Resist the devil . . . purify your hearts . . . be sad and mourn. (7b–9)
   A' Humble yourselves before the Lord. (10a)

The choice between the two approaches would probably not significantly affect the translation.

NOTES

4:7a Therefore The conjunction οὖν 'therefore' indicates that the exhortations that follow are based on what has just been said, primarily upon the 6b–d quotation from Prov. 3:34. However, commentators recognize a broader reference. Hiebert, for example, says, "'Then' (*oun* 'therefore, consequently') indicates that his injunctions are prompted by the condition just exposed"; and Ropes says that οὖν here means "in view of the relation of God and his service to the pursuit of worldly pleasures." It is functioning at the macrostructural level to introduce the 4:7–10 GENERIC APPEAL of the 4:1–16 subsection (see "Intent and Macrostructure" for 4:1–16).

submit yourselves (*or*, give your full allegiance) to God. The first imperative verb, ὑποτάγητε 'submit yourselves', stands almost as a "heading" over the following series of commands (Moo). The relation between this imperative and the eight that follow it is therefore generic-specific. Submission is more than obedience; it involves humility and a voluntary, total subordination to God and his will instead of friendship with the world, which is opposed to God (4:4). This is not just a passive act, as Burdick says: "Submission is the surrender of one's will and this leads to obedience." The alternative rendering of the verb is for languages in which the term 'submit' has a negative or derogatory connotation.

All ten imperatives in 4:7–10 are in the aorist tense, which denotes either a sense of urgency (Martin, Hiebert) or a call for decisive action (Lenski, Burdick). Kistemaker suggests that all these aorists are ingressive; that is, the focus is on beginning the action, implying they hadn't been doing it. In languages that have an ingressive aspect, it may be appropriate to use it here unless the focus is thereby distorted.

4:7b Resist the devil Davids (1982) calls this exhortation the first step in submission. The verb ἀνθίστημι 'resist' establishes a verbal link with v. 6, since it is in the same semantic domain as ἀντιτάσσω 'oppose, resist' in v. 6. It emphasizes the necessity of making a choice: one must resist the devil or he will be resisted by God. While James earlier stressed the person's own evil desires as being responsible for sin (1:14, 4:1–3), he also recognizes that the devil as God's enemy plays a part. The desire to sin may be internal, but to give in to that desire is to yield to the devil.

4:7c and *as a result* he will run from you. The verb phrase φεύξεται ἀφ' ὑμῶν 'he will flee from you' expresses the direct consequence of resisting the devil. This result functions as a promise to motivate their action. If in the receptor language this metaphor is not well understood, one could say 'he will leave you alone' or express the concept idiomatically.

4:8a Draw near *spiritually* to God This clause is a counterpart to the exhortation in 7b to resist the devil. To draw near to God is to renew one's relationship with God. The verb ἐγγίζω 'draw near' was used of the Jewish priests' drawing near in worship. In this context, however, the meaning is not limited to worship or even prayer, but rather involves turning to God in genuine repentance. This does not refer to conversion but is addressed to believers who have compromised with the moral standards of the world. They need to renounce their evil practices and return to God. It is rendered literally as 'come near' or 'come close' in all the versions consulted. However, translators must be certain that such a literal rendering would not be taken in a physical sense. If the term for 'worship' in the receptor language is a meaningful one, it might be rendered 'truly worship God again'. Other suggestions are 'have fellowship with God again' or even 'repent and obey God again'.

4:8b and *as a result* he will draw near to you. The 8a–b construction is parallel with the one in 7b–c: an imperative followed by a future tense verb that conveys a promise. A wholehearted turning to God will be met by a full response from him. The verb phrase ἐγγιεῖ ὑμῖν 'he will draw near to you' denotes an assurance of God's readiness and availability to help (Stulac). Again, one must be careful lest a literal translation give the wrong idea. It might be rendered 'he will have fellowship with you' or even 'he will forgive and accept you'.

4:8c Stop doing wrong and do only good— The verb phrase καθαρίσατε χεῖρας 'cleanse your hands' is used figuratively here to refer to outward behavior that needs to be changed from the kind just condemned to behavior that God approves. Worship in the Old Testament required ceremonial cleansing and James applies this as a figure to the Christians who at present are unfit for worship because of sin in their lives. Both the negative aspect of turning from evil actions and the positive aspect of doing good need to be brought out in the rendering in order to properly convey the concept of 'cleanse'.

4:8d you *are* sinners (*or*, you *are* doing wrong). The vocative ἁμαρτωλοί 'sinners' is a term usually used of the unsaved, but in this context these are clearly believers, especially in view of the parallel vocative in 8f, 'double-minded'. James deliberately uses the harsh appellation 'sinners' to pierce the readers' consciences. In the light of the context, 'sinners' refers not only to people but also to the action they characteristically perform. If, in the receptor language, such a term as 'sinner' can be used as a vocative, this would be appropriate, especially if it is more forceful than a statement like the one here.

The communication relation between 8c and 8d can be understood as EXHORTATION-grounds. The readers' deplorable spiritual condition is what necessitates the exhortation.

4:8e And stop thinking wrongly and think only pure thoughts— With the verb phrase ἁγνίσατε καρδίας 'purify your hearts' James continues the theme of cleansing. The essential connection between external washing (mentioned figuratively in 8c) and inward purifying is an Old Testament theme. This internal cleansing is necessary for the readers to fulfill the command in 8a, 'draw near to God'. Moo says, "A note of blunt vividness is given the two clauses in the Greek by the lack of any articles or possessive pronouns." Again, both the negative and the positive need to be brought out in translating this: turning from evil thoughts to pure ones.

4:8f you *are* people who cannot decide *if you will commit yourselves to God*. Here James calls the readers δίψυχοι 'two-souled': they were trying to combine loyalty to God with their desire for worldly pleasures. This same term is used in 1:6–8 for persons who were unstable because they doubted God. The emphasis here is upon their divided affections. These two pejorative vocatives (in 8d and here) show the seriousness of their sins. If in the receptor language, there is an appropriate vocative, it could be very effective.

4:9a Be sorrowful and weep/mourn *because you have done wrong*. This begins the third of three couplets (7b–8b, 8c–f, 9a–c). It calls for deep, heartfelt sorrow for sin. Some consider the three imperatives in 9a synonymous (e.g., Moore, Bratcher). Others (e.g., Hiebert, Loh and Hatton) say that the first verb ταλαιπωρέω 'grieve, be distressed' denotes the feeling of misery and shame for sin, whereas the other two, πενθέω 'mourn' and κλαίω 'weep', are the outward manifestations of that grief. We follow the latter view and take 'mourn and weep' as a doublet. Mayor thinks that the meaning of the first verb, 'grieve' has retained its classical meaning of voluntary abstinence from luxuries. However, there is nothing in the context to suggest asceticism; rather, as most commentators say, the focus is on sorrow for sin. That it is for sin is indicated by the vocatives 'sinners' and 'double-minded' in v. 8. Thus the words 'because they have done wrong' are supplied in the rendering in the display. This helps avoid any misconception that God wants us to always be sad.

4:9b Don't laugh *flippantly* (*or*, don't laugh *enjoying just what you selfishly desire*), The imperative verb μετατραπήτω 'be turned' suggests that change is necessary for true penitence. The form is passive; but, following the NIV and TEV, it is translated here as active, since the focus of the entire paragraph is on personal responsibility. The subjects of this verb, γέλως 'laughter' and χαρά 'joy', are a doublet. This is not a condemnation of all laughter. The laughter referred to here is the hilarity of those involved in the pleasures of festivities (cf. 4:3d-e) or "a laughter born of flippancy, scorn and self-satisfaction" (Tasker). In the alternate rendering the implicit idea of self-centered pleasure is supplied.

4:9c but be sad *because you have done wrong*. There is a contrast in v. 9 between two pairs of nouns, γέλως 'laughter' and χαρά 'joy' and their opposite, πένθος 'grief' and κατήφεια 'dejection'. Moore (p. 60) describes each pair as a near-synonymous doublet. There are minor differences between the terms in each pair, as suggested by Huther, in that the first part of the clause (and consequently the nouns involved) refers to outward expression, whereas the second part refers to one's internal state. However, in this context these components are not in focus. This is an example of rhetorical parallelism for emphasis, so only one term for each pair is necessary as far as communicating informational content is concerned. At the same time, if in a given language all the terms can be easily expressed by complementary synonyms, the translator could use both terms if that is the appropriate way to convey emphasis. Louw and Nida (25.296) propose "Instead of laughing, mourn, and instead of being happy, become sad."

4:10a Indeed, humble yourselves before the Lord (*or*, *because* the Lord *is sovereign*, humble yourselves before him), The final imperative in this paragraph is ταπεινώθητε 'be humbled'. The majority of commentators consider it to be a summarizing exhortation. Although it is an aorist passive, most say that it is used in a middle sense, signifying a voluntary self-abasement. This call to humility is given in response to the promise made in v. 6 that God will help the humble. At the macrostructural level, v. 6 is a part of the second *basis* (vv. 4–6) for the vv. 7–10 GENERIC APPEAL.

The qualifying prepositional phrase ἐνώπιον κυρίου 'before/in the sight of the Lord' may simply mean 'in relation to Lord' (BAGD, 271.5b). It is so translated by most commentators and versions. However, others (e.g., Alford, Huther) say that it means an awareness of God's presence and providence, which brings with it a sense of our own total dependence upon him. In the display this view is the basis for the second alternative—a consciousness of his sovereignty. Either interpretation is acceptable. If the second alternative is chosen, the translator should take care that it does not take the focus off the need for humble repentance.

Regarding the referent of the noun κύριος 'Lord', commentators differ. The majority think it refers to God the Father, while a few (Lenski, Hiebert) say it probably refers to Christ. Either is acceptable but the former is preferable, since 10a is a restatement of the 7a GENERIC APPEAL and 'Lord' parallels the reference to God in 7a. The title κύριος clearly refers to God rather than Jesus in certain other verses in the epistle as well (e.g., 1:7, 5:4, 10–11).

4:10b and *as a result* he will exalt you *spiritually*. The promise given to those who humble themselves is expressed by the verb phrase ὑψώσει ὑμᾶς 'he will exalt you'. Although a few commentators (e.g., Martin) interpret this only eschatologically, the majority (e.g., Ropes, Alford) say that the exaltation is both in this life, in a spiritual sense, and hereafter. Stulac relates the promise of exaltation in v. 10 to the promise of grace in v. 6, which would imply all the spiritual blessings of forgiveness and restoration implicit in the intervening imperatives and explicit in the result clause in 8b. This phrase may be rendered 'and he will honor you', as in the CEV.

BOUNDARIES AND COHERENCE

The initial boundary of the 4:7–10 paragraph was discussed under 4:4–6. The next unit begins at 4:11, marked by the vocative ἀδελφοί 'brothers' and a change of topic: from the need for repentance to comments about judging a Christian brother.

The coherence of 4:7–10 consists in the common semantic domain of all the APPEALS. All of them pertain to some aspect of repentance. The first APPEAL and the last APPEAL (i.e., the generic appeal and its restatement) are essentially synonymous. Between the first and the last *APPEAL* are three couplets. The first couplet (7b–8b), which presents the basic choice between the devil and God, is clearly a pair because both imperatives are followed by a second verb giving a promise. The second couplet (8c–f), which addresses the need for cleansing from sin, is a pair in that the imperative in each clause is followed by its object with a disparaging vocative. The third couplet (9a–c), which deals with remorse for sin, though semantically unified, has a more complex structure. The first part consists of a series of three essentially synonymous imperatives. The second part has only one passive imperative but with two subjects, each followed by a prepositional phrase introduced by the same preposition, εἰς 'to'.

PROMINENCE AND THEME

In the 4:7–10 paragraph the *GENERIC APPEAL* and the *SPECIFIC APPEALS* are all naturally prominent, so the theme is drawn from each of them. One aspect of each couplet is represented in the theme so as to give the full picture of the process of repentance. The *restatement* of the *GENERIC APPEAL* is also represented in the theme along with its result (10b) since the result acts as a motivational basis for the *APPEAL*.

SUBSECTION CONSTITUENT 4:11–12
(Hortatory Paragraph: Specific Appeal₁ of 4:7–10)

THEME: Stop speaking evil against one another and thus condemning each other. Only God has the right to condemn others.

¶ PTRN	RELATIONAL STRUCTURE	CONTENTS
APPEAL		4:11a My fellow believers, stop speaking evil against one another,
	grounds	4:11b *since* the person who speaks evil against a fellow believer and *thus* condemns *one who is as close as* his own brother is speaking against what God commanded us to do, *that is, to love others*, and is saying that we don't have to do what he commanded.
	condition	4:11c If you(sg) say that you don't have to do what God commanded,
	contrast — CONCLUSION — CONSEQUENCE — negative	4:11d you(sg) are not obeying God;
	POSITIVE	4:11e rather, you(sg) are claiming that you *have the authority of* a judge (*or, to judge others*). [MET]
grounds — NUCLEUS		4:12a *But in fact* there is only **one** who has the authority to tell *people* what is right to do and to judge *them*.
	amplification	4:12b *God alone* is able to save *people* or to destroy/punish *them*.
basis — CONCLUSION		4:12c *Therefore* **you**(sg) certainly have no right to judge/condemn other people. [RHQ]

INTENT AND PARAGRAPH PATTERN

After a strong call to repentance in 4:7–10, James proceeds in 4:11–12 to give a specific example of how this repentance should apply in the personal relationships of his readers. Their evil speaking about each other does not reflect the necessary humility before God that is referred to in v. 10. Their critical remarks reveal a proud spirit that presumes to judge others (Davids 1982:169). His intent is to affect their actions by a warning command that such attitudes should cease, since they are usurping God's prerogative by condemning others.

The paragraph consists of an APPEAL (expressed by the imperative in 11a) and a *basis* (11b–12c). It is therefore hortatory. Within the *basis*, 11b provides the grounds for the CONCLUSION in 11c–e that the readers were wrongfully claiming authority to judge others. Verse 12 presents God as the only true source of authority, hence the final CONCLUSION in 12c that they have no right to condemn others.

NOTES

4:11a My fellow believers, stop speaking evil against one another, Again James uses an initial vocative ἀδελφοί 'brothers' here, after the three harsh vocatives in 4:4 and 8. This milder form of address may indicate affection, but probably it also prepares the way for the two occurrences of this term in nonvocative form in 11b. The triple repetition of 'brother' reinforces the APPEAL here.

The clause μὴ καταλαλεῖτε ἀλλήλων 'speak not against one another' is a prohibition. The verb καταλαλέω 'speak against' denotes critical derogatory speech intended to influence others against someone (Hiebert). Several versions (NIV, JB) use the term 'slander'. In contrast to the preceding ten aorist imperatives, this one is in the present tense. In this context, especially vv. 1–3 and 7–10, the present imperative with the negative particle is interpreted by most commentators as meaning to stop an action in progress.

4:11b *since* the person who speaks evil against a fellow believer Both Hiebert and Moo refer to 11b–12c as the "justification for the [preceding] prohibition." This relation is here rendered by the conjunction 'since', alerting the translator to the relation of APPEAL-*basis*, which should be expressed by whatever means is grammatically appropriate in the receptor language.

James repeats the verb used in 11a with the form καταλαλῶν 'speaking against'. It is the first of two participial phrases that are governed by only one article. This indicates that the two participles have the same subject.

and *thus* condemns *one who is as close as his own brother* The second participle κρίνων 'condemning/judging' is joined to the first by ἤ 'or'. Although a few commentators (e.g., Huther) consider the two verbs distinct ideas, the majority (e.g., Davids 1982, Tasker) say that they refer to the same activity from different aspects, as indicated by the use of only one article with both participles. The rendering 'and thus' rather than 'or' shows that the second verb, 'condemn', is the inevitable implication of evil speaking. Supporting this view is the double use of ἀδελφός 'brother' as object of each of the two participles. The first occurs without an article, indicating a fellow believer, whereas the second, which has both an article and the third person possessive pronoun (τὸν ἀδελφὸν αὐτοῦ 'his brother'), makes the accusation more personal and emphasizes the gravity of such a sin. Although the reference is not to a biological brother, the relationship is as close as if it were. This idea is supplied here, but in another language this distinction may result in an overly complicated and unnatural rendering.

is speaking against what God commanded us to do, *that is, to love others,* The noun νόμος 'law' occurs here without the article. A few commentators (e.g., Oesterley) claim that this refers to the Mosaic law, but there is nothing in the context to suggest that James is addressing any problem in the interpretation of the Mosaic law that might have existed in the early church among the Jewish Christians. Rather, as most agree, a reference to Lev. 19:18 is intended, since speaking against one another is a violation of that law. This same law was previously identified in 1:25 as 'the perfect law of liberty' and in 2:8 as 'the royal law' of love. That it is the law to love others is therefore supplied here.

and is saying that we don't have to do what he commanded. The verb phrase κρίνει νόμον 'he judges (the) law' implies setting oneself above God's law. Essentially, such judging is saying that it is not necessary to obey the law (Laws).

4:11c If you(sg) say that you don't have to do what God commanded, The opening δέ is not contrastive, as many versions (KJV, NASB, NJB, NRSV, REB) imply by the use of 'but'; rather it is marking a progression in the argument. The conjunction may be omitted as here, following the NIV, TEV, and TNT, or may be rendered 'and'.

The εἰ 'if' clause is a first-class condition, meaning that the reality of such a situation is assumed. The second person singular ending of the verb in νόμον κρίνεις 'you(sg) judge (the) law' confronts the readers individually with the consequences of criticizing fellow believers.

4:11d you(sg) are not obeying God; The apodosis begins with a negative clause: οὐκ εἶ ποιητὴς νόμου 'you(sg) are not a doer of law'. Obedience to God's commands is the expected response of the believer who has humbled himself before him. James has already devoted the entire second chapter to the importance of obeying the royal law of love (2:8) and the essential part that good deeds have in genuine faith (2:14–26).

4:11e rather, you(sg) are claiming that you have the authority of a judge (*or*, to judge others). The adversative conjunction ἀλλά 'but' introduces the positive statement of the apodosis, which consists simply of the noun κριτής 'judge'. This noun is a second complement of the verb εἶ 'you(sg) are' in 11d. Normally one would expect to translate ἀλλά as 'but' to express the contrast with the negative statement in 11d. However, at a higher level there is a greater semantic contrast, between 11e and 12a; so 'rather' is used here in the sense of 'on the contrary'.

Commentators differ in the interpretation of 'judge'. Some (e.g., Kistemaker), and many versions (e.g., TEV, NIV, REB, TNT), appear to consider this a judgment of the law itself: "speaks against the law and judges it" (NIV). Others (e.g., Ropes, Alford; JBP) say that νόμου 'law' is not to be understood after κριτής 'judge', since that has already been stated in 11b and this is really a step forward in the argument. As Tasker says, "When man ceases to be a *doer of the law*, he becomes *ipso facto a judge*, such a judge, James implies, as God and only God can be, for He alone is not under law." One of the meaning components in the word 'judge' is the authority to decide the question of legal right or wrong (Louw and Nida, 56.20). By their very act of harsh criticism some were in actuality making a claim to such authority. The rendering in the display reflects this latter interpretation.

4:12a *But in fact* Semantically there is a contrast between 11e and 12a, since the former presents a false claim, whereas the latter states the real source of authority to give and enforce the law. This contrast is rendered here by the conjunction 'but' and made emphatic by 'in fact'. (The only overt suggestion of this contrast is in v. 12's forefronted εἷς 'one'.)

there is only one who has the authority to tell *people* what is right to do The pronominal adjective εἷς 'one' is highlighted by fronting, hence the bold 'one' in the display. It may be seen as the subject of the verb ἐστιν 'is' or a numeral modifying both νομοθέτης 'lawgiver' and κριτής 'judge'. The decision rests partly on a textual variant involving these two nouns. Some manuscripts have a definite article ὁ 'the' before 'lawgiver', whereas others omit it. The GNT includes the article in brackets with a C rating, meaning that their decision is uncertain. One factor favoring its absence is that ὁ νομοθέτης is the more usual type of construction so ὁ could well be a scribal addition to conform to the usual pattern. But for a translator this is not a vital decision, since the literal rendering, 'one is the lawgiver', still emphasizes the uniqueness of the one who gives the law.

Although grammatically 'one' is most likely the subject of the sentence, the majority of versions make it a modifier (NIV, JB, REB, RSV), as we do: "there is only one lawgiver" (NIV). (See the note on 2:19a for a similar construction.) In some languages it would be better for clarity and prominence to follow TEV: "God is the only lawgiver." The identification of God as the only ultimate source of law is brought out in our rendering of 12b in order that the focus in 12a might be on 'one', as in the Greek.

and to judge *them*. Since God is the only judge, they have no excuse for judging others. James is not suggesting that there ought not be civil courts or human legislators. Nor does he rule out the need for honest discussion and constructive criticism, even among believers (Martin). His concern is the harsh, critical spirit that condemns people, usually behind their back. Such a spirit springs from jealousy and rivalry.

4:12b *God alone* is able to save *people* or to destroy/punish *them*. The participial phrase ὁ δυνάμενος σῶσαι καὶ ἀπολέσαι 'the one being able to save and to destroy' stands in apposition to εἷς 'one' in 12a (the subject of the verb ἐστιν 'is'). The 12b phrase amplifies the 12a clause. Only God has the authority and ability to give laws and enforce them. The aorist tense of these infinitives indicates the finality of God's decisions. These are general statements, but most commentators say that the eschatological verdict is primarily in view.

4:12c *Therefore* you(sg) certainly have no right to judge/condemn other people. The particle δέ 'but' marks a switch of topics from the sovereign God to the person who by censuring another person presumes to have authority to set the standard by which others are judged. The use of a forefronted free form, σύ 'you(sg)', heightens the contrast. This emphasis is brought out with 'one' in 12a, referring to God, and 'you' in 12c, both in bold type. In some languages the emphasis upon 'you' can be expressed by an emphatic affix or particle or perhaps by word order.

The interrogative pronoun τίς 'who?' introduces a rhetorical question that has the force of an emphatic negative statement, rendered as 'you certainly have no right'. Some commentators (e.g., Tasker, Adamson) say that the structure of the question makes it one of sarcasm or scorn. This may be indicated in other languages by affixes or some other grammatical device. The noun πλησίον 'neighbor' that is the object of the verb phrase ὁ κρίνων 'the one judging' occurred also in 2:8 and seems intended to recall the law of love described there. This is reflected in the display by the term 'other people' in an attempt to recall the use of 'neighbor' as interpreted by the same phrase in 2:8 (see the note on 2:8b).

BOUNDARIES AND COHERENCE

The initial boundary of the 4:11-12 unit was discussed under 4:7-10. The beginning of the next unit at 4:13 is marked by the prominence orienter ἄγε νῦν 'come now' and a change of topic: from judging a Christian brother to a warning against being presumptuous about the future. Lexical coherence in the 4:11-12 unit is shown by the use of the verb κρίνω '(to) judge' in both v. 11 (three times) and v. 12 as well as the cognate noun κριτής 'judge' in v. 11 and v. 12. The noun νόμος 'law' occurs three times in v. 11 with the related noun νομοθέτης 'lawgiver' in v. 12. None of these terms are found in contiguous passages. The double use of ἀδελφός 'brother' in v. 11 along with the noun πλησίον 'neighbor' in v. 12 provides referential coherence as does the use of the second person singular in the verb κρίνεις 'you judge' in v. 11 along with the emphatic personal pronoun σύ 'you' in v. 12.

PROMINENCE AND THEME

The theme of the 4:11-12 paragraph is drawn from both the *APPEAL* and its *basis* since these are integral parts of a hortatory paragraph pattern.

SUBSECTION CONSTITUENT 4:13–16
(Hortatory Paragraph: Specific Appeal₂ of 4:7–10)

THEME: You should not boast about what you will do in the future, since life is transitory; rather, you should plan to do whatever God wants you to do, since boasting about what you want to do, rather than considering the will of God, is sinful.

¶ PTRN RELATIONAL STRUCTURE	CONTENTS
prominence orienter	4:13a Listen *to me*.
hortatory problem — orienter	4:13b Some of you are *arrogantly* saying,
CONTENT	4:13c "Today or tomorrow we will go to a certain city. We will spend a year there and we will buy and sell and earn a lot of money."
MITIGATED NEGATIVE APPEAL	4:14a *You shouldn't say that* [4:13c]
basis for 14a — CONCLUSION	4:14b *since* you do not know what will happen tomorrow or *how long* you will live, [RHQ]
grounds	4:14c since you are *transitory like* a mist/vapor that appears for a short time and then disappears. [MET]
MITIGATED POSITIVE APPEAL — orienter	4:15a Instead of saying that [4:13c], you should say,
CONTENT — condition	4:15b "If the Lord wills,
CONSEQUENCE	4:15c we will live and do this or that."
basis for 15 — evidential grounds	4:16a But now you are boasting about all the things that you arrogantly *plan to do*.
CONCLUSION	4:16b You are doing evil when you boast like that [4:13c].

INTENT AND PARAGRAPH PATTERN

In the 4:13–16 paragraph James gives a second specific example of how the GENERIC APPEALS (4:7–10) should be applied in the readers' personal lives. Their confident plans for the future reveal an arrogance that is not in keeping with the humility called for in 4:10. James' intent here is to affect their actions by warning them that presumption is evil and will not be rewarded by God.

The initial *prominence orienter* (13a) goes with the entire paragraph and stresses the importance of all that follows. The rest of the paragraph consists of a *hortatory problem* (13b-c) followed by two mitigated APPEALS. The first one is negative (14a) and has its own *basis* (14b-c); the second one is positive (15a-c) and also has its own *basis* (16a-b). (For further evidence that this paragraph is hortatory, see the note for 15a.)

The arrogant plans of these believers are shown to be based on faulty reasoning—they are reckoning without considering their own human frailty. In the 15a-c positive APPEAL James points out that the proper response to life is to include God in one's plans. In the final *basis*, 16a-b, he asserts that their present attitude of boasting is sinful in God's sight. Martin concludes,

> To live in the recognition that God—not the human being—is in control is to choose a Christian life of humility before God; to live as though we ourselves—not God—have the final say is to adopt a proud and haughty attitude. (p. 166)

NOTES

4:13a Listen *to me*. The initial word in the introductory ἄγε νῦν 'come now' is a second person singular imperative form, but since this is a stereotypical phrase, the addressee may be in the plural, as it is here. The phrase is functioning as a *prominence orienter* to the entire paragraph. It implies disapproval and marks the transition to a new step in the discourse. The adverb νῦν 'now' is not temporal. It could be interpreted as meaning 'as far as the present situation is concerned' (BAGD, 546.2), but more likely it is a way of adding to the urgency of ἄγε. The phrase is variously rendered: "Go to now" (KJV), "Now listen" (NIV, TEV), "Look here" (NLT), "A word with you" (NEB), "Just a moment now" (JBP). All of these are idioms that call attention to the following quotation and its subsequent discussion. BAGD (p. 8) translates the expression as "come!" In the display we follow the NIV, except that we omit "Now," which might be construed as a temporal. In some languages, especially those in which kinship vocatives are commonly used to mark a new topic, a vocative such as 'brothers and sisters' or 'friends' may be used to make a more natural-sounding construction. Each language will have its own appropriate way of stating this.

4:13b Some of you are *arrogantly* saying, The phrase 'come now' is usually followed by a vocative, as it is here. However, this vocative is a participial phrase, οἱ λέγοντες 'the ones saying', and to propositionalize it, the phrase must be reworded using a finite verb. The definite article that is part of this participial phrase specifies the people making this boast. Commentators disagree as to who the addressees are. Some (e.g., Laws, Blue) consider them non-Christian Jewish traders, since ἀδελφοί 'brothers' is not used. However, others (e.g., Davids 1982, Mayor) hold that James' remarks to them imply that they are part of the Christian community. The latter is preferable for several reasons. First and foremost, vv. 15 and 17 presuppose a knowledge of biblical truth. In addition, James does not rebuke them with the finality of judgment that he uses toward the rich in chapter 5; rather, he is here warning all the believers of the danger of the attitude of presumptuously making plans without considering God. The fact that he does not address them as brothers may be explained as being a mild rebuke, since at this point they are not acting like believers. The address 'brothers' is also omitted in 4:1, 4:4, and other places in the epistle where he is clearly speaking to believers.

From the context, especially vv. 15–16 in which the remarks in 13b are referred to as 'boasting', it can be seen that these people have excluded God. This idea is expressed by the adverb 'arrogantly'.

4:13c "Today or tomorrow we will go to a certain city. There is a textual variant for the adverbial phrase σήμερον ἢ αὔριον 'today or tomorrow': rather than ἤ 'or', some manuscripts read καί 'and', which would imply a two-day journey. Although Huther prefers 'and' as showing greater confidence, the majority (e.g., Hiebert, Mayor) say that 'or' is better attested. The GNT has ἤ and does not mention a variant.

The elaborate plans proposed by these people reflect assurance and self-confidence with no thought of impediment. The verb πορευσόμεθα 'we will go' is the first of four verbs that are all in the future tense, indicating their "fixed certainty of the assumption" (Alford). In each case the finite form of the verb is used (none are participles) and all are connected by καί 'and', thereby putting emphasis on the different steps in the plan. The demonstrative adjective ὅδε 'this or that', in the prepositional phrase εἰς τήνδε τὴν πόλιν 'into this or that city', is used in the representative sense. A definite city was in the quoted speaker's mind, but since this is only a typical statement, James indicated the destination in an indefinite way (Huther).

We will spend a year there The verb phrase ποιήσομεν ἐκεῖ ἐνιαυτόν literally means 'do a year there'. It implies planned action and presumes control over their affairs for a long period of time.

and we will buy and sell and earn a lot of money." The verbs ἐμπορευσόμεθα 'we will trade' and κερδήσομεν 'we will make a profit' indicate the intended activity and the goal. James is not condemning work and profits as such but rather their proud complacency and their preoccupation with things of this world without any mention of God.

4:14a *You shouldn't say that* [4:13c] The connection between v. 13 and v. 14 is not readily perceived. Several versions therefore supply an introductory particle to mark a connection: "Why, you do not even know . . ." (NIV); "Yet you have no idea . . ." (NEB). Hill recognizes the need for a statement like the one supplied here in 14a, which he calls "an implicit evaluation proposition." This mitigated *APPEAL* is implicit, being a necessary part of the argument. It is clear from the context, especially 15a, that the reasoning cited here is inappropriate for a believer. Note that 15a begins with the prepositional phrase ἀντὶ τοῦ λέγειν ὑμᾶς 'instead of your saying', in which the preposition indicates an alternate, clearly implying that their remarks about the future reveal a wrong attitude. Hill observes,

> The force of ἀντί in v. 15 . . . sets the substantival infinitive τοῦ λέγειν ὑμᾶς in contrast to the substantival participle οἱ λέγοντες [in] v. 13 (see Robertson, p. 573). . . . "Instead you ought to say" is equivalent to: "don't say that but say this."

4:14b *since* you do not know what will happen tomorrow The first word in v. 14 is the relative pronoun οἵτινες '(you) who'; it is in apposition to the vocative phrase οἱ λέγοντες 'the ones saying' in 13b. Its use here puts emphasis upon the fact that by their very nature they do not know the future. All their elaborate planning is threatened by the uncertainty of what will happen. This uncertainty is the grounds (*basis*) for the implicit APPEAL 'you shouldn't say that' in 14a. That it is grounds is expressed in the display by 'since'.

There is a textual variant of the phrase τὸ τῆς αὔριον 'the thing of tomorrow'. Rather than the singular definite article τό, some manuscripts have the plural article τά; still others have no article. The GNT reads τὸ τῆς αὔριον 'the thing of tomorrow' with a B rating, "almost certain." The plural article may have been an emendation intended to harmonize this verse with Prov. 27:1. Whichever form is accepted, the meaning is essentially the same, that life itself in the future is uncertain.

or how *long* you will live, Commentators differ in how they punctuate the phrase ποία ἡ ζωὴ ὑμῶν 'of what kind your life'. The pronoun ποία is interrogative and may be used in direct or indirect questions. But some commentators (e.g., Martin, Stulac) say it is better to incorporate this phrase into what immediately precedes it: 'you do not know about tomorrow what your life will be' or, more naturally, as in NASB, "Yet you do not know what your life will be like tomorrow." Others (e.g., Hiebert, Moo, Tasker) say that it is preferable to see it as a separate question, 'What is your life?' The rendering in the display (although propositionalized as a subordinate clause) is based on seeing this as a rhetorical question in Greek, a device directing attention to the uncertain nature of their lives. Loh and Hatton observe, "James appears to be emphasizing the uncertainty and shortness of life." These boasters did not even know if they would be alive at a future date. The second view fits the context and flow of the argument better, especially the example that immediately follows. However, either view is acceptable, and, as Laws comments, the meaning is "not materially affected" by the choice between the two.

In some manuscripts γάρ 'for' occurs after ποία 'what sort', but the GNT omits γάρ here, giving its exclusion a B rating, indicating the opinion that it is almost certain it did not occur in the original text. It is omitted by most commentators and all English versions except KJV.

4:14c since you are *transitory like* a mist/vapor that appears for a short time and then disappears. In their boastful planning they did not consider the uncertainty or brevity of life. Some manuscripts omit γάρ 'for' after ἀτμίς 'mist'. The GNT includes it with a C rating, indicating difficulty in deciding whether or not to include it. Since most commentators accept it, it is included in the display. Another reason for including it is that γάρ introduces the grounds for the 14b CONCLUSION. All versions except RSV omit it, but probably for stylistic reasons only.

The other instance of a textual variant in 14c is that instead of ἐστε 'you are', some manuscripts read ἔσται 'it will be' and still others ἐστιν 'it is'. The GNT has 'you are', but with a C rating, influenced perhaps by its having been discussed along with the preceding γάρ 'for', which is given a C. Greenlee concludes that the C rating cannot apply to ἐστε. Indeed, it is read as 'you are' by almost all commentators and versions. Ropes says that the external evidence favors ἐστε. The verb 'you are' centers attention on the readers themselves and is therefore more vigorous (Hiebert).

In some languages the closest equivalent for the noun ἀτμίς 'mist/vapor' is steam rising from a boiling pot. What is important is the fact that it disappears so quickly. In this metaphor the topic is people, the image is mist or vapor, and the point of similarity is transitoriness. This may be represented best as a simile plus the point of similarity, as in the display. The word play involving the participles φαινομένη 'appearing' and ἀφανιζομένη 'disappearing' focuses further attention on the transitoriness of life.

4:15a Instead of saying that [4:13c], you should say, James now indicates the attitude these merchants should have. The prepositional phrase ἀντὶ τοῦ λέγειν ὑμᾶς 'instead of your saying' looks back to the vocative οἱ λέγοντες 'the ones saying' in v. 13 and the quotation. Thus v. 14 is in a sense parenthetical (Hiebert). If we omit v. 14, then vv. 13 and 15 flow as follows: Ἄγε νῦν οἱ λέγοντες, Σήμερον ἢ αὔριον πορευσόμεθα εἰς τήνδε τὴν πόλιν καὶ ποιήσομεν ἐκεῖ ἐνιαυτὸν καὶ ἐμπορευσόμεθα καὶ κερδήσομεν ... ἀντὶ τοῦ λέγειν ὑμᾶς, Ἐὰν ὁ κύριος θελήσῃ. ... 'Listen, you who say, "Today or tomorrow we will go into this city and we will do there a year and we will trade and make a profit" ... instead of your saying, "If the Lord wills. . . ."' Semantically v. 15 states the desired alternative to the remark in 13c in view of the uncertainty of life described in v. 14. Many commentators (e.g., Huther, Tasker, Moo) express this idea with 'should' or 'ought' in their discussions, as do all the English versions. They translate it as an independent clause, 'Instead you should say'; that is, they treat it as a mitigated appeal (see the discussion of mitigation in the note on 3:2b).

4:15b "If the Lord wills, The third-class conditional clause ἐὰν ὁ κύριος θελήσῃ 'if the Lord wills' implies uncertainty as to what God's will may be in a given situation, but the attitude James desires here is the willingness to accept whatever God's will is, based on confidence in the character of God. Various commentators (e.g., Ropes, Adamson) point out that the formula 'if God wills' or 'if the gods will' is widespread in ancient Greek philosophy and religion but is not found as such in the Old Testament. However, the concept permeates the Old Testament, as in Isa. 53:10 and Psalm 139 as well as in the accounts of Daniel and Esther's lives. In the New Testament the phrase *is* found, frequently, as in Acts 18:21. So it is not necessary to postulate that James has borrowed a pagan expression.

The common occurrence of this phrase in pre-Christian writings has led some commentators (e.g., Huther) to suppose that James may have non-Christians in view in this paragraph. However, it should not be overlooked that his use of 'the Lord', rather than 'God', is uniquely Christian. Almost all commentators agree that the noun phrase 'the Lord' refers to the Father here.

4:15c we will live and do this or that." Most commentators and versions take καί . . . καί in the verb phrase καὶ ζήσομεν καὶ ποιήσομεν τοῦτο ἢ ἐκεῖνο 'and we will live and we will do this or that' as 'both . . . and', connecting the two future indicative verbs in the apodosis of the conditional sentence: 'we will both live and do this or that'. A few commentators (e.g., Reicke) accept a variant reading of ζήσομεν 'we will live', the variant being the aorist subjunctive ζήσωμεν 'we should live'. The GNT does not deal with this variant, but such a reading, if accepted, would include ζήσωμεν as a part of the protasis of the condition: 'if the Lord should will and we should live, we will do this or that'. (In this view, the first καί would be a connector between the two subjunctive verbs in the protasis.) However, there are three good reasons for taking the meaning of these conjunctions as 'both . . . and': (1) Grammatically it is more correct to have only the one verb, θελήσῃ 'wills', dependent on ἐάν (so Alford). (2) The subjunctive reading does not bring out as clearly as the other the important truth that is stressed in v. 14, that we are dependent upon God for life itself (Tasker). (3) With the subjunctive reading there is a problem in handling the second καί.

The phrase τοῦτο ἢ ἐκεῖνο 'this or that' is a way of referring to a plan without being specific. James is not trying to banish planning from their lives but rather the kind of planning that ignores God. In all their planning they should acknowledge that God is in control and not they themselves.

4:16a But now you are boasting about all the things that you arrogantly *plan to do*. The phrase νῦν δέ 'but now' turns the attention back to the readers' arrogant attitude as set forth in v. 13. The verb καυχάομαι 'boast', although it can have a positive connotation as in Rom. 5:11, clearly has a negative connotation here.

The greatest difficulty in this verse is the meaning of the prepositional phrase ἐν ταῖς ἀλαζονείαις ὑμῶν 'in your arrogance' and its relationship to the verb 'boast'. The word 'arrogance' refers to a state of pride with the implication of a complete lack of basis for such an attitude (Louw and Nida, 88.219). But regarding the function of this phrase, commentators differ greatly. Some (e.g., Mayor, Laws) say that it is used adverbially, expressing manner: 'you boast arrogantly'. But others (e.g., Hiebert, Martin) point out that in the sixteen instances in the New Testament where 'boast' is followed by ἐν, the prepositional phrase expresses the object or content of the boast (Loh and Hatton), as in 'boast in/about one's high position' (1:9). A third view is held by Alford and Huther, who consider this phrase to express, not the content, but the source or reason for the boasting: 'you boast because of your arrogant confidence that your plans will succeed'.

The second view is the preferred one. For one thing, the noun 'arrogance' is plural, which would indicate that various situations are referred to. This idea is lost in the first view. Moreover, the consistent pattern of usage of this construction elsewhere in the New Testament carries a great deal of weight. Thus we conclude that the boasting is about their arrogant plans for the future, as stated in 13c, and this is supplied in the rendering here.

The adverb 'arrogantly' in the proposition is an expression of 'arrogant plans' rather than of the manner of boasting, as in the first view.

4:16b You are doing evil when you boast like that [4:13c]. The adjective πονηρά 'evil, wrong' is the verdict James pronounces on the remarks referred to in 16a (the remarks stated in 13c). The communication relation between 16a and 16b is therefore evidential grounds–CONCLUSION.

The adjective τοιαύτη 'such' modifies the word 'boasting'. It limits the judgment that boasting is evil to this particular kind of boasting. No distinction is drawn in vv. 16–17 between 'evil' here and ἁμαρτία 'sin' in 17 (Ropes). Stulac says, "The sin James is exposing is not merely a sin of omission (neglecting to recognize God's rule over their affairs); it is a sin of commission in that they even boast about their self-sufficiency."

BOUNDARIES AND COHERENCE

The initial boundary of the 4:13–16 unit was discussed under 4:11–12 and the final boundary under 4:1–16. Semantic coherence is shown by the contrastive content of remarks following the two occurrences of the verb λέγω 'say'. The first, in v. 13, states the addressees' present aspirations, which are self-confident and self-centered. The second, in v. 15, suggests the proper attitude toward life of dependence upon the will of God. This second remark is introduced by the prepositional phrase ἀντὶ τοῦ λέγειν ὑμᾶς 'instead of your saying', in which ἀντί signals a contrasting alternative (see the note on 15a).

Further coherence is provided by the sandwich structure at the beginning and end of the unit in v. 13 and v. 16:

A Some of you are saying, "Today . . . we will work and gain money." (13b-c)
  B Instead you should say, "If the Lord wills . . ." (15a-c)
A' But now you are boasting in your arrogance. (16a)

A few commentators make minor breaks at some point within the paragraph: following v. 13 (Blue), following v. 14 (Hiebert, Blue), or following v. 15 (Hiebert, Kistemaker). However, the theme of boasting runs through 13–16, which they would all acknowledge, and for this reason we consider that these breaks are simply between lower-level units.

PROMINENCE AND THEME

The theme statement of 4:13–16 is drawn from both of the *APPEALS* and *bases* since in a hortatory paragraph such as this, these are integral components of the paragraph pattern.

SECTION CONSTITUENT 4:17
(Expository Propositional Cluster: Axiomatic Basis of 4:1–16)

THEME: *Certainly if anyone knows the right thing that he ought to do yet doesn't do it, he is sinning.*		
RELATIONAL STRUCTURE		CONTENTS
condition	┌ concession ───────	4:17a Certainly `if` anyone knows the good/right thing that he ought to do,
	└ CONTRAEXPECTATION ──	4:17b `yet` he does not do it,
CONSEQUENCE	───────────────	4:17c he is **sinning**.

INTENT AND STRUCTURE

The 4:17 propositional cluster is an axiom. It functions in this context as a warning about the consequences of not heeding the exhortations given in 4:1–16 that clearly present what God desires. James assumes that as believers the readers will want to do the will of God. The unit is introduced by the conjunction οὖν 'therefore', which here may well mean 'to sum this up'. The unit consists of a condition (17a-b) and a CONSEQUENCE (17c) and functions at the macrostructural level (in the 4:1–17 section) as the *axiomatic basis* of the 4:1–16 APPEAL.

NOTES

4:17a Certainly The summary maxim with which James concludes the 4:1–17 section is very generic. Although a few commentators (e.g., Dibelius, Mitton) view it as an independent saying having no direct connection with what goes before or after it, most acknowledge some connection with what has gone before, based on the conjunction οὖν. Some (e.g., Mayor, Stulac) say that it summarizes all that has been said before in the entire epistle. Such verses as 1:22–25, 2:15–16, 3:1, 3:13, and 4:11 are mentioned. But if it were intended to serve as a general summary, the end of the book would be a more appropriate place for it, since there are other exhortations in chapter 5. The majority of commentators (e.g., Moo, Oesterley, Tasker) say that it sums up what has just been said, usually seen as the preceding paragraph, 4:13–16. Such topics as presumptuous self-confidence, boasting, and the transitoriness of life are specifically mentioned. However, there is the possibility, in view of the way James uses proverbs, that on a macrostructural level more than the immediately preceding verse or paragraph is being summarized: As Ropes points out, James has a characteristic method of "capping the discussion" of a topic with a proverb; earlier examples of such are in 1:18, 2:13, and 3:18. Adamson remarks that James "concludes this chapter, like each of the others, with a pointed sententious maxim ... which clenches the thoughts of the previous verses." This pattern is reflected in the display, where 4:17 is the *axiomatic basis* of 4:1–16 (see "Intent and Macrostructure" for 4:1–17). The need for obedience is not restricted to boasting, the topic of 4:13–16, but applies to all the other exhortations in 4:1–16 as well, especially to the ten that form the core of the 4:7–10 GENERIC APPEAL.

This verse states a very general principle. REB captures the idea with "What it comes to is that. . . ."

Note that since v. 17 is not in a conclusion-grounds relation to what precedes it, it is not quite appropriate to translate οὖν as 'therefore'. NLT has "Remember. . . ." In the display οὖν is rendered 'certainly' based on its use here as an emphatic (see BAGD, 593.3).

***if* anyone knows the good/right thing that he ought to do,** The first of the two dative participles here is εἰδότι 'knowing'. It occurs without an article, indicating that the reference is broad and indefinite, hence 'anyone'. The tone of the address changes because James is no longer speaking directly to those who make plans without including God but to anyone reading his epistle. Third person endings replace the second person endings because he is stating a general principle.

Commentators differ as to the content of 'knowing' here. Some (e.g., Alford, Huther) say that the object is the infinitive phrase καλὸν ποιεῖν 'to do good': "knoweth to do good" (KJV). However, it is also possible that the object is the adjective καλόν 'good' with the infinitive used epexegetically. This view underlies the NIV rendering: "knows the good he ought to do." Semantically, there is little difference between the two interpretations except, perhaps, a matter of emphasis. The latter seems preferable since such a rendering makes clearer that what is involved is not merely an intellectual understanding that one should do good but rather an emphasis upon doing the right thing. Martin says that once a merchant, or any Christian for that matter, "knows what is right, the same person is under moral obligation to do it." Moo and Blue seem to imply this and almost all versions follow this view.

4:17b yet he does not do it, The second dative participle is ποιοῦντι 'doing'. Like the first, it occurs without an article and is present tense, which indicates along with the negative that although there is knowledge nothing is being done about it. This participial phrase is connected with the one in 17a by καί 'and'; the two are translated as coordinate in almost all versions. Only NCV translates it as contrastive: "anyone who knows . . . but does not do it." However, what James seems to be saying is that the two behaviors are inconsistent, which is a relation of concession-CONTRAEXPECTATION, not contrast. (One would expect that a person who knew what was right to do would do it.) In the display this relation is expressed with 'yet' (BAGD, 392.I2g).

4:17c he is sinning. The noun ἁμαρτία 'sin' is forefronted, emphasizing that knowledge without obedience is certainly sin. While sins of omission are included, as many of the parables and other teaching of Jesus bring out (e.g., the parables of the talents in Matt. 25:14–30 and the teaching on the final judgment in Matt. 25:41–45), sins of omission are not the primary focus here because the merchants had not been charged with such sins. Rather, the focus is upon actively doing what one knows is right.

Because 17a–b is a type of conditional clause and the concept of 'ought' or 'should' is here, it would be possible to interpret this verse as implying an appeal: 'Therefore always do what is right'. However, it is not so treated here because of its function in the macrostructure of 4:1–17 as the *axiomatic basis* of the preceding APPEAL (see "Intent and Macrostructure" for 4:1–17).

BOUNDARIES AND COHERENCE

The initial boundary of 4:17 was discussed under 4:1–16 and the final boundary under 4:1–17. The verse coheres as one Greek sentence.

PROMINENCE AND THEME

The 4:17 propositional cluster consists of a condition-CONSEQUENCE, with the CONSEQUENCE being naturally prominent. Both components are represented in the theme, since the condition is obligatory to the sense of the whole sentence.

DIVISION CONSTITUENT 5:1–11 (Hortatory Section: Appeal₅ of 1:19–5:11)

THEME: The rich people who oppress you should weep because God will punish them. Therefore wait patiently for the Lord to return and judge all people fairly. Do not complain against each other lest he judge you when he returns. God blesses those who patiently endure suffering.

MACROSTRUCTURE	CONTENTS
basis	5:1–6 The rich people who oppress you should weep because they will suffer much. God will punish them because they have unjustly caused others to suffer.
APPEAL	5:7–11 Therefore wait patiently for the Lord Jesus Christ to return and judge all people fairly. Do not complain against each other lest he judge you when he returns. From the examples of the prophets and Job we know that God blesses and rewards those who patiently endure suffering.

INTENT AND MACROSTRUCTURE

Many of the trials faced by the believers to whom James writes were caused by the social structure in which they lived. They were often victims of injustice, oppressed by the wealthy landowners who controlled the political and judicial systems. James' intent in 5:1–11 is to encourage the believers to respond to unjust treatment with patient endurance, since God is in control.

The 5:1-11 section consists of a *basis* (vv. 1-6) and an APPEAL (vv. 7-11); thus it is hortatory. Although 5:1-11 is the fifth APPEAL unit of the 1:19-5:11 division, it differs from the preceding four in that it does not conclude with a proverb as its *motivational basis*. The reason for this is that the first four APPEAL units deal primarily with problems in the church and were prohibitory, whereas this fifth APPEAL has to do with creating rapport between James and the addressees—it is a unit of encouragement. However, it has ties with the fourth APPEAL (chap. 4) in terms of its general topic, which is riches. James speaks of covetousness and desire for riches at certain points in chapter 4 (e.g., vv. 1-4 and 13-16) and then in 5:1-11 speaks of the rich unbelievers who oppress the believers. Section 5:1-11 is thus more closely connected with what precedes it (4:1-17) than with what follows it (5:12-18).

To encourage patient endurance on the part of the readers, James shows how the wealthy landlords who had been oppressing them would suffer in the Day of Judgment. He exhorts them to wait patiently for the time when God will bring full justice. At the same time he cautions them to be careful that their own conduct would not also deserve judgment when the Lord returns. He encourages them to persevere by examples that show how God blessed and rewarded those who endured suffering patiently.

BOUNDARIES AND COHERENCE

The initial boundary of the 5:1-11 unit was discussed under 4:1-17 and the final boundary under 1:19-5:11. The two paragraphs that make up this section (5:1-6 and 5:7-11) are connected by the conjunction οὖν 'therefore' in v. 7.

The section's semantic coherence derives from its topic, suffering at the hands of unbelievers and in the difficult circumstances of life. This is brought out in 5:4-6, which speaks of the injustices perpetrated by the wealthy landowners, and in 5:10, which cites the ill-treatment endured by the prophets. Further coherence is seen in the various references in both paragraphs to judgment in the end times: 'the troubles that are coming upon you' (v. 1), 'the last days' (v. 3), the 'day of slaughter' (v. 5a), 'the Lord's coming' (vv. 7 and 8), and the figure of the judge standing at the door (v. 9).

Stylistic coherence is seen in the four occurrences of ἰδού 'behold' in vv. 4, 7, 9, and 11. In each of these occurrences, this particle functions as an interjection and signals an example or image that reinforces and clarifies the message of the entire unit. Van Otterloo classifies the four similarly: the one in v. 4 as "calling attention to grounds that require a logical conclusion to be drawn" (p. 52) and the other three as "calling attention to a situation that requires action" (p. 63). The particle ἰδού is found elsewhere in James only in 3:4 and 5.

Some commentators (e.g., Blue, Kistemaker) consider 5:1-20 as one high-level unit, but with a topic so general that it does not reflect the structure of the chapter: Blue calls it "Share with Concern," Kistemaker calls it "Patience," Adamson calls 5:1-18 "Conclusion." Furthermore, they overlook the major break at 5:12 (see "Boundaries and Coherence" of 1:19-5:11).

PROMINENCE AND THEME

The theme of 5:1-11 is drawn from both the APPEAL (vv. 7-11) and the *basis* (vv. 1-6), since both are integral to a hortatory unit.

SECTION CONSTITUENT 5:1–6 (Expository Paragraph: Basis of 5:7–11)

THEME: The rich people who oppress you should weep because they will suffer much. God will punish them because they have unjustly caused others to suffer.

¶ PTRN	RELATIONAL STRUCTURE	CONTENTS
orienter		5:1a This is what I say to the rich people who do not believe in Christ.
CLAIM	orienter	5:1b "Listen *to me*, you rich people.†
	RHETORICAL EXHORTATION	5:1c You should weep and wail
	rhetorical grounds	5:1d *since* you will experience terrible troubles. [PRS]
justification₁ — CONCLUSION	grounds — GENERIC	5:2a Your wealth *of various kinds* is *worthless as if it were* rotted.† [MET]
	specific₁	5:2b Your fine clothes are *worthless as if they were* ruined by moths [MET]
	specific₂	5:3a and your gold and silver are *worthless as if they were* rusted. [MET]
	NUCLEUS	5:3b This worthless wealth [MTY] will be evidence [PRS] *in the judgment* that you are guilty *of greed*, and as rust and fire *destroy*, you [SYN] will be severely punished *by God*. [MET, SIM]
	amplification	5:3c You have *in vain* stored up *wealth* (or, hoarded) in a time when *God* is about to judge *you*. [MTY]
justification₂	orienter	5:4a Think *about what you have done*.
	NUCLEUS₁ — REASON	5:4b You have not paid wages to the workmen who have reaped your fields for you
	result — REASON	5:4c *with the result that* they are crying out to God for him to help them. [PRS]
	result	5:4d And *as a result* the all-powerful Lord has **heard** their fervent cries.
	NUCLEUS₂ — NUCLEUS	5:5a You have lived in luxury and have indulged yourselves here on earth.
	comparison	5:5b *Just as cattle fatten themselves, not realizing that* they will be slaughtered, [MET]
	amplification - NUCLEUS	5:5c you have indulged yourselves [MTY], *not realizing that you will be severely punished by God*.
	NUCLEUS₃ — NUCLEUS	5:6a You have *caused* innocent people to be condemned.
	amplification - CONTRAEXPECTATION	5:6b You have *caused* some to be killed (or, to die),
	concession	5:6c *even though* the innocent ones were not *able to* resist you (or, were not resisting you)."
restatement of orienter		5:6d *That* [1b–6c] *is what I say to the rich people who oppress you.*

INTENT AND PARAGRAPH PATTERN

In the 5:1-6 paragraph James denounces the rich who are oppressing the poor. Although he is speaking rhetorically to unbelievers who will not be receiving this letter, his primary concern is for the readers. He has a twofold purpose: to encourage them, based on the fact that their oppressors will be justly judged some day, and to warn them to avoid becoming materialistic or envious of the rich. If this paragraph were meant for the rich people in order that they change their ways, it would be hortatory. But from the context it is clear that it was meant for the encouragement of believers. The imperative 'weep' and the participle 'wailing' that follows it (1c) are not addressed to the believers; this is a rhetorical way of saying to the rich people that they are in a terrible situation.

The 5:1-6 paragraph is expository, being composed of an *orienter* (5:1a), CLAIM (5:1b-d), two *justifications* (5:2a-3c and 5:4a-6c), and a *restatement of orienter* (5:6d). The claim that these rich people will experience terrible troubles is supported by the evaluation of their wealth as worthless and the certainty of God's inevitable judgment upon them. Added to this is a list of the charges against them: injustice, self-indulgence, and judicial murder. The rich should express grief over the certainty of punishment awaiting them.

NOTES

5:1a-b *This is what I say to the rich people who do not believe in Christ.* **"Listen *to me*, you rich people.** Verse 1 begins with the introductory phrase ἄγε νῦν 'come now' followed by the vocative οἱ πλούσιοι the rich ones'. This vocative identifies the group being addressed in the formal structure. Commentators differ somewhat as to their identity. Although a few (e.g., Bratcher, Tasker) believe James is addressing those within the Christian community who have become wealthy, the majority (e.g., Moo, Davids 1982, Hiebert) believe that the term refers to non-Christian owners of large estates in the area where the readers live. The latter is preferable for the following reasons:

1. James does not address them with the familiar greeting ἀδελφοί 'brothers' but rather 'rich ones'.
2. He does not exhort them to repent as he so often does to the believers either directly, as in 1:21 and 4:7-10, or by implication, as in 2:12-13 and 3:13-18. Here he speaks only of condemnation.
3. His style of speaking is strikingly parallel to that used in Old Testament passages that condemn rich oppressors (e.g., Isa. 10:1-4).
4. The attitudes and actions attributed to these rich ones resemble those in 2:6-7, in which the reference is clearly to unbelievers, and not those in 1:10, which refers to wealthy Christians, according to many.

Most commentators agree that the purpose of this paragraph was not to counsel the rich but rather to benefit the believers who would draw appropriate deductions from it (Laws). Stulac and others emphasize that James is speaking in a rhetorical style very similar to that used in the Old Testament in addressing foreign nations. In Isa. 13:1-22 and Amos 1:3-2:3, for example, judgment is pronounced on the nations in order to encourage the faithful. This literary device is referred to as apostrophe by a number of commentators (e.g., Hiebert, Ward, Burdick); others (e.g., Stulac, Laws) simply say that James is "speaking rhetorically." In the display an introductory statement is supplied to clearly identify the addressees as rich unbelievers.

The introductory phrase ἄγε νῦν 'come now' is the same formula used in 4:13. It is variously translated by versions as "And now" (TEV, JBP), "Now listen" (NIV), "Now an answer" (JB), "Next a word to you" (REB), and "listen" preceded by the vocative (NCV). CEV omits it. Our rendering follows the NCV but fills out the case frame with 'to me', as in 4:13.

In some languages, it might be better to omit the 1a orienter and to change the second person references to third person (both here and throughout 5:1-6), for example, 'Listen to what I have to say about rich people who do not believe in Christ. They should weep and wail . . .'. This is an alternative way of making it clear that the wealthy oppressors referred to were not members of the Christian community.

5:1c You should weep and wail The imperative κλαύσατε 'weep' conveys the idea of sobbing aloud and was used of mourning for the dead. James uses it in 4:9 of weeping in connection with repentance, but in this context it is a response of despair over judgment. It is followed by the participle ὀλολύζοντες 'crying aloud', an onomatopoeic word used frequently in the Septuagint, always in the context of judgment. When a participle follows an imperative verb, as here, it often has imperatival force and is so rendered in the display. The aorist imperative implies urgency and the present participle indicates action simultaneous with the action of the main verb. Moore (p. 60) labels κλαύσατε and ὀλολύζοντες a near-synonymous doublet, so they could be rendered as a single verb, but rendering them as two verbs is probably more forceful.

5:1d since you will experience terrible troubles. The call to lament in 1c is based on the prospect of upcoming calamities. The prepositional phrase ἐπὶ ταῖς ταλαιπωρίαις ὑμῶν ταῖς ἐπερχομέναις 'over the miseries coming upon you' describes this time of anguish that is so certain that it is pictured as already approaching. The verb form of the noun 'miseries' is used in 4:9 in an exhortation to grieve deeply over sin, but here the context shows that their concern should be for the punishment to come. A few commentators (e.g., Lange) say that this refers to the imminent destruction of Jerusalem, but the majority believe that the primary reference is eschatological, although they admit a possible preliminary fulfillment in the fall of Jerusalem. Some (e.g., Mitton) say 'miseries' refers to the final judgment; most (e.g., Alford, Hiebert) associate it with the return of Christ referred to in 5:7. The time of the judgment is not mentioned; it is the certainty of it that is in focus. The phrase 'miseries coming upon you' is a personification, which in many languages would be best expressed nonfiguratively as people experiencing great sufferings, as in the display. The communication relation between 1c and 1d is EXHORTATION-grounds, but it is a rhetorical exhortation, in that it is not directly addressed to the readers.

5:2a Your wealth *of various kinds* is *worthless as if it were* rotted. The Greek is ὁ πλοῦτος ὑμῶν σέσηπεν 'your wealth has rotted'. This is the first of three statements that James makes about the devastating effect of the coming judgment upon their wealth. One difficulty is the meaning here of the noun 'riches'. Many commentators (e.g., Laws, Davids 1982) say that it is a comprehensive term for all forms of wealth that men accumulate and that the following two statements in 2b and 3a give specific examples of that wealth. In this view, the verb σήπω 'rot/decay' is generally taken to be figurative. Others (e.g., Tasker, Oesterley) say that 2a–3a refers to three specific forms of wealth, and that the first, 'riches', is a reference to perishable grain. In this view 'decay' has its natural meaning. That is, the rich were allowing grain to rot in their fields rather than use it to alleviate the needs of others. Another proposed support for this view is that καί connects 2a and 2b (and 2b is also literal in this view). But the first view, that 'riches' is used generically in 2a, is preferable because of the focus in this paragraph. This is not a description of the natural result of greed and the reason for the judgment; rather, it is a description of the coming judgment with its effect on all the wealth they have valued so highly (Wiesinger, cited by Huther). Furthermore, to interpret 'riches' as a reference to crops, though not impossible, is nevertheless a bit forced (Loh and Hatton). Thus we take the communication relation between 2a and 2b–3a to be GENERIC-specific.

The verb σέσηπεν 'has rotted/decayed' is in the perfect tense, which refers to an action that has been completed and has a lasting effect. Commentators differ as to their interpretation of this tense here. Some (e.g., Alford, Mayor) call it a prophetic or proleptic perfect, denoting future events that are so certain that they can be spoken of as having actually happened. This is certainly possible. If it is so interpreted, Bratcher rightly suggests that in many languages it would be better to use the future tense to avoid misleading the readers into thinking that this had already happened: 'Your riches will rot'. But others (e.g., Hiebert, Laws, Loh and Hatton, Moo) say that the perfect tense here denotes the present worthless state of all their possessions—worthless, as Moo says, either for present spiritual benefit or for reward in the future judgment. The latter view is preferable for two reasons: (1) In v. 3 James changes to the future tense in describing the future role of these riches, and (2) in this context God's evaluation of hoarded wealth is clearly the focus. The rendering in the display is based on this view; however, the prophetic interpretation would be a valid alternative.

5:2b Your fine clothes One of the chief forms of wealth in the ancient world was fine clothing. The elaborate robes worn by the rich were a symbol of their wealth and prestige. This form of wealth is often mentioned in Jewish literature and in the Bible (e.g., in Matt. 6:19 and 23:5 and Acts 20:33). James mentions fine clothing as a sign of a rich person in 2:2–3, which may account for his choosing clothing as a specific example here of the transitoriness of riches.

are *worthless as if they were* **ruined by moths** The verb phrase σητόβρωτα γέγονεν 'have become moth-eaten' may be taken literally or figuratively. Those who take it literally join 2a and 2b and usually translate them with a past tense or perfect tense form. It is so translated in almost all versions. The NIV, for example, has "Your wealth has rotted, and moths have eaten your clothes." But in many languages such a literal rendering would be very confusing. Readers would take it to mean that these people's wealth had literally rotted, their clothes had been literally ruined by moths, and (in 3a) their money had literally rusted or corroded. If this proves to be a problem in the receptor language, it would be possible to translate using the future tense as suggested by Bratcher: "your fine clothes will be ruined by moths." However, the interpretation that is presented in the display (the one suggested by many commentators) is preferable, since it focuses on the worthlessness of what they considered their great riches. Also, it is more in keeping with the certainty of judgment to come.

5:3a and your gold and silver are *worthless as if they were* rusted. It is an accepted fact that gold and silver do not rust. Those who take the verb κατιόω 'become rusty' literally explain it in various ways. They say that it is merely an imprecise term, implying destruction (Alford), or that it means loss of luster or having become tarnished (Blue). However, many commentators (e.g., Ropes, Laws) interpret it figuratively. The NLT with "Your gold and silver have become worthless" is the only version that reflects this view. The rendering in the display is likewise based on its being figurative. Such a rendering clarifies the focus of the paragraph. However, the prophetic interpretation (see the final paragraph of the note on 2a) would also be valid: 'your gold and silver will be tarnished or corroded'.

5:3b This worthless wealth will be evidence *in the judgment* that you are guilty *of greed,* The wealth of the rich is declared to be not only worthless, but also something that will be counted against them personally in the Day of Judgment. Although the noun ἰός 'poison/rust' is used in 3:8 of deadly poison, here it clearly refers to the corrosion of gold and silver, followed as it is by the possessive pronoun αὐτῶν 'of them'. But it is a metonymy and is rendered nonfiguratively as 'worthless wealth' in the display. The verb phrase εἰς μαρτύριον ὑμῖν ἔσται 'will be for a testimony to/against you' indicates that this 'rust' will have an effect on their future. Whether this evidence will serve to enlighten the rich or to convict them can only be determined from the context. Some (e.g., Ropes, Mayor, Barclay) say that the rust will symbolize *to* them the perishability of wealth and their own certain destruction. But in view of the note of threat in the context, their corrupted wealth is more likely evidence *against* them (Laws). Most commentators (e.g., Tasker, Martin, Davids 1982) and virtually all the versions reflect the latter interpretation. Moo proposes that the reason for this judgment may simply be their unduly accumulated material wealth. Hiebert suggests that such wealth could be a testimony to their hard-heartedness or selfish hoarding. The main point, he concludes, is that it will verify their guilt. This idea is supplied in the display. It is further clarified by vv. 4–6, which specify the charges against them.

and as rust and fire *destroy*, you will be severely punished *by God*. The Greek is φάγεται τὰς σάρκας ὑμῶν ὡς πῦρ 'will eat your flesh like fire'. Moo cites Judith 16:17 ("The Lord Almighty will punish them on Judgment Day. He will send fire and worms to devour their bodies . . .") as evidence that this phrase is an image of God's judgment. The future tense verb ἐσθίω literally means 'eat, consume' but can be used figuratively to mean 'destroy'. Its object σάρκας is plural: 'fleshes'. Some commentators (Hiebert, Lenski) say that the plural may be used for the fleshy parts of the body, and that its use here focuses attention on their primary concern for their physical comforts. Ropes, however, contends that the plural is used in the same sense as the singular. In actuality, this is a synecdoche meaning the persons themselves and in most languages should be so translated. Martin supports this: "flesh (σάρξ, i.e., the person . . .)."

Most commentators connect the phrase ὡς πῦρ 'like fire' with 'will eat your flesh'. All versions translate it literally, as in the NIV: "and eat your flesh like fire." However, there is an unusual mixture of personification, metaphor, and simile here. Laws rightly declares,

> It is the judgment of God upon their worthless possessions that will really destroy the rich. Alternatively it may be justifiable to read in the allusion to fire the threat of Gehenna, the place of burning to which those condemned at the last judgment are consigned. . . .

The topic of the metaphor is the judgment of the persons themselves; the image is 'rust eating their flesh' (fire is another image if the simile is included); and the point of similarity is destruction. In the display 'rust' and 'fire' are combined to picture God's punishment, since both involve destruction.

5:3c You have *in vain* **stored up** *wealth* **(or, hoarded)** There has been much speculation as to the object of the verb ἐθησαυρίσατε 'you stored up'. According to Ropes, it must have an object. Grammatically, ὡς πῦρ 'as fire', which precedes ἐθησαυρίσατε, could be connected with this verb. If it is, ὡς would have to mean 'since'; the translation Ropes prefers is 'since you have stored up fire'. However, this is not the most natural way of grouping the words and it would rob this last clause of its irony (Tasker). Only the NJB and Berkeley follow Ropes's interpretation. Others propose 'wrath' as a possible object based on Rom. 2:5. This view is reflected in the NAB; but although it is semantically logical, there is nothing in the Greek text itself to validate this. Most commentators say that James assumes the readers will understand the object as 'riches' since this is the topic of the entire paragraph. Laws points out that 'stored up' is found in Luke 12:21 without an object. Moo claims that the verb without an object is a more striking image: hoarding itself is what is condemned.

in a time when *God* **is about to judge** *you.* The phrase ἐν ἐσχάταις ἡμέραις 'in/for the last days' was associated in the Old Testament with God's judgment upon people for their sin; that is, it refers to the end of the age when God will reward the righteous and punish the wicked, as in Isa. 2:2. New Testament writers applied this phrase to the period in which they then lived with the expectation that it would soon draw to a close by the intervention of God in judgment (Acts 2:17; 2 Tim. 3:1; 2 Pet. 3:3). Although some versions (KJV, NRSV, JB, NCV) translate the preposition ἐν as 'for', implying that such a time was in the unforeseeable future, most commentators translate it as 'in', as do many versions. NIV, for example, has "You have hoarded wealth in the last days." Most commentators (e.g., Adamson, Moo) consider it a summary statement of vv. 1–3 before the specific charges in vv. 4–6. Several (e.g., Mayor) point out the irony of continuing to amass wealth in the light of the rapidly approaching judgment.

5:4a Think *about what you have done.* The specific charges against the rich begin here. The particle ἰδού 'behold' at the beginning of v. 4 functions to call attention to important images and examples (Davids 1982). It is variously translated as "behold" (KJV, RSV), "look" (NIV, JBP), "listen" (JB, NLT, NRSV), or is omitted (REB). In the display the verb 'think' is used in order to avoid the misconception that the workmen's cries might actually be heard. The content of the thinking is supplied from the context.

5:4b You have not paid wages This is the first of three charges that James makes against the rich (see 5a and 6a for the second and third). The noun phrase ὁ μισθὸς τῶν ἐργατῶν 'the wages of the workmen' follows ἰδού 'behold'. The injustice done to the workmen is expressed by the participial phrase ὁ ἀπεστερημένος ἀφ' ὑμῶν 'being defrauded from/by you', which modifies 'the wages'. Most versions change the passive verb to active and supply the agent 'you' from the prepositional phrase 'by you': "Behold, the wages of the laborers who mowed your fields, which you kept back by fraud, cry out" (RSV) or "You have not paid the wages to the men who work in your fields" (TEV). The scene is set after the harvest, so the owners were certainly able to pay the wages to these day laborers who were so dependent on the money for their daily sustenance. (Prompt payment of laborers is commanded in Scripture in Lev. 19:13 and Deut. 24:14–15.) James' statement implies a threat of judgment.

There is a textual variant for the verb 'defrauded'. Instead of ἀπεστερημένος, some manuscripts read ἀφυστερημένος 'held back'. The GNT has 'defrauded' with an A rating, indicating the opinion that the text is certain. Commentators are about equally divided in their preference, but in either case there is little difference in meaning, since the term 'held back' certainly "connotes an illegitimate, fraudulent action." (Moo)

Most commentators (e.g., Adamson, Tasker) and all versions connect the phrase ἀφ' ὑμῶν 'from/by you' with 'being defrauded' as the agent. A few (e.g., Alford, Huther) connect this phrase with the following verb κράζει 'cries': 'the withheld pay cries out from you', meaning 'from your coffers' but this interpretation is improbable (Hiebert).

to the workmen who have reaped your fields for you The situation is further clarified by the verbs used to describe the workmen. The first description of the workmen is the participial phrase τῶν ἀμησάντων τὰς χώρας ὑμῶν 'those who have mowed your fields'. The aorist tense reflects the fact that they have completed the harvest. Virtually all commentators agree that these same workers are described by the later participial phrase τῶν θερισάντων 'of those who have reaped'. The two verbs 'mow' and 'reap' are used as synonyms in the Septuagint and also in Classical Greek in reference to harvesting (Mayor).

5:4c *with the result that* they are crying out *to God for him to help them*. The noun phrase ὁ μισθὸς τῶν ἐργατῶν 'the wages of the workmen' is the subject of the verb κράζει 'cries'. This is a personification. Inanimate things crying out is a familiar figure in the Old Testament; for example, in Gen. 4:10 the blood of Abel cries out to God for vengeance. Almost all versions retain the personification; only the TEV does not. Such a figure of speech is understood in English, of course, but in many languages it is necessary to replace the personification with a statement that the workmen themselves do the complaining. In fact, this is stated in the very next phrase in 4d, αἱ βοαὶ τῶν θερισάντων 'the cries of those who reaped', where it is rendered 'their fervent cries'.

The communication relation between 4b and 4c–d is reason-result. As a part of the justification for the rich people's need to weep and wail, 4b is prominent. But since result is more often the naturally prominent unit of the reason-result relation and the Lord's hearing the cries of the unpaid workmen may also be understood as a justification for the CLAIM, the result is also considered prominent.

5:4d And *as a result* the all-powerful Lord has heard their fervent cries. The Greek is καὶ αἱ βοαὶ τῶν θερισάντων εἰς τὰ ὦτα κυρίου Σαβαὼθ εἰσεληλύθασιν 'and the cries of those having reaped have entered into the ears of the Lord of hosts'. The name κυρίου Σαβαώθ 'the Lord of hosts' occurs only rarely in the New Testament but is well suited for this situation. The name was used in the Old Testament to suggest the sovereign omnipotence and majesty of God, who would indeed take vengeance (Tasker). Rather than translate it with the Greek word for 'almighty', James transliterates the Hebrew word 'hosts/almighty'. It is rendered 'all-powerful' in the display.

The 'reapers' mentioned here are the same people as the 'workmen' in 4b, and their cries are referred to both here and in 4c. These semantically equivalent references indicate marked emphasis, expressed in the display by the descriptive term 'fervent'.

Not only are the reapers' cries emphasized, but the fact that they have been heard is also emphasized, as shown by the forefronting of the prepositonal phrase 'into the ears of the Lord of hosts'. Note the anthropomorphism here (Adamson), which is a vivid way of saying that God not only listens but also responds to his people.

Both 'defrauded' (4b) and 'entered' are in the perfect tense, implying actions begun in the past the effect of which continues to the present. The injustice by the wealthy landowners continues and also the response by God: the cries of protest have been heard and have not been forgotten. God will surely vindicate them.

5:5a You have lived in luxury and have indulged yourselves James' second charge against the rich sets the pleasure-centered lifestyle of the rich in striking contrast to the hardships they have imposed on the poor. The lack of a connecting particle with v. 4 marks this as a new accusation against them. The two verbs τρυφάω 'live in luxury' and σπαταλάω 'live in self-indulgence' overlap in meaning. Laws claims that they are virtually interchangeable, though she admits that the latter is more pejorative. The first pictures their life of ease, which does not in itself imply wantonness, but its cognate noun in 2 Pet. 2:13 is translated "carouse" (NIV) and "dissipation" (JB). The second adds the thought of unrestrained or excessive self-indulgence. Its only other occurrence in the New Testament is in 1 Tim. 5:6, where a widow living in wanton pleasure is described. Ropes says that the word suggests lewdness and riotousness. Both τρυφάω and σπαταλάω are in the aorist tense, which here is constative, summarizing their way of life.

here on earth. The prepositional phrase ἐπὶ τῆς γῆς 'on the earth' has a negative connotation here. It suggests that their concerns were only for earthly things and may also highlight the contrast that awaits them in the Day of Judgment (Martin).

5:5b *Just as cattle fatten themselves*, The second half of v. 5 is a vivid metaphor that compares the rich to fattened cattle that will be slaughtered. The words here are supplied as an expression of the image, which is not explicit in the Greek.

not realizing that **they will be slaughtered,** The focal point of 5b–c is the phrase ἐν ἡμέρᾳ σφαγῆς 'in a day of slaughter'. Most commentators (e.g., Ropes, Davids 1982, Laws) consider this a metaphor referring to the Day of Judgment. A few (Adamson, Dibelius) say that, to the contrary, it is a continuation of the indictment of the rich: they indulge themselves like victorious warriors in a feast after a victory. This view, they say, fits best with the first part of v. 5 and with v. 6, and introducing the idea of judgment would interrupt the mounting climax of charges in 4–6. Despite these arguments, the view that it is a metaphor is preferable because the primary focus of the entire 5:1–6 unit is not on rich people's self-indulgence but on the judgment that is coming upon them. Also, the implication in this context is that it is the rich who will be slaughtered, which is the normal interpretation of the phrase 'day of slaughter'. The topic of the metaphor is the punishment of the rich, the image is the slaughter of fattened cattle, and the point of similarity is the lack of awareness of impending doom.

Commentators differ in their interpretation of the preposition ἐν 'in' in the phrase 'in the day of slaughter'. Almost all (e.g., Moo, Martin, Davids 1982) say that it means *in* the Day of Judgment, but a few (e.g., Ropes) prefer *for*, equating ἐν with εἰς. This would mean in preparation for the day of slaughter at some future time. The former is preferable, since it reflects the belief of the early church that the last days had already begun, as 2 Pet. 3:3, for example, indicates.

There is a minor textual variant in v. 5. Some manuscripts add ὡς 'as' before ἐν 'in'. Only the KJV includes this, following the Textus Receptus. It is best omitted because it lacks sufficient manuscript evidence. (It is not dealt with in the GNT.) Moreover, if 'as' is included, the allusion to the Day of Judgment is weakened; it is only a comparison of the self-indulgence of the rich to fattened cattle that will be slaughtered. In reality, there is a clear allusion to the Day of Judgment, not only here but in the entire paragraph. The verb 'slaughter' is used in the Old Testament (e.g., Jer. 25:34) to refer to God's judgment.

5:5c you have indulged yourselves, *not realizing that you will be severely punished by God.* The verb phrase ἐθρέψατε τὰς καρδίας ὑμῶν 'you nourished/fattened your hearts' is a vivid picture of the self-indulgent lifestyle of the rich. The verb means to satiate with food, but connected with 'your hearts', as here, it is figurative. The term 'hearts' is a metonymy, referring to their inner life, the source of their attitudes and values, or as in the display, themselves. Most versions translate this phrase literally: "fatten your hearts" (NASB, NRSV), "fatten yourselves" (TEV, NIV). Mayor (p. 229) paraphrases it: "thinks of nothing but personal gratification." This is a good nonfigurative rendering and is reflected in a few versions (e.g., JBP). In the rendering in the display the focus is on their self-indulgence or pleasure-seeking in an attempt to avoid the suggestion of literal obesity. The point of similarity, namely the lack of awareness of impending doom, is supplied here.

5:6a You have *caused* innocent people to be condemned. The third charge against the rich is that they have unjustly used their power to have the righteous condemned and oppressed, even to the point of death. The absence of any connecting particle marks it as an independent charge. The verb καταδικάζω 'condemn' is a judicial term implying that this was done through the Jewish court, as was hinted in 2:6, hence the word 'caused' in the display. Rich Jews controlled these courts by bribes and even used their influence with pagan judges to secure unjust verdicts against the poor (Hiebert). This was a common accusation made by Old Testament prophets against the rich. Perverting the legal process was how they had accumulated much of their wealth.

Most commentators interpret the phrase τὸν δίκαιον 'the righteous one' as a collective term. The article is generic with the reference to an individual as representative of his class. James is continuing the theme of the righteous poor who are oppressed by the ungodly, powerful wealthy. The term 'righteous' has several meaning components, one of which is 'innocent', as in Luke 23:47 (BAGD, 196.4). It is that aspect which is in focus in this context.

5:6b You have *caused* some to be killed (*or*, to die), Although a few (e.g., Oesterley) say that the verb φονεύω 'murder' means actual killing in this context, most (e.g., Hiebert, Moo, Davids 1994) interpret it to mean that at times the condemnation the rich secured in the courts resulted in the death of the innocent poor, in other words, judicial murder. Other commentators (e.g., Ropes, Kistemaker) mention the possibility that the reference could be to the taking of life by unjustly depriving the poor of the means of making a living, as in Ecclesiasticus 34:22: "As one that slayeth his neighbor is he that taketh away his living; and *as* a shedder of blood is he that depriveth a hireling of his hire." The second alternative in the display is based on this. James used the word 'murder' primarily as an indication of the lengths to which oppression could be carried (Laws). The aorist tense of both 'condemn' and 'murder' indicates a summary of actions done at various times. It is significant that there is no connector between these two verbs, an example of asyndeton that sharpens the climax. Note that both alternatives in 6b refer to passive rather than active murder.

5:6c *even though* **the innocent ones were not able** *to* **resist you (***or,* **were not resisting you).**" The Greek is οὐκ ἀντιτάσσεται ὑμῖν 'he does not resist you'. This final clause of v. 6 seems on the surface to be anticlimactic. To understand why James ended the paragraph like this, first its grammatical form should be determined. It is possible to translate the clause as a question based upon the punctuation in the Westcott and Hort Greek text. Hort proposes that it is a question that expects a positive answer. Ropes agrees: "Does not he resist you?" Then the subject of the verb ἀντιτάσσεται 'resist' could be 'God' (as in the TEV footnote) or 'the righteous', with the means of resistance being their prayers or their testimony against the rich in the Day of Judgment. However, the generally accepted view is that it is a statement of the nonresistance of the poor, and this is far more likely. It is more natural and more in keeping with the prophetic style characteristic of the whole passage (Oesterley). It would have been a more regular construction if the participle οὐκ ἀντιτασσόμενον 'not resisting' had followed δίκαιον 'the innocent one'; however, this direct statement is far more graphic (Mayor). The change from aorist to the present tense also makes the statement of nonresistance more vivid (Loh and Hatton).

Not resisting may mean patient acquiescence to ill-treatment, but in this context it is more likely here to mean their inability to withstand their powerful oppressors (Laws). The appeal for patient endurance in v. 7 would then seem more logical.

As to this statement's being anticlimactic, various responses are made by those who interpret it as a statement. Some (e.g., Adamson) say that by concluding with the helplessness of the victims the oppression of the rich is made all the more heinous. Huther proposes that the primary emphasis is, by implication, on the proximity of the vengeance of God, who is especially concerned for the suffering of the innocent, and this would lead naturally to the exhortation in v. 7. Either explanation is possible.

5:6d *That* **[1b–6c]** *is what I say to the rich people who oppress you.* Closure to the direct speech addressed to the rich in 5:1b–6c is supplied here. It functions as a transition to the following paragraph, in which believers are again addressed. Without it, the shift may be too abrupt. Furthermore, this transition is implied by the conjunction οὖν 'therefore' in 7a.

BOUNDARIES AND COHERENCE

The initial boundary of the 5:1–6 paragraph was discussed under 4:1–17. The beginning of the next paragraph at 5:7 is marked by the vocative ἀδελφοί 'brothers', indicating a change of those being addressed: in 5:1–6 it is rich unbelievers; in 5:7–11 it is poor believers. There is also a change of topic: from retribution for the rich to an exhortation concerning patience. In addition, the genre changes from expository to hortatory.

Lexical coherence is shown by the vocative πλούσιοι 'rich ones' in v. 1 and other nouns in the same semantic domain: πλοῦτος 'riches' in v. 2 and χρυσός 'gold' and ἄργυρος 'silver' in v. 3. Further coherence is shown by the contrast between the oppressive activities of the rich in vv. 4–6 and the nonresistance of those designated as the 'righteous' in v. 6.

PROMINENCE AND THEME

In the 5:1–6 paragraph the focus is on James' charges against the rich and the certainty of future punishment by God. The paragraph pattern is thus CLAIM-*justification*. Since both are integral to such a unit, the theme includes elements of both the 1b–d CLAIM and the 2a–3c and 4a–6c *justifications*. The theme is worded as a description of what will happen to rich oppressors, rather than as being directly addressed to them as in the Greek text. Such a wording fits better with the rest of the themes in the epistle and also reflects the fact that the direct address in Greek is not literally intended.

SECTION CONSTITUENT 5:7–11 (Hortatory Paragraph: Appeal of 5:1–11)

THEME: Therefore wait patiently for the Lord Jesus Christ to return and judge all people fairly. Do not complain against each other lest he judge you when he returns. From the examples of the prophets and Job we know that God blesses and rewards those who patiently endure suffering.

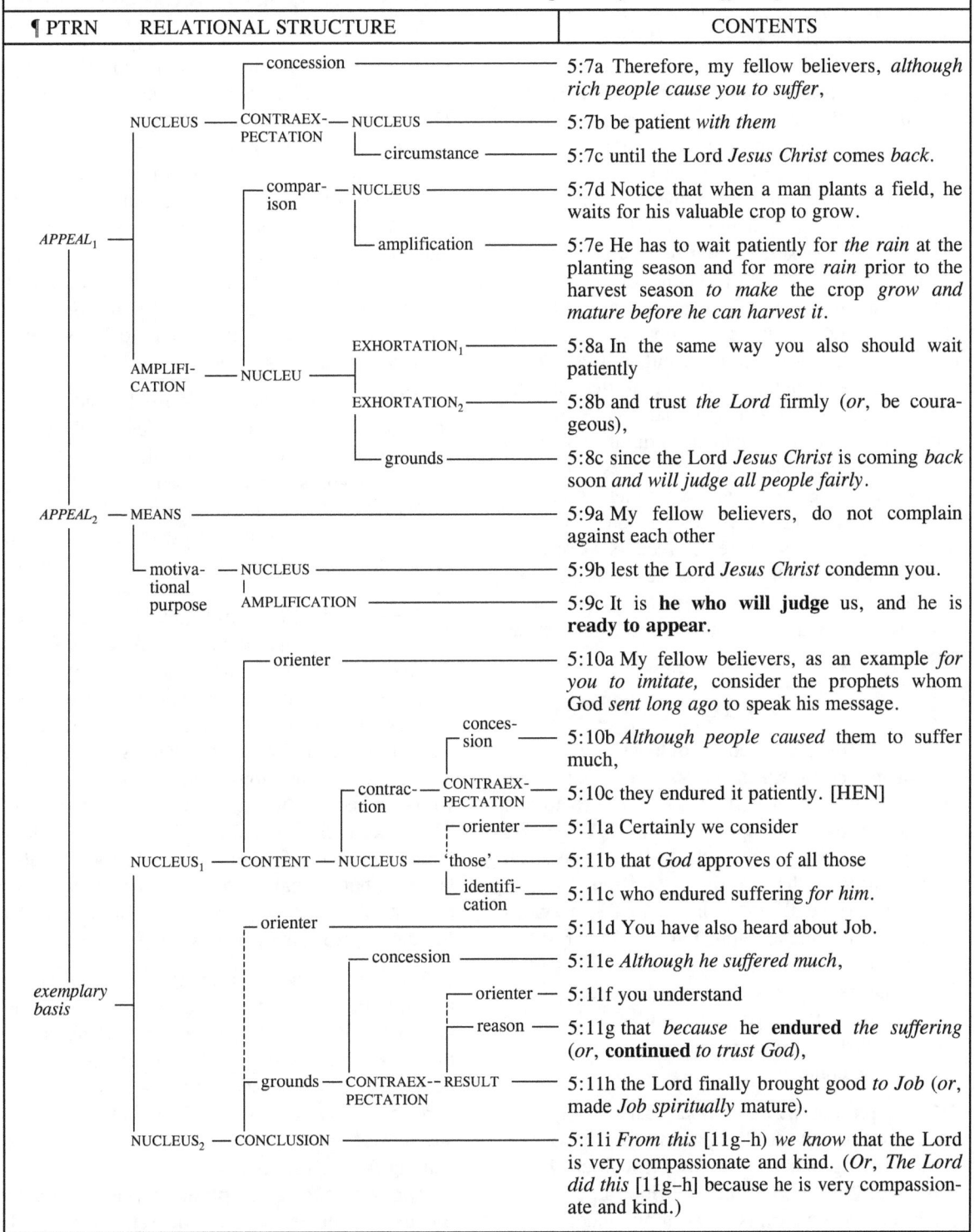

INTENT AND PARAGRAPH PATTERN

In the 5:7-11 paragraph James' intent of stimulating the readers to patient endurance of suffering is brought clearly into focus. The unit's internal structure is two APPEALS (7a-8c and 9a-c) and an *exemplary basis* (10a-11i), so this is a hortatory unit. (Within the first APPEAL there are three Greek imperatives and one in the second APPEAL.) In the first APPEAL the general exhortation to patience is reinforced by an example from nature that shows the necessity of waiting patiently for the final outcome. In the second APPEAL James makes a more specific application of the need for patience during a time of great stress by warning them of judgment if they do not stop acting impatiently toward fellow believers. He is urging the believers not only to have patience with unjust treatment but also with each other, since a bitter spirit manifested in the church has a dire effect upon harmony. Then he reinforces his call for patient endurance with an *exemplary basis*, providing examples from the Old Testament of those who were blessed and rewarded for enduring hardships patiently. His purpose in this is to motivate the readers to respond to their own difficult circumstances with the same patient endurance as the heroes of old. The *exemplary basis* is related to both APPEALS, not just the second one.

NOTES

5:7a Therefore, my fellow believers, *although rich people cause you to suffer,* Here there is an abrupt change of tone from the sharp rhetorical address to the rich oppressors in 5:1-6. This paragraph begins with the warm, personal address used earlier in the letter: the vocative ἀδελφοί 'brothers'. It is linked to the previous paragraph by the conjunction οὖν 'therefore', which contains the promise that God will punish their oppressors. This certainty provides a *basis* for the APPEAL to patience in 5:7-11. The situation that necessitates patience is supplied in 7a from the context.

5:7b be patient *with them* The meaning of the verb μακροθυμέω 'be patient' has to do with demonstrating patience despite difficulties (Louw and Nida, 25.168). Its initial position in the paragraph indicates that this is the topic under focus. James is urging the believers to exercise self-restraint and refrain from retaliation (Tasker). The aorist tense here is best viewed as constative, focusing on the attitude one should have in such situations. Such patience contrasts with the anger warned against in 1:20 and 3:14-16, which is the natural reaction to ill-treatment. Therefore the relation between 7a and 7b is concession-CONTRA-EXPECTATION.

5:7c until The preposition ἕως 'until' suggests the idea of a goal as well as a time period (Moo). The focus is not so much on time as on the significance of the occasion referred to.

the Lord *Jesus Christ* **comes** *back.* The noun παρουσία 'coming' was commonly used for the official visits of a monarch to a city under his rule. But in the early church the phrase 'the coming of the Lord' had become a technical term for the return of Christ. Virtually all commentators agree that κύριος here refers to Jesus Christ, so 'Jesus Christ' is supplied.

5:7d Notice The particle ἰδού 'behold' directs attention to the somewhat complicated illustration which follows, as in 3:4-5 and also 5:4.

that when a man plants a field, he waits James likens their situation to that of the farmer who must wait for an extended period of time before he can harvest the crop he has labored over.

for his valuable crop to grow. The Greek is τὸν τίμιον καρπὸν τῆς γῆς 'the precious fruit of the land'. Most English versions render this in terms of land producing or yielding a crop, but in another language it is important to seek the natural way of referring to a harvest. The crop is described as 'precious' or 'valuable'—it was valuable because it was needed to maintain life. This expression would help James' readers identify with the farmer, who was not a wealthy landlord but a small farmer who depended on his harvest for survival (Stulac). Because it is 'precious', it is also worth waiting for (Mayor).

5:7e He has to wait patiently The repetition of the first word in v. 7, μακροθυμέω 'wait patiently', puts emphasis upon patient waiting as the theme of this farming illustration. In its first occurrence an imperative form is used; the form here is a present participle, implying a constant attitude of expectancy throughout the time of waiting for the harvest.

for *the rain* **at the planting season and for more** *rain* **prior to the harvest season** The Greek is ἕως λάβῃ πρόϊμον καὶ ὄψιμον 'until it receives early and latter'. Almost all commentators agree that the referent of 'it/he', which is the subject of the verb 'receive', is not the farmer, but either the fruit or the earth. Some (e.g., Hiebert, Oesterley) prefer the earth, since at the time of the early rains the fruit was not yet in existence; but more (e.g., Ropes, Mayor, Davids 1982) favor the fruit. Most versions express this phrase in some natural, idiomatic way. The REB, for example, has "the farmer . . . can only wait in patience until the early and late rains have fallen." Every language will have its own natural way of expressing such rain and its effect on the land and the crops.

There is a textual variant here. Some manuscripts insert ὑετόν 'rain' before πρόϊμον 'early'. The GNT omits this word, giving the omission a B rating, "almost certain." However, even without it the reference is clearly to the rains. In the Septuagint the noun 'rain' always appears with these two adjectives. Furthermore, the readers knew the climate of Palestine and would have understood that these adjectives were referring to rain. The *early* rains came in late October and early November; they were needed to soften the hard-baked soil for sowing. The *late* rains came in late April and May; they were essential for the maturing of the grain. Descriptive phrases like those in the display may be needed so that the receptor audience will understand the situation clearly, especially in locations where there are no such distinctions in the time of essential rain.

to make **the crop** *grow and mature before he can harvest it.* The complement of the participle 'waiting patiently' is ἐπ' αὐτῷ 'over it', in which 'it' refers to the crop. It may be necessary to supply words about the function of the rains as in the display. In many languages it is also necessary to refocus on the farmer's goal, which was not rain but the harvesting of the crop.

5:8a In the same way you also should wait patiently The call for patience in v. 7 is repeated in 8a with the same imperative, μακροθυμήσατε 'be patient'. The repetition strengthens this important imperative. The next phrase, καὶ ὑμεῖς 'you also', refers back to the 7d illustration of the farmer: you also, like that farmer, should wait patiently. The communication relation between 7d–e and 8a–b is comparison-NUCLEUS.

5:8b and trust *the Lord* **firmly (***or***, be courageous),** The exhortation στηρίξατε τὰς καρδίας ὑμῶν 'strengthen your hearts' adds to the 8a exhortation to patience by focusing on their inner being. The word 'heart' includes their thoughts, attitudes, and motives. This phrase is variously translated as "stand firm" (NIV), "do not lose heart" (JB), "take courage" (NLT), and "keep your hopes high" (TEV). Some commentators say that this means a firm adherence to the faith (Moo), whereas others stress the need for hope, tenacity, and courage (Ropes). Both alternatives are given in the display as equally valid. In the context this inner strengthening is based on the hope of the return of Christ (see 8c). This same verb is used with 'God' as agent in 1 Thess. 3:13, where it is an encouragement to believers as they await Christ's return. Thus this work of inner strengthening is God's work in their hearts (see also 2 Thess. 2:17). However, the focus here is on their personal duty to develop an attitude of courage and firmness in facing difficulties.

5:8c since the Lord *Jesus Christ* **is coming** *back* **soon** The grounds for the preceding exhortations is the expected return of Christ. The noun phrase παρουσία τοῦ κυρίου 'the coming of the Lord' is repeated here to give hope to those who are suffering, a hope that should affect their attitudes and actions. This noun phrase is the subject of the verb ἤγγικεν 'has come near', which is in the perfect tense, indicating that it has already drawn near and is therefore imminent. The early church believed that Christ could return within a very short time, although Jesus himself warned against setting dates. The hope that he might return at any time is a vital influence on Christian living. If his return is relegated to a remote future, it ceases to be "a *living* hope" (Tasker). However, "James's point . . . is not the length of time between the present and the coming of Christ but how one deals with the interim of waiting" (Martin).

and will judge all people fairly. This implicit information is drawn from the picture in 7d of the harvest that the farmer was awaiting. The 'coming of the Lord' throughout the New Testament is associated with the end time, including, of course, the deliverance and reward of believers and the punishment of evil people who were oppressing them (Moo, p. 167).

5:9a My fellow believers, do not complain against each other Although some (e.g., Dibelius) do not see v. 9 as fitting with the context, most commentators consider it a specific application of the need for patience, that is, in their relationship with other believers. The vocative ἀδελφοί 'brothers' does not here indicate a change of topic, as it so often does, but rather shows the urgency of the appeal (Loh and

Hatton). The verb στενάζω 'grumble' means to sigh or groan because of an undesirable circumstance (BAGD, 766). It is only natural that oppressed people would feel frustrated, but the use of the phrase κατ' ἀλλήλων 'against one another' indicates that their frustration was being directed against their fellow believers. The imperative is in the present tense, which may indicate a habitual action; thus it could be rendered 'do not keep complaining'.

5:9b lest the Lord *Jesus Christ* condemn you. The subordinate conjunction ἵνα 'in order that' is used here with the negative μή, a construction that functions as a warning. James reminds his readers of the undesirable consequence to be avoided. The communication relation between 9a and 9b is MEANS-motivational purpose. The verb κρίνω 'condemn' is in the aorist tense, which indicates the finality of judgment. Any attitude other than patient endurance will bring judgment. Commentators differ in their view of who is doing the judging in v. 9. Some (e.g., Ropes, Laws) say that it is God because of the statement in 4:12 that there is only one Judge, which in that context is indisputably God, the giver of the Law. The majority, however (e.g., Martin, Hiebert), contend that in this context it is Christ, since he is the one whose coming they are anticipating.

5:9c It is he who will judge us, and he is ready to appear. James uses a very dramatic style for emphasis in describing the judgment. The initial particle ἰδού 'behold' calls attention to what follows. In addition, both the subject, ὁ κριτής 'the judge', and the prepositional phrase, πρὸ τῶν θυρῶν 'at the doors', are fronted. This phrase is an idiom indicating imminence, an event almost begun (Louw and Nida, 67.58). Although a few versions (KJV, NRSV, NLT) translate the particle as 'look' or 'see', a significant number simply omit it (NIV, TEV, CEV, NCV). JBP uses an emphatic pronoun for emphasis: "The judge himself is already at the door." The rendering in the display, which expresses the idiom nonfiguratively, is a cleft construction.

5:10a My fellow believers, as an example *for you to imitate*, For the sake of strengthening the exhortation to patience in 5:7-9 James cites the prophets as examples to follow. The noun ὑπόδειγμα 'example' stands first in the sentence, being the central concept of vv. 10-11. This term can be used negatively—conduct to be avoided, as in Heb. 4:11 and 2 Pet. 2:6. However, it is used positively here (cf. John 13:15); it is conduct that believers are to imitate. This idea is supplied in the display.

consider Although the verb λάβετε 'take/consider' is an imperative, it is not another APPEAL in sequence. Rather, it has to do with how the readers should handle the previous APPEALS in 5:7-9. It functions as an orienter, drawing attention to the example of the prophets that James expects them to emulate.

the prophets The word προφήτης 'prophet' is not limited to those who wrote prophetic books. It includes all the prophets of old whom God called to be his messengers (Hiebert). The reference is to the Old Testament prophets whom God used as his spokesmen.

whom God *sent long ago* to speak his message. The relative clause οἳ ἐλάλησαν ἐν τῷ ὀνόματι κυρίου 'who spoke in the name of the Lord' signifies that the prophets spoke as God's representatives and therefore with his authority. This is indicated in the display by 'sent long ago'. Note that what the prophets suffered (10b) was a result not of wrongdoing but of their obedience and faithfulness to God (Moo).

5:10b-c *Although people caused* them to suffer much, they endured it patiently. Much has been written about the relationship of the two nouns here, κακοπαθία 'suffering hardship' and μακροθυμία 'long-suffering'. Some commentators (e.g., Alford, Huther) say these are two distinct ideas: "As an example of suffering and patience" (RSV). They point to the definite articles before each noun as evidence that the prophets provide a twofold example, of suffering and of patience. However, a greater number of commentators (e.g., Laws, Ropes, Moo) interpret the phrase as a hendiadys. This interpretation is reflected in many versions: NIV has "as an example of patience in the face of suffering." The articles are articles of previous reference rather than an indication of two separate ideas. James' purpose is not to furnish an example of suffering as such, but an example of patience in suffering. Thus the relation between 10b and 10c is labeled concession-CONTRAEXPECTATION.

5:11a-c The 5:11a-c propositional cluster, building on the example of the prophets, makes a general statement about all who endure. It also prepares the way for the specific example of Job (Hiebert). While 11a-c may seem to be an amplification of 10b-c, yet it has the more prominent bit of information. Note also that the occurrence of ἰδού at this point in the argument creates emphasis on 11a–c. This is another reason to consider 11a–c more prominent than 10b–c. Thus the communication relation between 10b–c and 11a–c is seen as contraction-NUCLEUS.

5:11a Certainly The introductory particle ἰδού 'behold' calls special attention to the worthiness of perseverance under suffering. It is a call to closer consideration and contemplation (BAGD, 371.1c). Some versions translate it as "remember" (JB, JBP, NEB); others omit it (TEV, REB, NCV, NLT); CEV translates it "in fact." The word 'certainly' also fits the sense well in this context.

we consider The verb μακαρίζομεν 'we count blessed' has two meaning components. The first is 'count', which means to estimate the worth of something. The second is 'blessed', the content of the evaluation. The first component is expressed here. It functions as the orienter for 11b–c.

5:11b that *God* approves of all those The focus in vv. 10–11 is on three elements of the believer's life: suffering, perseverance, blessing (Stulac). These three develop in succession. Perseverance is the believer's proper response to suffering, which in turn results in blessing from the Lord, the second meaning component of the verb μακαρίζομεν 'we count blessed'. Moo rightly says,

> 'To be blessed' is not, of course, the same as being *happy* (despite the tendency of modern versions so to translate); 'happiness' normally suggests a subjective, emotional reaction; 'blessing' is the objective, unalterable approval and reward of God.

5:11c who endured suffering *for him*. In v. 11 there is a subtle shift of emphasis in the discussion of suffering. James changes from the verb μακροθυμέω 'be patient' in vv. 7, 8, and 10 to ὑπομένω 'endure', another verb in the same semantic domain. Both refer to responses to difficult circumstances in life. In some contexts the two terms are virtually synonymous. The difference may be that the former implies patience or self-restraint despite difficulties whereas the latter focuses on continuing to persevere in the face of difficulties. The emphasis here is less on patience and more on perseverance in the face of suffering.

Grammatically the participial phrase τοὺς ὑπομείναντας 'the ones having endured' is the object of the verb μακαρίζομεν 'count blessed'. It identifies the ones who are considered blessed. They were approved because of their perseverance under difficult circumstances.

Although it is not mentioned in the GNT, there is a minor textual variant in 11c. Instead of the aorist participle ὑπομείναντας 'having endured', a few manuscripts read the present participle ὑπομένοντας 'enduring'. It may be that copyists changed the aorist participle to the present tense participle because they wanted the text to refer to people still alive (Martin). However, the aorist reading is the best authenticated one. The aorist indicates a reference to people in the past; thus the emphasis in 11a–c is on the full enjoyment of the state of blessedness enjoyed by those who persevered to the end of their lives. This emphasis is in no way incompatible with the challenge to the readers to persevere in order to enjoy God's blessing and approval; the present tense *is* used in 1:12 ('Blessed [is] the man who endures trials').

5:11d You have also heard about Job. James' second example for the readers to imitate is a specific individual, Job, whose story was well known to the readers. The reference to having heard about Job may mean that they had heard readings in the synagogue or that Job's story was common knowledge (Huther).

5:11e *Although he suffered much*, The noun ὑπομονή 'endurance, perseverance' has two meaning components: endurance in suffering. The relation between suffering and endurance is best described as concession-CONTRAEXPECTATION. The 11e proposition is supplied here to express the concession, and this is followed by the CONTRAEXPECTATION in 11f–h. In many languages it will be necessary to state the full meaning of ὑπομονή in two or more clauses rather than in one word.

5:11f you understand The verb here is εἴδετε 'you saw', which is figurative. The sense is mental perception. Although most versions translate it literally, terms such as 'notice', 'recognize', and 'understand' are suggested by BAGD (578.1cα). The rendering in the display follows the NJB: "You have heard of the perseverance of Job and understand the Lord's purpose. . . ."

5:11g that *because* he <u>endured the suffering</u> (or, <u>continued to trust God</u>), The primary lesson from Job's life is summed up in the noun ὑπομονή 'endurance', which is here fronted for emphasis (see the note on 11c for a discussion of its meaning components.) Kistemaker elucidates the nature of Job's endurance: "He is known for his steadfastness, that is, his persevering faith that triumphed in the end." Since the word 'endurance' is aspectual, indicating a process that continues over time, it implies an action and the action is trusting. Therefore the idea of 'perseverance' is given in the display as the second of two acceptable alternatives. Either one is a good expression of the reason for the 11h RESULT that the Lord brought to Job.

5:11h the Lord finally brought good *to Job* (or, made *Job spiritually* mature). There are three main interpretations of the noun phrase τὸ τέλος κυρίου 'the end of the Lord'. (1) Several older theologians (e.g., Augustine) as well as Lange say that it refers to the death of Jesus as another example of perseverance; however, such an interpretation does not fit either the preceding or following context. (2) Many commentators (e.g., Ropes, Laws, Adamson) say that 'of the Lord' is a subjective genitive and refers to the outcome brought about for Job by the Lord. They mention the concept of reward, although some do not limit the outcome to the purely physical restoration of Job's family and possessions. For example, Mayor says it is best understood as "the end appointed by the Lord, viz. Job's final prosperity and the declaration of his integrity against Satan and the friends. . . ." Proponents of this view defend it as the more usual meaning of the word 'end' and more appropriate in a context where James is encouraging his readers to hope for an intervention of God as the end of their time of suffering (Laws). In most versions 'the end of the Lord' is translated in accord with this view. For example, REB has "how the Lord treated him in the end," and TEV has "how the Lord provided for him in the end." (3) Other commentators (e.g., Martin, Oesterley) say that 'end' should be rendered as 'purpose', as in the NRSV, meaning that it is the end designed by the Lord. Martin presents this view very convincingly:

> There is a reason for suffering and that is to produce Christians who are mature and complete (1:4; 3:2; cf. Rom. 5:1-5). . . . Job came to understand God's faithful nature (Job 42:5) before his material possessions were restored, and as he persevered, he found his closest communion with God in the midst of adversity.

In the display the second view, which is the generally accepted one, is presented as a very generic statement. The third view is also given as a valid alternative. Both are possible meanings of 'end' in this context. BAGD (811.1c) gives the meaning as "*end* or *goal* toward which a movement is being directed, *outcome*." Hiebert seems to accept both, presenting them as two different uses of the word 'end' without any expression of preference. He mentions both "appropriate reward" (view 2) and the purpose of the Lord "to refute Satan's slander . . . and to vindicate and strengthen Job's faith" (view 3). In some languages, aspects of both views could be used, if they are meaning components of 'end'—the views are not necessarily mutually exclusive. In view of the total content of the epistle, it would be well to include the concept of spiritual maturity in the outcome.

5:11i *From this* [11g-h] *we know* that the Lord is very compassionate and kind. (*Or, The Lord did this* [11g-h] because he is very compassionate and kind.) Commentators differ in their translation of the initial conjunction ὅτι 'that/because'. Some (e.g., Huther, Mayor, Hiebert) interpret it as epexegetic: '(showing) that God is compassionate and merciful'. Interpreted thus, the clause that it introduces further explains the preceding one: the way God acted toward Job is the way he acts in general. "All of this demonstrates the character of the Lord, which is finally what James wants his readers to know with confidence" (Stulac). Such a view of God, as seen in the ending of Job's story, is what would give the readers hope. Based on this interpretation, the communication relation between 11e-h and 11i is shown as grounds-CONCLUSION in the display and ὅτι may be rendered 'that' (KJV, NASB, NJB), 'how' (NRSV, WEY) or be omitted (NAB, NIV, TNT, NCV). The other interpretation is that ὅτι expresses the cause (e.g., Alford, Adamson, Martin): 'the Lord dealt well with Job because he is compassionate and merciful'. In this case the communication relation between 11e-h and 11i is RESULT-reason. The REB, TEV, CEV, NLT, and Berkeley so render it. Both interpretations are valid, although the former is preferred.

The two coordinate adjectives that describe 'the Lord' are closely related in meaning. Moore (p. 60) calls them a near-synonymous doublet. Therefore it would be acceptable to use only one adjective in translating them, but using the two may add emphasis to the concept and bring out the subtle difference in meaning between them. The first, πολύσπλαγχνος 'very compassionate', is not found elsewhere in the New Testament or in the Septuagint. James may even have coined it (Hiebert). Louw and Nida (25.52) say that it has to do with "great affection and compassion." The second adjective, οἰκτίρμων 'merciful/kind', occurs frequently in the Septuagint. It is plural, perhaps to express the varied outward manifestations of this abstract concept (Hiebert). This implies not only an attitude but also actions motivated by a merciful attitude. In the Greek the concept 'compassionate-merciful' is emphasized both by the forefronting of one of its representations ('compassionate') and also by the use of two words to represent the one concept.

BOUNDARIES AND COHERENCE

The initial boundary of the 5:7–11 paragraph was discussed under 5:1–6, and the final boundary under 1:19–5:11. Lexical coherence is shown by the verb μακροθυμέω 'be patient' in vv. 7 (twice) and 8 along with the cognate noun μακροθυμία 'patience' in v. 10 as well as by a verb in the same semantic domain, ὑπομένω 'endure', and its cognate noun ὑπομονή 'endurance' both in v. 11. The farmer analogy in v. 7 and the examples of the prophets and Job in vv. 10–11 provide further coherence. Semantic coherence is seen in the concept of judgment that is implied by 'the coming of the Lord' in vv. 7–8 along with the verb κρίνω '(to) judge' and its cognate noun κριτής 'judge' in v. 9.

PROMINENCE AND THEME

Since the *APPEAL* and the *basis* are integral to a hortatory paragraph pattern, the theme of the 5:7–11 paragraph includes prominent elements from both *APPEAL* units and the *exemplary basis*. The motivational purpose clause following the second *APPEAL* is also included since it functions as motivational grounds for carrying out that *APPEAL*.

PART CONSTITUENT 5:12–18
(Hortatory Division: Concluding Appeals of 1:2–5:18)

THEME: Always tell the truth. Whatever your circumstances are, pray and God will help you. So confess your sins to each other and pray for each other.

MACROSTRUCTURE	CONTENTS
APPEAL₁	5:12 Don't say, "If I am lying, may God punish me." Instead, always tell the truth lest God condemn you.
APPEAL₂	5:13–18 Whatever your circumstances are, pray with faith and God will certainly help you, both physically and spiritually. So confess your sins to each other and pray for each other, since God answers prayer.

INTENT AND MACROSTRUCTURE

James is now ready to end his letter, so he concludes with significant pastoral instructions to summarize his main message (see "Intent and Macrostructure" under 1:2–5:18). His intent is to encourage these suffering believers to persevere; he wants to instill in them the proper response to the difficulties of life.

The 5:12–18 division is hortatory, being composed of conjoined *APPEALS*. The first (5:12) is an exhortation concerning oaths, which addresses the problem of the tongue again as well as the coming judgment. The second (5:13–18) counsels prayer in distress and sickness. Both *APPEALS* relate to the religious expression of strong emotion (Ropes).

BOUNDARIES AND COHERENCE

The initial boundary of the 5:12-18 unit has already been discussed under 1:18-5:11 and the final boundary under 1:2-5:18. It should be mentioned that a number of commentators consider either 5:12-18 (e.g., Martin, Ropes) or 12-20 (e.g., Laws, Lenski) a macrostructural unit, with a major break before v. 12. Laws affirms that "a train of thought, if not always a tightly logical one, may be discerned running through it [i.e., 5:12-20]." Martin unites v. 12 with vv. 13-18 under the theme of community issues, including oath-taking and reactions to problems and sins. Others, however (e.g., Dibelius), dispute the unity of vv. 12-18.

A few commentators (e.g., Blue, Hill) unite v. 12 with vv. 7-11 at a macrostructural level (Blue on the basis of the topic of patience and Hill interpreting πρὸ πάντων δέ as indicating that the command in 5:12 is more important than that of 5:9). However, a greater number (e.g., Ropes, Laws, Martin, as just mentioned) unite v. 12 with the verses that follow at the macrostructural level.

The 5:12-18 division begins with the phrase πρὸ πάντων δέ 'above all' (see the note on 12a) and contains topics commonly treated in the closing of a Greek letter: an oath formula and health and prayer (Martin, p. xcix, and Davids 1982:25-26). But the oaths that were used in Hellenistic epistography were for the purpose of proving the writer's trustworthiness, and what James says in 5:12 is not such an oath. Whether his mention of oaths at the end of his letter has any relation to the oaths in Greek letters is not clear. However, even the topic of oaths in this strategic place might indicate an association in James' mind with the conclusion of his epistle.

The coherence of the 5:12-18 unit lies in its emphasis upon the believers' conduct in their community. This is marked by the personal pronouns ὑμεῖς 'you(pl)' in vv. 12, 13, and 14 and of ἡμεῖς 'we' in v. 17 as well as by the reciprocal pronoun ἀλλήλων 'each other' in v. 16.

As the close of the letter is anticipated, James includes a reminder of many of the epistle's important themes. They are woven together into a coherent whole in the final unit of the body. Some of the key motifs repeated here are: speech and judgment in v. 12, trials and testings in v. 13, prayer in vv. 13-18, faith in v. 15, and repentance and righteousness in v. 16. Johnson (p. 184) observes,

> It is surely not by accident that James' composition begins and ends on the topic of prayer, since prayer is the activity that most fundamentally defines and expresses that construal of reality called "faith."

James mentions all these topics here to summarize his major concerns.

PROMINENCE AND THEME

Both of the *APPEALS* of 5:12-18 are naturally prominent. The theme is therefore drawn from both.

DIVISION CONSTITUENT 5:12 (Hortatory paragraph: Appeal₁ of 5:12–18)

THEME: *Don't say, "If I am lying, may God punish me." Instead, always tell the truth lest God condemn you.*	
¶ PTRN RELATIONAL STRUCTURE	CONTENTS
orienter	5:12a Also, my fellow believers, *I want to say* something important *about how you talk.*
NEGATIVE APPEAL — NUCLEUS	5:12b Don't say, "If I am lying, may *God in* heaven [MTY] punish me."
└ amplification	5:12c Don't even say, "If I am lying, may *the one who rules* the earth [MTY] punish me." Don't say anything like that.
POSITIVE APPEAL	5:12d Instead, *always speak the truth, so that people will believe you if you only* say "yes" or "no,"
motivational basis	5:12e lest *God* condemn you.

INTENT AND PARAGRAPH PATTERN

The stress upon oaths in the 5:12 unit at such a strategic place in this epistle seems strange to the modern mind. However, in the ancient world, both Jewish and Greek, oaths played an important role. In the Sermon on the Mount Jesus dealt with his contemporaries' misuse of oaths (Matt. 5:33-37); they frequently used subtle distinctions of form to avoid binding themselves to an obligation. In the Greek culture, authors of formal letters customarily wrote an oath at the end of their letters to guarantee their truth (Davids 1982).

James' intent in 5:12 is different. He wants to point out the necessity of total honesty toward God and toward men when responding to the problems of life. Consequently, although this verse has an element of prohibition, its primary focus is positive. This is reflected in 12d and in the theme statement.

There are two imperative forms in the 5:12 paragraph, one negative and one positive, hence the *NEGATIVE APPEAL* (12b-c) and the *POSITIVE APPEAL* (12d). They are followed by a *motivational basis* (12e). Thus the unit is hortatory. The threat of being condemned by God is a great inducement to complete integrity in speech.

NOTES

5:12a Also, my fellow believers, Here δέ functions grammatically to indicate the switch of topic from patient endurance to swearing. Since δέ acts together with πρὸ πάντων 'above all' (see 12b) to introduce the unit, it is not necessary to translate it explicitly in English. In fact, the majority of versions do not translate δέ here (TEV, NIV, NRSV, REB, NCV, CEV, JBP). However, it is rendered as 'also' in the display to indicate the switch to a new topic.

I want to say something important *about how you talk*. Much has been written about the significance of πρὸ πάντων, which may be understood in three different ways. (1) Some (e.g., Lenski) hold that its force is temporal: those who swear must stop doing that before they proceed to anything else. (2) Others say it refers to importance compared with something else, but James does not state what this is. Most commentators agree that it does not mean that swearing is a worse sin than stealing, adultery, or murder. Some (e.g., Adamson) say that the comparison is only with the previously mentioned sins of speech. Although many languages require that a comparison be complete, we have not attempted to complete this one since to do so would be pure speculation and would change the focus of the passage. (3) There are still other commentators (e.g., Moo, Davids 1982) who interpret πρὸ πάντων as an emphatic introductory phrase calling attention to what follows. Laws says that it performs "an intensifying function, identifying something as particularly important in its own right, and not necessarily in comparison with other ideas." This third view is preferable and is the one reflected in the rendering in the display with the implicit actor, action, and topic supplied from the context. Several commentators, including Martin, Moo, Moffatt, and Kistemaker, point out that the phrase is intended to signal the final section of the letter in much the same way as the adverb λοιπόν 'finally' in 2 Cor. 13:11.

Proposition 12a functions as an orienter to the entire paragraph. Loh and Hatton summarize its function well:

> **But above all** is literally "Before everything (else)." This can be taken to mean that the exhortation introduced by this formula is the conclusion of a series of exhortations and is the most important of them all. However, it seems best to take it as a transition to a new line of thought with emphasis. The phrase **above all**, as used here, does not have to mean that the warning against swearing is more important than other exhortations; it probably means that what follows as a whole is important. It also signals that James is bringing his letter to a close. The familiar expression **my brothers** (meaning "brothers and sisters" or "fellow believers") also serves to mark the transition, in addition to **above all**.

5:12b Don't say, "If I am lying, may *God in heaven* punish me." The negative imperative μὴ ὀμνύετε 'do not swear' is in the present tense. As with other prohibitions in the present tense, this could be translated as 'stop swearing'; but there seems to be no indication that swearing was a particular problem in the early church (Johnson). Louw and Nida (33.463) define the verb 'swear' as "to affirm the truth of a statement by calling on a divine being to execute sanctions against a person if the statement in question is not true." The phrase μήτε τὸν οὐρανόν 'neither by heaven' invokes God's name; that is, 'heaven' substitutes for God's name. Unless the receptor language has a word or set expression that contains most of the components of this definition of swearing, it will be necessary to express it in a verbal clause, as in the display. The command to not swear is reminiscent of Matt. 5:34-37 and contains remarkable parallels. There are minor differences such as the fact that James uses only two examples whereas Matthew has four, and James does not include the explanations that Jesus gave. James also uses the accusative following the verb, which is a classical construction, whereas Matthew has ἐν with the dative, a Hebraism. Nevertheless, the primary focus is the same: our truthfulness should be so consistent and dependable that we do not need an oath to support it (Moo).

Some commentators (e.g., Huther, Alford) contend that 'swear by heaven' does not mean swearing by the name of God and that the prohibition is against frivolous oath-swearing. In similar fashion others (e.g., Kistemaker) believe that James is referring to the Jewish custom of making nonbinding oaths by the avoidance of God's name. Ropes, however, interprets James' concern to be about irreverently calling upon God in their distress with an emphasis also on the importance of truthfulness. Although no version uses the name of God here, many commentators (e.g., Hiebert, Martin) imply that the ultimate appeal in all of these oaths *was* to God. Therefore it seems preferable to consider 'heaven' a typical Jewish metonymy for the name of God. The word 'heaven' could be omitted in the rendering if it is expressed as 'God', but note that 'heaven' does tie in with 'earth' in the next proposition.

Care should be taken in the receptor language not to confuse swearing with cursing:

> A wrong turn is given to this injunction when swearing and cursing are combined, or when swearing is connected with the sufferings that are mentioned in the preceding section. This view confuses swearing and cursing. A man who is in distress utters no more oaths than one who is not in distress. (Lenski)

Several commentators (e.g., Reicke, Moffatt) reflect this confusion. They mention impatience as the cause of the problem or "hasty swearing and imprecations" (Alford).

5:12c Don't even say, "If I am lying, may *the one who rules* the earth punish me." The phrase μήτε τὴν γῆν 'nor by the earth' has to do with swearing by things considered holy, a kind of oath that was common. This, like swearing in the name of God, was forbidden. The reference to earth is clearly linked to God, since in Matt. 5:35 earth is called God's footstool (an indirect reference to Isa. 66:1). This is brought out in the rendering as '*the one who rules* the earth'.

Don't say anything like that. Although James does not mention all the kinds of oaths listed in Matt. 5:34-37, he does cover them by the additional phrase μήτε ἄλλον τινὰ ὅρκον 'nor any other oath'. The question is, Does this prohibit all swearing? Moo points out that historically some Christians, such as the Anabaptists, answered yes to this question—they refused to take oaths even in the courtroom—yet Paul used oaths (Rom. 1:9, 2 Cor. 1:23). What James denounces is the use of oaths in everyday conversation to prove integrity (Davids 1982).

5:12d Instead, *always speak the truth, so that people will believe you if you only say "yes" or "no,"* The imperative clause ἤτω δὲ ὑμῶν τὸ Ναὶ ναί, καὶ τὸ Οὒ οὔ 'but let your yes be yes and no be no' is the positive counterpart of the negative exhortation in 12b. Ropes, citing a similar example from noncanonical Jewish literature, says that this expression "seems to correspond to a current Jewish mode of describing truthfulness." The function of this expression is supplied in the display in addition to the 'yes' and 'no'. In some languages it would be better to express this in terms of fulfilling a promise: Bratcher suggests "Just say 'I promise to do it' or 'I promise not to do it,' and keep your promise." Or it could be stated as keeping one's word: 'If you say, "I'll do something," do it. If you say, "I'll not do something," don't do it.'

5:12e lest *God* condemn you. One major difference between Matt. 5:34-37 and what James says here in v. 12 is that the latter concludes with a warning of judgment in which the implicit agent is God (cf. 4:12). The warning is expressed as a purpose clause: ἵνα μὴ ὑπὸ κρίσιν πέσητε 'lest you fall under judgment'. A similar warning occurs in 5:9. The theme of judgment is prominent in chapter 5, especially vv. 1-6, 9, and 12. There is also an implicit reference to a time of judgment in 7-8 in the phrase ἡ παρουσία τοῦ κυρίου 'the presence/coming of the Lord'.

There is a minor textual variant here, which the GNT does not mention. The text of Erasmus, followed by Tyndale, reads 'lest ye fall into hypocrisy'. This may have been an attempt to bring the passage more into line with Matt. 5:37, but it lacks adequate manuscript support and fails to provide the motivation for the strong appeal to total truthfulness.

BOUNDARIES AND COHERENCE

The initial boundary of the 5:12 unit was discussed under 1:19-5:11. Its closing boundary and the start of the next unit at 5:13 is marked by a rhetorical question and a change of topic, from oaths to praying. The coherence of the 5:12 unit consists in its being one Greek sentence. The twofold exhortation about swearing oaths also provides coherence.

PROMINENCE AND THEME

Both the NEGATIVE APPEAL and the POSITIVE APPEAL in the 5:12 unit are naturally prominent, and the theme is drawn from both. Since the *basis* is integral to any hortatory paragraph pattern, it is included in the theme as well.

DIVISION CONSTITUENT 5:13–18 (Hortatory Paragraph: Appeal₂ of 5:12–18)

THEME: Whatever your circumstances are, pray with faith and God will certainly help you, both physically and spiritually. So confess your sins to each other and pray for each other, since God answers prayer.

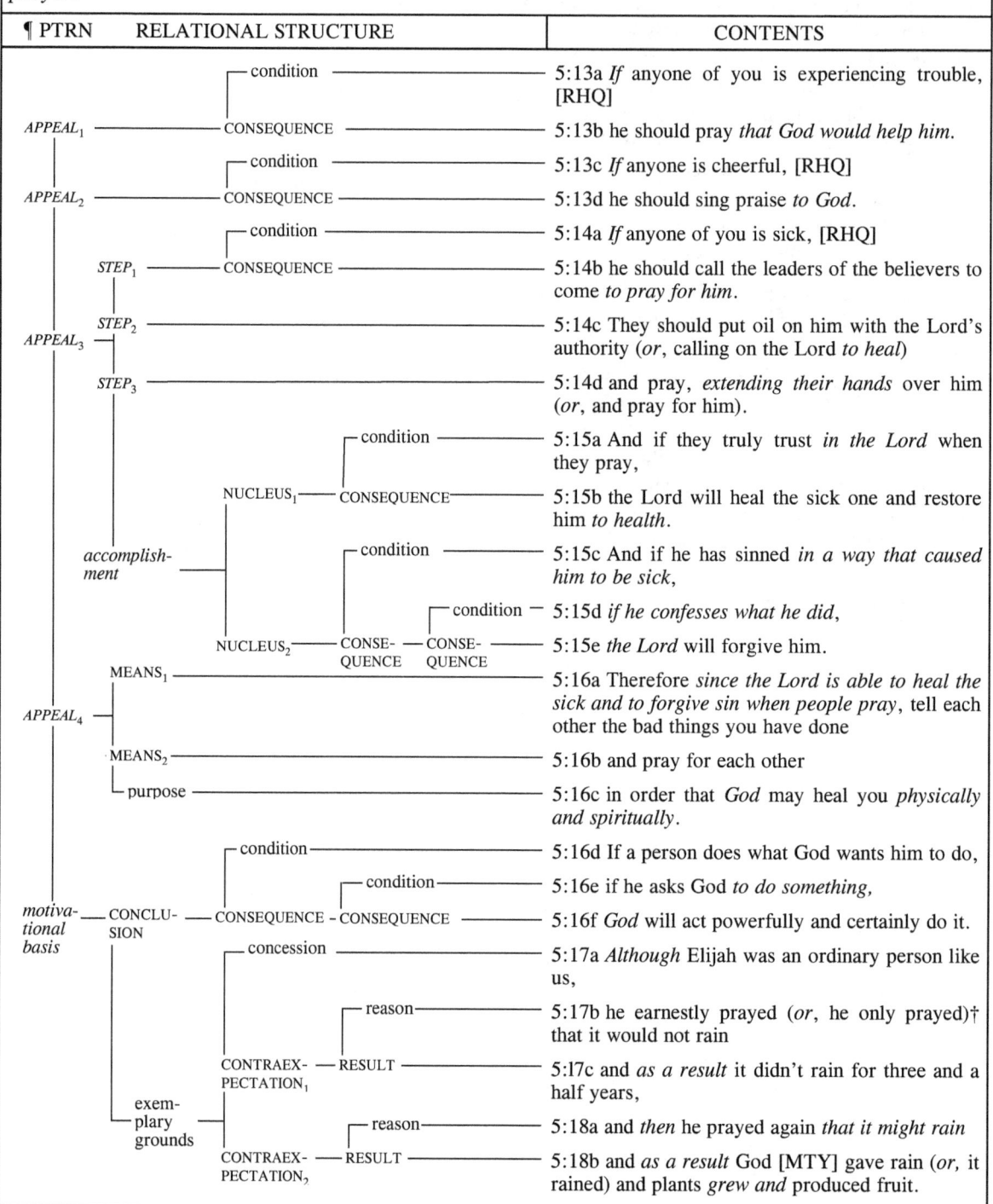

INTENT AND PARAGRAPH PATTERN

The 5:13–18 paragraph comprises four *APPEALS* followed by a *motivational basis*, all of which deal with the need for prayer. In the first two *APPEALS* (13a–b and 13c–d) the readers are exhorted to pray when they find themselves in certain conditions, namely, when they experience trouble and when they feel cheerful. The third APPEAL (14a–15e) contains detailed instructions for praying in the specific situation of sickness. Within this third APPEAL there is an embedded procedural paragraph pattern consisting of three STEPS (14a–b, 14c, and 14d) that culminate in the *accomplishment* (15a–e). (While there is an occasion-outcome relation between 14a–b and 14c–d, it seems better to handle all three as STEPS since the genre is procedural.) The STEPS are imperatives, hence prominent, with the labels in upper-case letters. The final APPEAL (16a–c) challenges the whole Christian community to mutual confession of sin and prayer for each other. The *motivational basis* (16d–18b) includes the promise that prayer will be answered (16d–f) as well as an example from the life of Elijah demonstrating the effectiveness of prayer (17a–18b).

NOTES

5:13a If anyone of you is experiencing trouble, The Greek is κακοπαθεῖ τις ἐν ὑμῖν 'suffers hardship anyone among you'. A few commentators (e.g., Dibelius) interpret this clause as a declarative statement: 'Someone among you suffers'. However, the vast majority consider it a rhetorical question, this being characteristic of James' style throughout the book (cf. 2:14, 3:13, and 4:1), a very vivid style typical of a diatribe (see the discussion of diatribe on p. 7 of the introduction). In many languages, however, rhetorical questions, if they occur at all, do not have the function that they have in a diatribe. Here the rhetorical question is followed by an imperative and may be translated as a conditional clause. In fact, Martin calls this clause "quasi-conditional"; and Tasker says that it is "in effect the protasis of a conditional sentence." Although the majority of versions (e.g., NIV, NRSV, TEV) translate it as a rhetorical question, a few (JB, JBP, and CEV) translate it as a conditional clause. In the display the conditional is given.

The verb 'suffers hardship' is a general term referring to the misfortunes of life. It would include persecutions like those the prophets endured. (The cognate noun is used in 5:10 with the same meaning.) Davids (1982) says that it emphasizes the inner feelings resulting from misfortune.

5:13b he should pray *that God would help him*. The imperative προσευχέσθω 'let him pray' gives the proper response to the trials of life. The present tense indicates habitual practice whenever troubles come. The content of the prayer is not explicit. Bratcher suggests that the prayer should be understood as asking for God's help; Laws says "presumably for relief or deliverance"; but most commentators (e.g., Martin, Moo) stress that in view of the context it is prayer for the strength to endure. The display follows Bratcher's suggestion since it is the most generic way of expressing it in this context.

5:13c If anyone is cheerful, The verb εὐθυμέω 'be cheerful' refers to a heart attitude of cheerfulness not dependent upon circumstances. It is the word used in Acts 27:22 and 25 as Paul encouraged the crew just before the shipwreck off Malta: 'be of good cheer'. (See the note on 13a for an explanation of the grammatical forms here.)

5:13d he should sing praise *to God*. In Classical Greek literature the verb ψάλλω refers to the playing of a stringed instrument. In the Septuagint it is used of playing but also of singing to such an accompaniment. In the New Testament it is used of singing without reference to any instrument. In 1 Cor. 14:15 it is closely associated with prayer; as Moo says, it can be regarded as a form of prayer. Normally this verb is followed by a dative noun referring to the one to whom the praise is intended (see Eph. 5:19). Here there is no explicit dative form, but it is supplied from the context to fill out the case frame.

5:14a *If* anyone of you is sick, This is a third circumstance in which prayer is the proper response. The verb ἀσθενέω means 'be without strength'. Throughout the Gospels this word clearly refers to physical illness (e.g., Mark 6:58, Acts 9:37, Phil. 2:26). But in the Epistles it is also used of general weakness (e.g., 2 Cor. 12:10) and figuratively of moral weakness (Rom. 4:19). Virtually all commentators agree that James here refers primarily to physical sickness. However, there is also a spiritual dimension in this context—see 15c–e and 16a–c, where confession of sin and forgiveness are addressed.

5:14b he should call the leaders of the believers to come This is the CONSEQUENCE following the quasi-condition in 14a. The 14a–b pair, which is more complex than the two preceding condition-CONSEQUENCE pairs (13a–b and 13c–d), is best considered as an embedded procedural paragraph pattern (see "Intent and Paragraph Pattern"). In such a situation of sickness, it is the sick person himself who is to take the initial STEP, perhaps as an expression of faith. The group to be summoned is identified as 'the elders of the church', πρεσβύτεροι 'elders' meaning 'older ones', a term commonly used for the elders or leaders both of Jewish communities and Christian (as in Matt. 16:21 and Acts 14:23). The noun used here for 'church' is ἐκκλησία. Although in 2:2 James used συναγωγή 'synagogue' to refer to the assembly of believers, ἐκκλησία is the more frequent term. Thus those to be summoned are the leaders of the local assembly, the older, spiritually mature men, typically. Martin points out that it was the elders as a group who were to perform this ministry, not a particular individual with the gift of healing (see 1 Cor. 12:9).

to pray for him. The purpose of summoning the elders was that they might pray. This implicit purpose is supplied based upon the Greek clause 'and let them pray over him' (14d). In Greek this clause directly follows 'let him call the elders', but in the semantic analysis the order of the propositions is different.

5:14c They should put oil on him Prayer was to be accompanied by anointing the sick one with oil. Almost all commentators stress the fact that prayer rather than anointing was the primary act. Lenski comments that since 'anointing' is a participle, it "marks the minor and subsidiary act, a fact that should be noted." The participial phrase ἀλείψαντες ἐλαίῳ 'having anointed (him) with oil' follows the main verb phrase, προσευξάσθωσαν ἐπ' αὐτόν 'let them pray over him', which is an imperative. When joined to an imperative, as here, a participle often has imperatival force as well. Commentators differ in their interpretation of the function of this aorist participle and the sequence of the events of anointing and praying. Some (e.g., Hiebert, Johnson) say that anointing probably preceded the prayer, but the majority (e.g., Kistemaker, Martin, Laws) say simply that the anointing accompanied prayer. The aorist participle does not necessarily imply that anointing should precede the prayer—it may refer to the completeness of the process. However, it *can* mark action before that of the preceding finite verb, as in Mark 1:31: ἤγειρεν αὐτὴν κρατήσας τῆς χειρός 'he raised her holding her hand' (BDF, §339). If in the receptor language the sequence needs to be specified, it would be preferable to state the action of anointing as preceding the prayer.

There are several different views of the significance of this anointing. Some (e.g., Burdick, Wilkinson) regard it as medicinal. Oil was widely used in the ancient world for medicinal purposes (see Luke 10:34). Others consider the purpose of the anointing as symbolic, representing God's healing power (Martin), the Holy Spirit (Hoyt), or the power of prayer (Davids 1989). Other interesting speculations as to its use are to awaken faith (Mitton) or to reduce the temptation to use charms, incantations, or other such pagan devices (Ropes). The symbolic interpretation is probably preferable. However, it is not necessary in a translation to make the function of the anointing explicit. The most important point is that this is an activity subsidiary to the praying. In languages where the concept of anointing is unfamiliar, it may be helpful to specify that only a small amount of oil was used. Furthermore, the manner of application may need to be specified. TEV has "rub," and NCV "pour," but the right word in translation will to some extent be based on the receptor language usage.

with the Lord's authority (*or*, calling on the Lord *to heal*) The phrase ἐν τῷ ὀνόματι τοῦ κυρίου 'in the name of the Lord' is more naturally connected with 'anointing', although some (e.g. Mitton, Hiebert) say that it modifies both 'anointing' and 'pray'. As to the meaning of 'in the name of the Lord', there are two main views: (1) acting with the Lord's authority (Laws, Moo), and (2) invoking the name of Jesus, that is, appealing to the Lord to heal, as in Acts 3:6 and Luke 10:17 (Huther, Dibelius). In the display both alternatives are given. The latter alternative is suitable for languages in which there is no idiomatic way to express doing something with the authority of another.

A few manuscripts have Ἰησοῦ or Ἰησοῦ Χριστοῦ after κυρίου, but the GNT, which omits this, gives its own text an A rating, indicating the opinion that it is certain. Although most commentators agree that κυρίου refers to Jesus Christ, undoubtedly the additions to the text were scribal emendations.

5:14d and pray, *extending their hands* over him (*or*, and pray for him). The finite verb προσευξάσθωσαν 'let them pray' marks prayer as the main focus of the elders' ministry in the healing. It is in the aorist tense, probably to stress urgency (Martin). The prepositional phrase ἐπ' αὐτόν 'over him' emphasizes motion or direction

(Dana and Mantey, p. 106). Many commentators say this should be taken literally, either as describing the elders standing by the bedside or possibly extending hands over, or even laying hands upon, the sick one. It is also possible to understand it as simply prayer directed toward the sick man (Davids). Both alternatives are acceptable.

5:15 The v. 15 *accomplishment* involves two conjoined NUCLEI. The first (15a–b) addresses the primary condition for healing, the prayer of faith; the second (15c–e) addresses the forgiveness of any sins that could have caused the sickness.

5:15a And The initial καί indicates a continuation of the situation described in v. 14. In some versions (e.g., TEV, JB, REB, NRSV, CEV, JBP) it is not translated. In a few the connection is indicated by some other grammatical device, such as the demonstrative pronoun in TEV: "This prayer made in faith will heal the sick person. . . ." The conjunction καί here introduces a result, this being one of its several functions according to BAGD (392.2f). In a procedural paragraph pattern it marks an *accomplishment*.

if they truly trust in the Lord when they pray, Prayer is clearly James' main focus in the 13–18 paragraph. This is reflected in the fact that the anticipated healing is attributed not to the anointing but rather to the elders' prayers. The noun phrase ἡ εὐχὴ τῆς πίστεως 'the prayer of faith' signifies "the prayer which expresses trust in God and flows out of commitment to him" (Davids 1982). The genitive 'of faith' is a descriptive genitive: the prayer that is based on faith. But this does not "imply that if only there is a sufficient degree of faith, prayer will be answered" (Tasker). Although this statement is unconditional and could refer to general faith in God, several factors indicate that 'the prayer of faith' is a special term in this context:

1. The word used here for prayer is unusual. It may mean a fervent wish or petition as in Acts 27:29 and Rom. 9:3. It is also used for 'vow', hence is a strong word.
2. The definite article is used with both 'prayer' and 'faith', making the expression specific to the context.
3. Even the words σώσει 'will heal' and τὸν κάμνοντα 'the one being sick' are not the usual technical terms used for physical healing and sickness. (See the note on 15b for a full discussion of these words.)

Moo sheds light on the meaning of this phrase as follows:

> This faith, while certainly including the notion of confidence in God's ability to answer, also involves absolute confidence in the perfection of God's will. A true prayer of faith, then, always includes within it a tacit acknowledgment of God's sovereignty in all matters; that it is *God's* will that must be done. . . . Therefore, the "faith" that is the indispensable condition for our prayers for healing to be answered—this faith being the gift of God—can be truly present only when it is God's will to heal.

All English versions render this phrase with a general, unconditional sense. In some languages a statement of general faith may be adequate, but in others it may be necessary to show that more than general faith is involved, hence the word 'truly' in the display. Hiebert says,

> . . . it is not just an ordinary prayer for another, however good and sincere it may be, but the prayer prompted by the Spirit-wrought conviction that it is the Lord's will to heal the one being prayed for.

While this is a very biblical concept, it is not explicit in this verse.

5:15b the Lord will heal the sick one James' choice of Greek terms presents ambiguities and challenges. The verb σῴζω 'save/heal' that is used here can have the eschatological sense of salvation in the last days, as it does in 2:14, 4:12, and 5:20. For this reason Martin says that some scholars see in its use here deliverance from spiritual death. However, the majority of commentators agree that in this context it is far more likely to refer to physical healing.

One other view deserves consideration. Some (e.g., Blue) consider that the verb 'save/heal' and related terms in vv. 14–15 are being used figuratively. The one said to be sick in v. 14 (ἀσθενέω 'be weak/sick') is here referred to as τὸν κάμνοντα 'the one being sick/discouraged'. Thus the healing could be viewed as a restoration from discouragement and spiritual defeat rather than as recovery from an illness. This argument is supported by the fact that the most common verb for heal ἰάομαι 'heal' is not used until 5:16. But we take this to be physical sickness, remembering, however, that there may well be a spiritual dimension to the sickness, since the term has mental and emotional aspects.

In translating σῴζω 'save/heal', it is preferable to consider the primary focus in this context to be upon physical healing, for the following reasons:

1. The verb 'save/heal' is commonly used of physical healing throughout the Gospels (see, e.g., Matt. 9:21-22 and Mark 6:56).
2. The use of oil (14c) seems to imply a physical condition.
3. Although the verb 'be sick/discouraged' is used figuratively in its only other New Testament occurrence (Heb. 12:3), it commonly has the meaning 'be sick' in Classical Greek.
4. The example of Elijah's prayer for rain in vv. 17-18 involves physical elements.
5. The language is too specific to mean spiritual health rather than physical (Huther).

The vast majority of commentators (e.g., Davids 1982, Adamson, Moo) believe that this person was physically ill. However, they point out that the rest of the verse indicates that the man's spiritual condition is also involved. In addition, Johnson points out that in New Testament literature when the word 'save' is combined with 'faith', it tends to mean 'saved' in a religious sense. So if in another language there is a broader term that would indicate *both* physical and spiritual healing here, it could well be used.

and restore him *to health*. The verb ἐγείρω 'raise up' is, like σῴζω 'save/heal', ambiguous. It is commonly used of the resurrection, but most (e.g., Alford, Huther) agree that here it means to raise him up from his bed of sickness. Louw and Nida (23.140) cite this verse as an example of the figurative extension of the meaning of 'raise up': to restore a person to health. Ropes says that this word is virtually synonymous with 'heal/save', intended as a repetition of the same concept.

The subject of ἐγείρω 'raise up' is ὁ κύριος 'the Lord', showing that it is the Lord who is the true source of the restoration (Hiebert). Commentators agree that this is a reference to Jesus.

5:15c And if he has sinned *in a way that caused him to be sick*, The connective κἄν 'and if, even if' is a contraction of καί and ἐάν (a crasis). Huther and Alford contend that this is not a copula ('and if') and should be rendered 'even if' with the implication that the sickness was the result of sin. While it is true that in most of the occurrences of κἄν in the New Testament 'even if' is more appropriate, in Mark 16:18 and Luke 13:9 κἄν does have the copulative force. The vast majority of commentators take it as a copulative here also, as do we. It is important not to imply that all sickness is a result of sin in the life of the sick one.

The noun ἁμαρτίας 'sins' is fronted, indicating that it is the new topic. It is plural, implying repeated occasions. Some commentators (e.g., Mayor, Ropes) say that the sins referred to here are sins that caused the sickness, which idea is supplied in the display. Clearly, in view of the conditional, not all sickness is due to sin (see also John 9:2-3). Yet there is the possibility that *this* sickness was the result of sin. This idea is supplied in 15c since the perfect tense of the participle πεποιηκώς 'having committed' implies that the person is abiding under the consequences of his past sins (Hiebert).

5:15d *if he confesses what he did*, Proposition 15d is clearly implied by the context, especially v. 16. Confession is an important step in the process of seeking forgiveness. Commentators all assume the necessity of confession. Adamson says that the service "would obviously include at least the patient's confession of sin"; and Martin concludes, "If illness is related to sin, the asking of forgiveness of sin (as confessed both to God and to the injured party) will lead to healing. . . ."

5:15e *the Lord* will forgive him. The verb ἀφεθήσεται is a future passive indicative, an impersonal construction meaning that forgiveness will be given. The use of the singular verb form together with the phrase αὐτῷ 'to him' implies that 'his sinning' is the understood subject. However, since in many languages it is necessary to express the implicit agent of forgiveness, this is supplied here as 'the Lord', based on the clear teaching of Scripture.

5:16a Therefore *since the Lord is able to heal the sick and to forgive sin when people pray*, The conjunction οὖν 'therefore' indicates a close connection between 16a and what has gone before. James now appeals for a wider application as a general deduction drawn from the situation of vv. 14-15. In the rendering this connection is supplied in an abbreviated summary form. However, this relation is not shown in the left side of the display because to diagram the relation would be too complex: Both 14–15 and 16a-c are *APPEAL* units, yet they are in a GROUNDS-CONCLUSION relation, as signaled by οὖν.

A few manuscripts omit οὖν 'therefore', but the most reliable, ancient ones include it. It is rendered in all versions except KJV. GNT does not even mention the omission as a variant. The presence of οὖν can be accepted with confidence.

tell each other the bad things you have done The verb ἐξομολογέω 'confess' is a compound verb in which the initial ἐκ- is an intensive, implying confession of specific sins, not just of personal sinfulness (Hiebert). This is corroborated by the use of the plural object τὰς ἁμαρτίας 'the sins'. Although the GNT does not mention a variant, some manuscripts have the noun phrase τὰ παραπτώματα 'the trespasses' instead of 'the sins'. All versions except the KJV have 'the sins'. The text does not specify what sins should be confessed. Hiebert says that certainly sins that spoil fellowship are intended, but other sins that burden the conscience may also be included. The main purpose for such confession is ultimately for communal healing.

The reciprocal pronoun ἀλλήλοις 'to each other' that follows the verb stresses that this is a group activity.

5:16b and pray for each other The second imperative in v. 16 is the verb phrase εὔχεσθε ὑπὲρ ἀλλήλων 'pray on behalf of each other'. The two imperatives in 16a-b are connected by the conjunction καί and need to be associated together since prayer is the chief focus of v. 16. Both of the imperatives are in the present tense, indicating a habitual practice. Whereas in vv. 14–15 the elders were the ones to pray for healing, here the whole church body is to be involved. The power to heal is invested in prayer, not in the elders (Moo). The exhortation to confess their sins and pray for one another is based on v. 15: ". . . since prayer has such power [to bring about healing and forgiveness per v. 15], pray for each other; and, that you may be able to do this better, confess your faults to each other . . ." (Mayor).

5:16c in order that God may heal you physically and spiritually. The conjunction ὅπως 'so that' introduces the purpose for the mutual confession of sins and prayer. An understanding of the meaning of the verb ἰάομαι 'heal' in this context is crucial for the proper interpretation of v. 16. There are three main views:

1. Some (e.g., Ropes, Alford) say that only physical healing is involved here. If so, v. 16 would be a concluding exhortation to the discussion of sickness started in v. 14.
2. Others, especially Laws, make a strong case for spiritual healing. She contends that the sickness referred to in v. 15 raises the possibility of sin so that in v. 16 James turns to deal with healing from sin and its consequences (which may or may not include physical suffering). Wells points out that while it is true that the verb 'heal' used here usually refers to curing physical sickness, it also occurs in passages in which the reference is clearly to spiritual healing, as in Matt. 13:15 (quoting Isa. 6:10), Heb. 12:13, and 1 Pet. 2:24 (quoting Isa. 53:5).
3. A number of commentators (e.g., Tasker, Stulac, Hiebert) believe that the healing is both physical and spiritual:

> The reference to the confession and forgiveness of sins in the context makes this broader scope of 'healing' probable. For James and the readers, the thoughts of physical and spiritual healing were closely related. (Hiebert)

The rendering in the display is based on this third view. In translating this word in another language it would be well to include both aspects of healing, if at all possible. As Wilkinson (p. 344) concludes, "Sickness and healing always have more than a physical dimension."

5:16d If a person does what God wants him to do, The one praying is described as δίκαιος 'righteous', an adjective used substantivally. The same adjective is used in 5:6, where the meaning component 'innocent' is the focus. In this context the term more probably calls attention to the ethical character of a person who does God's will. Since 'righteous' in this context can be seen as referring to actions, it is rendered as a clause in the display.

5:16e if he asks God *to do something*, Three different words are used for prayer in this paragraph. The noun in 16e is δέησις 'petition', which is largely restricted to petitionary prayer, though some say there is little difference in meaning between it and εὐχή (v. 15) and προσευχή (v. 17). The lack of an article leaves the petition undefined.

Since prayer is an action, an event concept, it is expressed as a verbal clause in the display. Note that the communication relation between

16e and 16f is condition-CONSEQUENCE, the same relation as between 16d and 16e-f. The 16d condition, however, is more inherent to the argument, the 16e condition being circumstantial. If in the receptor language the concept of a righteous person can be naturally expressed as the subject of the verb in 16e, it would be possible to combine the 16d and e propositions as one conditional clause preceding the 16f CONSEQUENCE. The combined clause would read 'if a righteous person asks God *to do something*'.

5:16f *God* will act powerfully The verb is ἰσχύει 'is strong', referring to capability. In other contexts this verb is used of physical health or strength. Here it expresses the powerful effect of petitionary prayer. James emphasizes prayer's efficacy with the modifier πολύ 'very'.

and certainly do it. The participle ἐνεργουμένη 'being made effective' is a nominative singular feminine form, which would seem to indicate that it modifies, or at least is in agreement with, the noun 'petition'. However, its function in the sentence is not clear. Some (Dibelius, Laws) consider it equivalent to an adjective describing prayer. (JBP has "the earnest prayer"; KJV and WEY are similar.) If this participle is so interpreted, it could also be rendered as an adverb, 'fervently' in 16e: 'fervently pray'. The majority (e.g., Moo, Stulac, Hiebert), however, say that the participle is more directly related semantically to the verb. Some (e.g., Mayor, Davids 1982) interpret it as passive: '(prayer is very powerful) when it is energized by God'. TNT has ". . . because God is at work in it." Others (e.g., Moo, Stulac) say it is in the middle voice: '(prayer is very powerful) in its working or in its effect'. The latter is more likely. Many versions render it as a predicate adjective: "The prayer of a righteous man is powerful and effective" (NIV). The idea of effective prayer is expressed here as the certain fulfillment of the thing petitioned. Several versions treat the two ideas in one clause; TEV, for example, has "The prayer of a good man has a powerful effect" and NCV has "When a believing person prays, great things happen."

5:17a *Although* Elijah was an ordinary person like us, James cites the Old Testament prophet Elijah as an illustration of the truth of 16d-f. Elijah was one of the most popular of all the Old Testament prophets because of his miracles and also because he was the one who would pave the way for the messianic age. Numerous traditions grew up around him, ascribing superhuman traits to him (Hiebert). But James stresses his humanity by the descriptive phrase ὁμοιοπαθὴς ἡμῖν 'of like feeling to us'. This adjective means 'with the same nature', referring to "similar feelings, circumstances, experiences" (BAGD, 566). Its only other occurrence in the New Testament is in Acts 14:15, where Paul and Barnabas responded to the people who mistook them for gods. This adjective's root, πάθος 'suffering, passion', refers to suffering and vicissitudes that come to all human beings, which would be especially apropos to James' readers. His intent is to challenge them to pray by reminding them that any human being who is righteous can offer an effective prayer.

5:17b he earnestly prayed (*or*, he only prayed) The account of Elijah's effective prayers is introduced with the connective καί, which links 17b–18b to the assertion of Elijah's humanity in 17a (Hiebert). The connective καί, which may function adversatively (Dana and Mantey, p. 250), is so taken by JBP: "He was a man as human as we are but he prayed. . . ." More precisely, the relation can be labeled as concession-CONTRAEXPECTATION, with 'although' expressing the 17a concession. Two CONTRAEXPECTATIONS follow the concession, the first in 17b–c and the second in 18a–b.

Although the account in 1 Kings does not state that Elijah prayed that the rain would cease, some infer the idea of a prayer from the words 'As the Lord the God of Israel lives, before whom I stand' in 1 Kings 17:1 (so Ropes). In addition, prayer was prominent in Elijah's other great miracle in 1 Kings 17:17–24. Evidence also exists of a tradition that associated the drought with Elijah's praying (mentioned in the Apocrypha in Ecclesiasticus 48:2–3 and 2 Esdras 7:109).

The verb phrase προσευχῇ προσηύξατο 'in prayer he prayed' reflects the influence of a Hebrew idiom. The reduplication of the root term conveys an intensive force (Wilkinson). (Similar reduplications occur in Luke 22:15, "with desire I desired," and in John 3:29, "with joy he rejoices.") The intensity has been interpreted in two different ways. (1) Some commentators (e.g., Moo, Martin) and almost all versions say that it means that he prayed fervently. (2) Others (e.g., Alford, Ropes) say that this idiom emphasizes the significance of the prayer itself. Huther says,

"This addition of the substantive serves to bring out the verbal idea . . . , not to denote that the prayer of Elias was *earnest* . . . but that nothing else than *his prayer* produced the long drought." The first view is preferable as more fitting in the context, but the second also has merit and is given as a valid alternative. It might be effectively stated as 'he did no more than pray'.

that it would not rain The phrase τοῦ μὴ βρέξαι 'not to rain' is an articular infinitive construction that normally expresses purpose (e.g., in Matt. 2:13, '. . . Herod sought the child to destroy him [τοῦ ἀπολέσαι αὐτό]'). However, when this construction follows verbs of saying such as 'pleaded' in Acts 21:12 or 'prayed' as here, it expresses content.

A translator should consider giving a footnote about the background of Elijah's prayer from 1 Kings 18:18 so that the receptor audience does not get the wrong idea that Elijah's prayer for a drought was because of anger or revenge. Rather it was because of the spiritual and moral degradation of the people of Israel at that time.

5:17c and *as a result* it didn't rain for three and a half years, The communication relation between 17b and 17c is reason-RESULT. The conjunction καί introduces the 16c result of Elijah's prayer. Commentators speculate much about the apparent discrepancy between the length of time specified here and in the Old Testament account (esp. in 1 Kings 18:1). Some of the explanations are (1) that a more specific figure is given here for what was a rounded-off three years in 1 Kings (Kistemaker); (2) that three years and six months is possibly a symbolic figure referring to a period of judgment (Moo); and (3) that three years and six months was just a stock phrase for a considerable period (Laws). Interestingly enough, three years and six months is also mentioned in Luke 4:25 in reference to this drought. But an explanation of the number, if included at all, should be only in a footnote or glossary, not in the text.

The phrase ἐπὶ τῆς γῆς 'on the earth' is rendered in most versions (e.g., NIV, TEV, JBP, NEB, NCV), but in many languages it might be awkward and confusing—where else would it rain? For this reason we omit it. It is also omitted in JB, CEV, and NLT. In translating, a natural, idiomatic expression for rain should be used.

5:18a and *then* he prayed again *that it might rain* After the three and a half years of drought Elijah's prayer was effective once again. The lapse of time may be signaled by 'then', as in several versions (JB, NCV, NLT, JBP). The Old Testament account does not explicitly mention that Elijah prayed, but his posture in 1 Kings 18:42 was obviously a posture of prayer. Bratcher recommends not saying 'the next time he prayed' since that might imply that he had not prayed for three and a half years.

The content of the prayer is not mentioned in the Greek, but for languages in which it is necessary to express the content, the content is easily derived from the context. Like several other versions, CEV has "But when he did pray for rain, it fell." The content is also supplied in the display.

5:18b and *as a result* God gave rain (*or*, it rained) and plants *grew and* produced fruit. The verb phrase ὑετὸν ἔδωκεν 'gave rain' here occurs also in 1 Sam. 12:17, 1 Kings 18:1, and Acts 14:17, in each of which its subject is 'God'. The subject here is the noun οὐρανός 'heaven', a typically Jewish substitute for God's name, hence 'God' in the display.

As in 17c, whatever is the natural way of speaking of rain should be used in translating 'God gave rain'. The REB has "the rain poured down." This rain was the result of the second prayer mentioned in 18a. (Together 18a and b function as the second CONTRAEXPECTATION of the 17a concession.)

The result of the rain is expressed in the clause ἡ γῆ ἐβλάστησεν τὸν καρπὸν αὐτῆς 'the earth brought forth its fruit'. In the display this is rendered in terms of the growth of plants that produce fruit.

The discourse structure of some languages may be such that the paragraph needs a concluding remark in the form of a mitigated appeal. If so, an appeal such as 'Therefore, trusting in God, let us earnestly pray to him' may be supplied here.

BOUNDARIES AND COHERENCE

The initial boundary of the 5:13-18 paragraph was discussed under 5:12 and the final boundary under 1:2-5:18. Coherence is shown by the topic of prayer in every verse in the unit: προσεύχομαι 'pray' in vv. 13, 14, 17, and 18; εὐχή 'prayer' in v. 15; εὔχομαι 'pray' in v. 16; and δέησις 'petition' in v. 16. Further lexical coherence is marked by verbs denoting healing or restoration: σῴζω 'save/heal' in v. 15; ἐγείρω 'raise up' in v. 15; and ἰάομαι 'heal' in v. 16. Semantic coherence is evident in the interrelationship of the physical and the spiritual aspects of healing: In 14a–15b the reference is primarily to physical healing, whereas in 15c–16c, though still in the context of the physical, the need for spiritual healing is focused upon by addressing sin and confession.

A few commentators and versions make various other paragraph breaks: before v. 16 (NLT, CEV, WEY), before 16d (Hiebert; JBP); before v. 17 (Martin; NIV). However, the topic of prayer begun in 5:13 is continued through v. 18. Specifically, 16d–f is a promise closely following upon the 16a–c encouragement to pray, and 16d–f is followed by the 17a–18b illustration about the efficacy of prayer.

PROMINENCE AND THEME

Since *APPEALS* and their *bases* are essential parts of a hortatory paragraph pattern, all four of the *APPEALS* as well as the *motivational basis* are represented in the theme of the 5:13–18 paragraph. But since the themes of these *APPEALS* are closely related, a generic summary of them has been made for the theme statement.

EPISTLE CONSTITUENT 5:19–20 (Hortatory Paragraph: Closing of Epistle)

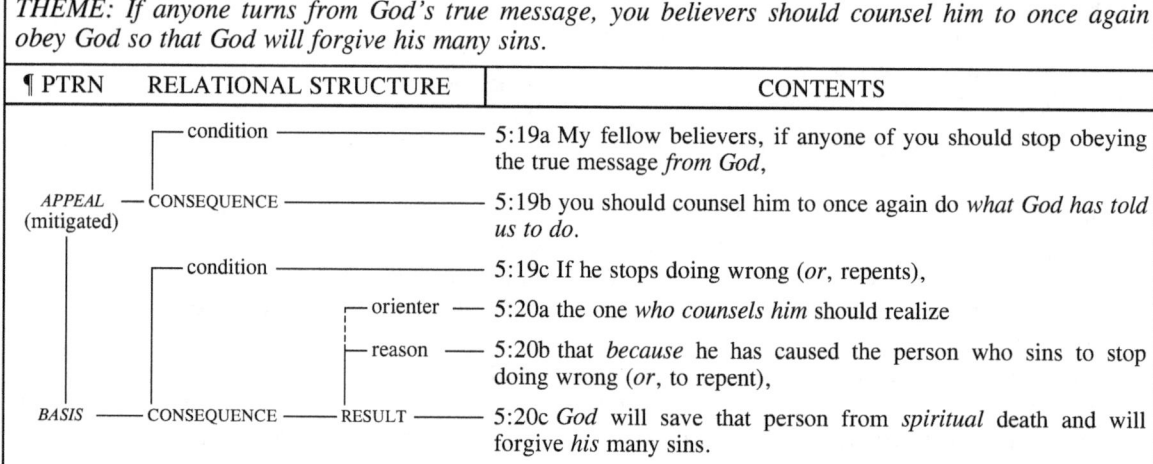

INTENT AND PARAGRAPH PATTERN

The 5:19–20 paragraph is the closing of the epistle, and here James focuses on the matter of dealing with sin within the Christian community. Since the same topic was just considered in 5:15–16, some commentators (e.g., Mayor, Mitton) say James is reverting to the themes of sin and pardon that are expressed there. However, it is more likely that vv. 19–20 emerge "from the content of the Epistle as a whole" (Adamson). The warning against straying found here is also in 1:16; the concept of 'the truth' that is in 5:19a is also in 1:18; and these themes are developed in succeeding chapters. James censures wrong conduct of various kinds throughout the letter, but here he makes it clear that his intent is not to condemn but to restore (Hiebert).

In the Greek text the only imperative in this paragraph occurs in 5:20a. However, 5:19a–b is considered to be a mitigated *APPEAL*, with 5:19c–20c its *BASIS*. Thus the paragraph is hortatory. Proposition 19b deals with an action that James deems necessary for the addressees to take, and 20a–c involves motivation for such an action. The fact that there is an imperative in 20a marks the 19c–20c cluster as very prominent. Thus the *BASIS* is seen as equally prominent with the *APPEAL*.

In the *APPEAL* James presents his readers with the need to bring back the believers who are in great danger of abandoning their faith or of not applying the truth of the gospel in their personal relationships. They are to be brought back into fellowship not only with God but also with the rest of the Christian community. In one sense, unity in the church as a result of personal spiritual renewal is James' goal in the entire epistle. The result of such restoration, presented in the BASIS, provides strong motivation for the readers to heed the 19a–b exhortation.

NOTES

5:19a My fellow believers, if anyone of you should stop obeying the true message *from God*, For the last time James addresses the readers by the familiar vocative ἀδελφοί μου 'my brothers'. It signals that this verse is the beginning of a new paragraph and also conveys affection and concern for the readers. Only here and in 2:1 does it occur first in the sentence.

The third-class conditional clause introduced by the conjunction ἐάν 'if' indicates a hypothetical situation that is viewed as very probable, especially in the light of rebukes given throughout the letter (e.g., 1:21, 2:6, 3:10, 4:1-4). The phrase τις ἐν ὑμῖν 'anyone among you' indicates that the person James is focusing on is a member of their local group.

The situation about which he is concerned is expressed by the verb πλανάομαι 'wander', bringing to mind the metaphor of sheep going astray, though 'wander' here is no doubt a dead metaphor. It is used here to refer to moral straying and is followed by the prepositional phrase ἀπὸ τῆς ἀληθείας 'from the truth', 'truth' meaning the body of truth contained in the gospel. Moo aptly states, "This truth is something that is to be 'done' as well as believed. . . ." The stress throughout the letter is on practical faith that results in right conduct.

Some interpret the verb 'wander' as a passive, but it is probably in the middle voice, in which case the idea of personal accountability is present (Hiebert). The aorist tense indicates not a single act of disobedience but rather a departure from the Christian principles of life.

5:19b you should counsel him to once again do *what God has told us to do*. The conjunction καί connects two coordinate conditional clauses (19a and 19c), their respective verbs being πλανηθῇ 'should wander' and ἐπιστρέψῃ 'should turn back'. The latter is a transitive verb in the active voice, 'turn someone from something', and is used of a change of mind or of a course of action (BAGD, 301). In this context, in view of the meaning of ἀλήθεια 'truth' in 19a, it is a course of action. Two meaning components of 'turn back' are significant in this context. One is the effort on the part of someone to affect a restoration—here it is τις 'anyone' that is the subject of the verb. (The other meaning component of this verb is discussed in the note on 5:19c.) The verb ἐπιστρέψῃ is in the subjunctive and is expressed in the display as a mitigated appeal. (See the note on 3:2b for a discussion of mitigation as proposed by Longacre and Tuggy.)

The indefinite pronoun τις 'anyone' occurs twice in v. 19. The first is in 19a; the second is here in 19b, where it shows that the duty of spiritual restoration was not confined to the elders but was the responsibility of each member of the church (Hiebert). Since 'anyone' is singular, it may be acceptable to translate the pronoun as 'one of you'. However, in the display the plural 'you' is used to convey the idea of group responsibility and avoid the misconception that only one person should counsel. The goal of the counseling is restoration, shown by the verb 'turn back'.

5:19c If he stops doing wrong (*or*, repents) The meaning component of ἐπιστρέφω 'turn back' that is in view in 19c is the response of the person who has morally wandered. Note that the verb occurs only once in v. 19 but with the meaning both of someone causing the wanderer to turn back and the wanderer himself turning back (see the note on 19b for the other meaning component). Although this verb can be used to describe an initial turning to God for salvation, as in Acts 14:15, it can also refer to a wandering believer's turning back to the faith, as in Luke 22:32. The context shows that it is the latter sense that is in focus here. The church is to have a vital part in bringing about such restoration. This proposition underlies the second conditional clause following ἐάν and functions in the semantic analysis at the higher level as the beginning of the BASIS for the APPEAL in 19a–b.

5:20a the one *who counsels him* should realize The verb γινωσκέτω 'he should know' is a third person singular imperative. But although it is an imperative, it functions as the orienter for 20b–c.

Some manuscripts read γινώσκετε 'know', which is a second person plural imperative. This textual variant is most probably a scribal amelioration introduced either to conform to 'my brothers' in 19a or to avoid ambiguity as to which is the subject, the brother who has wandered or the one who brings him back (Metzger, p. 615). The GNT has 'let him know' with a B rating, indicating the opinion that that text is almost certain. In some versions (KJV, JB,

RSV, WEY, JBP) it is rendered as a third person imperative, but in most (TEV, NIV, NCV, NRSV, NLT, REB) as a second person imperative. REB has "you may be sure of this," chosen probably because it avoids ambiguity and fits better into the context, since vv. 19–20 are addressed to the whole group of believers. The display follows the text preferred by GNT but specifies the subject of the verb as 'the one who counsels him'.

5:20b that *because* he has caused the person who sins to stop doing wrong (*or*, to repent), The final clause of v. 19, ἐπιστρέψῃ τις αὐτόν '(if) anyone turns him' is repeated in 20b as ὁ ἐπιστρέψας ἁμαρτωλόν 'the one who turns a sinner'. Some have questioned the reason for this repetition. Hiebert says that it stresses the point, which is crucial. But it is more likely that it functions to avoid ambiguity as to the subject of the verbs in 20c (Mayor).

The prepositional phrase ἐκ πλάνης ὁδοῦ αὐτοῦ 'from the error of his way' is variously rendered as "from his erring ways" (NJB, REB), "from his wrong way" (TEV), and "from his error" (NIV). These are all essentially equivalent. The noun 'way' in the Greek is used of a way of acting or conduct (BAGD, 554.2b), and 'error' contrasts with 'truth' mentioned in 19a. The nature of the error is most probably moral rather than doctrinal error.

These two phrases combine as one subordinate phrase functioning in relation to 20c as the reason for the 20c result. In other words, the action of turning a sinner back to the truth results in his being saved and forgiven. This reason-RESULT relation is expressed by the conjunction 'because'.

If there is a suitable noun for 'sinner' in the receptor language, it would be appropriate here: 'because he has caused the sinner to repent'. It is also acceptable to use a pronoun, for example, 'someone', since the concept of wrongdoing occurs immediately following; to say 'has caused one who does wrong to turn from doing wrong' would be tautological.

5:20c *God* will save that person from *spiritual* death Hiebert summarizes v. 20 by saying, "James approves and encourages this work of restoration by urging his readers to recognize its important results." These results are stated in 20c. (Instead of "results" Laws uses the term "outcome" to refer to the spiritual renewal that James is urging.) The first result is expressed in the verb phrase σώσει ψυχὴν αὐτοῦ 'he will save his soul', in which the word 'soul' is a Hebraism meaning the whole person (used also in 1:21). Here the saving of a soul is attributed to the action of a person (as also in Rom. 11:14, 1 Cor. 7:16, and 1 Tim. 4:16). However, it is understood that God is the primary actor and the individual is just the instrument God uses. The rendering in the display brings this out. (See 20b for the human role in bringing about salvation.)

It is true that since in this context, especially 5:15, illness is associated with sin, the noun θάνατος 'death' could refer to physical death; but almost all commentators agree that the reference here is to spiritual death, eternal death. A few (e.g., Burdick, Ward) hold that the sinner was not a genuine believer before this time. Most (e.g., Adamson, Laws), however, believe that this is an erring Christian who needs to be restored to fellowship. The latter view is better because of the connotation of 'wandering' and because the whole book addresses believers and their problems. Stulac says,

> If we make this verse merely an occasion to argue whether Christians can lose their salvation, we will miss the real impact James wants to make on his readers. He is again, with passion and forcefulness, warning his readers that genuine faith includes repentance for sin and a life of obedience to Christ as Lord. What James is saying in 5:20 is simply consistent with his view throughout the letter. See the discussion of 1:15, where he first brought up the notion of death. His point is not that true believers may lose their salvation by sinning, but that sin full-grown ultimately destroys the sinner, and that genuine faith compels us to flee from sin and to help each other do the same.

and will forgive *his* many sins. This clause expresses the second result of reclaiming one who has wandered from the true message. It is joined to the previous clause by the conjunction καί. The verb phrase καλύψει πλῆθος ἁμαρτιῶν 'he will hide/cover many sins' is frequently associated with Prov. 10:12; however, in that context 'hide/cover' refers to the eagerness of love not to expose or gloat over the sins of others (Tasker). Here the term implies forgiveness, as it does also in Ps. 32:1.

Commentators are divided as to whose sins are covered. Some (e.g., Moffatt, Adamson, Ropes) believe the reference is to the sins of the reclaimer. They contend that if it were the sins of the converted person, it would be anticlimactic and a kind of tautology. In defense of their position, they cite Jewish sources and church fathers such as Origen who said converting a sinner was one method of securing forgiveness of one's own sins. However, the majority (e.g., Alford, Hiebert, Davids 1982, Martin, Blue) contend that the primary reference is to the sins of the erring one, although, several say, this does not rule out some type of blessing for those who reclaim the sinner. The latter view, that James is referring to the sins of the wandering one, is preferable for the following reasons:

1. The concept that forgiveness can be won by any type of works is wholly alien to the New Testament.
2. The sequence of thought in the verse makes it awkward to refer the covering of sins to a person different from the one who has been saved from death.
3. Although this second clause may sound anticlimactic, there is a possible progression of thought. Not only is the person rescued from peril but he is also blessed by the forgiveness from all his sins (Knowling, cited by Tasker).

Although this ending sounds very abrupt, it is striking and is a distinct call to action. Stulac summarizes James' closing message in this way: "As you hold onto the truth and trust God in prayer during your trials, keep helping others to do the same."

BOUNDARIES AND COHERENCE

The initial boundary of 5:19–20 was discussed under 1:2–5:18. The final boundary coincides with the end of the epistle. The unit coheres as one Greek sentence.

PROMINENCE AND THEME

The theme of the 5:19–20 unit includes a representation of the *APPEAL* and *BASIS*, since both are essential parts of a hortatory paragraph pattern. The *BASIS* has equal prominence with the *APPEAL* itself, which is mitigated. Moreover, the *BASIS* is comprehensive in that it provides motivation for obeying all the exhortations throughout James' letter. Indeed, 5:19–20 is a fitting conclusion for the letter.

BIBLIOGRAPHY

SELECTED COMMENTARIES, LEXICONS, AND OTHER GENERAL REFERENCES

Adamson, James B. 1976. *The Epistle of James*. New International Commentary on the New Testament. Grand Rapids: Eerdmans.

Alford, Henry. [1871] 1968. *The Greek Testament*, vol. 4. Chicago: Moody.

Banker, John. 1996. *A semantic and structural analysis of Philippians*. Dallas: SIL.

Barclay, William. 1960. *The letters of James and Peter*. The Daily Study Bible Series. 2d ed. Philadelphia: Westminster.

Bauer, Walter, William F. Arndt, and F. Wilbur Gingrich. 1979. *A Greek-English lexicon of the New Testament and other early Christian literature*. 2d ed. Revised and augmented by F. Wilbur Gingrich and Frederick W. Danker from Walter Bauer's 5th edition, 1958. University of Chicago Press.

Beekman, John, and John Callow. 1974. *Translating the Word of God*. Grand Rapids: Zondervan.

Beekman, John, John Callow, and Michael F. Kopesec. 1981. *The semantic structure of written communication*. 5th rev. ed. Dallas: SIL.

Bennett, W. H. n.d. *The General Epistles: James, Peter, John, and Jude*. The Century Bible: A Modern Commentary, ed. H. H. Rowley and Matthew Black. London: Blackwood, Le Bas.

Blass, R., and A. Debrunner. 1961. *A Greek grammar of the New Testament and other early Christian literature*. A translation and revision of the 9th-10th German edition by Robert W. Funk. University of Chicago Press.

Blue, J. Ronald. 1983. James. In *The Bible knowledge commentary: New Testament*, ed. John F. Walvoord and Roy B. Zuck, 815-36. Wheaton, Ill.: Victor.

Bratcher, Robert G. 1984. *A translator's guide to the Letters from James, Peter, and Jude*. Helps for Translators. New York: UBS.

Brooks, James A., and Carlton L. Winbery. 1979. *The syntax of New Testament Greek*. Lanham, Md.: University Press of America.

Bullinger. E. W. [1898] 1968. *Figures of speech used in the Bible*. Grand Rapids: Baker.

Burdick, Donald W. 1981. James. In *The expositor's Bible commentary*, ed. Frank E. Gaebelein, vol. 12, 159-205. Grand Rapids: Zondervan.

Burns, John A. 1986. James, the wisdom of Jesus. *Criswell Theological Review* 1:1:113-35. (Dallas: Criswell College.)

Buth, Randall. 1980. Troubleshooting in James. *Selected Technical Articles Related to Translation* 2:3-15. (Dallas: SIL.)

Callow, Kathleen. 1998. *Man and message*. Lanham, Md.: University Press of America.

Coutts, John. 1976. *The soldier's armoury*. Jan.-June.

Cranfield, C. E. B. 1965a. The message of James. *Scottish Journal of Theology* 18:2:182-93. (London: Cambridge University Press.)

———. 1965b. The message of James continued. *Scottish Journal of Theology* 18:3:338-45. (London: Cambridge University Press.)

Crofts, Marjorie. n.d. Metaphors of the New Testament: Their interpretation and translation. Prepublication draft. (Dallas: SIL.)

Dana, H. E., and Julius R. Mantey. 1949. *A manual grammar of the Greek New Testament*. New York: Macmillan.

Davids, Peter H. 1982. *The Epistle of James*. New International Greek Testament Commentary. Grand Rapids: Eerdmans.

———. 1989. *James*. New International Biblical Commentary. Peabody, Mass.: Hendrickson.

———. 1994. James. In *New Bible Commentary: Twenty-first century edition*, 1354-68. 4th ed. Leicester, England; Downers Grove, Ill.: InterVarsity.

Deibler, Ellis W., Jr. 1998. *A semantic and structural analysis of Romans*. Dallas: SIL.

Dibelius, Martin. 1976. *A commentary on the Epistle of James*. Revised by Heinrich Greeven, translated by Michael A. Williams. Philadelphia: Fortress.

Dockery, David S. 1986. True piety in James: Ethical admonitions and theological implications. *Criswell Theological Review* 1:1:51–70. (Dallas: Criswell College.)

Ekstrom, J. O. n.d. The discourse structure of the Book of James. Unpublished draft. (Dallas: SIL.)

Friberg, Barbara, and Timothy Friberg. 1981. *Analytical Greek New Testament*. Grand Rapids: Baker.

Fry, Euan. 1978. The testing of faith: A study of the structure of the Book of James. *The Bible Translator* 29:427–35.

Greenlee, J. Harold. 1993. *An exegetical summary of James*. Dallas: SIL.

Hiebert, D. Edmond. 1992. *The Epistle of James: Tests of a living faith*. Chicago: Moody.

Hill, Ralph. n.d. An analysis of James 3–5 to the paragraph constituent level. Unpublished. (Dallas: SIL.)

Hort, F. J. A. 1909. *The Epistle of St. James*. New York: Macmillan.

Huther, Johann Eduard. 1887. *Critical and exegetical handbook to the General Epistles of James, Peter, John, and Jude*. New York: Funk & Wagnalls.

Johnson, Luke Timothy. 1995. *The Letter of James: A new translation with introduction and commentary*. The Anchor Bible, ed. W. F. Albright and D. N. Freeman, vol. 37A. New York: Doubleday.

Kistemaker, Simon J. 1986. *Exposition of the Epistle of James and the Epistles of John*. New Testament Commentary. Grand Rapids: Baker.

Lange, J. P., and J. J. Van Oosterzee. 1960. The Epistle General of James. In vol. 12 of *Lange's commentary on the Holy Scriptures*. Translated and edited from the 2d revised German edition, n.d. Grand Rapids: Zondervan.

Larson, Mildred L. 1984. *Meaning-based translation: A guide to cross-language equivalence*. Lanham, Md.: University Press of America.

Laws, Sophie. 1980. *A commentary on the Epistle of James*. London: Adam & Charles Black.

Lenski, R. C. H. 1966. *The interpretation of the Epistle to the Hebrews and the Epistle of James*. Minneapolis: Augsburg.

Levinsohn, Stephen H. 1992. *Discourse features of New Testament Greek*. Dallas: SIL.

Loh, I-Jin, and Howard A. Hatton. 1997. *A handbook on the letter from James*. UBS Handbook Series. New York: UBS.

Longacre, Robert. 1996. *The grammar of discourse*. 2d ed. New York: Plenum.

Louw, Johannes P., and Eugene A. Nida, eds. 1988. *Greek-English lexicon of the New Testament based on semantic domains*, vol. 1. New York: UBS.

MacArthur, John F. 1990. Faith according to the Apostle James. *Journal of the Evangelical Theological Society* 33:13–34. (Jackson, Miss.: Evangelical Theological Society.)

MacDonald, William. 1995. The Epistle of James. In *Believer's Bible Commentary*, ed. Art Farstad, 2215–389. Nashville: Thomas Nelson.

Manton, Thomas. 1995. *James*. Crossway Classics Commentaries, ed. Alister McGrath and J. I. Packer. Wheaton, Ill.: Crossway.

Martin, Ralph P. 1988. *James. Word Biblical Commentary*, vol. 48. Waco, Tex.: Word.

Mayor, J. B. [1897] 1954. *The Epistle of St. James*. Grand Rapids: Zondervan.

Metzger, Bruce M. 1994. *A textual commentary on the Greek New Testament*. 2d ed. Stuttgart: German Bible Society.

Miller, Neva, and Catherine Rountree. 1989. James: Analyzed translation. Unpublished draft. (Dallas: SIL.)

Moffatt, James. 1928. *The General Epistles: James, Peter, and Judas*. Moffatt New Testament Commentary. London: Hodder and Stoughton.

Moo, Douglas J. 1985. *The Letter of James: An introduction and commentary*. Tyndale New Testament Commentaries. Grand Rapids: Eerdmans.

Moore, Bruce R. 1993. *Doublets in the New Testament*. Dallas: SIL.

Motyer, Alec. 1985. *The message of James*. The Bible Speaks Today, ed. John R. W. Stott. Downers Grove, Ill.: InterVarsity.

Moulton, James Hope. 1963. *A grammar of New Testament Greek*. Edinburgh: T. & T. Clark.

Oesterley, W. E. 1967. The General Epistle of James. In *The Expositor's Greek Testament*, ed. W. R. Nicoll, vol. 4, 385–476. Grand Rapids: Eerdmans.

Pope, Tony. n.d. Translator's notes on James. Preliminary draft. (Dallas: SIL.)
Rakestraw, Robert V. 1986. James 2:14–26: Does James contradict the Pauline soteriology? *Criswell Theological Review* 1:1:31–50. (Dallas: Criswell College.)
Reicke, Bo. 1973. *The Epistles of James, Peter, and Jude*. The Anchor Bible, ed. W. F. Albright and D. N. Freeman, vol. 37. Garden City, N.Y.: Doubleday.
Richardson, Kurt A. 1997. *James*. New American Commentary, vol. 36. Nashville: Broadman & Holman.
Robertson, A. T. 1934. *A grammar of the Greek New Testament in the light of historical research*. Nashville: Broadman.
Ropes, J. H. 1916. *A critical and exegetical commentary on the Epistle of St. James*. International Critical Commentary. Edinburgh: T. & T. Clark.
Ross, Alexander. 1954. *The Epistles of James and John*. New International Commentary on the New Testament. Grand Rapids: Eerdmans.
Rountree, Catherine. 1976. Further thoughts on the discourse structure of James. Unpublished draft. (Dallas: SIL.)
Sherman, Grace E., and John C. Tuggy. 1994. *A semantic and structural analysis of the Johannine Epistles*. Dallas: SIL.
Sloan, Robert B. 1986. The Christology of James 1. *Criswell Theological Review* 1:1:3–29. (Dallas: Criswell College.)
Songer, Harold S. 1972. James. In *The Broadman Bible Commentary*, ed. Clifton J. Allen, vol. 12. Nashville: Broadman.
Sterner, Robert H. 1998. *A semantic and structural analysis of 1 Thessalonians*. Dallas: SIL.
Stulac, George M. 1993. *James*. Downers Grove, Ill.: InterVarsity.
Tasker, R. V. G. 1957. *The General Epistle of James: An introduction and commentary*. Tyndale New Testament Commentaries. Grand Rapids: Eerdmans.
Terry, Ralph Bruce. 1992. Some aspects of the discourse structure of the Book of James. *Journal of Translation and Textlinguistics* 5:2:106–25. (Dallas: SIL.)
Tuggy, John C. 1992. Semantic paragraph patterns: A fundamental communication concept and interpretive tool. In *Linguistics and New Testament interpretation: Essays on discourse analysis*, ed. David Alan Black, 45–67. Nashville: Broadman.
Van Otterloo, Roger. 1988. Towards an understanding of 'lo' and 'behold' functions of ἰδού and ἴδε in the Greek New Testament. In *Occasional Papers in Translation and Textlinguistics* 2:1:34–64. (Dallas: SIL.)
Ward, Ronald A. 1970. James. In *New Bible commentary, revised*, ed. D. Guthrie and J. A. Motyer, 1222–35. Grand Rapids: Eerdmans.
Wells, C. Richard. 1986. The theology of prayer in James. *Criswell Theological Review* 1:1:85–112. (Dallas: Criswell College.)
Wilkinson, John. 1971. Healing in the Epistle of James. *Scottish Journal of Theology* 24:326–45. (London: Cambridge University Press.)
Zerwick, Maximilian. 1963. *Biblical Greek illustrated by examples*. Adapted from the Latin by Joseph Smith. Rome: Biblical Institute Press.

GREEK TEXTS AND TRANSLATIONS

Aland, Kurt, Matthew Black, Carlo M. Martini, Bruce M. Metzger, and Allen Wikgren, eds. 1993. *The Greek New Testament*. 4th rev. ed. Stuttgart: UBS.
Friberg, Barbara, and Timothy Friberg, eds. 1981. *Analytical Greek New Testament*. Grand Rapids: Baker.
Good news for modern man: The New Testament in today's English version. 1976. New York: ABS.
Goodspeed, Edgar J. 1923. *The New Testament: An American translation*. University of Chicago Press.
The Holy Bible. Authorized (or King James) version. 1611.
The Holy Bible: The Berkeley version in modern English. 1959. Grand Rapids: Zondervan.
The Holy Bible: Contemporary English version. 1995. New York: ABS.

The Holy Bible: New century version. 1993. Dallas: Word.
The Holy Bible: New international version. 1985. Grand Rapids: Zondervan.
The Holy Bible: The new Jerusalem Bible. 1985. New York: ABS.
Holy Bible: New living translation. 1996. Wheaton, Ill.: Tyndale.
The Holy Bible: New revised standard version. 1989. Nashville: Thomas Nelson.
The Holy Bible: Revised standard version. 1971. New York: Thomas Nelson.
The Jerusalem Bible. 1968. Garden City, N.Y.: Doubleday.
The new American Bible. 1971. Nashville: Thomas Nelson.
The new American standard Bible. 1977. Nashville: Holman.
The new English Bible New Testament. 1970. Oxford University Press; Cambridge University Press.
Phillips, J. B. 1972. *The New Testament in modern English*. New York: Macmillan.
The revised English Bible. 1989. Oxford University Press; Cambridge University Press.
The translator's New Testament. 1973. London: British and Foreign Bible Society.
Westcott, Brooke Foss, and Fenton John Anthony Hort. 1925. *The New Testament in the original Greek*. 1966 reprint. New York: Macmillan.
Weymouth, Richard Francis. 1943. *The New Testament in modern speech*. 5th ed., revised by J. A. Robertson. Boston: Pilgrim.
Williams, Charles B. 1952. *The New Testament: A translation in the language of the people*. Chicago: Moody.

www.ingramcontent.com/pod-product-compliance
Lightning Source LLC
Chambersburg PA
CBHW060253240426

43673CB00047B/1918